Arthurian Literature
by Women

ARTHURIAN LITERATURE BY WOMEN

ALAN LUPACK
BARBARA TEPA LUPACK
Editors

GARLAND PUBLISHING, INC.
A member of the Taylor and Francis Group
New York and London
1999

P N
6071
.A84
A 74
1999
40675004

This book is dedicated to our sister
Donna Schurmann

Copyright ©1999 Alan Lupack and Barbara Tepa Lupack
All rights reserved

Library of Congress Cataloging-in-Publication Data

Arthurian literature by women / edited by Alan Lupack and Barbara Tepa Lupack.
   p. cm. — (Garland reference library of the humanities ; v. 2137)
 Includes bibliographical references and index.
 ISBN 0-8153-3305-6 (alk. paper). – ISBN 0-8153-3483-4 (pbk. : alk. paper)
  1. Arthurian romances—Adaptations. 2. Knights and knighthood—Literary collections.
3. Kings and rulers—Literary collections. 4. Women and literature. 5. Literature—Women
authors. I. Lupack, Alan. II. Lupack, Barbara Tepa, 1951– . III. Series: Garland
reference library of the humanities ; vol. 2137.
 PN6071.A84A74 1999
 808.8'0351—dc21   99–11197
                      CIP

Printed on acid-free, 250-year-life paper
Manufactured in the United States of America

Augustana College Library
Rock Island, Illinois 61201

Contents

Introduction

Texts

Foreword

In recent years, women have been increasingly associated with the Arthurian tradition. From the historical retellings of the legendary stories to the original reworkings of them, from the versions set in Arthur's day to those set in modern times, from fantasy and science fiction to mystery and children's literature, contemporary Arthurian novels by women have garnered critical attention and gained popular acclaim.

Readers are probably most familiar with authors like Vera Chapman, whose "Three Damosels" trilogy—*The Green Knight* (1975), *The King's Damosel* (1976), and *King Arthur's Daughter* (1976)—popularized the device of female narration in contemporary fiction; or Mary Stewart, whose classic Merlin trilogy (*The Crystal Cave* [1970], *The Hollow Hills* [1973], *The Last Enchantment* [1979]) blends traditional and nontraditional accounts of Merlin, the self-tutored bastard son of Ambrosius Aurelianus and eventual overseer of Arthur's reign, and whose later novel *The Wicked Day* (1984) features a sympathetic Mordred who becomes the unwilling instrument of his mother Morgause's revenge against Arthur; or Rosemary Sutcliff, whose *Sword at Sunset* (1963) allows Arthur to tell his own story in the first person. Andre Norton, in her clever science fiction novel *Merlin's Mirror* (1975), in which Merlin is the product of cross-breeding with aliens, and in her many juvenile Arthurian fantasies, including *Steel Magic* (1965), *Dragon Magic* (1972), and *Witch World* (1963), the first volume of her most extensive and imitated series, helped to establish a new genre of Arthurian fiction—a genre that includes C. J. Cherryh's *Port Eternity* (1982), which features a marooned spacecraft peopled by clones modeled on Arthurian characters from Tennyson's *Idylls of the King*, and Sanders Anne Laubenthal's *Excalibur* (1973), which brings the quest to the New World and Excalibur itself to Mobile, Alabama. Novels like *Merlin's Booke* (1986) and the "Young Merlin Trilogy"—*Passager* (1996), *Hobby* (1996), and *Merlin*

(1997)—by prolific author JaneYolen and Katherine Paterson's *Park's Quest* (1988), which entwines the Grail theme with a young boy's odyssey to understand Vietnam and discover his heritage, have introduced the Arthurian world to children as well as to adults. Series like Fay Sampson's "Daughter ofTintagel" sequence about Morgan le Fay (*Wise Woman's Telling* [1989], *White Nun's Telling* [1989], *Black Smith's Telling* [1990], *Taliessin's Telling* [1991], and *Herself* [1992]) and trilogies by Gillian Bradshaw (*Hawk of May* [1980], *Kingdom of Summer* [1981], and *In Winter's Shadow* [1981]) and Persia Woolley (*Child of the Northern Spring* [1987], *Queen of the Summer Stars* [1990], and *Guinevere: The Legend in Autumn* [1991]) have explored at greater length and often from nontraditional perspectives the tales of traditional Arthurian characters. And, of course, for many, women's Arthurian literature is epitomized by Marion Zimmer Bradley's best-selling and much emulated novel *The Mists of Avalon* (1982), which focuses on the legend's women—Igraine; Morgaine, her daughter by Gorlois; Morgause, Igraine's younger sister, later Lot's queen; Viviane, the Lady of the Lake, Igraine's half-sister, and mother of Lancelot; Niniane and Nimue; and Gwenhwyfar, Arthur's queen—and by its sequel, *Lady of Avalon* (1997), which spans the creation of Avalon and foreshadows the birth of Arthur.

Given the amount and scope of recent popular Arthurian women's fiction, it is surprising that there is so little awareness among readers and scholars alike of the significant earlier—and ongoing—tradition of Arthurian literature by women. That tradition goes back to the nineteenth century, to writers like Letitia E. Landon and Elizabeth Stuart Phelps, who were popular and widely read in their own day but who are now largely forgotten; and it continues into the twentieth century with Sara Teasdale, Edna St. Vincent Millay, and Dorothy Parker, among others. That tradition incorporates a broad spectrum of Arthurian works, some of which are remarkably prescient in their attitudes towards social problems, religion, philosophy, and feminism. The position of Guinevere, who must serve as wife to an uncaring husband/king, is a recurring concern in this literature, as is the desire to discover—usually in the enchanted isle of Avalon—a place in which women can find refuge and a society in which they can at last achieve equality with men.

In fact, many of the techniques that are considered to be contemporary have their roots in the earlier neglected tradition of Arthurian women's literature. The device of female narration, for instance, in which female characters relate their stories in their own voices, is anticipated in several nineteenth-century works and realized in the early twentieth-century Guinevere poems ofTeasdale and Parker. Numerous other seemingly recent devices—from the emphasis on the role of women in the legends to the underscoring of the women's strength and will, from contemporized story settings to fantastic travels, from interesting and unconventional uses of traditional characters to the creation of new ones— also harken back to this forgotten tradition. Moreover, notions like the redemption of King Mark, the recasting of Morgan le Fey as healer rather than destroyer, or the depiction of King Arthur as "brother" to the common man, and the introduction of characters like the peasant girl who proves more noble than all the ladies and lords of Arthur's court, the page boy who wins a seat at the Round Table by "keeping tryst," or the dwarf who curses the holy cup but who eventually achieves the Grail when noble knights like Sir Lancelot cannot, seem like very modern twists to the familiar Arthurian stories; but all are actually the innovations of authors who wrote their poems and tales almost a century or two ago.

The purpose of *Arthurian Literature by Women: An Anthology* is to explore that rich but forgotten tradition and to afford it some of the attention it deserves. To that end, the volume does not reproduce works (or portions of works) that are readily available to contemporary readers—Bradley's *Mists of Avalon*, for instance, or excerpts from Vera Chapman's trilogy. Rather, it attempts to introduce less known, but no less significant, Arthurian works that are out of print or otherwise difficult to access. Insofar as possible, those works are presented in their entirety; and the broadest selection of genres of women's writing is represented. Included, among others, are lais by Marie de France (newly translated for this volume by Norris Lacy); a translation of a tale from the *Mabinogion* by Lady Charlotte Guest; short fiction by Elizabeth Stuart Phelps and Mrs. T. K. Hervey; poems by Anne Bannerman, Jessie Weston, and Aline Kilmer; a short romance by Annie Fellows Johnston; a fantastic tale by Dinah Maria Mulock Craik; and a play by Martha Kinross. Two comprehensive bibliographies document the remarkable range of Arthurian fiction and of Arthurian poetry and drama by women. For it is only with a proper understanding of this forgotten tradition that the many recent developments in Arthurian literature can be fully appreciated and that the Arthurian canon can be redefined to incorporate the achievements of a number of these women writers.

Acknowledgments

We are sincerely grateful to Norris Lacy for providing new translations of *Chevrefueil* and *Lanval* for this volume and to Kristi Long of Garland Publishers, Inc., for her support of this project.

We would also like to acknowledge the many women whose contributions to Arthurian studies have enriched the field and influenced our own work, in particular:

Freya Reeves, publisher of *Avalon to Camelot*

Sally Slocum, the founder and for many years chair
of the Arthurian section of the Popular Culture Association

Elizabeth Sklar, the current chair
of the Arthurian section of the Popular Culture Association

Maureen Fries, who has written widely on matters Arthurian
and generously encouraged younger Arthurian scholars

Mildred Leake Day, editor of *Quondam et Futurus*

Bonnie Wheeler, editor of *Arthuriana*

Arthurian Literature by Women

Introduction

The Forgotten Tradition

ALAN LUPACK AND BARBARA TEPA LUPACK

Arthurian literature is traditionally considered the domain of men. The legends themselves are dominated by men, and the major canonical examples of the story are written by men. For the English-speaking world, Sir Thomas Malory's fifteenth-century *Morte d'Arthur* established and continues to define the tradition, so much so that even later versions of the tales that bear little resemblance to what Malory actually wrote pay homage to him and suggest that he is their source. And, apart from Malory, the best-known versions of the Arthurian story claim descent from other male writers, in particular Alfred, Lord Tennyson and T. H. White.

Even those who are interested in women's literature and women in literature have typically been compelled to discuss the legend's women as treated by the men who wrote about them, as illustrated by a recent article like "What Tennyson Did to Malory's Women." Volumes such as *Arthurian Women: A Casebook* and *Women and Arthurian Literature*, whose titles imply a strong emphasis on women writers, focus instead primarily on male authors. And courses dealing with women in the Arthurian legend teach works almost exclusively by men.

Although traditionally women have not been associated with the creation of significant versions of the Arthurian story until the burgeoning of the fantasy novel in the late twentieth century, there is in fact a considerable body of women's Arthurian literature dating back as far as the early nineteenth century. (Admittedly, before that time—with the brilliant exception of two lays by Marie de France—women wrote very little about the Matter of Britain.) Much of that forgotten and neglected Arthurian literature is by authors who never achieved canonical status or whose Arthurian works, by deviating from convention, place them outside the main tradition. Yet several of these writers were tremendously popular in their day. Elizabeth Stuart Phelps, for example, the author of more than fifty books, had an international reputation; and Dorothy Parker, Sara Teasdale, and

Edna St. Vincent Millay enjoyed a large and enthusiastic following as well. Others, like Letitia E. Landon, who wrote under the pseudonym L. E. L., are only now being rediscovered by a new generation of readers. Many of these writers, however, remain obscure; for a few, it is difficult even to establish their dates of birth and death. But all of these authors wrote notable versions of one or another of the Arthurian legends, and their combined works suggest that there are indeed certain traditions common to women writing on Arthurian themes.

Many of the women, for instance, demonstrate a willingness to depart from the familiar stories and the expected interpretations of the characters—a willingness, even a desire, to turn aside from the usual manner of telling and the conventional concerns of the Arthurian world, to "rebel," in Phelps's words, "against the story." Sometimes their reinterpretations of the received versions of the legend are radical, as in the redeeming of characters like King Mark who have been condemned in other accounts, or in the prominence of female characters like Guinevere or Isolt who are allowed to tell their own stories, often in their own voices. Sometimes the reinterpretations are topical, as in the tendency among some American women writers to democratize the legends by downplaying the notions of kingship and recognizing the nobility in the most common of characters. And sometimes the reinterpretations are highly individualized, as women writers concentrate on certain themes and motifs and adapt them to their own purposes. The legendary isle of Avalon, where Arthur is said to rest until he is needed again, for instance, is particularly popular; for many women writers it becomes a symbol of refuge and reconciliation, an emblem of a state of equality that is rarely achieved by women in mundane society.

While the taking of liberties with the Arthurian stories is not exclusive to women—Bulwer-Lytton, after all, sent his King Arthur to the Arctic to battle Eskimos and walruses; and American Arthurian authors, both male and female, routinely invent incidents quite alien to the original legends—it seems clear that women, by virtue of being outside the mainstream of Arthurian tradition, have been more inclined to radical reinterpetations and innovative reworkings of it. An excellent example is Mrs. T. K. (Eleanora Louisa Montagu) Hervey, whose *The Feasts of Camelot* (1863) is one of the earliest works of original Arthurian fiction by a woman and still one of only a few unified collections of short Arthurian fiction. Though Hervey's book consists of a series of tales modeled more on Chaucer's *Canterbury Tales* than on Malory's *Morte d'Arthur* and though individual tales seem more Gothic than Arthurian, her story of Tristram, Isond (Hervey's name for Isolt), and Mark diverges both from the traditional medieval and from other Victorian versions of the tragic love. Hervey relates the account of these characters over three chapters of the *Feasts*, beginning, in Chapter III, with an atypical tale of the typically evil "Mad King Mark." Tristram, called upon to fight for Mark's sovereignty, objects because he recognizes only Arthur as king in Britain. After Sir Maurice of Ireland taunts Tristram and repeats the stories of his cowardice spread by Mark, Tristram enters into the combat. (By contrast, in the traditional story Tristram is eager to fight to end the allegiance owed by Cornwall to Ireland.) After defeating, but not killing, Maurice, Tristram is sent to Ireland with a sealed message that contains two requests: that Tristram, suspected of plotting to usurp Mark's lands, be watched and that Mark be granted Isond's hand in marriage.

And Hervey again breaks from convention as she tries—at least by Victorian standards—to redeem Tristram and Isond by having them refrain from any adulterous or illicit acts. In fact, Hervey's Isond remains faithful to Mark, even proclaiming his kindness toward her before Arthur and his court. And Tristram, after escaping from Ireland through a bizarre plot devised by Isond, goes (as she has instructed) to her namesake in Wales. There he falls truly in love with and marries Isond of Wales. Tristram and his wife, the second Isond, are still happily wed as the tales at Camelot are being told.

Hervey's desire to redeem her characters extends even to the most traditionally wicked; at the end of Chapter III, for instance, she offers a defense of Morgan. When Merlin criticizes the bards who dare "to call our gracious lady Morgana, the 'Fay-lady,'" Guenever explains that it is because Merlin himself "taught her so many things that women seldom know of, that rumour has fixed upon her the blame of dealing with unlawful magic." This sympathic depiction of Morgan (paralleled in the Victorian age only in one other work—and that, unsurprisingly, by another woman, Dinah Maria Mulock Craik) is striking, particularly since it is couched in terms that are critical of male responses to women who attempt to exceed their expected roles. To set things right, Merlin takes steps to record the true story in books that are "fast locked in the great pyx" in the church of St. Stephen. "Heaven grant they never be lost," he adds, "or a sorry history will be given of us all in the ages to come!" The sorry history is obviously the traditional account of the unredeemed Merlin and Morgan and Tristram and Isond and Mark. And it is precisely such an account that Hervey, in the tales in *The Feasts of Camelot*, intends to correct.

Later, in Chapter XI, Isond relates Mark's "One Good Deed." Most of her telling, however, concerns not Mark but rather the deeds and misdeeds of two brothers, the elements of whose tale are reminiscent of events in Malory's account of Balin and Balan. One brother, Bertrand, is responsible for the death of the other, Walter, and at least in part because of the guilt he feels, dies shortly thereafter. Mark's good deed is to have the body of Walter brought back to his castle to be buried beside the woman he loved and to have prayers said for both of them. Of course, as Arthur says, "It could be wished that the living rather than the dead had been so humanely dealt with."

The redemption of Mark is completed in Chapter XII, the last in the *Feasts*, which introduces the character of Alisaunder, the Alysaundir the Orphelyn who is "slayne by the treson of kynge Marke" in Malory. But here Alisaunder is not slain. In fact, it is he who responds to Arthur's request for a tale revealing that someone of Mark's "blood and race" has done "acts of nobleness and generosity, whence we may infer that nature is not all in fault, but that circumstance has wrought in him some of the ill that he has done." Alisaunder tells of the young Tristram's forgiveness of his wicked stepmother who twice tried to poison him. Tristram's intercession not only saves her from his father Meliodus' condemnation to death but also transforms her into a devoted woman who "loved him tenderly ever after" and a penitent who "scourged herself and wore sackcloth for her sin." After hearing the story, Arthur is forced to admit that Tristram, Alisaunder's father (Mark's brother), and Alisaunder himself show that there are "traits of nobleness and self-denial in the blood of King Mark's line."

According to Hervey, Mark's misdeeds—a fault of "circumstance," not of "nature"—can be traced to rumors about a prophecy by Merlin that "one near akin" to Mark "should usurp his power, and hold him captive till his death-day." Not knowing "from which hand his doom is to come, he [Mark] wages an unnatural war with all his race." Yet his cruel and unjust acts are committed only because he is "led to suspect treachery through a foolish rumour." Even Isond, who typically suffers most from Mark's abuse, confirms that "King Mark has ever been kind and tender to me." Once the reason for Mark's earlier unchivalrous conduct is properly understood, he is given a place of honor as Arthur's guest and invited to join in the feasting and fellowship. "And many a pleasant tale and touching song wiled away the last trace of care from the softened heart of King Mark."

An even more radical departure from the tradition occurs in Antonia R. Williams' play *Isolt* (1900), subtitled "A New Telling." Although it is one of the least successful of the seventeen Tristan and Isolt plays written in the first three decades of the twentieth century, *Isolt* takes a decidedly new approach to the material, first by turning the story into a rather heavy-handed allegory of "Two Ideas in Conflict: Love and Fear" and then by giving the tragedy a happy ending. Unfortunately, Williams' approach sacrifices too much of the tradition to originality; and ultimately her "New Telling" is just too artificial to be good.

A better play—in fact, among the most fascinating of all the Tristan plays—

is Martha Kinross's *Tristram & Isoult* (1913), which, despite its title, focuses on Isoult by juxtaposing her with Guinevere. Whereas Malory highlighted the tragedy of Arthur by contrasting his nobility to Mark's mean-spiritedness and cowardice, Kinross makes Guinevere a foil by means of which Isoult's independence and courage are revealed.

Early in the play, Guinevere says: "Isoult the fearless, I have envied thee / Thy Joyous Gard, and the avowéd years / Lived open to King Mark and to the world." This openness, coupled with a strength rare—or at least rarely emphasized—in the typical portrayal of Isoult, makes Kinross's heroine a compelling character. Isoult's fearlessness, from which her strength derives, is dramatically depicted when Mark confronts her in a tower at Tintagil. "I never fear," she tells him; and he, recalling an incident in which she gave the death blow to a bayed stag that was slashing her hunting hounds with its horns, replies "almost I believe thy vaunt." Determined nevertheless to break her spirit, he declares that it is "the end I set my life" to "make thee fear," and he forces her towards a broken parapet. But Isoult proclaims herself "undizzied," draws her dagger, and orders him to "take off thy hands." Her open confrontation amounts not just to contemptuous insult of Mark, whom she compares to a dog that sniffs "at the thresholds / Of doors are shut to thee," but also to an admission of her love for Tristram.

As the tower scene demonstrates, Isoult is no stereotypical damsel in distress; rather, she is a forerunner of the overtly feminist heroines of recent Arthurian literature. Her only real "fear," unconfessed to Mark, is that Tristram will forget her; yet even that fear grows not from weakness but from a passion as strong and as undiminished as Isoult's character itself. At the end of the play when, with Tristram dead, she drinks a poisoned cup that she refers to as "the Grail upraised," she again asserts her independence from conventional moral standards. By inverting the traditional life-giving and religious associations implied by the Holy Grail, Isoult affirms that she will define her own faith, choose her own values, and determine her own life and her own death.

Reinterpretations of the story of Isolt and Tristan, though not always as good as that of Kinross or as original as those of Hervey or Williams, have long offered women a vehicle for treating, in nontraditional ways, a traditional plot created and passed on by male authors. Of the twentieth-century dramatic versions of the story, three others—apart from those already mentioned—are by women. *Tristram and Isolt* (1905), by Martha Austin, uses Malory's conception of the characters and his contrast of the Tristram-Isoult-Mark triangle with that of Lancelot, Guinevere, and Arthur; but the play is best when Austin avails herself of the "privilege" (6) of poetic licence. In a blending of legends, for instance, her

Tristram—who generally lacks guilt over his actions—goes so far as to compare the cup from which he drank the love potion to the Grail and Isoult to the "angel of the Grail" (48). Yet, while Tristram has the most dramatic potential, none of Austin's characters is developed fully enough to make the reader experience their tragedy as something personal yet legendary. Similarly, Amory Hare (a pseudonym of [Mary] Amory Hare Hutchinson) claims to use Bédier as a source, but her *Tristram and Iseult* (1930) is derivative and unfocused; and her notion of character creating destiny seems to be an afterthought rather than a determining force or an essential element in the development of the play. *The Tragedy of Pardon* (1911) by Katherine Harris Bradley and Edith Emma Cooper (writing under the pseudonym of Michael Field) begins on an exceptionally promising note: the prologue finds Queen Iseult of Ireland in a laboratory preparing the love potion, which is empowered by "star-rays" that "fall on the alembic and ignite it" (3). And the play itself is full of action—Tristan, for example, shoots the spying Marjodo with an arrow and Melot buries the body; Iseult undergoes the ordeal of the hot iron to prove her innocence. Although some of the characters are not always treated consistently, Field nonetheless demonstrates a talent for dramatic spectacle, as is apparent in the ending, in which Iseult uses not a black or white sail but a golden one to announce her presence; and as Iseult dies over the dying Tristan, her hair fans out so that he mistakes it for a golden sail, a sign of the spatial and temporal confusion of the dying man. Such visual effects abound in *The Tragedy of Pardon* and make for good theater.

Among women novelists, the story of Tristan and Isolt has also been popular—and handled variously, with varying degrees of success. Some retellings, like Rosemary Sutcliff's *Tristan and Iseult* (1971) and Dorothy James Roberts' *The Enchanted Cup* (1953), are fairly straightforward. Others address the traditional legend but add original—and sometimes unfortunate—twists; Ruth Collier Sharpe's *Tristram of Lyonesse: The Story of an Immortal Love* (1949), for instance, transforms the story into a long and sentimental Gothic melodrama with a happy ending, in which Mark gives Ysolt a "Bill of Divorcement" that allows her to become the Queen of Lyonesse. Still other retellings update the story by setting it in modern times, as Maria Kuncewicz does in *Tristan* (1974), or by applying its lessons to contemporary characters, as Mary Ellen Chase does in *Dawn in Lyonesse* (1938) and again in "A Candle at Night" (1942). Some novelists, like Anna Taylor in *Drustan the Wanderer: A Historical Novel Based on the Legend of Tristan and Isolde* (1971) and Hannah Closs in *Tristan* (1940), focus on Tristan and filter events through his mind or allow him to tell his own tale. Still other novelists focus on the legend's female characters, who often narrate their own accounts of the tragic love and its repercussions, as Iseult does in Dee Morrison Meaney's *Iseult: Dreams That Are Done* (1985) and Branwan, Esseilte's (Iseult's) cousin, does in Diana L. Paxson's *The White Raven* (1988).

Women poets have also been interested in the possibilities of the theme. The first to retell the story, or rather a carefully selected portion of the story, was the twelfth-century writer Marie de France. In her *Lanval*, Marie explored the romantic adventures of another knight, the title character Lanval, whose fairy lover swears him to secrecy; but when Guinevere makes advances to him, Lanval feels compelled to break the secret and reveal his love. All ends happily: despite his broken oath, Lanval is spared punishment by the timely arrival and intervention of his lady. *Chevrefueil* (*The Honeysuckle*), a much shorter lai, is no less important. It begins by acknowledging the ultimate tragedy but returns to a scene in the forest where Isolde and her exiled Tristan are enjoying a brief idyll. The passion of the lovers during their intense moment of love—and the entwining of their destinies—is evoked by the honeysuckle attached to a hazel branch.

Grace Constant Lounsbery depicts a similar moment of love in "An Iseult Idyll," which describes the instant when Tristram and Iseult first utter each other's names after drinking the love potion. Iseult's whispered "Tristram," in reply to his "Iseult," is followed only by "the sea's reverberate monotone, / With Love's own voice in unison." This interplay of soft sounds and silence ends the poem on exactly the right note of awe. But what is most interesting is that Lounsbery—as her title suggests—makes this an Iseult idyll: highlighted is Iseult's moment of awareness and not Tristram's, as is common in the versions of this story written by men. Likewise, Dorothy Parker portrays in her brief poem "Iseult of Brittany" a character even more neglected than her namesake from Ireland. Known as Iseult of the White Hands, Iseult of Brittany sees "a bitterness" in her hands, the physical feature that "might have been my pride" but which are "Too frail to cup a heart within, / Too soft to hold the free . . . ." Though Parker uses the word "cup" as a verb and not as a noun, she nevertheless evokes the image of the inevitable drinking of the love potion by Tristram and Iseult of Ireland; and she heightens the reader's awareness of the sadness that Iseult of Brittany's white hands, emblematic of her failure to "cup [Tristram's] heart within," represent to her.

By looking at the Arthurian legends in innovative ways, women writers create new versions of the familiar stories. One of the most frequent devices they employ is the placing of traditional characters in new roles or—as in "The Ylle Cut Mantell," the first American Arthurian work by a woman (the author identifies herself only as "a daughter of Eve")—by creating new characters to deconstruct the traditional tale. "The Ylle Cut Mantell," which appeared anonymously in *The*

Democratic Review in May, 1844, purported to be "A Romaunt of the Tyme of Gud Kynge Arthur Done into English from an Authentic Version," the authentic version being "The Boy and the Mantle," a ballad that Bishop Thomas Percy included in his widely read *Reliques of Ancient English Poetry* (1765). Percy's traditional ballad describes a test of faithfulness: putting on a mantle that "shall never become that wiffe, / That hath done amisse." Guinevere, of course, fails the test, as does Sir Kay's wife. Only the wife of Sir Craddocke, after confessing to the fault of having kissed her husband before their marriage, can wear the garment. While Guinevere, out of malice, accuses Craddocke's loyal wife of infidelity, two other tests, one with a carving knife and one with a drinking horn, ultimately confirm the mantle's judgment.

The American poem transforms Percy's ballad in some fascinating ways. Considerably longer than the earlier ballad, it presents the mantle as the only test of fidelity. As in the ballad, Guinevere fails the test; but in a departure from its source, the wife of "Caradois," here called Ella, also fails: the robe is too short on her "by half an ell." This is because "she had been faithless and untrue." There is no mitigating explanation, as in the ballad, that she had merely kissed her future husband. Following Ella's discomfiture, another character, Genelas, who has had many lovers, also fails; so do two hundred other ladies, all the women of Arthur's court, save one. That young woman, Coralie, had been brought to court to marry a lord named Hubert before "envious lips and lying tongue" poisoned his mind against her. Coralie, surprisingly, is only "a Norman peasant's child," a point the poem reinforces when the handsome young knight who brings the mantle to Arthur's court announces that "the magic robe was woven / for the poor Norman peasant girl" and proclaims her "of maids the pride and pearl."

In this way, "The Ylle Cut Mantell" rejects worth based on birth. As does much of the American Arthurian literature of the nineteenth and early twentieth centuries, it underscores the notion that virtue is more important than rank or wealth, a lesson Hubert appears to have learned when he takes Coralie back to her native village to wed her rather than "amid regal pomp and show" at court. The anonymous author of "The Ylle Cut Mantell" thus significantly reworks the earlier English ballad, not only to make her poem more democratic and therefore more suitable to the readers of *The Democratic Review*, but also to suggest the integrity of the overlooked peasant girl, a simple woman who is inherently more noble than all the lords—and ladies—of the court.

In a short prose work called *Keeping Tryst: A Tale of King Arthur's Time*, another woman, Annie Fellows Johnston, perhaps best known as the author of the "Little Colonel" series for girls, creates a character who is excluded from the world of knights and nobles until he proves his moral worth. Johnston tells the story of a page boy named Ederyn who asks a minstrel if it is possible for him to become a knight. The minstrel advises Ederyn that some win knighthood by slaying dragons or giants or by going on crusades but suggests that he forget his dreams of glory and be content to serve his squire. "For what hast such as thou to do with great ambitions?" he asks. "They'd prove but flames to burn away thy daily peace." A year later the minstrel returns with information that "there *is* a way for even such as thou to win the honours thou dost covet." The opportunity arises because of Arthur's desire to establish "round him at his court a chosen circle whose fidelity hath stood the utmost test. Not deeds of prowess are required of these true followers, . . . but they must prove themselves trustworthy, until on hand and heart it may be graven large, '*In all things faithful.*'" Ederyn is required to undergo and pass a series of tests of his faithfulness by keeping tryst despite obstacles and temptations. Since he answers each call without neglecting his duties as page and then as squire, he is finally knighted. Clearly, it is those qualities not immediately obvious and not related to birth and status—the numerous "little pearls" on his breast that he earns by his small deeds of devotion, not the few larger "jewels"— that make Ederyn suitable to serve the king.

Just as Johnston recasts the story of the achievement of knighthood by focusing on a simple page boy, another American woman, Sophie Jewett, retells the story of the Grail quest by focusing on another overlooked and underappreciated character. The protagonist in "The Dwarf's Quest" is Dagonet the dwarf, King Arthur's fool. The object of derision and even physical abuse by knights like Sir Kay, whose rude foot and fist "He bore with jest and sneer," Dagonet believes that he is not destined for the quest. But a divine voice gentler than Queen Guinevere's and "kinglier than the King's" informs him that "There waits one vision of the Cup / For thee and Galahad." This injunction to seek "the Cup" comes despite the fact that Dagonet, feeling hurt by his exclusion, had earlier "cursed" the Holy Grail. It is as if the King of Heaven, like the King of Camelot, can forgive the jester's biting words.

How different Dagonet is from the usual Grail knight is immediately apparent. In addition to being "an impish, mocking thing," he is "crooked and weak." By contrast, the face of Galahad, one of the traditional Grail knights, is "like a star"; and Galahad and Percivale ride in the "shining mail" that marks them as heroes of romance. But the divine voice deems Dagonet worthy of the quest because of his "heart's prayer." His physical deformity becomes less important than his moral qualities, which he demonstrates when he stops to care for Lancelot, who is seriously wounded.

As Dagonet tends to the unconscious Lancelot, he sees a bright light and four maidens, one of whom bears the Holy Grail. Thinking that Lancelot is the one for whom the vision has appeared, Dagonet tries unsuccessfully to rouse him; but his "answered prayer is punishment / Since my Lord might not see!" Indeed, as Dagonet hopes, Lancelot is cured by the presence of the Grail. Yet, unlike Dagonet, Lancelot fails in his quest to achieve it since he has not actually witnessed the Grail's appearance. When Dagonet returns to Camelot, he is mocked again for setting out on the quest "Till something in the rider's eyes / Silenced the merry jest."

In Jewett's poem, Galahad and Percivale also achieve the Grail; but Dagonet's role is unprecedented. Usually when there are three Grail achievers, the third is Bors. By substituting Dagonet the fool, Jewett redeems the character who initially curses the Grail, and she allows for a new kind of Arthurian hero, a typically American Arthurian hero: one who is not noble by birth and who is not skillful or strong but who has moral qualities that have been enhanced by his own suffering at the hands of those who considered themselves superior to him.

Another American writer, Katrina Trask, also takes a nontraditional approach in retelling the conventional Grail story in "Kathanal," one of three poems in her volume *Under King Constantine* (1892). Although Constantine is said by Malory to reign after the passing of Arthur, Trask admits her poems "have no legendary warrant." Nevertheless, they create a world different from the Arthurian only in the names of the knights and ladies who figure in them and in the lack of civil strife that earlier had wracked Britain, which now allows leisure for other knightly pursuits.

In "Kathanal," a poem that cries out for Freudian interpretation, Trask uses the Grail quest as a way of sublimating the love between the title character and Leorre, the wife of his "patron knight." Kathanal is drawn to the quest not by divine vision but by Leorre herself, who imposes it upon him as a way of dealing with their forbidden feelings for each other. Earlier in the poem, frustrated by his as yet unspoken love, Kathanal tears the plume from his helmet and tosses it into the sea. With his "knightly symbol lost," he feels dishonored, and his boyhood dream of being "a knight like Galahad, pure and true" seems unattainable. Having forgotten "loyalty / And truth and honour for the fair Leorre," Kathanal fears that if he stays near her "tempting charm"

> I shall, through some wild impulse, wantonly
> Fling my unsullied knighthood to the winds,
> As now I flung the plume from out my helm.

The poem then becomes a virtual orgy of sexual repression. Kathanal struggles between "deep yearning for some touch of love" and "brave endeavour for self-mastery." He proclaims his love to Leorre; she confesses that she reciprocates it. "My senses thrill," she tells him, "If you but touch the border of my robe." Leorre's confession prompts Kathanal to say he will remain with her, but she replies, "now, if ever, you will surely go." Lest their love become "inglorious" like that of Tristram and Isoud or of Launcelot and Guenever, she asks him to undertake the quest. Furthermore, to replace the purple plume from his helmet that her "longing gaze" often followed in tournaments, Leorre gives him "this spotless scarf, the girdle from my robe." Kathanal wavers but, resisting temptation, departs; and ultimately, through his self-denial, he achieves the Grail. His love for Leorre becomes "a glory, not a doom; / Love for love's sake, albeit bliss-denied."

Just as Leorre guides and inspires Kathanal's quest, another woman figures prominently in an equally unusual recasting of a Grail story, "The Christmas of Sir Galahad" by Elizabeth Stuart Phelps. Though now for the most part forgotten or overlooked, Phelps, author of scores of volumes of fiction, poetry, and essays, published three stories and a number of poems on Arthurian themes. In her own day, Phelps's writing was thought to have "vividness," "spiritual passion," and "the power to strike the human note"; and it was praised by prominent literary figures. She made her reputation writing fiction that was designed to console women who had lost loved ones in the Civil War as well as stories that commented on contemporary social problems, especially the question of women's rights and the treatment of women in a male-dominated society.

Given Phelps's social and feminist concerns, her Arthurian poems and stories at first seem hardly consistent with her other works. In fact, though, they are. In "The Christmas of Sir Galahad," perhaps the most didactic and melodramatic of her Arthurian stories, Phelps's Galahad is "Sir Galahad Holt," a worker in an organ factory who returns from his labor with "grimy, princely hands." He is in love with Rebecca Rock—the narrator calls her "Lady Rebecca"—who works in a necktie factory "cutting 'foundation' into strips for the public neck, eleven hours a day." Rebecca shares his feelings, but Galahad is married to Merry Ann, a "crazy" woman who "takes opium" and who, despite leaving him six years earlier, returns occasionally to his apartment. Galahad does not feel free to become involved with Rebecca; and so they wait four long years until Mery Ann finally dies.

The nobility of these characters, for Phelps, lies in their restraint. They never meet for a lover's tryst, never kiss, never even hold hands. In the romance terms that Phelps overlays onto their lives, Rebecca "had not even offered to embroider him a banner, nor to net him a silken favor, nor to fringe so much as a scarf for the next tournament to be held in Primrose Court [the courtyard on which their building is located]."The only sign of affection between them is Rebecca's act of darning Galahad's socks—and even that occurs after they ask the landlady if it is proper.This innate nobility of character raises them to the level of legendary figures.The narrator notes that "if Di Rimini had worked beside Rebecca at the necktie factory, she would have learned a royal lesson. And Abelard might well have sat at the feet of Galahad, making organs with his grimy hands. And if Eve or Isaac had wandered into the first floor front, or second back corner of $16^1/2$, on a lonesome, rainy evening, they would have wept for pity, and smiled for blessing, and mused much."

The Galahad of the story, as well as the woman he loves—for women are always a concern to Phelps—must live a lonely life until his first wife dies. But Phelps's version diverges from other Galahad stories because her protagonist is ultimately relieved of his loneliness; and that relief comes not by a vision of Christ and saints but by Rebecca, the woman who reveals his integrity.The narrator asks, "Did you ever know a lost knight to be found until a woman tracked him? Is it, therefore, surprising that if it had not been for Rebecca Rock, Sir Galahad Holt would have escaped recognition completely, and the modest number of men and women now admitted to the secret of the discovery have gone the hungrier and the sadder for the loss?"Thus, even in this story of a male hero who traditionally achieves his fame in part because he is so chaste that he rejects women totally, Phelps manages to make a woman central to the plot. By casting characters from the lower classes in terms of the Arthurian legends, thereby ennobling them, and then by reinterpreting the Grail story so that a woman becomes both the Grail and the discoverer of the nobility of the Grail knight, Phelps transforms her source material into an innovative, contemporary quest tale.

This tendency to shift the focus from traditional concerns and to give women prominent roles can be seen even in a short poem such as Sara Teasdale's "Galahad in the Castle of the Maidens." Based on one of the murals executed by Edwin Austin Abbey for the Boston Public Library, this sonnet focuses, in almost cinematic style, not on the triumphant figure of Galahad but on a particular figure among the group of maidens in the image, who has "hid her face away" because of "Love's shame and sweet humility." Her reaction contrasts with the others' "queenlike grace" and even with Galahad's "dim" eyes. The reader is left to wonder about the maiden who has such deep feelings for the young knight but who is unwilling or unable to express her desire directly.

Just as women writers tend to rework the Tristan legend by placing the emphasis on one or the other of the Isolts or to focus on women in retelling the

Grail story, so too do they tend, in the larger legend, to emphasize female characters who play a relatively minor part or whose roles are less than ideal in the
received versions by men. One such character is the figure who appears in the
dual guises of Elaine of Astolat and the Lady of Shalott.

One of the earliest treatments of the story, or more precisely an analogue
of the story, is by Letitia Elizabeth Landon, a poet and novelist who wrote under
the pseudonym L. E. L. Her poem "A Legend of Tintagel Castle," first published
in 1833, offers a fascinating variant of the Elaine of Astolat story, with a nymph
dying of unrequited love for Lancelot. The nymph takes Lancelot to her cave where
"They might have been happy" if, like the flowers, they could have dwelled in their
own private place. But Lancelot hears "the sound of the trumpet," a symbol for
the call of the world. As a result, "the wood-nymph was left as aye woman will
be, / Who trusts her whole being, oh, false love, to thee." She waits, like Elaine
of Astolat, for Lancelot to return, thinking that "every sun-beam that brightened
the gloom" is "the waving of Lancelot's plume." His love, however, is for "Genevra,"
and when the lady realizes that, she dies. Like the Lily Maid's, her body floats down
to Camelot in a barge:

> With purple sails heavily drooping around,
> The mast, and the prow, with the vale lily bound;
> And towed by two swans, a small vessel drew near,
> But high on the deck was a pall-covered bier.

Lancelot weeps at the sight. But the author, who recognizes the waste in the
nymph's death, observes that "Too late we awake to regret but what tears / Can
bring back the waste to our hearts and our years!"

A number of other women have also written short lyrical poems about the
tragic character of Elaine. Edna St. Vincent Millay's "Elaine," a monologue by the
title character, is notable less for its picture of Elaine's devotion than for revealing the desperation of her love, which even her studied composure can not hide,
and for the way that love hints at her impending tragic end: as Elaine pleads to an
absent Lancelot to return, she promises to be so unobtrusive that "You needs must
think—if you should think— / The lily maid had died." As in Landon's poem,
the shift of focus to the dying woman garners sympathy for her plight.

Elizabeth Stuart Phelps's "Elaine and Elaine," despite its title, deals with only
one Elaine, the Lily Maid who dies for love of Lancelot. Like the title, the poem
itself is somewhat cryptic: it seems to argue paradoxically for silence in the face
of the tragedy. The two sections of the poem end with questions about whether

we should speak about Elaine if the steersman of her barge "speaketh not a word" and whether "If she [Elaine] / Sayeth nothing, how should we?" It may be that Phelps wishes her readers to be silent so they can reflect on the fact that Elaine's position is representative, as is the fate of the Lady of Shalott in Aline Kilmer's poem "For All Ladies of Shalott," in which the circumstance of the towered lady becomes emblematic of that of many women. Phelps's penultimate stanza—"Oh! the river floweth fast. / Who is justified at last?"—implies that all people end their journeys through life without any ultimate justification for what they have, or have not, done.

The most interesting reinterpretation of the Elaine character by a woman is found in another of Phelps's works, the short story "The Lady of Shalott," which translates Tennyson's poem of that name into a nineteenth-century context, thereby making it more relevant and realistic. The title character, now a seventeen-year-old woman, was crippled at the age of five when "her mother threw her down-stairs by mistake, instead of the whisky-jug." This bit of information, the author adds, is one "fact which I think Mr. Tennyson has omitted to mention in his poem." The alcoholic mother dies a few years later, leaving the Lady of Shalott with only a sister, Sary Jane, for support. Her life becomes still more pathetic because her immobility prevents her from weaving—or from doing anything else. In Tennyson's poem, the function of weaving implies artistic creativity, and while it cannot alone provide fulfillment, it does offer some happiness: "But in her web she still delights / To weave the mirror's magic sights," wrote Tennyson. In Phelps's story, the weaver is not the title character but Sary Jane, who "made nankeen vests, at sixteen and three-quarter cents a dozen." Sary Jane must work hunched over under the eaves of the small garret room in which the young women live, and the earnings from her piecework barely allow the two to subsist.

Their apartment, described ironically as a palace, is another point of contrast between Tennyson's Lady and Phelps's character. The former lives in "Four gray walls, and four gray towers," which "overlook a space of flowers." The palace in the story

> measured just twelve by nine feet. . . . There were two windows and
> a loose scuttle to the palace. The scuttle let in the snow in winter and
> the sun in summer, and the rain and wind at all times. It was quite a
> diversion to the Lady of Shalott to see how many different ways of
> doing a disagreeable thing seemed to be practicable to that scuttle.
> Besides the bed on which the Lady of Shalott lay, there was a stove in
> the palace, two chairs, a very ragged rag-mat, a shelf, with two

notched cups and plates upon it, one pewter teaspoon, and a looking-glass. . . .

Moreover, Phelps's Lady of Shalott is trapped by her disability in a tower of sorts, for her room opens directly onto a flight of stairs so steep that in times of emergency they become a death trap rather than an escape route.

Phelps's narrative strategy here is obvious: looking to the traditional story, she offers analogous but more pathetic and oppressive details. Like the castle tower of Tennyson's Lady that becomes a slum apartment at the top of a dangerous flight of stairs, the river that flows past the tower in Tennyson's poem becomes "a dirty hydrant in the yard, four flights below, which supplied the Lady of Shalott and all her neighbors." And whereas the tower in the poem overlooks "a space of flowers," the only flowers in the life of Phelps's character are those provided by "the Flower Charity," which almost hide the odor of the slum. "You can 'most stand the yard with them round," says the Lady of the story. When Sary Jane brings her sister the flowers, however, the pathos of their situation is highlighted by the fact that they can afford only a single lemon between them for dinner.

But the primary correspondence between the poem and the story is the mirror through which Phelps's character sees her surroundings and the doctor, her Lancelot figure, who might have been her salvation. The smallness of her world is symbolized by the size of her mirror: "All the world came for the Lady of Shalott into her little looking-glass,—the joy of it, the anguish of it, the hope and fear of it, the health and hurt,—ten by six inches of it exactly."

The mirror is also used as a device for social commentary. Emphasizing the drastic inequalities in society, the narrator comments that "the Lady of Shalott would have experienced rather a touch of mortification than of envy if she had known that there was a mirror in a house just around the corner measuring almost as many feet. But that was one of the advantages of being the Lady of Shalott. She never parsed life in the comparative degree." Sometimes the mirror affords the Lady of the story views that disturb her, like the sad and hungry children in the window of the adjacent garret; and her only recourse is to tip her mirror so they do not come within its scope.

As in Tennyson's poem, the cracking of the mirror foreshadows the Lady of Shalott's death. In Tennyson's poem, the mirror cracks when the Lady sees Lancelot, and her world of shadows is no longer sufficient to sustain her. In Phelps's story, the mirror is cracked by a rock thrown by street urchins just after the Lady has seen in it the image of a doctor who is visiting the slum. In response to her cry, the doctor rushes to her room and takes pity on the sickly young woman.

Declaring her curable, he promises to tend "directly" to the terrible conditions outside the window in which Sary Jane sits and sews. (Although not described in detail, those conditions are gruesome enough to make the doctor turn away "with a sudden white face.") But two more days pass before the Board of Health arrives. They are met by "another board," a pine board on which the body of the Lady is being removed from her room. This Lady of Shalott does not rest in a wooden boat singing her last song but is carried, silent, on a plain wooden slab. Nor is there even the final compliment from her Lancelot figure—Tennyson's Lancelot says: "She had a lovely face; / God in his mercy send her grace"; but all the doctor can utter when he sees the body is: "We're too late, I see."

The plight of Phelps's Lady of Shalott is caused by a variety of social ills— her mother's alcoholism, the labor laws that allow her sister to be paid so little, the lack of adequate health care for the poor, and the slum conditions in which she is forced to live. Phelps's purpose undoubtedly is to call attention to these ills by means of analogy to Tennyson's familiar poem and by deromanticizing one of the most romantic and most recognizable images of the nineteenth century—that of the Lady of Shalott floating down to Camelot. There is nothing romantic about the pine board or the steep flight of stairs down which Phelps's Lady is brought.

While Elaine/the Lady of Shalott is truly a sad and compelling character, among the women of the Arthurian legends it is neither she nor Isolt who receives the most attention; rather, it is Guinevere. And it must be admitted that two Victorian men, Alfred, Lord Tennyson and William Morris, first perceived the possibilities inherent in the tale of the queen. Tennyson's first collection of idylls, *Idylls of the King* (1859), told the stories of four women: Enid, Elaine, Vivien, and Guinevere. Yet, in their final form, three of these idylls were retitled to include and even to give preeminence to male characters. "Enid" became two idylls: "The Marriage of Geraint" and "Geraint and Enid"; "Elaine" became "Lancelot and Elaine"; and "Vivien" became "Merlin and Vivien." Only the idyll "Guinevere" retained its original name and the corresponding emphasis on the female character. Of course, the picture of the queen presented by Tennyson is typically Victorian: on one level, at least, she is the wife who has failed her husband. The modern reader, however, understands Guinevere's situation and empathizes with her. Married to the near-perfect Arthur, she has no chance to fulfill her normal human desires—except by turning to Lancelot. No doubt that is why Tennyson's final image of Guinevere groveling before the austere Arthur, who magnanimously but without warmth forgives her, troubles modern readers and especially feminist critics. It also troubled Elizabeth Stuart Phelps, who responded to that image in her fiction.

The narrator of Phelps's "The True Story of Guenever" explicitly "rebel[s] against the story" as told by Tennyson because she "cannot bear to leave her [Guenever] there upon the convent floor." Phelps is, of course, alluding specifically to the passage in Tennyson's "Guinevere" in which Arthur visits his wife in the convent before the final battle:

> . . . She sat
> Stiff-stricken, listening; but when armed feet
> Thro' the long gallery from the outer doors
> Rang coming, prone from off her seat she fell,
> And grovell'd with her face against the floor.

This scene becomes for Phelps a symbolic icon of the distorted relationship between man and woman: Guinevere yearning for forgiveness before the masterful, royal, almost divine Arthur. In the image of Guinevere, she writes, "we see a delicate, high-strung, impulsive creature, a trifle mismated to a faultless, unimpulsive man. We shudder to discover in her, before she discovers it for or in herself, that, having given herself to Arthur, she yet has not given all; that there arises now another self, an existence hitherto unknown, unsuspected,—a character groping, unstable, unable, a wandering wind, a mist of darkness, a chaos, over which Arthur has no empire, of which he has no comprehension, and of which she—whether of Nature or of training who shall judge?—has long since discrowned herself the Queen."

In "The True Story of Guenever," Phelps appropriates to the female voice a traditionally male story and provides a resolution that prevents her Guenever from groveling—but only by having her accept a less than satisfactory marriage. And, in the end, the appropriation of the story is more interesting and makes more of a feminist statement than the narrative resolution. Phelps's "true story," she says, came to her through her washerwoman, not from any of the number of male authors who tell of the queen's shame. This rejection both of the male voice and of class privileging is in itself a comment on the original story and a means of achieving truth about female characters. Phelps writes:

> Who can capture the where, the how, the wherefore of a train of
> fancy? Was it because I thought of Guenever that I heard the story?
> Or because I heard the story that I thought of Guenever? My
> washwoman told it, coming in that bitter day at twilight and sitting
> by the open fire, as I had bidden her, for rest and warmth. What should

she know of the Bulfinch and Ellis and Tennyson and Dunlop, that had fallen from my lap upon the cricket at her feet, that she should sit, with hands across her draggled knees, and tell me such a story? Or were Dunlop and the rest untouched upon the library shelves till after she had told it? Whether the legend drew me to the fact, or the fact impelled me to the legend? Indeed, why should I know? It is enough that I heard the story. She told it in her way. I, for lack of her fine, realistic manner, must tell it in my own.

Phelps thus declares her version to be "the true story of Guenever the Queen," much as Hervey has her Merlin proclaim that the distorted image of Morgan le Fay is set right by the true account that he has locked in St. Stephen's Church.

In Phelps's redaction, Arthur—translated here into a master carpenter— is called "the blameless king." But obviously Phelps lays some of the blame for Guenever's actions upon him, for he fails to appreciate the delicacy and impulsiveness of her nature. Of late, Phelps says, Arthur "was often dull . . . what with being out of work so much, and the foot he lamed with a rusty nail." Arthur's dullness extends to his understanding of his wife's needs. At times he can hardly be more mistaken about what she wants. When Guenever has a toothache, Arthur's advice is merely to "Take some drops." But, as Phelps writes,

> There was nothing Guenever wanted to take. She wanted, in fact, to be taken; to be caught and gathered to her husband's safe, broad breast; to be held against his faithful heart; to be fondled and crooned over and cuddled. She would have her aching head imprisoned in his healthy hands. And if he should think to kiss the agonizing cheek, as she would kiss a woman's cheek if she loved her and she had the toothache? But Arthur never thought! Men were so dull at things. Only women knew how to take care of one another. Only women knew the infinite fine languages of love. A man was tender when he thought of it, in a blunt, broad way.

Phelps's Guenever is mismated not, as in Tennyson, because Arthur is so far above the average man that he is unable to understand human needs and desires, but rather because he is typical of the average man who, for Phelps, is unable to understand a woman's needs and desires. Arthur "supposed, if she had the toothache, she wouldn't want to be touched. He knew he shouldn't. So, not knowing what else to do, he just limped royally about and got the supper, like a dear old

dull king as he was." Launcelot—"the young bricklayer to whom Arthur and
Guenever had rented the spare room when the hard times came on"—is more
active in trying to help her; he goes to the druggist for laudanum to treat the pain.
Unfortunately, Guenever cannot tolerate the medication, and so it is useless. Similarly, Arthur is unable to give even a simple compliment. "Secretly he liked to see
Guenever in the bird-of-paradise chair, with the moody firelight upon her; but
he had never said so—it was not Arthur's 'way.' Launcelot, now, for instance had
said something to that effect several times."

In Phelps's "true story," as Guenever departs with her lover, she hears an
old gossip saying, "Guenever has fled with Launcelot. The Queen has left the King.
All the world will know it by to-morrow." Immediately she feels pangs of guilt.
There comes to her "a revelation awful as some that might shock a soul upon the
day of doom . . . that she was no longer a bewildered or a pitiable, but an evil
creature." She finds herself in a stormy wilderness with only Launcelot, who provides no comfort. A voice tells her she can never be clean, but she is unsure
whether the voice belongs to Launcelot or to "the deathly wind." When she says
"Perhaps I have been dreaming or have been ill. Let me go home at once to the
King!" the voice, "which seemed neither of Launcelot nor of the wind, but yet
akin to both," tells her that "there is no mistake," and that "you are not dreaming
and you can never return to the King. The thing that is done is done. Sorrow and
longing are dead to help you. Agony and repentance are feeble friends. Neither
man nor Nature can wash away a stain." But then another vision appears to her:

> It seemed then suddenly to the kneeling woman, that He whose body
> and blood were broken for tempted souls appeared to seek her out
> across the desolated moor. The Man whose stainless lips were first to
> touch the cup of the Holy Grael, which all poor souls should after
> Him go seeking up and down upon the earth, stood in the pure white
> snow, and, smiling, spoke to her.
>
> "*Though your sins,*" he said, "*are scarlet, they shall be white.*"

Having begged divine forgiveness, Guenever apparently receives it. But in a striking reversal, almost as if the word of Christ cannot be trusted, she finds no redemption. She is in the same position towards Christ that she is towards Arthur
in Tennyson's *Idylls*: "she groveled on the ground where the sacred Feet had stood,
which now were vanished from her. Wretched woman that she was! Who would
deliver her from this bondage to her life's great holy love? If Arthur would but
open the door for her in the fair distance, where the palace windows shone; if he

would take a single step towards her where she kneeled within the wilderness";
but "the King took no step toward the wilderness. The King was mute as death
and cold as his own white soul. On Arthur's throne was never more a place for
Guenever." Guenever remains groveling, wretched because she must depend on
Christ, who seems to deceive her, or on another man, Arthur, who is cold and
uncaring, to deliver her from her bondage. And neither does so. It is up to the
narrator, or the washerwoman who is her source, to give the Guenever of the
tale what little relief she can obtain. Despite the statement of Launcelot, another
unreliable male voice—if indeed it is his voice—that what has happened is no
dream, Guenever wakes to find herself in Arthur's sheltering arms. She has been
redeemed by the storyteller's suggestion that her escape with Launcelot was only
a nightmare induced by too much laudanum. Thus the Queen can wake, morally
unblemished, to a loving Arthur.

This ending raises Guenever from the convent floor and eradicates her "disgrace, exile, and despair." Yet the price she pays is certainly high: a tepid relationship with a man who holds typically nineteenth-century attitudes. By accepting
the limitations of such an arrangement, she attains a modicum of peace and re-
spectability but not the Holy Grail of female fulfillment, which Phelps's fiction
suggests is an ideal not yet achievable by women in this world.

Another important figure in the development of the character of the queen,
William Morris, was among the first writers to give Guinevere her own voice.
By allowing her to speak for herself, Morris afforded genuine insight into her
psyche and into her society. In Morris's poem "The Defence of Guinevere," the
queen uses her wits to delay Arthur's death verdict. But, for all of her rhetorical
cleverness, she remains a damsel in distress who does not act independently but
instead awaits rescue by her knight in shining armor.

Later women poets also utilized the device of woman's narration to explore
the queen's real position as a woman married to a king who places political above
personal affairs. For example, in Sara Teasdale's "Guenevere," a monologue in the
tradition of Morris's "Defence of Guenevere," the queen complains of being
"branded for a single fault"; describes vividly her meeting with Lancelot; and reveals, with great emotion, her frustration with those who expect her to play a
particular role, to "be right fair, / A little kind, and gownèd wondrously." Teasdale's
accent grave on the e in "gownèd" highlights, simultaneously, the word itself and
the artificiality of the role into which Guinevere is forced. The whole poem, in
fact, can be read as a woman's rejection of the demand to conform. Woman is
valued, the speaker of the poem seems to be saying, not for her own ideas or
emotions but for her doll-like elegance. And when she fails to live up to expecta-

tions, she is branded, like the Guinevere in Phelps's story, a "hated thing," even by the beggars and kitchen maids.

Dorothy Parker's "Guinevere at Her Fireside" presents a very different kind of woman. Her thoroughly modern and more cynical queen respects the king but is unhappy that her bed has become just "a thing to kneel beside." Arthur's lack of attention to her because he is too involved with ruling, his inability to champion her because he is king (a motif found, for example, in Malory), is translated into sexual terms. As Parker's Guinevere explains in her own words, she decided to turn to Lancelot in order to compensate for Arthur's neglect. (Tristram, in her estimation the better catch, "was busied otherwhere.")

The tradition of giving voice to Guinevere is continued by contemporary writers like Wendy Mnookin. The very title of Mnookin's *Guenever Speaks* underscores the fact that the volume is a first-person account of the events that affect the queen. And that acccount is significantly different from the usual male-oriented versions of her story: Mnookin's poems treat subjects that are far removed from or neglected in more conventional tellings. In one poem, Guenever recalls a childhood incident; in others she prays for a child and then loses the baby. "Guenever Retreats to Almesbury After Arthur's Death" describes the simple sensuous act of working in the convent's herb garden and the subsequent modest activities of Guenever's day, which are charged with emotion and meaning because of the contrast they offer to her former life. And in the poem "Guenever Returns from the Garden," the queen declares her intention never to leave the nunnery or to look again on Lancelot—not because of an asceticism she has learned through the consequences of their love but because she "cannot lose him / again."

The sense of love of life and its pleasures that makes the confinement in Almesbury so tragic for Mnookin's Guenever is also evident in "Guinevere in Almesbury Convent" by Lizette Woodworth Reese, a poem published a century earlier and told not in the queen's voice but with some of the same empathy for her. Guinevere, though retired to the convent, is not yet resigned to her life there. In the opening stanza, as she "pores the missal on her knee," she catches by chance a sound or a smell that frees her "From the long days of fast and prayer; / And all about comes Camelot." The beauty of the Almesbury lilies or the song of the nightingales that Guinevere continues to notice enhances the pathos of her situation; and the reader realizes that she remains a woman with a great love for wonder, a woman who is ill-suited to her new life in the nunnery.

While many works focus on other figures, Guinevere is still the central female character in the Arthurian tradition, just as Arthur is the central male character. Therefore, it is not surprising that in addition to the poems discussed above, a spate of recent novels by women have retold the story of Camelot from the queen's perspective (the device of female narration in popular contemporary fiction having been popularized by Vera Chapman in her "Three Damosels" trilogy— *The Green Knight* [1975], *The King's Damosel* [1976], and *King Arthur's Daughter* [1976]). The trilogies by Sharan Newman (*Guinevere* [1981], *The Chessboard Queen* [1983], and *Guinevere Evermore* [1985]) and by Persia Woolley (*Child of the Northern Spring* [1987], *Queen of the Summer Stars* [1990], and *Guinevere: The Legend in Autumn* [1991]), like Nancy McKenzie's historical novels (*The Child Queen: The Tale of Guinevere and King Arthur* [1994] and *The High Queen: The Tale of Guinevere and King Arthur Continues* [1995])—offer Guinevere's own views of her youth, her difficulties adjusting to the sweeping and radical social changes inherent in Arthur's reign, and her attempts to maintain her own independence, particularly in the face of patriarchal attitudes toward women.

Of course, Guinevere's story, like Arthur's, ends tragically. Perhaps it is this fact that prompts so many women to set all or part of their retellings in Avalon, a place of refuge and escape. For novelists from Anya Seton in her *Avalon* (1965) to the pseudonymous Mary J. Jones, author of the "lesbian Arthurian romance" *Avalon* (1991) in which Gwenhyfar's daughter becomes the Lady of the Lake and defends Avalon in the name of the Goddess against the evil queen Annis, the island of Avalon is both magical and mystical. Modern readers are probably most familiar with Marion Zimmer Bradley's presentation of the enchanted isle as a sanctuary where women have real power in her wildly popular novel *The Mists of Avalon* (1982) and its sequel *Lady of Avalon* (1997), which offers a similarly strong feminine presence as it spans the creation of Avalon and foreshadows the birth of Arthur.

But Avalon also figures in the writings of nineteenth-century women. In "The Prophecy of Merlin" (1802), Anne Bannerman depicts Avalon as the place where Arthur is destined to remain until it is time to fulfill Merlin's prophecy of his return. As Arthur arrives at the "charmed Isle," he is greeted by a beautiful woman who gives him a cup from which to drink. As he does, he sees in the woman's face "a demon-smile"; but she is demonic only in the sense that she is otherworldly. In fact, she is performing a necessary function by helping Arthur to sleep—albeit for a long time—and thus to prepare for his eventual return. The poem ends on an appropriately peaceful note: nothing reaches Arthur's "burial place" except "the murmurs of the wave."

A much more unusual use of Avalon (or Avillion) appears in the story "Avillion," written in 1853 by Dinah Maria Mulock Craik. A newlywed nineteenth-century couple, the sickly Wilfred Mayer and his wife Lilias Hay, embark on an ocean voyage during which they meet Herr Foerster, a German physician. Foerster is nearly monomaniacal in his quest for "the Island of the Blest," which he has been seeking at sea for ten years and where he believes he will find happiness and eternal life. Despite Wilfred's reservations, Lilias consults the physician about her husband's illness; and "she had her way, for it was the right way." Foerster gives a "rare drug" to Wilfred, who seems to die (although he never loses awareness of the events that follow, including his own burial at sea).

When Wilfred wakes, he finds himself in "the Happy Isles" of Greek mythology, where—in a conversation with Ulysses—he learns that "there was no to-morrow," no thought of the future, no goals or striving. But, realizing that he is different from those who inhabit this region, Wilfred decides he must leave. Seeing the moon create a "glimmering bridge of light" on the water, he determines to follow that bridge, whether it be "to Infinity or Nothingness," and he begins walking on the water away from the isle. Soon he sees another island, representing "another sphere of being," whereon is built a splendid palace.

As the light vanishes from beneath his feet, Wilfred sinks into the water. In answer to his prayer for aid, a boat appears and he is pulled from the sea by its pilot, who turns out to be Sir Galahad. Apparently, Wilfred has reached the isle of Avillion "where dwell many good Christian knights, with those knights of Faërie who serve God." This is a middle point in what is almost an evolutionary process, for Wilfred will pass on to "Eden-land, or the Happy Isle," a place surprisingly like the real world, or at least like a somewhat idealized version of the real world, where he feels the chill of autumn and discovers that the inhabitants perform productive labor.

Avillion is a step towards this third stage, for in the isle of Arthur, as Merlin tells Wilfred, there "is intermixed just so much of evil and of suffering as will purify and lift us one stage nearer to divine perfection." This view of Avillion as a stage in the improvement of its inhabitants is certainly unique, since traditionally there is neither sorrow nor suffering on the isle. But in Craik's Avillion—unlike the classical Isle of the Blest—people have desires: Merlin is still tempted by visions of Vivienne, and, except for Galahad, each of the inhabitants faces some kind of trial.

A significant aspect of "Avillion" is its portrayal of some of the women of the Arthurian legend. In his book *King Arthur's Laureate*, J. Phillip Eggers points out a remarkable anticipation of Tennyson's "Guinevere" idyll in Craik's depiction of a stern Arthur confronting the sinful Guinevere and sees this parallel as a sign of "the distinctively Victorian sentiments" of the idyll because they are so close to those in "this popular piece of fiction." But it may be more than just a case of two writers reflecting parallel sentiments. It may be that in his depiction of some of the women of the *Idylls* Tennyson actually used Craik's piece as a source. It may even be that he got the notion of dividing the women of Camelot into the true and the false from the references in Craik's story to "the false queen" and again to the "false queen, false wife, false woman." In fact, the tale of Elaine might have suggested the frame for Tennyson's idyll of the Lily Maid, whose basic story duplicates some of the details of Craik's account. When Elaine says, "it is no more Sir Lancelot's fault / Not to love me, than it is mine to love / Him," her statement is similar to that of Craik's Elaine, who says to Lancelot: "Nay: it was no sin of thine. I worshipped thee, as one should only worship Heaven." And Craik's reference to the "cruel scorn which, knowing her pure love, instead of requital offered pitiful gold" may have been reworked into Lancelot's offer to Elaine in the idyll that should she marry a poor knight, he would "Endow you with broad land and territory / Even to the half my realm beyond the seas."

The brief description of Vivienne in Craik's account seems even more likely to have provided material for Tennyson. Craik's Vivienne is a young temptress, of whom the elderly Merlin says, "Dost thou not feel her young breath, that once came upon my already wrinkled brow like the breath of spring?" And the "lithe form" of Craik's Vivienne is reminiscent of the "lithe arm" that Tennyson's Vivien tightens and loosens serpentlike around Merlin's neck, just as Merlin's memory of Vivienne's "light laugh" that he hears just "as the spell-closed rock shut down upon me" suggests the scornful shriek of "O fool" that echoes in Merlin's ears at the moment he is entrapped in the oak in Tennyson's poem. Tennyson's reinterpretation of Merlin as an aged man, not as the young man or child typically depicted in literature of the Middle Ages, may also have been based on his knowledge of "Avillion."

Even if Craik's influence on Tennyson is not as direct as such strong parallels would indicate, her view of the Arthurian women is nonetheless as interesting as it is distinctive. Morgan le Fay, for example, is a character ignored by Tennyson and generally avoided by other male Victorian poets. But Craik gives her "Morgue la Faye" an important and unusual role as a figure in whom "woman's soul" shines "tearfully in her majestic eyes." She reminds the narrator of his beloved Lilias (though at the time he cannot remember enough of his earthly life to know of whom she reminds him). When Morgue looks on Wilfred, "a gleam of womanly pity softened the steel-like brightness of her eyes." Most notably, she restores his memory of the world he has left behind. In contrast to her villainy in some medieval works and in J. Comyns Carr's play *King Arthur*, one of only a few Victorian pieces to treat her, Craik's Morgue la Faye is both healer and wise woman.

Though the story of "Avillion" ends as a dream that Wilfred experiences while under the influence of the German doctor's medicine, the dream concludes with Wilfred's forgiveness of Foerster after he hears his story in the Happy Isle.

Wilfred awakens cured from his fatal illness—he and Lilias live happily and "shall grow old among our children's children"—but his redemption is as much spiritual as physical.

Craik's atypical concept of Avillion as a temporary refuge, a step on the way to another level of human awareness, may also have been suggestive to Tennyson. The laureate's Arthurian world is, after all, only a stage of development. In Darwinian fashion, that world takes people beyond where they were—moves them away from the beasts who dominate Camelot at the beginning of the *Idylls* and towards the angels. Similarly, Craik's Arthurian realm is a stage in the development of humanity. In both cases, the old order must change and yield place to the new, "lest one good custom corrupt the world."

Craik, however, was not the only woman to make such symbolic use of Avalon; another is Sallie Bridges. Though virtually unknown today and apparently little recognized in her own day, Bridges wrote a sequence of Arthurian poems that is of considerable interest largely because of the ways in which she recast some of the traditional material. The sequence "Legends of the Round Table," which appears in her collection entitled *Marble Isle, Legends of the Round Table, and Other Poems*, contains fourteen poems that tell Arthur's story from the pulling of the sword from the stone to his resting in Avalon ("Avilion" in Bridges's poem). Bridges says pointedly that she got the ideas for many of her poems "several years before reading a line of Tennyson" when she "met with the old romance of 'Prince Arthur' translated from the French," by which she means Malory's *Morte d'Arthur*.

While most of the poems in Bridges' sequence are straightforward retellings of tales from Malory, a few are genuinely original. "Avilion," the final poem—and the best—in the sequence, owes the least to her source. Its narrator tells of her sorrow that her work will soon be forgotten, and she wishes that she could go to rest in the Happy Isle as Arthur did. The action of the poem begins with a striking image:

> And so I closed my tired eyes, that press'd
> Two tears between the lids, that, as they touch'd
> The level ground, into a wonder grew;
> For, lo! a lake that spread its waters up
> Nigh to my feet, while through the sunset glow
> A black barge hove in sight, like one that came
> For wounded Arthur, only now it bore
> No fair, crown'd queens, no hooded, weeping dames!
> Only a pallid steersman stood at helm,

> With white garb stirless as a statue's robe
> That seem'd to sweep adown o'er folded wings.

The Avalon she reaches is an idyllic place where she is aware of the meaning of "earth's great riddle" and the "grand significance e'en evil took." She encounters there "one that I knew" but who had died before her and who awaits her arrival, finding even the joys of Avilion incomplete without her.

In the Happy Isle, the narrator also meets Arthur, Guinevere, and Lancelot. The former lovers are purified of their passion for one another. And Arthur is the ideal ruler. He is "grand in presence" and yet has "Such courteous, kindly mien, that one who begg'd / Might call him 'brother.'"Thus the Arthur of Bridges' poem is like many other American Arthurs and Arthurian characters in that he is not separated from the common person and in that he realizes he must serve those who trust in him. When Arthur asks if men still hope for his return "To do my best to win for them the right," he is touched by the narrator's response. She gives him "a picture of the times, / And how the nations groan'd because was found / No strong, true leader pure in life and aim." So he decides "The time is ripe" for him to come back "To lead the way to truth through seas of blood!"The poem ends after Arthur announces to the knights who would join him that he must go alone. And then something, perhaps the flapping of the barge's sail in the wind, breaks the spell and she finds herself:

> . . . once more within this world,
> On which the shades had gather'd into night,
> And mid the throng that wait the Coming King!

"Avilion" is remarkable not only for its depiction of Avalon but also for its call for Arthur's return. Although no specific allusion is made to contemporary events, the reader cannot help but wonder if the poem is really a comment on the Civil War. This seems a plausible interpretation since, in the same volume, another poem entitled "The Question of the Day in 1860" ponders the "dissolution of the Union," which Bridges clearly thinks would be a great tragedy. She writes:

> Dissolve this Union, and dear hope dies out
> In all the eager souls that watch its stars
> Rise steadfast o'er the earth with growing light.

Bridges calls her "young and lovely land" that is "Throned on two seas" the "Queen of nations." Perhaps it is the threat to this queen that causes the "nations" to groan in "Avilion"; and perhaps when Arthur says the time is ripe for him to return "To lead the way to truth through seas of blood!" it is the bloodshed of the Civil War and the truth of maintaining the Union to which Bridges alludes.

For Bridges, then, as for other writers, part of Avalon's appeal rests in the hope of the return of Arthur and in the idea of a second chance for the ideal he represents, the opportunity to set things right the second time around. But, as the poem "From Avalon" (1896) by Emily Huntington Miller demonstrates, the enchanted isle is also a symbol of refuge from the world. Miller describes Avalon as:

> . . . that green and tranquil isle,
> Encircled by the arms of summer tides
> That sway and smile, and whisper of the sea.

It is a place that is "not far away," at least to the imaginative person. Miller observes that

> Oft have I found its shelter. When the stress
> Of warring winds, and sharp tumultuous storms
> Have left me spent and breathless on the field,
> Then my swift thoughts, for healing and for rest,
> Bear me away to peaceful Avalon.

As a sanctuary and as a site of personal renewal, Avalon offers some relief from the harsh tragic conclusion of the Arthurian story. As such, it is perhaps analogous to the redemption of characters discussed above.

The hope for a second chance also underlies a recent poem, Valerie Nieman's beautifully crafted "The Naming of the Lost." Approaching the Arthurian tradition in a highly original way, Nieman reunites Merlin and Nimue in a strange setting, twentieth-century West Virginia. The Southern countryside is infused with great mythic significance: a simple oak chair with a broken rung becomes a Siege Visionary in which the lost and nameless wanderer discovers her identity as Nimue and is reconciled with Merlin. Their reconciliation, which is also Nimue's redemption for her act centuries earlier of imprisoning Merlin, is described in evocative imagery and a blank verse that flows as smoothly as the river of the poem and the water with which Nimue is associated. She tells Merlin that she remains:

the water-flow, and you the lasting stone.
Can you embrace, and not be worn away?
Can I be held and not break free to foam,
or chafe myself, confined, to stagnancy?

Merlin's reply is that their incompatibility was in the former time, the age of Camelot, but that "there are times between the stars / when all the elements are joined." With a touch, Merlin lifts Nimue from the chair and says, "We'll sing together a song, and arches raise / of a new Camelot which shall not fall," a Camelot built not on political struggles but on their singular and enduring love. In a deft contrast of images, "The chair crumbles, falls fine to ash and sifts / upon the flowered lawn," just as the two mythic figures raise, through their reunion, the new Camelot of personal happiness.

Nieman, like many of the women who rewrite Arthurian stories, asserts a personal vision that differs sharply from that of her male counterparts. Taking radical liberties with the traditional material, she emphasizes the female character and offers to both her female and male characters a possibility of redemption and renewal that is often lacking in more conventional retellings. It is precisely these qualities that define the forgotten tradition of Arthurian literature by women.

Arthurian Literature by Women

Texts

The Honeysuckle

MARIE DE FRANCE

(TRANSLATED BY NORRIS J. LACY)

I am both pleased and very eager to tell you the truth about a lay entitled *Chevrefueil*: why it was composed and how it came about. Many people have recited it to me, and I have also found it in written form. It concerns Tristan and the queen and their wondrous love, which brought them great pain and eventually caused the two of them to die on the very same day.

King Mark, angry with his nephew Tristan, banished him from his land because of the young man's love for the queen. Tristan made his way to his own land and could not return. He spent a full year in South Wales, where he had been born. But then he risked death and destruction. You should not be surprised at that, for anyone who loves with true love is in distress and sorrow when he cannot satisfy his desires. Tristan was distraught and melancholy, and as a result he left his land and went directly to Cornwall, where the queen lived. So as not to be seen, he stayed in the forest all alone, showing himself only in the evening when it was time to find shelter. At night he took lodging with peasants and poor people. He asked them for news of the king's actions, and they told him they understood that there was a proclamation summoning the barons to Tintagel. There the king wanted to hold court at Pentecost, and everyone would be present. There would be much celebrating and rejoicing—and the queen would be with them.

Tristan was overjoyed to hear this news, for if she traveled there, he could not fail to see her pass by. On the day the king set out, Tristan entered the forest by the road he knew the procession would take. He cut a piece of a hazel branch and squared it. After preparing the stick, he carved his name on it with his knife. If the queen saw it—and she would surely be watching for it, since she had seen the same thing once before—she would know that the stick was placed there by her lover. It symbolized what was in a message he had sent to her: that he had been there for a long time, watching and waiting, to learn how he might be able to see her, for he could not possibly live without her. The two of them were like the honeysuckle that clings to the hazel: when it has attached itself to the wood and has twined around it, they can survive together; but should anyone try to separate them, the hazel quickly dies, and the honeysuckle with it. "My love, so it is with the two of us: you cannot live without me, nor I without you."

The queen rode along. She looked down at the sloping path, saw the piece of wood, and understood what it was. She recognized the letters and ordered the knights with her to stop, saying that she wished to dismount and rest. They did as she commanded, and she moved away from her companions, accompanied only by her faithful servant Brangain. She went a short way off the path, and in the forest she found the man who loved her more than any living thing. Both of them were overcome with joy. They told each other everything that was in their hearts. Then she explained how he might be reconciled with the king and told him how distraught she had been when the king, because of an accusation made against Tristan, banished him from his land. Then she departed, leaving her lover behind, and at that moment they both began to weep.

Tristan returned to Wales, where he stayed until his uncle sent for him. At the queen's suggestion, Tristan, who was a skilled harpist, composed a new lay to commemorate what he had written and the joy he had experienced at seeing his beloved. I will briefly name it: the English call it *Goatleaf*, and the French, *Chevrefueil*. This is the truth about the lay I have told you here.

Lanval

MARIE DE FRANCE

(TRANSLATED BY NORRIS J. LACY)

I will tell you the story of another lay, just as it happened. It is about a very worthy young man whose name, in Breton, is Lanval. King Arthur, who was valiant and courtly, was at Carlisle, because the Scots and Picts were laying waste the country: they had invaded the land of Logres and were frequently pillaging it. The king was there in summer, at Pentecost.

He distributed rich gifts to his counts and barons and to the knights of the Round Table, whose equal did not exist in all the world. He gave wives and land to all, except to one who had served him. That was Lanval, whom he forgot about. No one called the king's attention to him, for many were jealous of Lanval, because he was worthy, generous, handsome, and valiant. Some feigned affection for him, but they would not have been saddened if some misfortune had befallen him. He was the son of a king and thus of noble lineage, but he was far from his land. He belonged to King Arthur's household, but he had spent all his wealth, for the king gave him nothing, and Lanval asked him for nothing. Now Lanval was downcast and overcome with sadness. That, my lords, is hardly surprising: a disconsolate man in a strange land can be very forlorn when he has nowhere to turn for help.

This knight whom I am telling you about had long served the king. One day he mounted his horse and went away to amuse himself. He left the city and, all alone, came to a meadow. He dismounted beside a flowing stream, but his horse was trembling violently. He loosened the saddle girth, and the horse went away from him to roll around on the meadow. Lanval lay down with his cloak folded beneath his head. He was distraught because of his misfortune, and nothing around him pleased him.

As he was lying there, he looked downstream and saw two young women coming toward him. Never had he seen more lovely women. They were richly dressed in fitted tunics of dark silk, and their faces were very beautiful. The older of them—I am telling you the truth about this—carried a pair of basins made of finely crafted gold, and the other carried a towel. They came straight to the place where the knight lay. Lanval, who was well-mannered, stood up as they approached. They greeted him first and gave him their message: "Sir Lanval, my lady, who is noble and wise and fair, sends us to you; now come with us. We will take you safely to her: see, her pavilion is nearby."

The knight went with them, paying no attention to his horse, which was grazing on the meadow. They led him to the tent, which was beautiful and luxurious: neither Queen Semiramis, however much wealth, power, and knowledge she had, nor Emperor Octavian could have afforded even the flap of the tent. On top of it was a golden eagle; I cannot even guess the value of it, or of the ropes and poles that supported the walls. No king on earth, no matter how extravagant he might be, could have afforded it.

In the tent was the maiden. Neither the lily nor the rosebud, when it first appears in summer, could match her beauty. She lay on a fine bed, the coverings of which were worth a castle, and she wore only a shift. Her body was shapely and beautiful. To protect herself from the sun, she had covered herself with an expensive mantle of white ermine trimmed with Alexandrian silk, but her face, neck, breast, and side were uncovered. Her skin was whiter than the hawthorn blossom.

The knight approached, and the maiden called to him; he sat down beside the bed. "Lanval," she said, "fair friend, for your sake I left my land; I have come far to seek you. If you are worthy and noble, no emperor or count or king has ever had such joy or profit as you will, for I love you more than anything."

He looked at her and saw that she was beautiful, and Love's flame was kindled in his heart. He answered her in seemly fashion: "Fair lady," he said, "if it pleased you to love me—if I were so fortunate—I would obey your every command, whether it be foolish or wise. I will do your will, and for you I will abandon the company of others. I never want to leave you: this is what I most desire."

When the maiden heard the words of the man who loved her so much, she granted him her love and her body. Now Lanval's fortunes have changed!

Afterwards she gave him a boon: he would have in abundance whatever he most wanted. He could give gifts and spend liberally, and she would provide whatever he needed. Lanval was well provided for: however generously he spent, he would always have more gold and silver.

"My love," she said, "now I warn you and command and entreat you never to reveal this to anyone. And I will tell you the truth: if our love were ever revealed, you would lose me forever. Never again could you see me or possess me."

He answered that he would do as she commanded. He lay down beside her: now he was well provided for indeed! He stayed with her all afternoon and until evening fell, and he would have stayed longer if he had been able and if his lady had permitted it.

"My love," she said, "get up. You can remain no longer. Go now, and I will stay here. But I tell you this: when you wish to speak with me, you have only to think of a place where one could be alone with his lady without reproach or shame, and I will be there to do your bidding. No one except you will see me or hear my voice."

Hearing this, he was overjoyed. He kissed her and then stood up. Those who had led him to the tent dressed him in rich garments. Thus dressed, he was the most handsome of young men, and he was by no means foolish or ill-mannered. They gave him water to wash his hands and a cloth to dry them; then they brought him food. He supped, as was proper, with his lady. He was graciously served, and he accepted it with pleasure, and there was one abundant dish that pleased him in particular: he repeatedly embraced and kissed his lady.

When they had finished eating, his saddled horse was brought to him. Lanval had been well served there. He took his leave, mounted, and set out for the city. He often looked back, very uneasy. He was pensive and fearful because of his adventure; he was astonished and confused, and he could hardly believe that it had happened.

He returned to his lodging, where he found his men finely dressed. That evening he was a generous host, but no one knew how he had the means to afford it. In the city, there was no knight in need of lodging whom he did not summon and serve generously and well. Lanval gave rich gifts; Lanval pardoned prisoners; Lanval outfitted jongleurs; Lanval performed noble acts. There was neither stranger nor friend to whom Lanval would not give money. Lanval had great joy and pleasure, for by day or by night he could see his lady frequently, and she was completely at his command.

I believe it was that same year, after the feast of Saint John, when some thirty knights sought amusement in a grove beneath the tower in which the queen was staying. Gawain was with them, as was his cousin, the handsome Yvain. The noble and valiant Gawain, who was loved by all, said, "By God, my lords, we are treating our friend Lanval badly by not bringing him along, for he is generous and courtly and his father is a powerful king." Then they turned back, went to his lodging, and invited Lanval to accompany them.

The queen, who had three ladies with her, was at a window carved from the stone. Seeing the king's retinue approach, she recognized Lanval and looked at him. She called one of her ladies and had her summon her most attractive and beautiful maidens, who were to go with her to enjoy themselves in the garden where the others were. She took thirty or more with her. They descended the stairs, and the knights, delighted to see them, came forward to meet them. They took the women by the hand and engaged them in courtly conversations.

Lanval went aside, well away from the others; he was impatient to hold his lady and to kiss, embrace, and touch her. The joy of others meant little to him if he could not take his own pleasure. When the queen saw him alone, she went straight to him. She sat down beside him and spoke to him about what was on her mind: "Lanval, I have greatly honored and cherished and loved you. You can have all my love. Now tell me what you desire. I grant you my love, and you should be very happy to have me."

"Lady," he said, "leave me alone! I have no desire to love you. I have long served the king, and I do not wish to betray my faith. Never will I wrong my lord for you or your love."

The queen became angry and spoke outrageously. "Lanval," she said, "I do not think you have a taste for that kind of pleasure. I've often been told that you are not interested in women. While training young men, you have taken your pleasure with them. Lowborn, evil coward! It is tragic that my husband has tolerated you near him. I fear that he is damned for doing so."

When he heard that, he was pained, and he was not slow to reply. In his anger he spoke words that he would often regret. "Lady," he said, "I lack skill in the kind of work you mention; rather, I love and am loved by a lady who deserves to be prized over all others. And I will tell you something, and you can be certain of this: even her poorest servant girl is more worthy than you, my dear queen—in body, face, wisdom, and goodness!"

Then the queen left, returning to her room in tears. She was distraught and outraged at his insult. She took to her bed, ill, saying that she would never get up if the king did not see that justice was done in regard to her complaint.

The king returned from the forest, where he had spent a joyful day. He entered the queen's chambers. When she saw him, she complained aloud, fell at his feet, implored his mercy, and said that Lanval had shamed her by asking for her love; when she refused, he insulted and vilified her. He boasted that he had a lady who was so refined and noble and proud that even her poorest chambermaid was more worthy than the queen.

The king was extremely angry and swore that he would have Lanval burned or hanged if the knight could not defend himself in court. The king left the room and summoned three of his barons. He sent them for Lanval, who was very pained and distraught. He had returned to his lodging, and he understood that he had lost his lady by revealing their relationship. He was all alone in a room, downcast and tormented. He frequently called to his lady, but to no avail. He lamented and sighed and often fainted, and he asked a hundred times that she have mercy on him and speak to him. He cursed his heart and his mouth; it is a wonder that he did not kill himself! No matter how much he wept and wailed, struggled and strained, she would not take pity on him, not even so far as to let him see her. Alas, what could he do?

The men sent by the king arrived and ordered him to come to court immediately: the king had sent them to summon him, for the queen had made an accusation against him. Lanval, distraught, went to court; he would have been happy to have them kill him. Sad and without speaking, he came before the king; his great sorrow was evident.

The king said to him angrily, "Vassal, you have greatly wronged me. You acted unworthily in shaming and insulting me and in vilifying the queen. You made a foolish boast: your lady is very noble indeed if her serving girl is more worthy than the queen."

Lanval categorically denied that he had dishonored or shamed his lord and insisted that he had not sought the queen's love, but he acknowledged the truth of what the king had said otherwise, about the love of which he had boasted. Now he was in despair because he had lost her, and he said that he would accept whatever the court decreed in this matter.

The king, who was very angry but did not want his actions to be considered improper, asked his advisors to tell him what he should do. They had no choice but to do as he had ordered: they gathered and decided that Lanval should be tried. But he should provide his lord with pledges to ensure that he would await his trial and return at the proper time. (That way the court could be enlarged, for only the king's household was there at this time.) The barons returned to the king and presented their conclusions to him.

The king demanded pledges, but Lanval was alone and had neither relatives nor friends there. Gawain came forward and presented himself as a pledge, and all his companions did so as well. The king told them, "I entrust him to you, and his presence at trial will be guaranteed by everything—lands and fiefs—that each of you holds from me."

When the pledges were made, nothing remained to be done. Lanval returned to his lodging, accompanied by the knights. They repeatedly criticized and chastised him, urging him not to be downcast, and they cursed such a foolish love. They went to see him daily, for they wished to be sure that he was taking proper nourishment; and they feared that he would harm himself.

On the designated day, the barons assembled. The king and queen were there, and those who had pledged themselves brought Lanval to court. Everyone felt great sorrow on his account. I believe that there were at least a hundred who would have done anything to see him freed without a trial, for he had been wrongly accused. The king asked for a verdict based on the charge and the denial; now it was up to the barons to make their decision. Undertaking their deliberations, they were very concerned and troubled on account of this man from another land, who was now in such dire straits. Some wanted to punish him according to their lord's desire.

The Count of Cornwall said, "We will not fail in our duty. Right must prevail, like it or not. The king lodged a complaint against his vassal whose name, I understand, is Lanval. He accused him of a crime and a misdeed concerning a love of which he boasted, angering the queen. Only the king is making that accusation. Upon my faith, there truthfully should be no need for a rebuttal, were it not that one should honor his lord in all things. An oath will bind Lanval, and the king will then release us. And if Lanval can prove his claim—if his lady presents herself and if what he said that angered the queen is true—then he will be acquitted, since he did not say it out of spite. And if he cannot prove his claim, we should inform him that he must leave the king's service and be banished."

They sent word to Lanval that he was to have his lady come there to defend and protect him. He told them that that was impossible, that he would have no help from her. The messengers returned to the judges, who were not expecting help to come for Lanval. The king pressed them because the queen was waiting for them.

As they were about to render their verdict, they saw two maidens approaching on fine ambling horses. The maidens were very attractive; they were dressed in purple taffeta, worn next to their bare skin. The judges watched them with interest. Gawain, along with three knights, went to Lanval and recounted this to him and pointed out the two women. Gawain was happy about this and asked if one of them was Lanval's ladylove. Lanval replied that he did not know who they were or where they had come from or where they were going.

The women rode on. They dismounted before the dais where King Arthur was sitting. They were very beautiful, and they spoke in a most refined manner: "King, make your chambers available, and have them hung with silk in preparation for my lady, for she wishes to take lodging with you." He granted this willingly; he summoned two knights to accompany them up to the chambers. For the moment they said nothing more.

The king asked his barons for their verdict and said that they had greatly angered him by delaying for so long. "Sir," they said, "we were deliberating, but we did not reach a verdict because of the maidens we saw. Now we will resume our deliberations." They reconvened, very troubled, and there was a good deal of contentious debate.

As they were arguing, they saw two other maidens, who were beautifully dressed in Phrygian silk, riding down the street on Spanish mules. The vassals were delighted and said to one another that the worthy and courageous Lanval was now saved. Yvain and his companions went to Lanval. "Sir," he said, "rejoice! In God's name, speak with us. Two attractive and beautiful damsels are coming: one must certainly be your lady." Lanval immediately responded that he did not recognize, know, or love them.

Then the women arrived and dismounted before the king. Many who were there praised their figures, their faces, their complexions. Each of them was more worthy than the queen had ever been. The older one was refined and wise, and she delivered her message in courtly fashion: "King, now make chambers available to lodge my lady; she is coming here to speak with you." He ordered that these women be taken to the others who had arrived earlier. No attention was paid to the mules. When the women had gone, the king sent word to his barons that they were to render a verdict. There had been too much delay, and the queen, who had been kept waiting too long, was angry.

As they were about to deliver their verdict, a maiden came riding through the city. In all the world there was not a more beautiful woman. She rode a white palfrey, which carried her properly and elegantly. Its neck and head were finely formed; there was no more beautiful animal in the world. This palfrey was richly equipped, and no count or king under heaven could have afforded it without selling or pledging his land.

The woman was dressed in a white linen shift and robe, and at the sides her body was visible through the laces. Her body was beautiful, her hips low, her neck whiter than snow on a branch; she had bright eyes, a white face, a beautiful mouth and a well-formed nose, brown eyebrows and an attractive forehead, and curled blond hair. A gold thread does not shine as brightly as her hair did in the sun. Her cloak was of dark silk, and she had wrapped its hem around her. She held a sparrow-hawk on her hand, and a greyhound followed her. No one in the town, rich or poor, young or old, could take his eyes off her, nor did anyone jest about her beauty. She approached slowly. The judges, seeing her, thought it was a marvel, and every one of them felt true joy.

Those who loved Lanval came to him and told him that the maiden who was arriving would save him, God willing: "My lord, a lady is coming here. Her hair is neither red nor dark, and she is the most beautiful lady in the world."

Lanval heard this and raised his head; he knew who she was, and he sighed and blushed. He spoke without hesitation: "By my faith," he said, "this is my ladylove! Now I am healed by the very sight of her, and if she has no mercy on me, I hardly care if I am killed."

The lady entered the palace; never had such a beautiful woman been there. She dismounted before the king, where everyone could see her clearly, and she removed her cloak, the better to display her beauty. The king, who was well mannered, rose to meet her; and all the others honored her and offered her their service.

When they had looked at her intently and had praised her beauty at length, the lady, having no desire to linger, said, "King, I have loved one of your vassals. Here he is: it is Lanval. Because of what he said, he was accused in your court, and I do not want any harm to come to him. Know that the queen was wrong: he never asked for her love. If I can prove that the boast he made was true, he should be freed by your barons."

The king agreed to abide by what the judges legally decided. There was not one among them who did not consider Lanval to have been properly defended. He was freed by their decision, and the maiden, with her many servants, left: the king could not keep her there.

Outside the room there was a large stone of dark marble, where the heavily armed men mounted their horses when they left the king's court. Lanval stood on it, and when the maiden came riding through the door, Lanval leapt on the palfrey behind her. The Bretons tell us that he went with her to Avalon, to a beautiful isle. The young man was taken there, and no one ever heard of him again. Nor is there anything more to tell.

The Prophecy of Merlin

ANNE BANNERMAN

For three long nights had King Arthur watch'd,
The light from the turret shone!
For three long nights had King Arthur wak'd,
He pass'd them all alone!

On the fourth, at the first hour's summon bell,
As the warder walk'd his round,
A figure cross'd at the postern gate,
That enters underground;

All wrapt it was in a monkish cowl,
By the gate-lamp burning dim,
When a double shadow slid across,
And another stood by him!

In low and broken tones they spoke,
Till the fourth hour ceas'd to ring:
That monk had Merlin's giant form,
The other was the king.

The morning shone on Camlan hills,
And the summon horn was blown;
But not a knight would mount the tow'r
Where Arthur watch'd alone!

When noon was past, the king came down,
He bore his dragon shield;

And dark and dread was his clouded brow,
On the eve of Camlan field!

Slowly past that fateful eve,
And sad it wore away;
And sad and silent was the king
As he watch'd the break of day;

All down the slope of Camlan hill,
And along the river's side,
The rebel bands were posted round,
Since the fall of eventide:

From the signal posts the shout begins,
When the sky was bright and clear;
And the red sun shone on the steel dragon,
On King Arthur's standard-spear!

Above the rest was Britain's crest
In living flame enroll'd!
And the Virgin's form, in silver wrought,
With the brazon dragon bold![1]

O! in the field of Camlan fight,
Ere the burning noon was o'er,
The red blood ran, like a river-wave,
On the dry and parched shore:

King Arthur spurr'd his foaming horse
Amid that living flood![2]
And twice he wav'd his witched sword
Where the dauntless Modred stood!

But who could stand by Arthur's side,
When that steel of terror shone?
When the fire of wroth was in his eye,
And he rais'd his arm alone!

That sun that blaz'd in middle sky,
And flam'd on hill and dell;
Its westering light had sunk in night,
When the mighty Modred fell!

But the blood that flows is Arthur's blood,[3]
His fiery eye is dim!
And a dew like death is on his face,
And over every limb!

He lean'd him down on his dragon shield,
He clasp'd his beaver on!
And the gushing blood it ceas'd at once,
But they heard no dying groan.

O! how they strove till the night came on,
And all to raise that masque again!
And every arm by turns had tried,
But every arm was vain!

They held him in their arms, and wept
With tears of deep despair!
Till they fear'd to touch that plate armour,
For the sound was hollow there!

Then they drew that witched sword,
And they heard the armour ring!
They wav'd it twice in Merlin's name
Before they touch'd the king.

At once the cross-lace open'd wide,
They felt the rushing air!
But that mail was hollow as the grave,
Nor form, nor body there.

As wild they gaz'd, the iron rings
Were clasped as before!

But the tongue that call'd on Merlin's name
Was dumb for ever more!

Mean time, the king was borne away,
In deep and death-like sleep the while,
To the charmed sea, by magic spell,
By the Queen of the Yellow Isle!

And when his tranced soul was rous'd,
He thought, and thought how this might be,
For there was nought but sea and sky
As far as he could see.

King Arthur gaz'd on the calmed surge,
So clear beyond compare!
But neither the form of living man,
Nor the sound of life was there:

The ship it mov'd on the sleeping wave
Like a bird upon the air;
He knew it gained on the deep,
But he felt no motion there!

O, then! he had no trace of time
How long he was on that pathless sea!
But he could have rested there for aye,
So sweet it seem'd to be!

How many times he watch'd the sun,
And saw it sink, he never knew;
For it ne'er was more than faint twilight
In that sky of stainless blue!

Ah! then he thought, within that ship
He ever more was doom'd to be!
And he had not once bethought him yet
Of Merlin's prophecy!

Those sleepless nights he watch'd alone,
When the damps of midnight fell!
That voice, of more than human tone,
He heard in Merlin's cell;[4]

That night, the eve of Camlan fight,
When he felt his courage fail;
When the chill of death was on his brow,
Like a bloodless vision pale;

That night, his knocking knees refus'd
To bear him from the cave;
When, press'd in his, the hand of blood
Its deadly pressure gave!

Clear was the sky, and O! with this
What summer could compare?
What woes could press on Arthur's heart,
When he breath'd that blessed air?

Clear was the sky! the ship drew near
Without the aid of wind or toil!
And, lighted by the morning sun,
He saw the charmed Isle!

The ship was steady on her keel,
Wash'd by that soft and lovely flood;
And, blushing, on the yellow beach,
The Queen of Beauty stood.

High in one hand, of snowy white,
A cup of sparkling pearl she bore;
And she reach'd it to the tranced king
As he knelt upon the shore:

All pallid now was Arthur's brow,
While he took the draught she gave;

For he thought on what the hand of blood
Had mingled in the cave:

He thought on what the fiend pronounc'd,
That Merlin's spirit brought;
And he fix'd his eyes on that ladie's face,
And trembled at the thought.

Ah! in these eyes, of softest blue,
What magic dwells, to lull the soul!
And Arthur saw their mild reproach,
And rais'd the fraughted bowl!

His lips have drain'd that sparkling cup,
And he turn'd on her his raptur'd eyes!
When something, like a demon-smile,
Betray'd the smooth disguise!

He started up! he call'd aloud!
And, wild, survey'd her as she stood:
When she rais'd aloof the other arm,
And he knew the hand of blood!

The voice, that answer'd to his call,
Was that he heard within the cave!
When the mighty form of Urien
Was roused from the grave![5]

It told him, that the hour was come
He too must slumber in the cave;
When nought would reach his burial-place,
But the murmurs of the wave!

It told him of the years to pass
Before his kingdom he could see:
And Arthur knew he would return,
From Merlin's prophecy.[6]

King Arthur's body was not found,
Nor ever laid in holy grave:
And nought has reach'd his burial-place,
But the murmurs of the wave.

Author's Notes to "The Prophecy of Merlin"

1. Arthur's shield had on it the picture of our Lady, and his helm, an engraven dragon.

—Selden's Notes to the *Poly. Olb.* Song IV.

2. Pendragon's worthie sonne, who waded there in blood.

—*Poly. Olb.* Song IV.

3. King Arthur, according to our ancient historians, slew Modred with his own hand; but received his death-wound himself, and retired to Ynys Ofallon, or Glastenbury, where he soon afterwards died. His death was politically concealed, lest it should dispirit the Britons. Hence arose so many fabulous stories about it.

—Evans's *Specimens of Welsh Poetry*.

4. There the wise Merlin, whilome wont, (they say,)
   To make his wonne, low underneathe the ground
   In a deep delve, farre from the vew of day
   That of no living wight he mote be found,
   When so he counseld, with his sprights encompast round:
   And if thou ever happen that same way
   To traveill, go to see that dreadful place:
   It is an hideous hollow cave, (they say,)
   Under a rock.

—Spenser's *Faery Queene*. Book III. Can. III.

5. Urien Regen, king of Cambria and a great part of Scotland, as far as the river Clyde. His brave actions are celebrated by Taliessin.

—Evans's *Specimens*.

6. The bard-songs suppose, that, after the battle of Camlan in Cornwall, where Modred was slain and Arthur wounded, Morgan le Fay, an elfin lady, conveyed the body to Glastenbury, to cure it; which done, Arthur is to return to the rule of his country.

By prophecy Merlin set the date,
Among princes king incomparable,
His seat againe to Carlian to translate.
The Parchas sustren sponne so his fate,
His epitaph recordeth so certaine
Here lieth King Arthur that shall raigne againe.

—Dan Lidgate, See Notes to the *Poly. Olb.* Song III.

It will not perhaps be very consonant to popular feeling, that legendary tradition has been violated in the fate and disposal of this great, national hero. But it is all fairy-ground, and a poetical community of right to its appropriation has never been disputed.

A Legend of Tintagel Castle

LETITIA ELIZABETH LANDON

Alone in the forest, Sir Lancelot rode,
O'er the neck of his courser the reins lightly flowed,
And beside hung his helmet, for bare was his brow
To meet the soft breeze that was fanning him now.

And "the flowers of the forest" were many and sweet,
Which, crushed at each step by his proud courser's feet,
Gave forth all their fragrance, while thick over-head
The boughs of the oak and the elm-tree were spread.

The wind stirred the branches, as if its low suit
Were urged, like a lover who wakens the lute,
And through the dark foliage came sparkling and bright,
Like rain from the green leaves, in small gems of light.

There was stillness, not silence, for dancing along,
A brook went its way like a child with a song:
Now hidden, where rushes and water-flags grow;
Now clear, while white pebbles were glistening below.

Lo, bright as a vision, and fair as a dream,
The face of a maiden is seen in the stream;
With her hair like a mantle of gold to her knee,
Stands a lady as lovely as lady can be.

Short speech tells a love-tale;—the bard's sweetest words
Are poor, beside those which each memory hoards:

Sound of some gentle whisper, the haunting and low,
Such as love may have murmured—ah, long, long ago.

She led him away to an odorous cave,
Where the emerald spars shone like stars in the wave,
And the green moss and violets crowded beneath,
And the ash at the entrance hung down like a wreath.

They might have been happy, if love could but learn
A lesson from some flowers, and like their leaves turn
Round their own inward world, their own lone fragrant nest,
Content with its sweetness, content with its rest.

But the sound of the trumpet was heard from afar,
And Sir Lancelot rode forth again to the war;
And the wood-nymph was left as aye woman will be,
Who trusts her whole being, oh, false love, to thee.

For months, every sun-beam that brightened the gloom,
She deemed was the waving of Lancelot's plume;
She knew not of the proud and the beautiful queen,
Whose image was treasured as hers once had been.

There was many a fair dame, and many a knight,
Made the banks of the river like fairy-land bright;
And among those whose shadow was cast on the tide,
Was Lancelot kneeling near Genevra's side.

With purple sails heavily drooping around,
The mast, and the prow, with the vale lily bound;
And towed by two swans, a small vessel drew near,
But high on the deck was a pall-covered bier.

They oared with their white wings, the bark thro' the flood,
Till arrived at the bank where Sir Lancelot stood:
A wind swept the river, and flung back the pall,
And there lay a lady, the fairest of all.

But pale as a statue, like sunshine on snow,
The bright hair seemed mocking the cold face below:
Sweet truants, the blush and the smile both are fled—
Sir Lancelot weeps as he kneels by the dead.

And these are love's records; a vow and a dream,
And the sweet shadow passes away from life's stream:
Too late we awake to regret—but what tears
Can bring back the waste to our hearts and our years!

The Ylle Cutt Mantell

A Romaunt of the Tyme of Gud Kynge Arthur

Done into modern English from an authentic version.

ANONYMOUS

It fell, upon a Pentecost,
Of which the date has long been lost,
That Arthur, the gentle and the bold,
Summoned his vassals all, to hold
The gayest court that e'er was known
Since he ascended England's throne.

Nor was such ever seen again;
For at the call of their suzerain,
From east and west, from south and north,
The bravest and the best went forth.
Counts and earls, and dukes and kings,
Barons and squires and underlings,
Warriors heralded by fame,
And minstrels, to the revels came.

And with him every loyal knight
  The ladye of his love must bring,
Whose colors graced him in the fight,
  Whose praises he was bound to sing.
For in the days of chivalry
Each cavalier had his amie,
  His arm her shield, his heart her throne,
He lived and loved and fought for her alone.

The gentle king with joy beheld
How every hour the numbers swelled.

The shrill trump rang upon his ears,
 Mingled with the armor's clang,
 As from his steed each rider sprang;
The air with banners and pennoned spears
Was gay; the sun so brightly shone
On polished shield and morion,
On burnished gold and precious stone,
That its reflected radiance
Wearied the dim and dazzled glance;
And with her train each noble dame
On jennet and gentle palfrey came;
Till of the valiant and the fair
A goodly company, I ween, was there.

It was as if throughout the world
Beauty's banner had been unfurled,
And her most peerless votaries,
 At her command,
 From every land,
Had come to celebrate her mysteries.
Maids were there whose joyous glance
Was lit beneath the sun of France;
Some whose melancholy smiles
Told of Grecia's captive isles;
Some from Cambria's wilds might be,
Some from classic Italie.

There were those dark eyes whose flashes,
Are softened by long silken lashes;
And those blue eyes, so sad and deep,
Which look as they were made to weep,
And eyes of sober, tender grey,
And eyes that ever seemed at play,
And eyes that took you by surprise,
 And eyes that now were bent on earth,
 Now sparkled with malicious mirth,—
In short, there were all kinds but "evil eyes."

There were all kinds of ladyes, too,
Fair and false ones not a few.
Some were young and some were old,
Some were shy and some were bold,
Some were gentle, some were wild,
Some were haughty, some were mild,
Some were graceful as the fawn,
Some were haggard and care-worn,
Some were buds about to blow,
Some were wreaths of new-fall'n snow,
Some were alarmed and some alarming,
   Some shrank from notice, and some sought it,—
Variety is always charming,
   At least, so men have always thought it.

"Wassail and wine in the palace halls!
Mirth and music within its walls!
Let the echoing laugh resound,
And merriest measures beat the ground!
Minstrel, tune to joy thy lyre!
Maiden, don thy best attire!
Wreathe with flowers and with pearls
Youthful brows and clustering curls;
Let your robes be all of white,
Your lips all smiles, your eyes all light!
And he that here wears look of wo,
Arthur of England will deem his foe!"

How lightly danced each fair one's heart,
   As to the well-loved task she flew,
And strove with many a curious art,
   To give her cheek a fresher hue;
To borrow from the rose its dyes,
From many a flower its fragrant sighs;
To range the mantle's draperies,
Until its graceful folds displayed
The beauty they appeared to shade;
In braid and ringlet to confine

The flowing tresses' wavy line,
And clasp with glittering gold and gem
The form that had no need of them.

I cannot well describe in rhyme,
The female toilet of that time;
I do not know how trains were carried,
How single ladies dressed, or married;
If caps were proper at a ball,
Or even if caps were worn at all;
If robes were made of crape or tulle,
If skirts were narrow, gored, or full.

Perhaps, without consulting grace,
The hair was scraped back from the face,
While on the head a mountain rose,
Crowned, like Mont Blanc, with endless snows;
It may be that the locks were shorn;
    It may be that the lofty puff,
    The stomacher, the rising ruff,
The boddice or the veil, were worn.
Perhaps mantillas were the passion,
Or féronières were just in fashion,—
I will not, because I cannot, tell,—
(An omission for which, as a daughter of Eve
Myself, I very profoundly grieve)—
But this one thing I wot full well:
That every ladye there was dressed
In what she thought became her best.

Each joy has its attendant woes;
There lurks a thorn 'neath every rose,
    To pierce unwary fingers;
In life's most sparkling blush of wine,
Mid the sweet goblet's sunniest shine,
    Some bitter drop still lingers;
Pride is oft coupled with disgrace,—
And so, alack! it happened in this case!

There was a wicked little fairy
   Whom the good king had not invited
   And who thereby felt sadly slighted.
She was wily and she was wary,
She was wrinkled and cross and thin,
Foul without and fouler within;
The fairy of a nursery tale,
Whose mention hushes the infant's wail;
Not much larger than a shrimp,
The very essence of an imp.
She was jealous of the queen,
And eke of Launcelot, who had been
Her lover, when in fair disguise
She had arisen before his eyes.
Ginevra! well for thee at least,
If thou hadst asked her to thy feast,
For then, perhaps, this honeyed chalice
Had not been poisoned by her malice!

The gentlemen were all assembled,
   Clad in silk and jewels sheen;
And the illumined hall resembled
   In splendor some enchanted scene.
The King was seated on his throne,
While in their tiring-rooms, alone,
The damozels impatient wait
The welcome summons to the fête.

But, hark! at the palace gate a knock!
And then the turning of the lock
Is heard. The blow was quick and hard,
And soon the portal is unbarred.
The door of state is open flung,
And lo, appears a knight as young,
Of form as noble, brow as fair,
As any already seated there.
I ween he was full gaily dressed,
Bright jewels glittered in his crest;

His velvet cap and falling plume
Shaded a cheek whose peach-like bloom
With the most blushing maiden's vied.
A slender sword hung at his side,
While over his graceful shoulders rolled
His hair in waves of paly gold.
Who could have dreamed that he was sent
To be of ill the instrument?

Beneath one arm a case he bore,
Of velvet richly broidered o'er,
Crimson deep with golden bars,
Wrought in flow'rets and in stars.
This at the monarch's feet he laid,
And bending low before him prayed
The royal ear for his request.
A motion of the hand expressed
The King's approval:—"Speak, my son;
What wouldst thou, or what hast thou done?"

In honeyed tones and accents sweet
Did the fair youth his charge repeat:
"The loveliest lady in this isle,
One who has oft received your smile,
By me, her loyal knight and true,
Doth her petition make to you.
Ah, sire! did you but know how fair
My ladye is, you'd grant her prayer!"

The noble Arthur shook his head,
And paused awhile—then smiling said:
"Fair youth, I something might complain
That I should be compelled to grant
The prayer of unknown suppliant;
Yet none shall say that in my reign,
    And the reign of gentle chivalrie,
A maiden aught should ask in vain,
    So as she wills it let it be!

But, pray you, bear your ladye word,
Her boon was given ere 't was heard,
Here, in the presence of my peers,—
You're witness to the pledge, messires!"

The knight the coffer's clasp undid,
And drew from beneath its silken lid
A robe, which he with care displayed,
The fairest robe that e'er was made.
Its like had never been seen before,
Its like will never be looked on more.
'Mid all her sumptuous garbs the queen
Had naught so beautiful, I ween;
For the fairy Morgue had made it so,
And had woven it all from top to toe;
Nor stitch had it nor slope nor seam,
    And none could tell its shape or hue;
'Twas like the tracery of a dream
    Or those fleecy clouds the sun shines through,
    When the summer sky is bright and blue.

"My noble ladye greeting sends,
And this rich garment, to her friends;
And asks that in Ginevra's court
The queen and ladies every one,
Will they, nill they, shall try it on;
And she for whom 'tis not too short,
And not too long, and not too wide,
    She whom it shall exactly fit,
Be she wife or widow, maid or bride,
    Will graciously please accept of it."

These words somewhat alarmed the king,
Who saw that in this simple thing
More than met the eye was meant,
And that some deep design was blent
With one which so innocuous seemed.
The fairy Morgue, he almost deemed,

With her attendant imps lay hid
Beneath the velvet coffer lid.
He wished he had lost his witless head
Ere the rash promise had been made!
He might at least have seen the dress—
Who ever heard of such hastiness!
In vain he sighed, and in vain he frowned,
 He could not solve the mystery;
But his royal and knightly faith was bound,
 And he would not break his pledge—not he!
So he craved the queen and the ladies all
To hasten to the banquet hall.

They came, for once obedient,
But, ah! had they known with what intent
The king had sent for them, not one
Had to the royal presence gone;
For this strange garment could reveal
All that the faithless might conceal;
None but the true in heart could wear it—
What wonder then that few would dare it?

First came the queen, whose stately charms
 Had ripened gloriously to their full;
 'Tis known how her beauty's magic rule
Commanded hearts and eyes and arms.
Launcelot of course was at her side,
Launcelot who for her had died.
Slowly she walked, while all around,
In joyous troop, with flowers crowned,
Came her maidens with her, like laughing elves;
Like living flowers they seemed themselves;
Or like the stars in a night of June,
  Stealing forth
  From the dusky north,
To pay their happy homage to the moon.

"Ginevra! a fair dame has sent

This mantle, with the kind intent
That she whom it becometh best
Shall wear it,—such is her request.
To you of course belongs the right
To try it first."With quick delight
The queen the splendid garment took,
And its transparent tissue shook
Around her, with majestic grace,—

But she saw a smile on every face,
Which the best courtiers could not hide,
Though they bit their lips till they almost cried,
As Ginevra the magic ordeal tried.
'Twas a world too long, and would not fit,
Though she did her best to manage it.
It clung too closely to her vest,
    Beneath her feet the drapery trailed;
She never had been so badly dressed;
    Her color rose, and her proud eye quailed
'Neath the ill veiled sarcasm in the gaze
Of those once foremost in her praise.
Then first the truth she understood,
    As the stranger youth had already told it
    To the knights there gathered to behold it.
But curbing well her angry mood,
Though the fairy's work in her heart she cursed,
And only wished she had known it erst,
She flashed a proud smile around the ring,
And took her seat beside the King.

The youth meanwhile, malicious sprite!
Could scarce dissemble his delight
At poor Ginevra's sore vexation,
And the good Arthur's indignation.
He laughed a moment in his sleeve,
Then spoke:—"Fair sovereign, much I grieve
My lady's gift suits not your pleasure,
    And may not grace a form so fair,—

She should have taken your beauteous measure,—
    But surely some one here can wear
My robe,—yon fair-haired maid is loyal,
Perhaps, although she be not royal.
It will become her well,—if not,
    Pass it on
    To the nearest one;
The promise must not be forgot."

Through all the ranks the word had passed,
But every one shrank back aghast;
Every lady's courage failed,
Each cheek in sad foreboding paled;
Not one of all that trembling crowd
But would almost rather have donned her shroud,
Than venture the magic mantle's trial—
Alas! the knight would list to no denial!

Young Caradois stood at the side
Of Ella, his affianced bride.
Faultless was she in form and feature,
Eye never looked on a fairer creature.
Her lover deemed he well might trust
That cloudless face and brow august,
Statue-like, save that lips of marble
Have never so been heard to warble,
Since the sun on Memnon shone,
And drew a sigh from a heart of stone.
She was his peerless queen of song;
He knew she could not do him wrong,
And was impatient to see her try
The robe which Ginevra had thrown by.

But another at her feet had knelt,
Her heart another's power had felt,
And one dark spot lay hid below
The dazzling surface of all that snow.
The lover turned to his amie:

"Ella, my Ella, thou alone
    Shalt call this magic robe thine own!
I know that it was made for thee,
Thou flower of faith and constancy!
Haste, haste to win it then, I pray—
Essay it, dearest, without delay!
Receive the homage of all the brave,
And forge new fetters for thy slave!"

The maiden's eye was wild with terror,
As if some deep and deadly error,
Some ghastly spectre of affright,
Had sudden arisen before its sight.
Unhappy girl! too well she knew
She had been faithless and untrue;
And that by Caradois that spot
Once seen could never be forgot.
    A few faint words first murmured she,
    Of deference and humility;
But when her prayers availed her not,
A moment more she backward hung,
A moment to her lover clung,
While a half breathed confession died
    Upon her lips—but ere 'twas spoken
The words were smothered by her pride,
    So soon to be for ever broken.
Then as about to hear her doom,
She sought the centre of the room,
And from the knight's impatient hand
Received the mantle's glittering band.
The courtiers laughed, the king looked grave,
A stifled shriek poor Ella gave,
And Caradois' gay visage fell—
It was too short by half an ell!

A moment there she stood alone,
As if she had been turned to stone,
Gazing on the vacant air,

In all the wildness of despair.
Upon her icy cheek one tear
    Descended, and in falling froze;
But madness had been less to fear
    Than that unnatural repose.
She did not hear the whispered jest,
    The smothered laugh, the cutting word.
But, deep and still within her breast,
    A sterner monitor she heard.
That mocking gaze, those looks of scorn,
If undeserved, she might have borne.
But worse, oh! infinitely worse,
Was the slow torture of remorse;
The sense of guilt, the consciousness
That she, so formed to love and bless,
With Caradois' young heart had played,
Forgot her vows, his trust betrayed,
And dashed to earth his hopes and joys,
As infant tramples on its toys.

The spell was broken, gone the dream,
    The flimsy veil was rent,
Which at some moments made her deem
    Almost, that she was innocent.
And each remembrance, every thought,
With it a sharper arrow brought;
Till she no longer could resist—
Before her eyes there rose a mist,
She shuddered, slowly drooped her head,
And fell, for consciousness had fled.

There's nothing earthly more convenient
    Than a well managed fainting fit;
The sternest heart 'twill render lenient,
    And ladies now so practise it,
That (I am told), whene'er they please,
They faint away quite at their ease.

Genelas was a rich brunette
A flirt, a romp, a sad coquette,
For such there are in every clime,
And such there were in every time;
Full of frolic and full of fun,
She had lovers many a one,
But would promise faith to none.
She shrank not from the general titter,
When the charmed mantle did not fit her:
For though of proper length before,
Behind, it trailed upon the floor;
But laughing, said, "it might be seen,
She was not taller than the Queen;"
And threw it by with gesture wild,
Impatient as a wayward child;
And shook her finger at the foe,
In sportive mimicry of wo,
While mischief sparkled in her glance;
Then with a playful reverence,
Drew back, and at Ginevra's feet
Sought gaily her accustomed seat.

Another, and another came,
But to depart in grief and shame;
The freshest rosebuds of the court,
Young, timid girls, who had been thought
Blameless, if aught on earth might be,
    And haughty prudes, whose long discretion
Had been renowned prodigiously,
    Were all convicted of transgression.
But soon there were none left to laugh,
For all the bitter cup must quaff,
    And every fond confiding knight
Insisted that his ladye fair
The magic robe would win and wear,
    Till, one by one, their hopes took flight,
And e'en the stranger knight relented,—
All, all, their curiosity repented.

Two hundred dames the garb had tried,
And thrown it in disgrace aside;
Two hundred, for whose faith, that morn,
A thousand knights their arms had borne;
And either in tournay or deadly strife,
Had perilled estates, and lands, and life,
The very models of perfection,
   Were seated there, and strove to hide
   The agonies of wounded pride,
At so unlooked for a detection.
Some burned with rage, some sadly wept,
While some an unmoved visage kept;
Some wore a look of cold disdain,
   And some implored to be forgiven,
And some essayed to mend the chain
   Whose links had been so rudely riven.

Meanwhile King Arthur wore an air
   Timid as that of startled rabbit;
And fidgeted upon his chair,
   Which is a most ungraceful habit;
His hospitality was foiled,
His feast was marred, his sport was spoiled;
Here was a pretty mess of fish,
In place of his own dainty dish!
And all this grief and trepidation,
Caused by his own precipitation!
He had a ready wit, 'tis true,
But now he knew not what to do.
It would be vain to call on Merlin,
For he had lately gone to Berlin;
And, as the royal mouth was muzzled,
The royal brain was sadly puzzled.
At length his voice the silence broke,
In tones of stifled rage he spoke:
"Accursed goblin, away apace!
   Or thy malicious head one blow
   From my good sword shall lay full low!

In this the fairy's hand I trace;
Go, bear her back her mantle, but
Tell her it's very badly cut;
And say that she shall dearly pay
For this, at no far distant day."

Small fear had he of Arthur's ire;
But answered: "Much you wrong me, sire.
A moment be your anger stilled,
Your promise is not all fulfilled;
There yet remains one beauteous dame
Who to my robe has not laid claim."

Who this might be, no one could guess,
Until Ginevra answered: "Yes,
Will't please your majesty to send
For the Lord Hubert's gentle friend?"

A squire was sent for Coralie,—
A Norman peasant's child was she,
Whom Hubert from her home had brought,
To grace awhile Ginevra's court.
Her beauty many a lay inspired,
And yet, 'mid all the show of state,
She wept in secret o'er her fate;
For envious lips and lying tongue,
Essaying oft to do her wrong,
At length had poisoned Hubert's mind,
And made him jealous and unkind.
Frankly and innocently gay,
Childlike, and thoughtless of display;
A wild flower in a rich parterre;
A breath of pure, untainted air
Chance-wafted into crowded rooms
'Mid sickly odors and perfumes;
What wonder that a soul so artless
    Should droop and pine, where all was art?
What wonder that the false and heartless

Should slander one that was all heart?

Upon her couch, in slumber laid,
The squire found the gentle maid.
One slender hand upheld her head,
All moistened with the tears she'd shed.
And one the tuneful chords had swept
With careless lightness e'er she slept.
She had been musing on the past,
For her fair brow was overcast;
And the light cloud that o'er it hung
Told she had suffered, though so young.
Some deep and poignant grief had stolen
    From her rich cheek its wonted rose,
And her soft eyelids were so swollen
    With weeping, they might scarce unclose.
Yet, o'er her parted lips the while,
There played a sweet though pensive smile,
The shadow of some happy dream.
As he approached, with start and scream
She wakened into life again.

"Oh! chase these spectres from my brain!
They come with yon familiar strain;
And well known forms before me flit
Like phantoms in a fever fit.
Mother! methought that thou wert near;
Thine accents soothed my dreaming ear;
I flew to thee, and hid my face
In my sweet sister's fond embrace.
I heard the music of the rills
Which dance among the sunny hills
Of my own Normandy;
    And the same wind, whose wailing sigh
    Was mingled with my lullaby,
A welcome breathed to Coralie.
Dear, happy home! Oh! take me there!
I pine to breathe my native air!"

The squire beheld her with surprise,
And prayed her straightway to arise,
And in the sumptuous banquet hall,
Attend the queen and ladies all.

"I cannot join the feast to-night,
    For I have wept all day,
I cannot sparkle with the bright,
    Or frolic with the gay,
My bosom throbs, my eyes are dim,
I tremble too in every limb;
I'm sick at heart, and faint and chill,—
Pray tell the queen you found me ill!"

But when he told her what had passed,
    And why her presence was required,
    She rose as with delight inspired,
Exclaiming, "Gracious heaven! at last
Thou wilt allow thy child to prove
That she deserves her Hubert's love!
For thou art witness that her heart,
Has never been bestowed in part!"
Then followed him with joyous bound,
And step that scarcely touched the ground.

High voices raised in words of wrath
    At her approach were instant hushed;
    But, as into the hall she rushed,
The jealous Hubert crossed her path.
"Rash girl! and art thou come," he cried,
"To sit yon perjured queen beside?
To tell how fondly I believed,
How I was toyed with and deceived!
Back to thy room! thou'rt false, I know;
But no one here shall call thee so!
Away, this arm is thy defence;
King Arthur dare not draw thee thence!"

"Peace, Hubert! was it to receive
    This insult at thy cherished hand,
That I was well content to leave,
    For thy dear sake, my native land?
Was it for this, that I have borne
Foul calumny and cutting scorn,
Yet in my heart my sorrow kept,
Lest thou shouldst grieve because I wept?
And thou canst doubt my constancy!
Put up thy sword, for Coralie
Asks and accepts of no defence,
Save her own conscious innocence."

She spoke, and with undaunted look
From the fair youth the mantle took;
Then, nothing fearing, tried it on,—
A shout proclaimed that she had won!
Around her graceful waist it clung,
Thence to the slender ancle hung;
It fitted well on every side;
'Twas not too long, too short, too wide;
Its folds her sylphlike form displayed,
As if for her it had been made.
The stranger, gaily smiling, said:
"Sweet Coralie! thy faith is proven;
    Thou art of maids the pride and pearl!
Ladies! the magic robe was woven
For the poor Norman peasant girl!"

Wonder on every visage dwelt,
    Ginevra started from her seat;
    And, low before the maiden's feet,
The now repentant Hubert knelt,
Like a despairing penitent
    Who scarcely hopes he may be shriven;
His fearful glance on earth was bent,
    —I need not say he was forgiven.

Not amid regal pomp and show
   Were Coralie and Hubert wed,
But ere another sunset's glow
   On Albion's hills its light had shed,
Back to her home, the Seine beside,
In triumph, Hubert bore his bride;
Where sister hands of wild flowers wove
The garlands of unchanging love;
Where faces glowing with delight,
And parents, graced the solemn rite.
There, long in peace and happiness,
Content each other's lot to bless,
They lived, and when at last they died,
There were they buried side by side.
I know on whom the mantle fell,
But I have promised not to tell.

The Lady of the Fountain

TRANSLATED BY

LADY CHARLOTTE GUEST

King Arthur was at Caerlleon upon Usk; and one day he sat in his chamber; and with him were Owain the son of Urien, and Kynon the son of Clydno, and Kai the son of Kyner; and Gwenhwyvar and her hand-maidens at needlework by the window. And if it should be said that there was a porter at Arthur's palace, there was none. Glewlwyd Gavaelvawr was there, acting as porter, to welcome guests and strangers, and to receive them with honour, and to inform them of the manners and customs of the Court; and to direct those who came to the Hall or to the presence-chamber, and those who came to take up their lodging.

In the centre of the chamber King Arthur sat upon a seat of green rushes, over which was spread a covering of flame-coloured satin, and a cushion of red satin was under his elbow.

Then Arthur spoke, "If I thought you would not disparage me," said he, "I would sleep while I wait for my repast; and you can entertain one another with relating tales, and can obtain a flagon of mead and some meat from Kai." And the King went to sleep. And Kynon the son of Clydno asked Kai for that which Arthur had promised them. "I, too, will have the good tale which he promised to me," said Kai. "Nay," answered Kynon, "fairer will it be for thee to fulfil Arthur's behest, in the first place, and then we will tell thee the best tale that we know." So Kai went to the kitchen and to the mead-cellar, and returned bearing a flagon of mead and a golden goblet, and a handful of skewers, upon which were broiled collops of meat. Then they ate the collops and began to drink the mead. "Now," said Kai, "it is time for you to give me my story." "Kynon," said Owain, "do thou pay to Kai the tale that is his due." "Truly," said Kynon, "thou art older, and art a better teller of tales, and hast seen more marvellous things than I; do thou therefore pay Kai his tale." "Begin thyself," quoth Owain, "with the best that thou knowest." "I will do so," answered Kynon.

"I was the only son of my mother and father, and I was exceedingly aspiring, and my daring was very great. I thought there was no enterprise in the world too mighty for me, and after I had achieved all the adventures that were in my own country, I equipped myself, and set forth to journey through deserts and distant regions. And at length it chanced that I came to the fairest valley in the world, wherein were trees of equal growth; and a river ran through the valley, and a path was by the side of the river. And I followed the path until mid-day, and continued my journey along the remainder of the valley until the evening; and at the extremity of a plain I came to a large and lustrous Castle, at the foot of which was a torrent. And I approached the Castle, and there I beheld two youths with yellow curling hair, each with a frontlet of gold upon his head, and clad in a garment of yellow satin, and they had gold clasps upon their insteps. In the hand of each of them was an ivory bow, strung with the sinews of the stag; and their arrows had shafts of the bone of the whale, and were winged with peacock's feathers; the shafts also had golden heads. And they had daggers with blades of gold, and with hilts of the bone of the whale. And they were shooting their daggers.

"And a little way from them I saw a man in the prime of life, with his beard newly shorn, clad in a robe and a mantle of yellow satin; and round the top of his mantle was a band of gold lace. On his feet were shoes of variegated leather, fastened by two bosses of gold. When I saw him, I went towards him and saluted him, and such was his courtesy that he no sooner received my greeting than he returned it. And he went with me towards the castle. Now there were no dwellers in the castle except those who were in one hall. And there I saw four-and-twenty damsels, embroidering satin at a window. And this I tell thee, Kai, that the least fair of them was fairer than the fairest maid thou hast ever beheld in the island of Britain, and the least lovely of them was more lovely than Gwenhwyvar, the wife of Arthur, when she has appeared loveliest at the Offering, on the day of the Nativity, or at the feast of Easter. They rose up at my coming, and six of them took my horse, and divested me of my armour; and six others took my arms, and washed them in a vessel until they were perfectly bright. And the third six spread cloths upon the tables and prepared meat. And the fourth six took off my soiled garments, and placed others upon me; namely, an under vest and a doublet of fine linen, and a robe, and a surcoat, and a mantle of yellow satin with a broad gold band upon the mantle. And they placed cushions both beneath and around me, with coverings of red linen; and I sat down. Now the six maidens who had taken my horse, unharnessed him, as well as if they had been the best squires in the island of Britain. Then, behold, they brought bowls of silver wherein was water to wash, and towels of linen, some green and some white; and I washed. And in a little while the man sat down to the table. And I sat next to him, and below me sat all the maidens, except those who waited on us. And the table was of silver, and the cloths upon the table were of linen; and no vessel was served upon the table that was not either of gold or of silver, or of buffalo-horn. And our meat was brought to us. And verily, Kai, I saw there every sort of meat and every sort of liquor that I have ever seen elsewhere; but the meat and the liquor were better served there than I have ever seen them in any other place.

"Until the repast was half over, neither the man nor any one of the damsels spoke a single word to me; but when the man perceived that it would be more agreeable to me to converse than to eat any more, he began to inquire of me who I was. I said I was glad to find that there was some one who would discourse with me, and that it was not considered so great a crime at that Court for people to hold converse together. 'Chieftain,' said the man, 'we would have talked to thee sooner, but we feared to disturb thee during thy repast; now, however, we will discourse.' Then I told the man who I was, and what was the cause of my journey; and said that I was seeking whether any one was superior to me, or whether I could gain the mastery over all. The man looked upon me, and he smiled and said, 'If I did not fear to distress thee too much, I would show thee that which thou seekest.' Upon this I became anxious and sorrowful, and when the man perceived it, he said, 'If thou wouldest rather that I should show thee thy disadvantage than thine advantage, I will do so. Sleep here to-night, and in the morning arise early, and take the road upwards through the valley until thou reachest the wood through which thou camest hither. A little way within the wood thou wilt meet with a road branching off to the right, by which thou must proceed, until thou comest to a large sheltered glade with a mound in the centre. And thou wilt see a black man of great stature on the top of the mound. He is not smaller in size than two of the men of this world. He has but one foot; and one eye in the middle of his forehead. And he has a club of iron, and it is certain that there are no two men in the world who would not find their burden in that club. And he is not a comely man, but on the contrary he is exceedingly ill-favoured; and he is the woodward of that wood. And thou wilt see a thousand wild animals grazing around him. Inquire of him the way out of the glade, and he will reply to thee briefly, and will point out the road by which thou shalt find that which thou art in quest of.'

"And long seemed that night to me. And the next morning I arose and equipped myself, and mounted my horse, and proceeded straight through the valley to the wood; and I followed the cross-road which the man had pointed out to me, till at length I arrived at the glade. And there was I three times more as-

tonished at the number of wild animals that I beheld, than the man had said I should
be. And the black man was there, sitting upon the top of the mound. Huge of stature as the man had told me that he was, I found him to exceed by far the description he had given me of him. As for the iron club which the man had told me was
a burden for two men, I am certain, Kai, that it would be a heavy weight for four
warriors to lift; and this was in the black man's hand. And he only spoke to me in
answer to my questions. Then I asked him what power he held over those animals. 'I will show thee, little man,' said he. And he took his club in his hand, and
with it he struck a stag a great blow so that he brayed vehemently, and at his braying
the animals came together, as numerous as the stars in the sky, so that it was difficult for me to find room in the glade to stand among them. There were serpents,
and dragons, and divers sorts of animals. And he looked at them, and bade them
go and feed; and they bowed their heads, and did him homage as vassals to their
lord.

"Then the black man said to me, 'Seest thou now, little man, what power I
hold over these animals?' Then I inquired of him the way, and he became very rough
in his manner to me; however, he asked me whither I would go? And when I told
him who I was and what I sought, he directed me. 'Take,' said he, 'that path that
leads towards the head of the glade, and ascend the wooded steep until thou comest
to its summit; and there thou wilt find an open space like to a large valley, and in
the midst of it a tall tree, whose branches are greener than the greenest pine-trees.
Under this tree is a fountain, and by the side of the fountain a marble slab, and on
the marble slab a silver bowl, attached by a chain of silver, so that it may not be
carried away. Take the bowl and throw a bowlful of water upon the slab, and thou
wilt hear a mighty peal of thunder, so that thou wilt think that heaven and earth
are trembling with its fury. With the thunder there will come a shower so severe
that it will be scarce possible for thee to endure it and live. And the shower will
be of hailstones; and after the shower, the weather will become fair, but every
leaf that was upon the tree will have been carried away by the shower. Then a flight
of birds will come and alight upon the tree; and in thine own country thou didst
never hear a strain so sweet as that which they will sing. And at the moment thou
art most delighted with the song of the birds, thou wilt hear a murmuring and
complaining coming towards thee along the valley. And thou wilt see a knight upon
a coal-black horse, clothed in black velvet, and with a pennon of black linen upon
his lance; and he will ride unto thee to encounter thee with the utmost speed. If
thou fleest from him he will overtake thee, and if thou abidest there, as sure as
thou art a mounted knight, he will leave thee on foot. And if thou dost not find
trouble in that adventure, thou needest not seek it during the rest of thy life.'

"So I journeyed on, until I reached the summit of the steep, and there I found everything as the black man had described it to me. And I went up to the tree, and beneath it I saw the fountain, and by its side the marble slab, and the silver bowl fastened by the chain. Then I took the bowl, and cast a bowlful of water upon the slab; and thereupon, behold, the thunder came, much more violent than the black man had led me to expect; and after the thunder came the shower; and of a truth I tell thee, Kai, that there is neither man nor beast that could endure that shower and live. For not one of those hailstones would be stopped, either by the flesh or by the skin, until it had reached the bone. I turned my horse's flank towards the shower, and placed the beak of my shield over his head and neck, while I held the upper part of it over my own head. And thus I withstood the shower. When I looked on the tree there was not a single leaf upon it, and then the sky became clear, and with that, behold the birds lighted upon the tree, and sang. And truly, Kai, I never heard any melody equal to that, either before or since. And when I was most charmed with listening to the birds, lo, a murmuring voice was heard through the valley, approaching me and saying, 'Oh, Knight, what has brought thee hither? What evil have I done to thee, that thou shouldst act towards me and my possessions as thou hast this day? Dost thou not know that the shower to-day has left in my dominions neither man nor beast alive that was exposed to it?' And thereupon, behold, a Knight on a black horse appeared, clothed in jet-black velvet, and with a tabard of black linen about him. And we charged each other, and, as the onset was furious, it was not long before I was overthrown. Then the Knight passed the shaft of his lance through the bridle rein of my horse, and rode off with the two horses, leaving me where I was. And he did not even bestow so much notice upon me as to imprison me, nor did he despoil me of my arms. So I returned along the road by which I had come. And when I reached the glade where the black man was, I confess to thee, Kai, it is a marvel that I did not melt down into a liquid pool, through the shame that I felt at the black man's derision. And that night I came to the same castle where I had spent the night preceding. And I was more agreeably entertained that night than I had been the night before; and I was better feasted, and I conversed freely with the inmates of the castle, and none of them alluded to my expedition to the fountain, neither did I mention it to any; and I remained there that night. When I arose on the morrow, I found, ready saddled, a dark bay palfrey, with nostrils as red as scarlet; and after putting on my armour, and leaving there my blessing, I returned to my own Court. And that horse I still possess, and he is in the stable yonder. And I declare that I would not part with him for the best palfrey in the island of Britain.

"Now of a truth, Kai, no man ever before confessed to an adventure so much to his own discredit, and verily it seems strange to me, that neither before nor since have I heard of any person besides myself who knew of this adventure, and that the subject of it should exist within King Arthur's dominions, without any other person lighting upon it."

"Now," quoth Owain, "would it not be well to go and endeavour to discover that place?"

"By the hand of my friend," said Kai, "often dost thou utter that with thy tongue which thou wouldst not make good with thy deeds."

"In very truth," said Gwenhwyvar, "it were better thou wert hanged, Kai, than to use such uncourteous speech towards a man like Owain."

"By the hand of my friend, good Lady," said Kai, "thy praise of Owain is not greater than mine."

With that Arthur awoke, and asked if he had not been sleeping a little.

"Yes, Lord," answered Owain, "thou hast slept awhile."

"Is it time for us to go to meat?"

"It is, Lord," said Owain.

Then the horn for washing was sounded, and the King and all his household sat down to eat. And when the meal was ended, Owain withdrew to his lodging, and made ready his horse and his arms.

On the morrow, with the dawn of day, he put on his armour and mounted his charger, and travelled through distant lands and over desert mountains. And at length he arrived at the valley which Kynon had described to him; and he was certain that it was the same that he sought. And journeying along the valley by the side of the river, he followed its course till he came to the plain and within sight of the Castle. When he approached the Castle, he saw the youths shooting their daggers in the place where Kynon had seen them, and the yellow man, to whom the Castle belonged, standing hard by. And no sooner had Owain saluted the yellow man than he was saluted by him in return.

And he went forward towards the Castle, and there he saw the chamber, and when he had entered the chamber he beheld the maidens working at satin embroidery, in chairs of gold. And their beauty and their comeliness seemed to Owain far greater than Kynon had represented to him. And they arose to wait upon Owain, as they had done to Kynon, and the meal which they set before him gave more satisfaction to Owain than it had done to Kynon.

About the middle of the repast, the yellow man asked Owain the object of his journey. And Owain made it known to him, and said, "I am in quest of the Knight who guards the fountain." Upon this the yellow man smiled, and said that he was as loth to point out that adventure to Owain as he had been to Kynon.

However, he described the whole to Owain, and they retired to rest.

The next morning Owain found his horse made ready for him by the damsels, and he set forward and came to the glade where the black man was. And the stature of the black man seemed more wonderful to Owain than it had done to Kynon, and Owain asked of him his road, and he showed it to him. And Owain followed the road, as Kynon had done, till he came to the green tree; and he beheld the fountain, and the slab beside the fountain, with the bowl upon it. And Owain took the bowl, and threw a bowlful of water upon the slab. And, lo, the thunder was heard, and after the thunder came the shower, much more violent than Kynon had described, and after the shower the sky became bright. And when Owain looked at the tree, there was not one leaf upon it. And immediately the birds came, and settled upon the tree, and sang. And when their song was most pleasing to Owain, he beheld a Knight coming towards him through the valley, and he prepared to receive him; and encountered him violently. Having broken both their lances, they drew their swords, and fought blade to blade. Then Owain struck the Knight a blow through his helmet, head-piece and visor, and through the skin, and the flesh, and the bone, until it wounded the very brain. Then the black Knight felt that he had received a mortal wound upon which he turned his horse's head, and fled. And Owain pursued him, and followed close upon him, although he was not near enough to strike him with his sword. Thereupon Owain descried a vast and resplendent Castle. And they came to the Castle gate. And the black Knight was allowed to enter, and the portcullis was let fall upon Owain; and it struck his horse behind the saddle, and cut him in two, and carried away the rowels of the spurs that were upon Owain's heels. And the portcullis descended to the floor. And the rowels of the spurs and part of the horse were without, and Owain, with the other part of the horse remained between the two gates, and the inner gate was closed, so that Owain could not go thence; and Owain was in a perplexing situation. And while he was in this state, he could see through an aperture in the gate, a street facing him, with a row of houses on each side. And he beheld a maiden, with yellow curling hair, and a frontlet of gold upon her head; and she was clad in a dress of yellow satin, and on her feet were shoes of variegated leather. And she approached the gate, and desired that it should be opened. "Heaven knows, Lady," said Owain, "it is no more possible for me to open to thee from hence, than it is for thee to set me free." "Truly," said the damsel, "it is very sad that thou canst not be released, and every woman ought to succour thee, for I never saw one more faithful in the service of ladies than thou. As a friend thou art the most sincere, and as a lover the most devoted. Therefore," quoth she, "whatever is in my power to do for thy release, I will do it. Take this ring and put it on thy finger, with the stone inside thy hand; and close thy hand upon the stone. And as long as thou concealest it, it will conceal thee. When they have consulted together, they will come forth to fetch thee, in order to put thee to death; and they will be much grieved that they cannot find thee. And I will await thee on the horseblock yonder; and thou wilt be able to see me, though I cannot see thee; therefore come and place thy hand upon my shoulder, that I may know that thou art near me. And by the way that I go hence, do thou accompany me."

Then she went away from Owain, and he did all that the maiden had told him. And the people of the Castle came to seek Owain, to put him to death, and when they found nothing but the half of his horse, they were sorely grieved.

And Owain vanished from among them, and went to the maiden, and placed his hand upon her shoulder; whereupon she set off, and Owain followed her, until they came to the door of a large and beautiful chamber, and the maiden opened it, and they went in, and closed the door. And Owain looked around the chamber, and behold there was not even a single nail in it that was not painted with gorgeous colours; and there was not a single panel that had not sundry images in gold portrayed upon it.

The maiden kindled a fire, and took water in a silver bowl, and put a towel of white linen on her shoulder, and gave Owain water to wash. Then she placed before him a silver table, inlaid with gold; upon which was a cloth of yellow linen; and she brought him food. And of a truth, Owain had never seen any kind of meat that was not there in abundance, but it was better cooked there than he had ever found it in any other place. Nor did he ever see so excellent a display of meat and drink, as there. And there was not one vessel from which he was served, that was not of gold or of silver. And Owain ate and drank, until late in the afternoon, when lo, they heard a mighty clamour in the Castle; and Owain asked the maiden what that outcry was. "They are administering extreme unction," said she, "to the Nobleman who owns the Castle." And Owain went to sleep.

The couch which the maiden had prepared for him was meet for Arthur himself; it was of scarlet, and fur, and satin, and sendall, and fine linen. In the middle of the night they heard a woful outcry; "What outcry again is this?" said Owain. "The Nobleman who owned the Castle is now dead," said the maiden. And a little after daybreak, they heard an exceeding loud clamour and wailing. And Owain asked the maiden what was the cause of it. "They are bearing to the church the body of the Nobleman who owned the Castle."

And Owain rose up, and clothed himself, and opened a window of the chamber, and looked towards the Castle; and he could see neither the bounds, nor the extent of the hosts that filled the streets. And they were fully armed; and a vast number of women were with them, both on horseback and on foot; and all the ecclesiastics in the city, singing. And it seemed to Owain that the sky resounded with the vehemence of their cries, and with the noise of the trumpets, and with the singing of the ecclesiastics. In the midst of the throng, he beheld the bier, over which was a veil of white linen; and wax tapers were burning beside and around it, and none that supported the bier was lower in rank than a powerful Baron.

Never did Owain see an assemblage so gorgeous with satin, and silk, and sendall. And following the train, he beheld a lady with yellow hair falling over her shoulders, and stained with blood; and about her a dress of yellow satin, which was torn. Upon her feet were shoes of variegated leather. And it was a marvel that the ends of her fingers were not bruised, from the violence with which she smote her hands together. Truly she would have been the fairest lady Owain ever saw, had she been in her usual guise. And her cry was louder than the shout of the men, or the clamour of the trumpets. No sooner had he beheld the lady, than he became inflamed with her love, so that it took entire possession of him.

Then he inquired of the maiden who the lady was. "Heaven knows," replied the maiden, "she may be said to be the fairest, and the most chaste, and the most liberal, and the wisest, and the most noble of women. And she is my mistress; and she is called the Countess of the Fountain, the wife of him whom thou didst slay yesterday." "Verily," said Owain, "she is the woman that I love best." "Verily," said the maiden, "she shall also love thee not a little."

And with that the maid arose, and kindled a fire, and filled a pot with water, and placed it to warm; and she brought a towel of white linen, and placed it around Owain's neck; and she took a goblet of ivory, and a silver basin, and filled them with warm water, wherewith she washed Owain's head. Then she opened a wooden casket, and drew forth a razor, whose haft was of ivory, and upon which were two rivets of gold. And she shaved his beard, and she dried his head, and his throat, with the towel. Then she rose up from before Owain, and brought him to eat. And truly Owain had never so good a meal, nor was he ever so well served.

When he had finished his repast, the maiden arranged his couch. "Come here," said she, "and sleep, and I will go and woo for thee." And Owain went to sleep, and the maiden shut the door of the chamber after her, and went towards the Castle. When she came there, she found nothing but mourning, and sorrow; and the Countess in her chamber could not bear the sight of any one through grief. Luned came and saluted her, but the Countess answered her not. And the maiden bent down towards her, and said, "What aileth thee, that thou answerest no one to-day?" "Luned," said the Countess, "what change hath befallen thee, that thou hast not come to visit me in my grief? It was wrong in thee, and I having made thee rich; it was wrong in thee that thou didst not come to see me in my distress. That was wrong in thee." "Truly," said Luned, "I thought thy good sense was greater than I find it to be. Is it well for thee to mourn after that good man, or for anything else, that thou canst not have?" "I declare to heaven," said the Countess, "that in the whole world there is not a man to equal him." "Not so," said Luned, "for an ugly man would be as good as, or better than he." "I declare to heaven," said the Countess, "that were it not repugnant to me to cause to be put to death one whom I have brought up, I would have thee executed, for making such a comparison to me. As it is, I will banish thee." "I am glad," said Luned, "that thou hast no other cause to do so, than that I would have been of service to thee where thou didst not know what was to thine advantage. And henceforth evil betide whichever of us shall make the first advance towards reconciliation to the other; whether I should seek an invitation from thee, or thou of thine own accord shouldst send to invite me."

With that Luned went forth: and the Countess arose and followed her to the door of the chamber, and began coughing loudly. And when Luned looked back, the Countess beckoned to her; and she returned to the Countess. "In truth," said the Countess, "evil is thy disposition; but if thou knowest what is to my advantage, declare it to me." "I will do so," quoth she.

"Thou knowest that except by warfare and arms it is impossible for thee to preserve thy possessions; delay not, therefore, to seek someone who can defend them." "And how can I do that?" said the Countess. "I will tell thee," said Luned, "unless thou canst defend the fountain, thou canst not maintain thy dominions; and no one can defend the fountain, except it be a knight of Arthur's household; and I will go to Arthur's Court, and ill betide me, if I return thence without a warrior who can guard the fountain, as well as, or even better than, he who defended it formerly." "That will be hard to perform," said the Countess. "Go, however, and make proof of that which thou hast promised."

Luned set out, under the pretence of going to Arthur's Court; but she went back to the chamber where she had left Owain; and she tarried there with him as long as it might have taken her to have travelled to the Court of King Arthur. And at the end of that time, she apparelled herself and went to visit the Countess. And the Countess was much rejoiced when she saw her, and enquired what news she brought from the Court. "I bring thee the best of news," said Luned, "for I have compassed the object of my mission. When wilt thou, that I should present to thee the chieftain who has come with me hither?" "Bring him here to visit me tomorrow, at mid-day," said the Countess, "and I will cause the town to be assembled by that time."

And Luned returned home. And the next day, at noon, Owain arrayed himself in a coat, and a surcoat, and a mantle of yellow satin, upon which was a broad band of gold lace; and on his feet were high shoes of variegated leather, which were fastened by golden clasps, in the form of lions. And they proceeded to the chamber of the Countess.

Right glad was the Countess of their coming, and she gazed steadfastly upon Owain, and said, "Luned, this knight has not the look of a traveller." "What harm is there in that, lady?" said Luned. "I am certain," said the Countess, "that no other man than this chased the soul from the body of my lord." "So much the better for thee, lady," said Luned, "for had he not been stronger than thy lord he could not have deprived him of life. There is no remedy for that which is past, be it as it may." "Go back to thine abode," said the Countess, "and I will take counsel."

The next day the Countess caused all her subjects to assemble, and showed them that her earldom was left defenceless, and that it could not be protected but with horse and arms, and military skill. "Therefore," said she, "this is what I offer for your choice: either let one of you take me, or give your consent for me to take a husband from elsewhere to defend my dominions."

So they came to the determination that it was better that she should have permission to marry some one from elsewhere; and, thereupon, she sent for the bishops and archbishops to celebrate her nuptials with Owain. And the men of the earldom did Owain homage.

And Owain defended the Fountain with lance and sword. And this is the manner in which he defended it: Whensoever a knight came there he overthrew him, and sold him for his full worth, and what he thus gained he divided among his barons and his knights; and no man in the whole world could be more beloved than he was by his subjects. And it was thus for the space of three years.

It befell that as Gwalchmai went forth one day with King Arthur, he perceived him to be very sad and sorrowful. And Gwalchmai was much grieved to see Arthur in this state; and he questioned him, saying, "Oh, my lord! what has befallen thee?" "In sooth, Gwalchmai," said Arthur, "I am grieved concerning Owain, whom I have lost these three years, and I shall certainly die if the fourth year passes without my seeing him. Now I am sure, that it is through the tale which Kynon the son of Clydno related, that I have lost Owain." "There is no need for thee," said Gwalchmai, "to summon to arms thy whole dominions on this account, for thou thyself and the men of thy household will be able to avenge Owain, if he be slain; or to set him free, if he be in prison; and, if alive, to bring him back with thee." And it was settled according to what Gwalchmai had said.

Then Arthur and the men of his household prepared to go and seek Owain, and their number was three thousand, besides their attendants. And Kynon the son of Clydno acted as their guide. And Arthur came to the Castle where Kynon had been before, and when he came there the youths were shooting in the same place, and the yellow man was standing hard by. When the yellow man saw Arthur he greeted him, and invited him to the Castle; and Arthur accepted his invitation, and they entered the Castle together. And great as was the number of his retinue, their presence was scarcely observed in the Castle, so vast was its extent. And the maidens rose up to wait on them, and the service of the maidens appeared to them all to excel any attendance they had ever met with; and even the pages who had charge of the horses were no worse served, that night, than Arthur himself would have been in his own palace.

The next morning Arthur set out thence, with Kynon for his guide, and came to the place where the black man was. And the stature of the black man was more surprising to Arthur than it had been represented to him. And they came to the top of the wooded steep, and traversed the valley till they reached the green tree, where they saw the fountain, and the bowl, and the slab. And upon that, Kai came to Arthur and spoke to him. "My lord," said he, "I know the meaning of all this, and my request is, that thou wilt permit me to throw the water on the slab, and to receive the first adventure that may befall." And Arthur gave him leave.

Then Kai threw a bowlful of water upon the slab, and immediately there came the thunder, and after the thunder the shower. And such a thunderstorm they had never known before, and many of the attendants who were in Arthur's train were killed by the shower. After the shower had ceased the sky became clear; and on looking at the tree they beheld it completely leafless. Then the birds descended upon the tree, and the song of the birds was far sweeter than any strain they had ever heard before. Then they beheld a knight on a coal-black horse, clothed in black satin, coming rapidly towards them. And Kai met him and encountered him, and it was not long before Kai was overthrown. And the Knight withdrew, and Arthur and his host encamped for the night.

And when they arose in the morning, they perceived the signal of combat upon the lance of the Knight. And Kai came to Arthur, and spoke to him: "My lord," said he, "though I was overthrown yesterday, if it seem good to thee, I would gladly meet the Knight again to-day." "Thou mayst do so," said Arthur. And Kai went towards the Knight. And on the spot he overthrew Kai, and struck him with the head of his lance in the forehead, so that it broke his helmet and the headpiece, and pierced the skin and the flesh, the breadth of the spear-head, even to the bone. And Kai returned to his companions.

After this, all the household of Arthur went forth, one after the other, to combat the Knight, until there was not one that was not overthrown by him, except Arthur and Gwalchmai. And Arthur armed himself to encounter the Knight. "Oh, my lord," said Gwalchmai, "permit me to fight with him first." And Arthur permitted him. And he went forth to meet the Knight, having over himself and his horse a satin robe of honour which had been sent him by the daughter of the Earl of Rhangyw, and in this dress he was not known by any of the host. And they charged each other, and fought all that day until the evening, and neither of them was able to unhorse the other.

The next day they fought with strong lances, and neither of them could obtain the mastery.

And the third day they fought with exceeding strong lances. And they were incensed with rage, and fought furiously, even until noon. And they gave each other such a shock that the girths of their horses were broken, so that they fell over their horses' cruppers to the ground. And they rose up speedily, and drew their swords, and resumed the combat; and the multitude that witnessed their encounter felt assured that they had never before seen two men so valiant or so powerful. And had it been midnight, it would have been light from the fire that flashed from their weapons. And the Knight gave Gwalchmai a blow that turned his helmet from off his face, so that the Knight knew that it was Gwalchmai. Then Owain said, "My lord Gwalchmai, I did not know thee for my cousin, owing to the robe of honour that enveloped thee; take my sword and my arms." Said Gwalchmai, "Thou, Owain, art the victor; take thou my sword." And with that Arthur saw that they were conversing, and advanced towards them. "My lord Arthur," said Gwalchmai, "here is Owain, who has vanquished me, and will not take my arms." "My lord," said Owain, "it is he that has vanquished me, and he will not take my sword." "Give me your swords," said Arthur, "and then neither of you has vanquished the other." Then Owain put his arms around Arthur's neck, and they embraced. And all the host hurried forward to see Owain, and to embrace him; and there was nigh being a loss of life, so great was the press.

And they retired that night, and the next day Arthur prepared to depart. "My lord," said Owain, "this is not well of thee; for I have been absent from thee these three years, and during all that time, up to this very day, I have been preparing a banquet for thee, knowing that thou wouldst come to seek me. Tarry with me, therefore, until thou and thy attendants have recovered the fatigues of the journey, and have been anointed."

And they all proceeded to the Castle of the Countess of the Fountain, and the banquet which had been three years preparing was consumed in three months.

Never had they a more delicious or agreeable banquet. And Arthur prepared to depart. Then he sent an embassy to the Countess, to beseech her to permit Owain to go with him for the space of three months, that he might show him to the nobles and the fair dames of the island of Britain. And the Countess gave her consent, although it was very painful to her. So Owain came with Arthur to the island of Britain. And when he was once more amongst his kindred and friends, he remained three years, instead of three months, with them.

And as Owain one day sat at meat, in the city of Caerlleon upon Usk, behold a damsel entered upon a bay horse, with a curling mane and covered with foam, and the bridle and so much as was seen of the saddle were of gold. And the damsel was arrayed in a dress of yellow satin. And she came up to Owain, and took the ring from off his hand. "Thus," said she, "shall be treated the deceiver, the traitor, the faithless, the disgraced, and the beardless." And she turned her horse's head and departed.

Then his adventure came to Owain's remembrance, and he was sorrowful; and having finished eating he went to his own abode and made preparations that night. And the next day he arose but did not go to the court, but wandered to the distant parts of the earth and to uncultivated mountains. And he remained there until all his apparel was worn out, and his body was wasted away, and his hair was grown long. And he went about with the wild beasts and fed with them, until they became familiar with him; but at length he grew so weak that he could no longer bear them company. Then he descended from the mountains to the valley, and came to a park that was the fairest in the world, and belonged to a widowed Countess.

One day the Countess and her maidens went forth to walk by a lake, that was in the middle of the park. And they saw the form of a man. And they were terrified. Nevertheless they went near him, and touched him, and looked at him. And they saw that there was life in him, though he was exhausted by the heat of the sun. And the Countess returned to the Castle, and took a flask full of precious ointment, and gave it to one of her maidens. "Go with this," said she, "and take with thee yonder horse and clothing, and place them near the man we saw just now. And anoint him with this balsam, near his heart; and if there is life in him, he will arise through the efficacy of this balsam. Then watch what he will do."

And the maiden departed from her, and poured the whole of the balsam upon Owain, and left the horse and the garments hard by, and went a little way off, and hid herself to watch him. In a short time she saw him begin to move his arms; and he rose up, and looked at his person, and became ashamed of the unseemliness of his appearance. Then he perceived the horse and the garments that were near him. And he crept forward till he was able to draw the garments to him from off the saddle. And he clothed himself, and with difficulty mounted the horse. Then the damsel discovered herself to him, and saluted him. And he was rejoiced when he saw her, and enquired of her, what land and what territory that was. "Truly," said the maiden, "a widowed Countess owns yonder Castle; at the death of her husband, he left her two Earldoms, but at this day she has but this one dwelling that has not been wrested from her by a young Earl, who is her neighbour, because she refused to become his wife." "That is a pity," said Owain. And he and the maiden proceeded to the Castle; and he alighted there, and the maiden conducted him to a pleasant chamber, and kindled a fire and left him.

And the maiden came to the Countess, and gave the flask into her hand. "Ha! maiden," said the Countess, "where is all the balsam?" "Have I not used it all?" said she. "Oh, maiden," said the Countess, "I cannot easily forgive thee this; it is sad for me to have wasted seven-score pounds' worth of precious ointment, upon a stranger whom I know not. However, maiden, wait thou upon him, until he is quite recovered."

And the maiden did so, and furnished him with meat and drink, and fire, and lodging, and medicaments, until he was well again. And in three months he was restored to his former guise, and became even more comely than he had ever been before.

One day Owain heard a great tumult, and a sound of arms in the Castle, and he enquired of the maiden the cause thereof. "The Earl," said she, "whom I mentioned to thee, has come before the Castle, with a numerous army, to sub-due the Countess." And Owain enquired of her whether the Countess had a horse and arms in her possession. "She has the best in the world," said the maiden. "Wilt thou go and request the loan of a horse and arms for me," said Owain, "that I may go and look at this army?" "I will," said the maiden.

And she came to the Countess, and told her what Owain had said. And the Countess laughed. "Truly," said she, "I will even give him a horse and arms for ever; such a horse and such arms had he never yet, and I am glad that they should be taken by him to-day, lest my enemies should have them against my will to-morrow. Yet I know not what he would do with them."

The Countess bade them bring out a beautiful black steed, upon which was a beechen saddle, and a suit of armour, for man and horse. And Owain armed himself, and mounted the horse, and went forth, attended by two pages completely equipped, with horses and arms. And when they came near to the Earl's army, they could see neither its extent, nor its extremity. And Owain asked the pages in which troop the Earl was. "In yonder troop," said they, "in which are four yellow standards. Two of them are before, and two behind him." "Now," said Owain, "do you return and await me near the portal of the Castle." So they returned, and Owain pressed forward until he met the Earl. And Owain drew him completely out of his saddle, and turned his horse's head towards the Castle, and, though it was with difficulty, he brought the Earl to the portal, where the pages awaited him. And in they came. And Owain presented the Earl as a gift to the Countess. And said to her, "Behold a requital to thee for thy blessed balsam."

The army encamped around the Castle. And the Earl restored to the Countess the two Earldoms he had taken from her, as a ransom for his life; and for his freedom he gave her the half of his own dominions, and all his gold, and his silver, and his jewels, besides hostages.

And Owain took his departure. And the Countess and all her subjects besought him to remain, but Owain chose rather to wander through distant lands and deserts.

And as he journeyed, he heard a loud yelling in a wood. And it was repeated a second and a third time. And Owain went towards the spot, and beheld a huge craggy mound, in the middle of the wood; on the side of which was a grey rock. And there was a cleft in the rock, and a serpent was within the cleft. And near the rock stood a black lion, and every time the lion sought to go thence, the serpent darted towards him to attack him. And Owain unsheathed his sword, and drew near to the rock; and as the serpent sprang out, he struck him with his sword, and cut him in two. And he dried his sword, and went on his way, as before. But behold the lion followed him, and played about him, as though it had been a greyhound that he had reared.

They proceeded thus throughout the day, until the evening. And when it was time for Owain to take his rest, he dismounted, and turned his horse loose in a flat and wooded meadow. And he struck fire, and when the fire was kindled, the lion brought him fuel enough to last for three nights. And the lion disappeared. And presently the lion returned, bearing a fine large roebuck. And he threw it down before Owain, who went towards the fire with it.

And Owain took the roebuck, and skinned it, and placed collops of its flesh upon skewers, around the fire. The rest of the buck he gave to the lion to devour. While he was doing this, he heard a deep sigh near him, and a second, and a third. And Owain called out to know whether the sigh he heard proceeded from a mortal; and he received answer that it did. "Who art thou?" said Owain. "Truly," said the voice, "I am Luned, the hand-maiden of the Countess of the Fountain." "And what dost thou here?" said Owain. "I am imprisoned," said she, "on account of the knight who came from Arthur's Court, and married the Countess. And he stayed a short time with her, but he afterwards departed for the Court of Arthur, and has not returned since. And he was the friend I loved best in the world. And two of the pages in the Countess's chamber traduced him, and called him a deceiver. And I told them that they two were not a match for him alone. So they imprisoned me in the stone vault, and said that I should be put to death, unless he came himself, to deliver me, by a certain day; and that is no further off than the day after to-morrow. And I have no one to send to seek him for me. And his name is Owain the son of Urien." "And art thou certain that if that knight knew all this, he would come to thy rescue?" "I am most certain of it," said she.

When the collops were cooked, Owain divided them into two parts, between himself and the maiden; and after they had eaten, they talked together, until the day dawned. And the next morning Owain enquired of the damsel, if there was any place where he could get food and entertainment for that night. "There is, lord," said she; "cross over yonder, and go along the side of the river, and in a short time thou wilt see a great Castle, in which are many towers, and the Earl who owns that Castle is the most hospitable man in the world. There thou mayst spend the night."

Never did sentinel keep stricter watch over his lord, than the lion that night over Owain.

And Owain accoutred his horse, and passed across by the ford, and came in sight of the Castle. And he entered it, and was honourably received. And his horse was well cared for, and plenty of fodder was placed before him. Then the lion went and lay down in the horse's manger; so that none of the people of the Castle dared to approach him. The treatment which Owain met with there, was such as he had never known elsewhere, for every one was as sorrowful, as though death had been upon him. And they went to meat; and the Earl sat upon one side of Owain, and on the other side his only daughter. And Owain had never seen any more lovely than she. Then the lion came and placed himself between Owain's feet, and he fed him with every kind of food that he took himself. And he never saw anything equal to the sadness of the people.

In the middle of the repast the Earl began to bid Owain welcome. "Then," said Owain, "behold, it is time for thee to be cheerful." "Heaven knows," said the Earl, "that it is not thy coming that makes us sorrowful, but we have cause enough for sadness and care." "What is that?" said Owain. "I have two sons," replied the Earl, "and yesterday they went to the mountains to hunt. Now there is on the mountain a monster who kills men and devours them, and he seized my sons; and to-morrow is the time he has fixed to be here, and he threatens that he will then slay my sons before my eyes, unless I will deliver into his hands this my daughter.

He has the form of a man, but in stature he is no less than a giant."

"Truly," said Owain, "that is lamentable. And which wilt thou do?" "Heaven knows," said the Earl, "it will be better that my sons should be slain against my will, than that I should voluntarily give up my daughter to him to ill-treat and destroy." Then they talked about other things, and Owain stayed there that night.

The next morning they heard an exceeding great clamour, which was caused by the coming of the giant with the two youths. And the Earl was anxious both to protect his Castle and to release his two sons. Then Owain put on his armour and went forth to encounter the giant, and the lion followed him. And when the giant saw that Owain was armed, he rushed towards him and attacked him. And the lion fought with the giant, much more fiercely than Owain did. "Truly," said the giant, "I should find no difficulty in fighting with thee, were it not for the animal that is with thee." Upon that Owain took the lion back to the Castle and shut the gate upon him, and then he returned to fight the giant, as before. And the lion roared very loud, for he heard that it went hard with Owain. And he climbed up till he reached the top of the Earl's hall, and thence he got to the top of the Castle, and he sprang down from the walls and went and joined Owain. And the lion gave the giant a stroke with his paw, which tore him from his shoulder to his hip, and his heart was laid bare, and the giant fell down dead. Then Owain restored the two youths to their father.

The Earl besought Owain to remain with him, and he would not, but set forward towards the meadow where Luned was. And when he came there he saw a great fire kindled, and two youths with beautiful curling auburn hair were leading the maiden to cast her into the fire. And Owain asked them what charge they had against her. And they told him of the compact that was between them, as the maiden had done the night before. "And," said they, "Owain has failed her, therefore we are taking her to be burnt." "Truly," said Owain, "he is a good knight, and if he knew that the maiden was in such peril, I marvel that he came not to her rescue; but if you will accept me in his stead, I will do battle with you." "We will," said the youths, "by him who made us."

And they attacked Owain, and he was hard beset by them. And with that the lion came to Owain's assistance, and they two got the better of the young men. And they said to him, "Chieftain, it was not agreed that we should fight save with thyself alone, and it is harder for us to contend with yonder animal than with thee." And Owain put the lion in the place where the maiden had been imprisoned, and blocked up the door with stones, and he went to fight with the young men, as before. But Owain had not his usual strength, and the two youths pressed hard upon him. And the lion roared incessantly at seeing Owain in trouble; and he burst through the wall until he found a way out, and rushed upon the young men, and instantly slew them. So Luned was saved from being burned.

Then Owain returned with Luned to the dominions of the Countess of the Fountain. And when he went thence he took the Countess with him to Arthur's Court, and she was his wife as long as she lived.

And then he took the road that led to the Court of the savage black man, and Owain fought with him, and the lion did not quit Owain until he had vanquished him. And when he reached the Court of the savage black man he entered the hall, and beheld four-and-twenty ladies, the fairest that could be seen. And the garments which they had on were not worth four-and-twenty pence, and they were as sorrowful as death. And Owain asked them the cause of their sadness. And they said, "We are the daughters of Earls, and we all came here with our husbands, whom we dearly loved. And we were received with honour and rejoicing. And we were thrown into a state of stupor, and while we were thus, the demon who owns this Castle slew all our husbands, and took from us our horses, and our raiment, and our gold, and our silver; and the corpses of our husbands are still in this house, and many others with them. And this, Chieftain, is the cause of our grief, and we are sorry that thou art come hither, lest harm should befall thee."

And Owain was grieved when he heard this. And he went forth from the Castle, and he beheld a knight approaching him, who saluted him in a friendly and cheerful manner, as if he had been a brother. And this was the savage black man. "In very sooth," said Owain, "it is not to seek thy friendship that I am here." "In sooth," said he, "thou shalt not find it then." And with that they charged each other, and fought furiously. And Owain overcame him, and bound his hands behind his back. Then the black savage besought Owain to spare his life, and spoke thus: "My lord Owain," said he, "it was foretold that thou shouldst come hither and vanquish me, and thou hast done so. I was a robber here, and my house was a house of spoil; but grant me my life, and I will become the keeper of an Hospice, and I will maintain this house as an Hospice for weak and for strong, as long as I live, for the good of thy soul." And Owain accepted this proposal of him, and remained there that night.

And the next day he took the four-and-twenty ladies, and their horses, and their raiment, and what they possessed of goods and jewels, and proceeded with them to Arthur's Court. And if Arthur was rejoiced when he saw him, after he had lost him the first time, his joy was now much greater. And of those ladies, such as wished to remain in Arthur's Court remained there, and such as wished to depart departed.

And thenceforward Owain dwelt at Arthur's Court greatly beloved, as the head of his household, until he went away with his followers; and those were the army of three hundred ravens which Kenverchyn had left him. And wherever Owain went with these he was victorious.

And this is the tale of The Lady of the Fountain.

Avillion; or, The Happy Isles

A Fireside Fancy

DINAH MARIA MULOCK CRAIK

"I am going a long way,
With these thou seest—if, indeed, I go—
(For all my mind is clouded with a doubt)
To the island-valley of Avillion."

—Tennyson

Chapter I

We sat together on the deck, Lilias and I, listening to the boom of the wide Atlantic, and looking into each other's eyes. A thriftless occupation, but infinitely sweet. We had not grown tired of it yet, though we had been married three weeks; our love was not even a shadow the less. It seemed impossible for us to date its beginning; Heaven grant we may never know its end!

We had been wedded three weeks. Three weeks! Could it be, then, that only one little month had passed since that day—the day of days!—when—But I will tell all concerning it. I will chronicle its every hour, whether of suffering or joy; for now both are alike written goldenly on this happy heart of mine.

I had been ill for a long time—indeed, from my youth up I have rarely known the blessing of continuous health. But though this circumstance gave a languor and a half-melancholy dreaminess to my whole character, I think, too, it made me more humble, more loving, more thankful for all the love which was showered upon me. And when my long illness came, this blessing increased tenfold. I heard people compassionate "poor Wilfred Mayer," and say how hard it was that a young man should have the strength and glory of his youth brought thus low. I did not feel it so; I knew that there was power, aye, and beauty, in my soul; and I cared not for the feeble body. Besides, I lived in such an atmosphere of love. There was my father; my bold, frank-hearted brother, younger than I, yet assuming all the tender protection of eldership; Hester, the most loving of sisters; and one, dearer than any sister—Lilias Hay.

But the day—that day! In the morning I, feeble always, seemed feebler than ordinary. I lay back in my arm-chair, listening to the soft pattering of the April rain upon the window-sill, without any connected thought, except a fear that the weather might keep Lilias Hay in-doors: and I did not like to miss seeing her, even for a day. I heard the sound of an opening door; but it was only the physician—accompanied by a second, whom I had not seen before. I was disappointed, and paid little heed to either, until I noticed that they drew my sister aside, and spoke earnestly. While she listened, Hester turned pale, looked at me, and began to weep. Her tears seemed to fall on my heart like ice-drops, piercing me with a shuddering dread. I felt, I knew, that that smooth-tongued stranger had, with his calm, stolid lips, pronounced my death-doom.

And I must die! The Shadow, hovering near me so long that I had ceased to regard it, was then close at hand—its very breath was upon me! I MUST DIE!

Hester came to my side with the second physician. I looked fixedly upon *him*, my doomer. I believe I said some words which betrayed my thoughts; for he answered, with a bland, cheerful smile, "that I must not imagine anything so serious; a voyage, perhaps a summer in Madeira, would soon—"

I turned away; I would hear no more of the smiling lie. Thank God, it was not breathed by Hester's lips! No; she only wept, and kissed me once or twice softly.

"In a week he must go!" I heard the physician whisper. Then I knew there was no hope. They went away, and left me alone.

I tried to think of peace, of religion; I tried to say, "Thy will be done;" but the strong writhings of human passion shut out from me even the face of God. To die, to leave all my dear ones, to part from Lilias Hay!—I uttered her name almost with a groan—the thought was horrible. In this fearful moment I knew how madly, how despairingly, I loved her. She knew it, too, though I had never told her so. There was no need. The deep tenderness between us had grown from year to year, until it became a part of our life. I say *our life*; for we seemed to have but one. Neither said, "I love;" but the daily tide of our existence as it flowed harmoniously on, cried out with its thousand voices, "See, how these two love one another!"

I had hitherto been content that it should be so, knowing well that Lilias would wed no man save me, and that one day the loving friendship between us would be changed for a closer bond. But now I must die—die without having called her wife, without even having taken her once to my heart. O misery! that blessed, long-dreamed-of moment would never come; I must go down into the dark grave; I must lay my head in the dust *there*, and not on the pure, faithful bosom of my Lilias Hay!

I groaned aloud; I writhed in my anguish. Life and youth were yet strong within me. *I could not die*. Sometimes I resolved at all hazards to tell Lilias of my love. Perhaps I might draw life from the lips of my betrothed; perhaps a wife's prayers might yet stand between me and the Destroyer. I would risk it! I would ask her to wed me now—at once. What,—wed youth with sickness, peace with misery, life with death? God forgive the sinful thought! No; rather let me die alone, with dumb lips that carried their eternal secret mournfully to the grave. Best so— best even for *her* sake.

I grew calmer. My frozen despair melted into a dew of tears. I began to pray the prayers that my dead mother had taught me when I was a child. They made me feel like a child now, peaceful and humble. When Hester came in again, I was able to look in her face and smile. She did not weep, but talked with me calmly and affectionately, about my journey. I said I would rather remain at home; but she prayed—nay, they all prayed—that I would embrace any chance that might spare me longer to their dear love. I promised. Then my sister left the room, and brought in Lilias Hay.

Lilias was very pale but composed and tearless. She came and sat down beside me, in her usual place. I laid my hand on her lap; she took it, and held it for a long time without a word.

"You know all, Lilias; that I am going to Madeira?"

"Yes."

I marvelled, nay, I was almost pained, that she said no more. My Lilias! I did not know thy heart even then!

They were all in the room: my father, Charles, Hester, and one who was to be Hester's bridegroom that very month. As they began to consult as to who would accompany me on this voyage of doom, young Fortescue drew her nearer to him with an anxious look. Hester cast her eyes down; but I saw the struggle in her heart. I would not put the claim of even a dying brother before that of an affianced husband. I said I would rather have Charles with me; and, after some resistance, Hester assented. They soon went away, and left me, as they often did, alone with my friend Lilias.

My friend! Was it friendship, when her every tone, her every movement, caused my heart to thrill, even through the cold sluggish pulses of disease. How keenly I suffered! How I yearned to lay my cheek on the dear hand I held, and pray her to take my poor dying head to her bosom, and let my last breath utter the life-long love which on earth might never be fulfilled. But I uttered it not. Even when, speaking of my going away so soon, her words came brokenly, and she leaned her brow against my chair in a long tearful silence, I only laid my hand softly on her hair, and bade "God bless her." Better, I thought, that she should mourn as a *friend* than as a widow.—Lilias, my faithful one, was I right?

Then we talked in a quiet, ordinary way, about my journey and its arrangements.

"Hester will go with you surely; of course, Hester must go," said Lilias.

"No, Hester must not, ought not," I answered earnestly. "Nothing should divide two who love one another." And then I trembled at my words, and I saw Lilias tremble too. But soon after she spoke of some indifferent subject, and continued to do so until the time came for her to go home. We bade each other "good-night" (we dared not say "good-bye"), parting as usual with the long, lingering hand-clasp only. She walked slowly to the door, her step seeming to me like the rending of soul and body. Whether by gesture or groan I betrayed the agony I know not; but Lilias turned round. The next moment she had flung herself on her knees beside me.

"Wilfred, Wilfred! in life or death I cannot part with you. Hush!"—and her voice grew solemn with unutterable tenderness—"do not speak. Let me say the truth, long known to us both—that—" But she could not say it. Only she caught my hands—wildly, fondly, fast—"Oh, Wilfred! do not—nay, you shall not go alone. Friend! lover! *husband!* take me with you!

I fell forward—my head on her shoulder. My lips asked feebly and blindly for the holy seal of troth-plight. I felt it—the first pure kiss of Lilias Hay; and then I felt no more, but sank into a swoon of joy.

It lasted not long; for with returning consciousness came that iron will of self-martyrdom, which would have made me die with my love unspoken: I lifted myself from her enclasping arms.

"Lilias," I cried, "this must not be. You would give me life, and I you—death. I dare not take the boon."

She arose; quick blushes diffused her face and neck, and then faded away. O love! my faithful love! I could dream I saw thee now, leaning over me with that white marble brow, and low, solemn voice.

"Wilfred, you think of yourself alone—you have not remembered *me.* Your love is my life—you have no right to take that from me. If I must suffer, better— better a thousand times that I should suffer with you than apart." And she sank once more on her knees beside me. "Oh, Wilfred! my only comfort—my only hope in this world—cast me not from you. Let me be your wife, to watch, tend, and cherish you, until—until you go away, and then to follow—soon, oh, soon!"

I opened my arms, crying, "Lilias, come." And thus, in one long embrace, silent as death—or love, we plighted our troth to each other.

A week after I and *my wife* were in the midst of the wide ocean, on our way to Madeira.

Reader, you do not wonder now that it was almost heaven to me to lie silent on the twilight-shadowed deck, doing nothing, save look into the eyes of my Lilias.

They were eyes, now bright with hope as well as love: for it seemed as though the shadows of doom were passing away from mine. I drank in the soft breezes of the southern sea; they gave me new life, as all said. But I knew, O my wife! that this new life was brought by that precious love of thine.

Chapter II

It was a pleasant voyage—by day under the sunny heaven, by night beneath the stars. Many a time Lilias and I sat for hours together on the deck, hand in hand like little children, pleased with the veriest trifles—a cloud on the sky, a flying fish on the water—talking sweet idleness, half sense, half nonsense, as loving and happy ones ever will; and then my wife would shake her head with a mock reproof, and say, we ought to be ashamed of ourselves—we, burthened between us with the conjoined weight of nearly fifty years. She was so happy, that she even used to sport with me, sometimes jesting about my having compelled herself to become the wooer at last. She kept buzzing about me like a merry little bee, her blithe voice lulling me either by song or speech, until, still feeble, I often sank to sleep on the deck, with my head on her lap. And then, many and many a time did I wake, feeling my hair wet with the dew of passionate tenderness which had rained on me from those dear eyes. "Thank God, thank God, for the blessedness of love!" was all my heart could cry. But thus it did cry, day and night, in a loud pæan of joy that even angels might hear.

Friend reader, I dare say thou thinkest we were a couple of simpletons! We smile on thee calmly. Poor fool! thou hast never loved.

One night we watched the twilight into starlight, and could not tear ourselves from the quiet, lonely deck. It was a strange and awful thing to be sweeping in the darkness over that vast, desolate sea, with not a sound near us, save the flapping of a sail and the wind in the cordage singing almost like a human voice,

or one which, though all spiritual now, yet comes laden with the echo of its remembered mortal wail. Our converse partook of the character of the scene, and
glided from the sweet trifling of contented earthly love, into the solemn communion of two spirits, wedded not only for life but for immortality. We spoke of
the deep mysteries of our being, of the unseen and immaterial world. All these
things were ever to me full of a strange fascination, in which Lilias shared. Why
should she not? All our lives we had thought alike, she following whither I led.
But she ever walked meekly, knowing that the man is the head of the woman. Her
wisdom was born and taught of love, as a woman's should be. And to me it brought
not weariness but strength; I thanked Heaven that the wife of my bosom was also
the wife of my soul!

In the midst of our talk there came by our only fellow-passenger, a German doctor. He startled us both, as he moved from behind a sail, the setting moon
lighting up his always pallid face and long, gray hair. He seemed to us, in our
present visionary mood, almost phantom-like in his appearance.

Lilias started, and then laughed. "It is only Herr Foerster. Let us speak to
him."

"No," I said, for I did not like the man. He was a mystic. He vexed me with
his wild aspect, his floating locks, and his perpetual harangues about Kant and
Swedenborg, and Jacob Bœhmen. Dear Lilias combated my prejudice in her own
gentle way. Where I condemned the eccentric philosopher, who hung out his wisdom as a sign to catch men's eyes, she pitied the strange old man, half-mad, and
wholly desolate.

"See, Wilfred, how wistfully he is looking out over the waters. We know
not what sorrowful thoughts may be in that poor brain of his. You will let me speak
to him, dearest?"

She had her way, for it was the right way, and I knew it. In a few minutes
the old German was sitting with us, inclined to begin his fantastic lore. But the
mood had changed since yesterday, and his speech was less mystic, and more full
of dreamy poetry. I was thankful that he had forgotten Kant. As his countenance
lighted up, and his speech grew earnest, I began to feel that there was sincerity
even in his eccentricities, and method in his madness.

"You were standing mute and absorbed when I spoke to you, Herr Foerster,"
said Lilias. "Were you thinking about home?"

"I have no home."

There was scarcely any sorrow in his eye or tone. He had passed these human weaknesses.

"But I was watching for a home, a true home—one in search of which I have traversed these seas for ten years. I shall find it some time—I know I shall."

Lilias looked at him compassionately; and then glanced involuntarily—first to the sea, then upwards to the starry, steel-blue sky.

"No: you mistake;" and the old mystic shook his head with a half-scornful smile, "I seek nothing so vague as that: I have no wish to die. Perhaps"—and his voice grew mysterious—"Perhaps I never may die."

My wife crept nearer me, and gazed earnestly on the man whom I now thought surely mad; but there was no sign of frenzy in his manner. Reassured, Lilias again spoke.

"Where and what is this home you seek?"

He pointed to the young moon just dipping into the western sea, amidst a bank of fantastic clouds—"Look there! do you not see beyond that pale crescent, where sea and sky meet, a luminous verge, resembling white hills and shining towers? *Resembling*, did I say? Nay, it is! That is the very spot I seek—the land beyond sunset—the Island of the Blest."

Surprised and somewhat startled by his sudden vehemence, neither Lilias nor I made any answer. He went on, changing abruptly from the energy of enthusiasm to the calmness of eager reasoning.

"You will doubt this, I know. You will think me mad. Many have done so—but I smile at them. The same was said of the great Ithacan—of Columbus—of other noble spirits who have set out on a like track."

"But none have ever found its ending, Herr Foerster," said I. "No man ever yet reached the Island of the Blest."

"Rather say, no man ever came back from thence. How should he?" And the German smiled a calm superior smile. As he went on, his plain, well-arranged arguments almost staggered my doubts as to his insanity. His speech was so like truth.

"Men in all ages have believed in the existence of this land. Legends, variously modified by different ages and climes, have all agreed in this universal fact, that far westward, in the midst of the vast mysterious ocean, untraversed and untraversable by man, lies an island, whose dwellers have all joys of humanity without its pain—all the sensuous delights of earth, combined with the purity of heaven. Who knows but that the angels carried God's Eden and planted it there in the midst of the sea?"

"This faith is very beautiful," said Lilias, attracted even against her will. "I had rather believe thus, than believe that the divine garden—trodden of angels, visited by God—was transformed into a howling wilderness."

I could not but smile at her graceful fancy; but the influence of this strange man was upon me also. "You say, Herr Foerster, that this belief has extended over all ages. How so?"

"Is it not among the Greeks? Listen to Homer." And with his grand, rich German accent, he poured out in kindred strength a torrent of that majestic Greek, which was in truth worthy to be the speech of Olympus—

"The large utterance of the early gods."

"It sounds glorious," murmured Lilias; "but I am a woman, and have only a woman's learning. I should like to hear it in our English tongue."

Herr Foerster obeyed.

"Thus it runs, then:—

> 'But thee the ever-living gods will send
> Unto the Elysian plain and distant bounds
> Of earth—
> There life is easiest unto men: no snow,
> Or wintry storm, or rain, at any time
> Is there; but evermore the ocean sends
> Soft-breathing air of Zephyr to refresh
> The habitants.'

"So says the blind seer and poet—for poets are all seers. Hear, too, the grand Pindar, still speaking the belief of his country—as in those days bard, prophet, and priest were one:—

> 'They speed their way
> To Kronos' palace, where, around
> The Island of the Blest, the airs
> Of ocean breathe, and golden flowers
> Blaze: some on land
> From shining trees, and other kinds
> The water feeds. Of these
> Garlands and bracelets round their arms they bind.'

"—Do you hearken, friends?"

We did indeed sit listening, in a silence that was not without awe. The scene, the hour, the gestures and tones of this man, carried with them a supernatural influence. More and more he spoke, collecting with infinite learning every mythical fable that could suggest or confirm this belief; the story of Ulysses, who sailed far into the wild desert of waters in search of the land beyond the sunset; the Roman superstition of the Island of Atlantis, which ancient fable, if fable it were, had left its impress on the Atlantic; the legends of mediæval lore, that spurred on to enterprise a Columbus and a Gama; the fantastic romance concerning the "happy land of Faerie," the Island of Avalon and its dwellers, once of earth—King Arthur, Sir Launfal, Ogier le Danois—all these fanciful creations of history and fiction were brought together by our companion—enthusiast, or madman, whichever he were—with a reality utterly astounding.

"You see," he continued, "that each legend coincides in one fact—the Happy Islands that lie in the western sea. Universal fable proves individual truth—at least, I believed so; and when the world became desolate to me, I turned my thoughts to a new land—the land of the blest."

"You have suffered, then," whispered Lilias' tender voice.

"Few men long so ardently for another world, as they whose hope is gone from this. But I must not speak of these things now: all are past—long past. Why did you make me think of them? You—oh, you twain have no need to seek the Happy Isles."

He drooped his face a moment, and then went on, harshly and wild as before. "I dreamed this dream, night and day, until I was convinced it was a truth. I squandered all my wealth—for whom should I keep it?—and then set sail. Ten years, ten long years, have I spent on these seas, passing from ship to ship—suffering famine and drought, fire and wreck; yet never, oh! never have I touched the land of the blest. But, hark you!" and he caught my hand—"I know they are here, in this very ocean. I see them sometimes—at sunset, or at dawn, far off in the horizon; they never come nearer. But they will come near: ah, yes! I know that some day I shall find the Happy Isles."

He stretched his clasped hands towards the ocean in full confidence of faith.

"Poor dreamer!" I thought. "Are they wise or mad—to be envied or pitied—the many who, like thee, toss blindly on the world's dark sea, vainly seeking the Happy Isles?"

But I had not time for more speech; for suddenly there seized me a racking pain, darting arrow-like through breast and brain. It was the fore-warning of sufferings I well knew of old. They came upon me, thronging thick and fast, sharp rending pains which lowered my manhood to the shrieking agony of a child. And there, alone beside me, sat the faithful one who had followed me over the seas—true woman, true wife! Thank Heaven—it was her thought as well as mine—thank Heaven! that she *was* my wife now; that it was hers to fold her cool hands round my brow, to gather me to her bosom as a mother would a sick child. Every form and phase of tenderest love—sister-love, mother-love, wife-love—seemed mingled into one, and poured out upon me from the heart of my Lilias. I knew now—would that every man on earth knew!—how infinite a faithful woman's love can be!

Stronger and stronger grew these torturing pains, until my senses became dim. I scarce felt even the winding arms of my Lilias, until they were removed, and I perceived bending over me the German mystic. He spoke, I thought, of some rare drug which would surely lull my sufferings.

"It is very fearful—this new power!" answered Lilias.

I heard *her* voice, every tone.

Those around her spoke a few words. I only knew their effect by her convulsive shudder and smothered cry; but soon after she said—

"Herr Foerster, you are a good man; I trust you with my life—more than my life, remember! Let my husband try this, and God be merciful to him and me!"

The German stooped down. To my distempered fancy his eyes appeared to flame like demons', and his tongue to hiss in her ear—

"You have no fear?"

"No!" she replied.

"It is well—and you are wise! Two hours more of these tortures, and—"

I heard no more; but as he went away I felt Lilias shiver; she drew me closer to her, and kissed passionately my lips and eyes. I strove to speak, but my mind would not concentrate itself so as to frame one intelligible sentence. The German came back. He knelt before me, and I perceived a faint fragrance that diffused itself on the air I breathed. One struggle I made to convince myself that all was real—that I was clasped safe in my wife's arms—and then I gave myself to the delicious numbness which stole over me. My eyes closed; the gathering lights that flitted before them disappeared: it was as though some spirit hand were folding over sight and hearing a dim, gray veil. A few times I felt my heart booming up and down, like a creature of life; I seemed almost to behold it beating in my bosom—its great pulses heaving continually louder and higher, like waves of the sea; and once or twice I distinguished those rending pains—pains darting lightning-like—pains that could be seen as well as felt: for in this strange spell all the various senses seemed to be confounded and mingled.

Then all grew peace. Closer and closer gathered over me the solemn veil: one by one my heart's leaping pulses sank lower and lower—as if dull fingers pressed them into stillness. All pain ceased, and with it all perception of being. I faintly stirred my hand, to convince myself of my bodily existence. I tried to make my lips express the thoughts which dwelt in my still conscious mind.

"I sleep, Lilias, I sleep!" It sounded less like my own human voice than that of a spirit; but it was answered.

"Yes, my own dearest, you will sleep soon."

Then all the outward world became dim—the sounds and sights about me fading as earth-landscapes fade before one who voyages through the air, rising higher and higher, until cities, towers, and trees—are all an undistinguishable mass. Thus I seemed to soar out of my bodily organs into a new existence. All sensation vanished: I no longer breathed; yet I seemed to feel no need of vital air. My heart lay still; but its hushed pulses gave me no pain. I no longer bore the burden of a weary body: it was as though I had become incorporeal, and had passed out of the world of matter into that of spirit.

I said to myself, "This is death!" but the thought found no echo on my lips— they would not give forth one sound. Then I knew more clearly the change that had taken place. It seemed at first that I was really dead—become a disembodied spirit. Yet my soul was not free from the clay which it no longer had power to animate into living and breathing man. It roved hither and thither, within its lost tabernacle, and could not flee away. My brain yet maintained power of thought and perception; through it I heard, and saw, and felt, though my outward senses were benumbed. Then, when the first delicious torpor had gone by, there came upon me a vague horror. Could it be that I was dead, yet not dead—a tranced body tenanted by a living soul? Was this my fearful doom?

It broke upon me with the first sound conveyed by my incorporeal senses— the cry of my wife Lilias! Then I heard—what no man on earth ever heard be- fore—the wail of his beloved over his own dead corse!

Chapter III

In a dark cabin—around all coldness, silence, death—they left me; *me*, still me, for the eternal essence had not quitted, could not quit, its clay tenement. I knew all they did to me—the demons, with that arch-demon looking on, smiling at his hor- rible work! I felt it all—my palsied limbs being straightened, the deadweights laid on my eyes, my helpless hands decently composed;—with my spirit's senses I saw and heard every whit, and yet my corporeal life was gone. Wonder, rage, terror, swept over my soul as vainly as blasts over a frozen lake—no sound, no movement, enabled the bodily organs to reflect the mind; I had power over them no more.

The German with his fellow-ministers left me, and I lay wrapped in ter- rible repose. I, of all human flesh, was the first who had *felt death*. There was a marvel, a mystery, even a pride, in this awful thought. I shrouded myself in it, and, piercing through the terror and the gloom, my soul went travelling over every phase of wild speculation. I, the immortal, indivisible *I*, looked down almost pityingly upon that poor atom of helpless mortality that was myself. It was a dear self—dear, with all its imperfections; for it was the human form which Lilias held precious, even beautiful. The pale, powerless head she had cherished on her bosom; the cold, nerveless hands had lain, hour after hour, enfolded tenderly in hers.

They were so folded once more; but it was the frenzied clasp of the widow, not the wife.

She came—Lilias, my beloved; her footsteps sounded through the stillness of the death-chamber; her sobs pierced the darkness of the desolate night. Oh, fearful spell! that not even such a cry could break!

I knew her hand was upon my pulseless heart; I knew her kisses were showered on my dumb lips; yet I could not answer; no more than the corpse which I appeared. A veil, far wider than that between the dead and the living, was drawn between me and the beloved of my soul. How I longed to rend at once the feeble thread that linked me to mortality, and pass—through any agony, soever great—into the state of a disembodied spirit. Then, perchance, I might hold communion with her, as the departed are sometimes permitted to do.

She would not believe that the life had entirely gone from my poor shrouded form. She wrapped the cold hands in her bosom; she laid her cheek beside mine on the same pillow; and so, weeping bitterly until her strength failed, she fell asleep. But she awoke soon, calling wildly on my name. Oh God! I would have almost perilled the immortal soul Thou gavest me to answer her. Why, thou Divine, didst Thou make this terrible human love so strong?

Lilias, shuddering, let my hands fall. *When they fell*, impassive as clay, she uttered a cry such as would almost have broken a death-slumber. It could not break mine.

She seized the lamp, and held it so that the light fell on my face. There was one start, one gasping sigh, and then she stood calm. Over her terror, her grief, her despair, had passed the awful peace given by the presence of Death.

She laid down the light, moving slowly, with hushed steps. Then she came, and knelt down, not by my pillow, but at the couch's foot. She kissed me no more, she clasped me no more; I was no longer her living husband, I was the solemn image of Death. That image froze her human love into mute awe. Her tears ceased, her sobs stilled. For a moment she hid her face as if to shut out from sight the dead face, once so beloved; and then she paused. It was beloved still! But as she gazed, there was in her look less of passionate earthly love than of the sublime

yet awful tenderness with which one would behold an angel of God or a departed soul.

After a while, Lilias lifted her voice and prayed—the widow's first prayer.
Yet it began with a thanksgiving. She thanked Heaven for all I had been to her; for
the love which had awakened her girlhood's soul, calling into life its strength, joy,
and beauty; for the blessed fate which had worked out, in due time, that love's
fulfilment, so that every dower of her rich heart might be poured in a full tide on
him who was its awakener. No murmurings were there for the love taken away;
but blessings for the love that *had been*.

"And thou, my husband!" she cried, "my own beloved! who art not here,
not in this form lying cold before me, but now standing a spirit among the immortal ones, glorious and beautiful as they, forsake me not! Live thou in my heart;
change this human anguish into a memory peaceful and divine! Love me, love me,
up in heaven as I love thee on earth! Oh, thou who wert—who art—my soul's
soul, through life and *after*, what shall part thee from me!"

She looked—not down towards the pale figure beside which she knelt, but
upwards into heaven. Thither her lifted hands were stretched, thither her eyes were
turned; and I, yet prisoned in that dull clay, mourned not that she regarded it no
more, but rejoiced in the immortal strength and purity of the devotion which had
loved, not my poor dying body, but *me*.

There came faces and voices to the door, and Lilias arose. She arose, not
the weeping, broken-hearted girl, stricken and desolate, but the widow of the
dead—calm, patient, almost sublime in her sorrow. Many pitying friends gathered round her; there was only one which stole in the rear, glaring at her and at
me from amidst his gray elf-locks—the Destroyer—who had worked upon us
this doom.

They besought Lilias to take some rest; but she meekly refused. Covering
my face, she took her seat at the head of what she deemed her husband's corpse;
and there remained, motionless and mute, a solemn watcher over the living Dead.
At last, her human strength yielded to this weight of woe; she sank down, slowly,
slowly, on the breast that could shelter her no more. Falling thence she lay a dull,
unconscious heap on the cabin floor.

It marked her, even there, that flaming, fiendish eye. It watched her everywhere—her and me. Creeping snake-like into the chamber, the Mystic gathered
her in his foul clutch, indifferently, as though that precious form had been some
victim slain by his hand. He bore her away, with a triumphant smile; and I, her
husband, bound in adamantine bonds, lay a living spirit prisoned in a dead corse.

Again I was alone. The wind rose, and the ship rocked madly on the deep.

I, lying there, might have been a stone. All sense, all power, was dead within me. Only the brain was alive—alive with sight, and sound, and perception. Phantom after phantom rose, peopling the vessel's hold. They danced in the darkness, like motes in a sunbeam; they shrieked in the blast, a whirlwind of unearthly voices; they filled the very air, the air that I had once breathed.

Thus I lay amidst these horrors, until a human presence, more demon-like than themselves, put them to flight. The German Mystic came and stood over his victim.

Love had been powerless to unloose the spell; how then should Hate have strength to break it? I, who would have heaped worlds upon worlds to crush my enemy, soul and body, into ashes—was doomed to lie still as a sleeping babe, while his cursed fingers wandered over my dead heart, my sunken pulse; while, in his ghastly mirth, he bent my helpless limbs, making me assume mocking attitudes of life.

At last, he dropped upon my lips some liquid, and my tongue felt itself unloosed. I howled upon him imprecations, threatenings, prayers; but he only smiled! I shrieked, until I thought the sound might pierce to the ocean's depths; and still he only smiled.

"Poor deceived one, it is vain!" he cried: "thy voice rings no louder than the sigh of a summer wind. No human ear could hear it, save mine, which is deaf as the rock. I must work my will."

He laid his fingers on my lips, and they were sealed as with an iron band. He began to speak once more.

"Listen, thou dumb one who hearest all! Against thee I bear no malice, no revenge; thou art but my instrument to work out the great end. Through thee I must find the Happy Isles. Thou, whose bliss on earth seemed so secure that it took from thee all desire for heaven—thou art the one chosen for this work. Therefore, I must send thee—a living, trance-bound human soul—to the place where the dead lie; to the unfathomable depth of the great sea, that there, perchance, thou mayst discover the way to the Land of Immortality."

At this my soul within me sent up a cry, such as might have risen to the crystal walls of heaven when the Son of the Morning fell. But it could not pass my frozen lips.

"Patience, poor struggler against destiny!" answered that voice of doom, and yet it now seemed not fierce but pitiful, even mild. "Is it so hard that thou, who hast been most blessed—who, loved and loving, hast found earth a very heaven—shouldst sacrifice a few years more of an existence that haply may soon become wretched as mine, in order that a fellow-being, equal to thyself in all but happiness, may exchange a life which to him has been a long torture, for rest and peace?"

His voice became plaintive, nay, humble. But I saw only the hand that rent from me love, hope, life, and I cursed him still.

"I hear thy unspoken thoughts," he replied. "But they avail not. Thou hast no pity on me—me on whom neither God nor man ever took pity. Thou hast no tenderness for thy brother-man, towards whom the human eye was never turned in love. Now, then, I stand as an avenger. I make thee a sacrifice for all the suffering and outcast of thy kind. Thou shalt go first, and find out the pathway on which they may follow to the land of peace. It is just, and I am a righteous instrument to fulfil this doom. The time is at hand."

While he spoke the hurricane rose louder and louder, and amidst its boomings came the din of clamorous voices, calling aloud that the dead should be brought forth. The sea would not rest, they said, until it had received its lawful prey.

The Mystic met them at the cabin door. "It shall be done now, at once, while the widow sleeps. Poor mourner! It will save her one parting pang the less."

He was a demon incarnate, with that cast-down eye—that silvery tongue!

They swathed me—me—living me, in the cerements of the grave; they bore me, a loathed weight, to the poop. There, out in the midnight blackness, they stood, unconscious murderers; he leading them on. Above the howl of the seething waves, I heard his low voice breathing the mockery of a funeral prayer. A lifting up—a plunge—and I sank down, down—into the yawning ocean-hell.

Chapter IV

I believe that death itself—the real parting of soul and body—is less horrible than many tortures, not only mental but corporeal, which we endure during life. Many a man has dreamed that he was dying—has felt vividly all the circumstances of that supreme hour—the gradual ebbing away of existence, or the passing suddenly from life into eternity. May it not be that this kind of dream, in which we rarely suffer any pain, whether seeming to die slowly or by violence, is but the striving of the spirit within us to foreshadow the moment of its departure; to make known, in the only possible way, the solemn secret which none who have passed death's portals can ever return to unfold?

Thus I died, if death it could be called, as softly, as painlessly, as one dies in dreams. "In a moment, in the twinkling of an eye," the change came. I sank down, down into an abyss of blackness, silence, and nothingness! and then I rose up— rose like a bird, or a cloud in the air. I beheld light, I heard sounds. I felt a life within me; richer, fuller, than any human life. Around me was neither void, nor spiritual heaven, nor terrible hell. It was earth—earth purified into Paradise.

I stood on the shore of the Happy Isles!

As the sunshine of that blessed land fell on me, my grave-cerements seemed to melt off like misty robes of air. With them melted the icy spell which had bound me. Once again I moved and breathed like living man—like that man of men who rose up beneath the finger of God from the life-pregnant dust of Eden.

As glorious as Eden itself was the land whereon I stood. Words cannot picture it. Perchance you may form the best image of its beauty, when you look up at those cloud landscapes which grow visible on summer-eves, and talk to your little son at your knee about the heavenly country which he dreams is something like that which his young eyes behold in the pictured sky. No other earthly similitude can approach so near to this vision of the Happy Isles.

Around them the sea folded itself like a girdle, a crystal circle, encompassing them with wide and loving arms, like Infinity. For there, Infinity and Eternity, the great mysteries into which the deepest and purest human faith cannot pierce without trembling, became near and familiar things. Still, the land was not heaven, but earth—earth with its curse taken away, and made pure and beautiful as it was in the Eden-time.

I walked with human feet along the lovely shore. I gazed with human eyes upon the view beyond—a region of pastoral, untrodden beauty, blue hills rising sky-wards, feathered down to the very strand with trees. The land, though unlike any which I had known on earth, was such as I had pictured many a time in fancy, when dreaming over that time of which Homer and Hesiod sung—the time when Hellas, the garden of the young world, was trodden by gods, demi-gods, and heroes.

It seemed that I beheld the golden age of Greece. On these purple hills the Latmian shepherd might have roved—amidst these thick woods Oreads and Dryads might have made their happy bowers. The sea itself, azure-shining and crystal-clear, seemed to catch its brightness from myriads of Nereid-eyes below, and the breeze that went sighing by was less an earth-wind than the audible breath of Zephyrus over his goddess-love.

Now I discerned the beauty of those ancient myths—suited to the time when the world was in its childhood, and needed to be taught by childish parables—which spiritualized all nature in poetic symbols, and filled the whole earth with the dim presence of half-understood Divinity.

I, too, felt within myself the spirit of the golden age. I was a Greek. I bounded over the strand, my bosom swelling with immortal fire—such as the great and glorious Titan poured into the soul of man. Life, young life, leaped in my veins; not that dull current transfused through eighteen hundred years—but the rich flood, sensuous yet pure, which coursed through the grand frames of the ancient heroes. I walked, I leaped, I ran; feeling no longer the pain and weakness of the body I had once borne, but a strength and beauty akin to that of the conqueror Theseus, or the goddess-born of Peleus.

Up from the sea-shore, across a sloping hill—such an one as might have blossomed beneath the footsteps of Paris and his woodland bride, ere Enone's wail had made fair Ida itself a place of desolation—up, higher and higher, I climbed; until from the hill summit I looked down on the scene below.

It was a deep vale, amphitheatred by forest and mountain. There, as in a nest of peace, dwelt the beings who peopled this new world; I saw them already— not with narrow human vision, but with an eye that seemed at once to behold and to know. They were human in semblance—in beauty superhuman. Their speech was music; their smile was sunshine: their very presence was an atmosphere of joy. But it was a joy such as immortals feel—calm, deep, tranquil. They had the power, never known on earth, to look on the noon-day sun of happiness with undazzled and unblinded eyes.

I stood on the mountain-top, and stretched forth my arms with a gesture of glad and yearning desire. The rising sun cast my shadow, dark and grand in its giant outline, upon the Happy Vale. Then I heard arising a billowy sound of many voices, swelling into a hymn. It came pealing on in the majestic cadences of Homer's tongue, and its burthen evermore ran thus:—

"Rejoice, rejoice! Another mortal has reached the Happy Isles!"

Winding up from the valley, the graceful procession neared me. Old men advanced first, rich in the beauty of age—for age has beauty as well as youth. Wisdom, peace, and tranquil thought, dwelt on each grave brow; the light of their eyes, though dimmed, was not obscure. Life's evening descended upon them in gray-clouded peace, bringing no regret nor fear.

Next came women—aged matrons, with their children's children clinging to their robes; young mothers, to whom mother-love was unmingled with fear, for their offspring would go down to the grave—if graves were here—sinless as on the day of birth. Then advanced Manhood—strong, mighty in stature, the perfect type of physical beauty, ennobled by the indwelling beauty of the soul. After this full development of humanity came young men and maidens, meek, tender, modest, who carried in their bosoms the rose of love; but it was a thornless rose. Last of all were seen the children—infant buds, wherein lay folded the perfect man.

These all cried aloud, with one voice of jubilant song, "Welcome! welcome to the Happy Isles!"

In the midst of them I passed on to the centre of the vale—a palace of verdure, branch-roofed, and fretted overhead with azure and gold—the blue sky and the darting sunlight. There was seen no work of men's hands.

Neither was there a throne—the ruler stood among his people like a father among his children. His only show of sovereignty was that which nature stamped upon his mien and gesture. These tokens pointed silently, "Behold a king among men!"

He *was* a king! I felt it as I looked upon him. He stood among them, loftiest in stature, grandest in beauty. It was meet that he should be so, for in this perfect land the symbol and the reality were one; the outward manifestation was complete as the inward truth. Therefore this kingly soul shone forth through a kingly semblance.—The temple was worthy of the god.

I say *god*, because there was something god-like in him. Perhaps the best type by which I can embody him is the Phidian Jove—but it was Jove unthroned, uncrowned, save by the circumfluent presence of his own deity.

I bowed myself before him, even to the ground, and my soul within me bowed likewise. He raised me, repeating the words of the choral salutation, "Stranger, whomsoever thou art, welcome to the Happy Isles!"

I have often thought that if there be one physical manifestation in which the indwelling divinity of manhood most shows itself, it is the human voice. From the moment I heard his voice I could have worshipped at the feet of that king. In its majestic sweetness was a pensive under-tone; speaking of endurance, but endurance sublimated into peace—of wisdom, but wisdom made holy by meekness—of power, but power softened by love.

"O thou Greatest One," I cried, "tell me—who art thou?"

He smiled: his smile was like that of Jove, which makes earth to laugh in sunshine.

"Askest thou this? Then, thou art not yet equal with us; but I will make thee so."

He placed one hand on my brow, the other on my heart; and his eyes looked solemnly into mine. An influence seemed to pass into my soul, raising me to a higher state of being. Hitherto, my existence had been one of mere sensation, like Adam's with the tree of wisdom untasted. In the deepest and most delicious sense, I had learned *to feel*—I now learned *to know.*

I sank before him, crying out,—

"Thou art the greatest, the wisest, of ancient heroes, the bold adventurer into unknown seas. Hail Ulysses, King of Ithaca!"

The monarch lifted his head with a noble pride.

"I *was* King of Ithaca; I *am* Ulysses. That name, which the Divine Spirit caused to be much honoured on earth, follows me here. My petty kingdom is forgotten; but Ulysses, the true Ulysses, reigns in the Happy Isles. And thou, O man! tell us,—for our knowledge extends not beyond these lands,—whence comest thou?"

I strove to answer the question; but a thick oblivion seemed to have gathered over my past life: only, as I gazed listlessly on the crowd that watched me with curious eyes, I saw two young lovers stand, leaning in each other's arms. The sight brought a passing gleam of remembrance, and then a sharp pang of regret.

"O King! all is dim with me; but it seems that I have been happy—have known love. I cannot rest, even here. Let me go back to earth once more."

"Is it even so?" And he cast on me a look of sublime compassion. "Drink peace and oblivion with the dews of the Happy Isles!"

He drew me beneath the spreading branches, and shook from them a shower of pearly drops, which fell, sweet as honey, on my lips and brow. As they touched me, I ceased to suffer and regret, and became altogether blessed.

I sat at the feet of the wisest of the Greeks while he judged his people. Little need of judgment was there, when there was no crime, and only enough of cloudy sorrow to show more clearly the eternal sunshine of happiness around them. They gathered round their king, drinking wisdom from his lips, and learning the few arts and sciences that their rich world needed. He blessed the young, he counselled those of maturer years, he spoke peace to the aged. As they departed each their several ways, I inwardly marvelled at many things concerning them, which even now seemed a mystery.

"Ulysses," I cried; "I, too, would fain learn of thee!"

The king bent his head in acquiescence.

"Tell me, then, of these thy people—did they journey with thee to the sunset? And if so, how is it that some are young, some aged? Is there birth and death here?"

He led me to a little distance, where stood a magnificent tree. Its branches bore at once foliage, flowers, and fruit. Of its leaves, some wore the tender green of spring, some the gold or ruddy hue of autumn; and as they fell—for they did fall—each, touching the earth, became a seedling plant, and so recommenced a new and different existence.

"Here," said the sage, "as the life of a tree, is the life of men: peacefully flow their fourscore years and ten; then they bid adieu to those they love, fall calmly asleep, and in that slumber the soul passes from the worn-out body into that of a new-born babe. Thus it is with the native dwellers in this land."

"But with those thou leddest from Greece, and with thyself?" I asked, gazing on the majestic form of perfect manhood, on which no added year might have passed since Calypso's immortal eyes, tear-dimmed, watched it disappear along the island-shore.

The Ithacan answered,—

"Men's souls differ from one another in greatness. I and my followers, though mortal, bore within us the germ of immortality, which gave us will to seek, and strength to find, the Happy Isles. Therefore, it needed not for us to pass through a succession of lives in order to attain perfection. We are already perfect."

"Then to thee and thine comes no change; but the body, now made the complete manifestation of the soul, is immortal as itself?"

"Even so. Now, come hither and behold!"

Still following him, I entered a pleasant glade, thick sown with amaranth and asphodel. Through it ran murmuring a little stream, in whose mirror looked the pale flower that wastes for love of its own image.

There was neither sun nor moon; but the whole atmosphere was pervaded with a serene twilight, like that of the dawn of day. It showed the quiet vale, and the countenances of those who dwelt therein. They were men of various mien; but over all was spread the same air of purity, happiness, and rest. The stalwart soldier leaned on his useless weapons; the poet, sitting on the flower-enamelled grass, sang his innocent songs, happy as a little child; the sage, lying calmly beneath the tree-shadows, found his deepest wisdom in the enjoyment of perfect peace.

It was a picture of the world's sinless infancy, when it lay, as a babe does, soul and body alike wrapped in slumbrous stillness. Would an awakening come? Or was this the culmination of existence?

As the idea crossed my spirit, I looked upon my guide. His face, too, wore the same expression—that of a soul which, desiring nought, or else having nought to desire, finds its struggles and sufferings merged into entire contentment.

In this Elysium, there seemed to be no future;—but was there a past? I turned unto the king, and said,—

"Tell me, Ulysses, have these all drunk of the Lethe dew, and lost the memory of their former life?"

"No!" he answered; "but they see it pictured dimly and painlessly like a remembered dream."

"And thou?"

His countenance shone with sublime triumph.

"To me the past is sweet as the remembrance of toil in rest: I look on it calmly, rejoicingly, as the victor of the goal looks back on the ended race."

So saying, the Ithacan turned from the entrance of the vale, and went on, I following his footsteps, to the margin of the sea.

Chapter V

On the verge of the strand Ulysses stood, and looked towards the vast ocean which had served as a pathway to his hero-feet. It kissed them now in tiny wavelets, obediently acknowledging his sovereignty. The moist touch seemed laden with some passing memories of earth; for the king stretched forth his arms and cried—

"Oh, life long past! oh, toils long conquered! oh, land long forsaken! must I then remember ye once more?"

He leaned against an overhanging rock: I crouching on the silver sands at his feet, looked up with wonder and reverence to the face of the son of Laertes.

"Wisest of the Greeks——" I began.

"Thou sayest right," interrupted he. "I *was* the wisest of the Greeks. The great gods poured wisdom into my soul when I yet hung upon the bosom of Anticlea. As a child, I yearned for the might and energy of youth; as a youth, I desired to attain the full knowledge of man. But when manhood came, the sceptre of Laertes only cumbered my hands; and the petty realm of Ithaca confined my soul.

"The wise men said to me, 'Son of Laertes, waste not thy strength in idle dreaming. Emulate Hercules and Theseus: take in thine hand arrow and spear, and rid the land of monsters.' And the young men whispered, 'Go forth with us, let us fight against men, and take captive fair women; this is glory.' But I knew that both voices were false: I felt within me something beyond the glory of the hunter or the warrior. So I stayed, vainly chafing at the limits of the narrow island.

"At last a vision came to me—'Go,' it said, 'wed the daughter of Jove—Helen—most beautiful of all the women of earth. Mingle thy mortal blood with that of divinity, and thou shalt become thyself divine.' I believed the deceitful dream, self-created out of the longings of unsatisfied youth; I went and stood with the princes of Greece at the court of Tyndarus."

Ulysses paused: and I, whose memory, while a blank as regarded my own past, went side by side with that of the mighty Ithacan—cried: "Tell me of that perfect type of woman—the ideal of beauty to the ancient world—tell me of Helen of Troy."

"Helen of *Lacedæmon* rises before me now," answered Ulysses. "She stands veiled at the foot of the throne. Around her are the young warriors, thirsting with ambition and eager love. Love! what was love to me? I sought not the fairest woman in Greece, but the being, Jove-born, whose embrace might impart unto my mortality the power and wisdom of the god.

"The veil was lifted: Helen stood revealed. The warriors knelt entranced before her. Fools! to mistake that incarnation of voluptuous human beauty for the divine Woman, the child of Jove! I turned away, half in sorrow, half in scorn, and wooed no more the daughter of Leda."

"But the son of Laertes returned not without a bride," I said, earnestly regarding the face of the king. Wisdom sat there—placid yet stern, unbending firmness, and indomitable will; but there was no sign of human tenderness. I saw that in the great Ithacan's soul an insatiable thirst for knowledge had filled the place of love.

He answered carelessly:—"My people said it was meet a woman should sit by the hearth of Ulysses, to tend the age of Anticlea, and bring up sons to mount Laertes' throne. So Penelope sailed with me in the black ships to Ithaca."

There was a silence—during which the little waves sang their under-melody, until it grew into the boom of the rising tide. The sea dashed and foamed against the rocks that confined it; and its loud roar sounded mournful even in the Happy Isles.

Ulysses beheld, and a new spirit dawned in his majestic eyes. "Child of the after world," he cried, turning suddenly round, "thou seest in that sea the image of my soul. It would not—could not stay murmuring among the golden sands: it must rise and rise, even though it dashed itself howling upon the bitter rocks. I sat, an enslaved king, upon my paltry throne, holding sway over the human beasts—for they were soulless as beasts—to whom the purple and the diadem made me appear divine; I ruled them, and then scorned myself for stooping to such a dominion. Why was I thus pent up within the limits of my narrow isle?—I for whose aspirings the world itself appeared too bounded and too small."

"Yet," I answered him, timorously and softly, "when the summons came, the monarch of Ithaca used his wisdom for a stratagem, rather than depart with those who warred for Helen, against Troy. Why did the kingly warrior pretend madness, and sow salt on the sea-shore?"

A look, as like human anger as that immortal face could assume, darkened the brow of the king. "Because the folly of mankind forced greatness itself to cunning. Was it meet that Ulysses, gifted in the wisdom of the gods, should go forth with a barbarian race to quarrel over an adulterous woman? But fate is stronger than human will: and so I, with my twelve ships, sailed for the Phrygian shore."

"And thou wert among the mightiest there?"

"I was *the* mightiest! Wisdom is greater than valour. It was I who ruled the wavering Agamemnon, and led the virgin-sacrifice to Aulis. I, by my counsels, caused the destruction of Troy."

As he spoke, there came before my mind's eye a vision of the pillaged city, the murdered Priam, the aged Hecuba grovelling in her children's gore. And I said, mournfully, "Alas, for Troy!"

The face of Ulysses expressed neither triumph nor compassion, as he answered. "Troy fell: it was destined that she should fall. The will of the Supreme must be accomplished. The world's tide must swell onward, whether men, cities, or kingdoms, lie engulfed in its course. Greece learned wisdom from that ten years' miserable war; and from the ravaged town may have arisen a new and a greater Ilion."

"It has—it has!" I answered, thinking of Eneas whose descendants builded Rome, and longing to impart the knowledge to which the wisest of the ancient world had not attained. But his impassive look asked it not. The perfection of his Elysium seemed to be, *never to desire*. Instead of speaking of a future which to him was indifferent, I pursued my questions concerning the past.

"Great Ulysses! to thy ten years before Troy succeeded another period of greater glory still—the glory of endurance. Let me bow, heart and soul, before the patient wanderer over many seas, the hero struggling with destiny, conquering alike the jaws of Scylla and the Sirens' song—enslaved neither by fear, ambition, nor love;" and here I paused, doubtful, remembering fair Circe's isle.

But the king answered unmoved. "If ever love subdued me, it was an immortal's love, which I thought might lift my being and endow it with something divine. But even Circe's charms were laid at my feet: I sought them not. And the winds that wafted our flying ship from the enchanted isle, testified that wisdom and virtue were dearer to Ulysses than the clasp of a goddess's imploring arms."

"Yet when the end was gained, the travail past, and the son of Laertes reached his native land, did that wisdom and virtue find their perfect fruition in happiness and peace? Else wherefore did thy bold feet quit for ever the Ithacan shore?"

Ulysses advanced a few paces, and lifted his hand in the attitude of speech. He stood as he might have stood before the throne of Agamemnon, his lips dropping words sweet as honey, but strong and all-subduing as the wine which Hebe poured out for Jove.

"I was a man before my age. I discerned faintly a higher life than that of brute warfare and sensual pleasure, and turned with loathing from my brethren.

I sought this diviner life everywhere—in the renown of battle, in the purer glory of travails conquered, in the delights of a goddess's love. But wisdom, which is alone happiness, ever flitted before me like a vain shadow: it was no nearer to me in Circe's or Calypso's island than in the gore-encrusted fields of Troy. So I turned my footsteps and sought it in my own home. I gave laws to my people; I taught them the lore of distant lands; I stooped my warrior's hand to guide the plough and melt the ore; I spoke of that wisdom which is better than physical prowess—of peace, which is more glorious than war."

"And they rewarded thee?"

"They muttered among themselves that fame had lied, and that the returned Ulysses was the same madman and coward whom their fathers had seen sowing the shore with salt. And throughout the isle men lived like brutes; each lifting his hand against his brother, as though Ulysses had never reigned in Ithaca."

"Alas!" I murmured. "Woe for him who is the herald of a coming age! But surely there was peace and content by the hearth of the returned spouse, the noble father, the duteous son? Surely there was rest for thee amidst thy kindred?"

He replied, calmly as ever; "A great man often finds no kindred but the gods. So it was with me and mine. I walked with them; I was not of them. Laertes looked on me and marvelled, as Typhon might have done at the monster offspring which called him sire. Anticlea 'was not.' Pale shade of mother-love, thou at least in thy solemn Hades hadst acknowledged thy Ulysses! Telemachus, dull follower of a past age's lore, with nought of fiery youth save its presumption, sought to guide into safe proprieties the errant sceptre held by his father's daring hand. Good he was—tender too; but the aged eagle despises the filial cares of the hooded crow. Ulysses was alone still."

"Yet Penelope?" I began inquiringly.

"Penelope sat by the hearth and span."

In that one sentence, where the only reproach was indifference, I read the sole atoning plea for the husband who once more quitted, and for ever, a wife faithful for twenty years. I saw before me the fair dull embodiment of virtuous inanities, fulfilling the lifeless round of conjugal and maternal duty, scared with horror at the bold soul that, over-leaping the world's boundary of assumed right and wrong, would fain dive for itself into the mysteries of the divine and the true. I knew how it was that not even the coldly-faithful Penelope could keep her lord within the bounds of Ithaca.

"But," I cried, "tell me how the end came; and how it was that thou and thy crew set sail for the Happy Isles?"

Ulysses paused, and a rapt expression, which might be either memory or prophecy, arose in his eyes, which were fixed on the distant cloud-hung main.

"I see my palace, as on that day of brutal feasting, when, moved to scorn and wrath, I stood in the midst, and called them beasts. They proved the justice of the name. They rose up against the hand that fed them: they would have torn asunder the only true man in Ithaca. Cowards! I hear their howling now. I see the white face of my son Telemachus, pleading caution, expediency, while on the other hand arise Penelope's weak railings against her rude, iron-hearted lord, whom she deemed the cause of all. But I stood up, among fools and beasts, A MAN—the man who had conquered gods and monsters, earth and hell—Ulysses."

"And Ulysses was victor once more," I cried eagerly.

"Go, ask the Ithacans, if Ithaca yet exist, concerning the aged monarch, whose age was more glorious than their puling youth. With me, to fight was to conquer. I crushed them like dust under my sceptre, and then I cast it among them—I would be no more their king."

"What followed?"

"I gathered from far and wide those tried companions of my ancient glory who yet breathed the upper air; neither them nor me did the dull world understand. Gladly they arose at their chieftain's summons—gladly they prepared to follow Ulysses to the West. Once more the old ship rocked in the bay, and on every aged cheek the sea-wind blew, alluring with delicious hope across the unknown wave. Thus Ulysses departed."

"But it was in peace?"

"Ay, in peace! From the tomb of Laertes to the strand did the crawling slaves track these footsteps, even with acclamations. The new-crowned head of Telemachus was bent for my blessing, and Penelope herself followed me to the shore. Her countenance expressed demure regret, but her eyes were bright, and not with tears. I saw that ere the prow had turned from the land, she likewise had turned away, hurrying joyfully to where the released people cried, 'Long live the King Telemachus!' He *was* a meet king for them."

"Even so, O great Ulysses! And thou—"

"I looked on Ithaca no more; but stretched my sail towards the boundless expanse of waters, where I might attain my full desire. So the shore faded from us for ever, and we sailed on and on, night and day, towards the sunset, until we reached the Happy Isles."

As Ulysses ceased, the sublime calm of his countenance deepened more and more. There was scarcely need for the question that burst from my lips—

"And they are, indeed, the *Happy Isles?* Thou art perfectly blessed?"

"Seest thou not I am," replied the king. "Here all desires are fulfilled—

we have wisdom, peace, virtue, glory, together with every delight of sense exalted into purity. We have no longings unattained—we live a life like that of childhood, one delicious present."

"But the future?" I said, as a doubt crossed my mind—a doubt that was not
reflected in the countenance of Ulysses.

"I understand not thy words," he said.

"Dost thou desire nought—expect nought? Is there not even here a something beyond—an Infinite, whereunto the soul may lift itself—a perpetual
Future?"

"What is the Future?" said the king's calm voice.

Then I knew that I was in an Elysium where there was no to-morrow. My
spirit, born in later time, possessed a power greater than that of the greatest in
the elder world—their heaven was sensuous delight and rest; mine—?

I knew not, as yet, what it was, or in what sphere of being. I only knew that
I was different from those among whom I moved. As Ulysses left me, passing with
slow, majestic footsteps across the shining sands, I felt that there was something
wanting even in this Paradise. The sea appeared no longer a loving guard, but a
crystal barrier, awful even in its beauty. And when the moon rose—looming out
of the waters like a thing of life, coming from—*whither?*—there rushed back upon
me the eternal secret, the thirst for the mysterious Beyond.

I lay beneath the shadow of the rock, immersed in thoughts too deep to
belong to the Happy Isles, but appertaining to another state of existence. Whether
that existence had been, or was to be, I knew not. The moon climbed higher in
the heavens, spanning the far sea with a glimmering bridge of light: it drew nearer
and nearer, until it reached my very feet—a silver pathway leading—was it to
Infinity or Nothingness?

Should I arise and follow? The impulse dawned, strengthened, grew into a
madness. The Island of the Blest, the peaceful vale—all faded from me. I yearned
for something to hope for—something yet to come. I looked at that unsubstan-
tial, dazzling line, and then at my own material frame, which, though spiritualized and made beautiful, bore yet a human likeness. Dare I walk the waves with
mortal feet?

I dare! for each earthly particle is interpenetrated with my immortal soul.
Faith, and Will, and Infinite Desire, can accomplish all things.

I turned one look on the beautiful land, sleeping beneath the curtain of
night—then I set my foot on the living line of radiance.

That immortal pathway sustained my immortal feet! On it I walked over
the fathomless abyss, on, on—whither?

Chapter VI

Out into the dim obscure, guided and sustained only by that slender moonlight line, I passed without fear. As I went, olden thoughts entered my mind; and this strange journey seemed a shadowing of something on earth—some wild ocean of fate, to be crossed by one pale ray.

Gradually the moon set, and the path was gone!

I felt it vanish from beneath my feet—with the darkness came imminent death! I cried out aloud, and the cry brought to me the knowledge that I had passed into another sphere of being—for, lo! in my despair I called upon God—the Christian's God!

At once, in a moment, the abyss of darkness was ablaze with light, showing me that I had almost reached the land. Looking up, I saw on the near shore a palace whose splendour lightened the whole isle, and glimmered even on the waves. But amidst these waves I was struggling still. I saw afar off life, safety, bliss, and yet Death was ready to engulf me.

There rose to my lips words faintly remembered as being known of old, solemn and holy—

"*What shall I do to be saved!*"

But still around me the greedy waves hissed and roared. Then the cry at my heart changed to one humble, helpless, yet not hopeless—

"Lord, what wilt *Thou* do, that I may be saved?"

Instantly I saw a light boat crossing the seething waters. In it stood a youth, pale, beautiful; serene and holy of mien as he who abode at Patmos—the beloved apostle John. Again I cried, and the answer was—

"Brother, peace! Help is near."

Then, his blessed hands lifted me out of that yawning grave, and I sank before him—saved!

He made on my forehead the sign of the cross, saying—

"Welcome, brother! This is the island of Avillion, where dwell many good Christian knights, with those knights of Faërie who serve God, and believe in His word. I, too, abide among them, because my life on earth was spent in faith and purity, and in the quest of the Sangreal."

"Who then art thou, my preserver?"

The youth put aside his shining helmet, looking upward a holy yet humble joy.

"I am Galahad, the only one of King Arthur's knights to whom God gave strength and patience to find the holy Greal."

As he spoke, the boat touched the strand. He signed me with the cross once more, leaped on the shore, and disappeared.

"Oh, leave me not!" I cried. "Good knight and true, I need thy guidance even here! How shall I tread alone the unknown isle; how enter the shining palace?"

And I looked tremblingly at the castle where dwelt King Arthur and Morgue la Faye; I knew it was so; for now all my prescience came back upon me, even as in the Island of Ulysses. But while I gazed, not daring to approach the presence of so great a hero, that which I had deemed a king's palace became a temple of the King of Kings. From the cathedral windows gleamed the altar lights, which I knew were burning round the Sangreal; and through the wide-opened doors came the holy matin-hymn, lifted ere yet the sky was purple with dawn. "*Dilexi quoniam*" began the psalm; and as it proceeded, verse after verse pealed on my heart and memory.

"*The sorrows of death compassed me, the pains of hell gat hold upon me. . . . Then called I upon the name of the Lord. . . .*

"*Thou hast delivered my soul from death, mine eyes from tears, and my feet from falling.*

"*I will walk before the Lord in the light of the living.*"

I entered the open temple-gate, and paid my vows at the threshold of the King of Heaven.

From thence I passed amid the train of worshippers—men and women, Christian knights, and ladies pure and fair—to the presence of Arthur and Morgue la Faye. They sat together on a throne, alike, and yet unlike; for she was the most beauteous dame in the whole land of Faërie, while on the face of her mortal brother lingered still the traces of his long warfare on earth. Yet he was a noble king to behold; and as he sat leaning upon Excalibur, his fair hair falling on either side his broad forehead, and his limbs showing grand and giant-like through his garments' folds, I felt rising within me the same ardour which had impelled so many brave knights to fight, bleed, or die, for Arthur of Britain.

Around the presence-chamber were grouped the most noted of the dwellers in Avillion. I beheld and knew them all. Side by side stood the two bold adventurers from the land of the Cymri, who sailed westward in search of the *Gwerdonnan Lian*—the Green Isles of the Ocean—and returned no more; Prince Madoc, and Merlin, the mightiest sage of those early days. Afar from these, half hid in a delicious twilight shadow, Sir Launfal, the pure and faithful knight, lay resting at the feet of the beloved Tryamour. Near the throne leaned Ogier le

Danois, the valiant and pious, who at his birth was chosen by Morgue la Faye to be her *loyal amoureux*. He ever kept at her side, looking up into her calm, queen-like eyes, and ready to obey her lightest behest, as true knight should for the sake of his dear ladye. But apart from all, kneeling in a little oratory, I saw Sir Galahad. His face was turned eastward, and the early sunbeams fell around his head like a glory. It seemed like the smile of God's love resting first and nearest upon him who on earth had loved God only.

Concealed behind the massive pillars which sustained the hall, I beheld all these, and then felt, piercing even to my hiding-place, the eagle glance of Arthur the king.

"Come forth!" he said. "Whence art thou?"

I answered trembling; for his voice was loud and deep, as the noise of many waters; and yet it sounded familiar, for the accents, though stronger and more rugged, were those of my native speech. The long-forgotten world, with all its memories, all its ties, rushed back upon my thought.

"Great king, I come from thine own far-off island in the northern seas. There, Arthur of Britain is remembered still."

His countenance changed, and his mailed fingers tightened over Excalibur.

"Is it so? Bringest thou tidings from my kingdom? Do the men of Carlyon ask for Arthur to return once more?"

And his frame, hitherto calm as a giant image of a marble knight, was stirred with human emotion. This land, then, was not like that of Ulysses, an elysium of undesiring repose.

"I cannot answer thee, O King!" I cried, while a confused mass of earthly memories struggled dimly in my brain.

But Morgue la Faye arose, and struck her wand on the area below the throne. Immediately the grounds divided, and formed a deep crystal well.

"Look down, and tell what thou seest," said the sweet tones of the Queen of Faërie.

"I see a land where men run about like ants, each laden with a golden burthen, or struggling to gain the same; I see palaces built for and inhabited by fools, and squalid huts where great and wise men grovel in misery."

"Oh, my Britain! oh, my country!" groaned the king. "The time is not yet come; they look not for Arthur!"

But his immortal sister said tenderly,—

"Wait! The ages that pass by but nearer bring the joyful day, when Arthur shall come on earth again. Child of man, look into the spring once more!"

"Aye, look!" cried the king. "Tell me of my palace, the many-towered

Camelot; of Tintagel, fair home of my mother Igrayne; of the plain near the sea, where my brave army fought with Mordred; of the valley, where I lay wounded and tended by Sir Bedivere!"

"I see a castle on a cliff."

"Ah!" eagerly interposed the king of knights, "it is my ancient castle of Dovor, where Sir Gawaine's ashes lie. Do they still say the masses for his soul, and does the passing bell ring nightly over the desolate sea shore?"

"It is a shore, not desolate but thronged with human habitations. The sea is black with ships, the hum of commerce rises up to the castle-wall. Men and women, their souls and bodies alike enfeebled by luxury and thirst of gold, tread mincingly over the bones of the stalwart-limbed and noble-hearted knight."

"Alas! alas!" Arthur again began, but the Faërie lady's hand was on his lips.

My vision continued. "I behold a plain, intersected far and near with iron net-work; over it speed, thundering and howling, breathing smoke and flame, giant-steeds stranger than those which Merlin harnessed to his chariot. He chained demons within the centre of the earth; this generation has created subject-demons from the dull dead metals that lie enwombed there."

"And these mighty dwellers in Britain have forgotten their fathers. Of Arthur and his bold knights no trace or memory remains on earth," said the King, while a shadow gloomed on his brow, like a cloud sweeping over a gray mountain-top.

"Not so," I answered. "The world's truths of mystical allegory are enduring as itself. The Round Table has crumbled into dust, and the raven hoots where stood the towers of Tintagel; but still many an old romaunt, and many a new poet's songs, keep up the name and the glory of Arthur."

The king folded his hands upon Excalibur, and leaned his forehead against the hilt. "Then I have lived," he said, and peace again stole over his majestic countenance.

Turning from the scene around me, I again sought the depths of the magic well. My vision obeyed now, not the command of Arthur, but the impulse of my own being. I saw no land, but a black heaving sea, upon which rode a single ship. Within its darkest cabin I beheld a woman sitting alone. She rocked herself to and fro in her desolation; she lifted helplessly her pale, sorrowful face.

Then I leaped up with a great cry, and from my now conscious heart burst forth the name of *Lilias*.

But immediately Morgue la Faye bound round my temples a slender circlet of gold. As it touched my brow all memory vanished, and I fell down in a swoon.

Chapter VII

When I awoke, or seemed to awake, the presence-chamber, and all the beautiful and noble forms with which it was thronged, had disappeared. I lay in a dim cavern that was hollowed out of a basaltic rock. Huge pillars sustained the roof; glistening stalactites peopled the place with fantastic images of natural objects, animals and even the human form. These icy phantasms of life grinned from dim hiding-places, making the solitude horrible. It was as though a troop of spectres had suddenly been congealed into material form; each grotesque or ghastly shape still transparent as air, but fixed in an awful immobility.

As I beheld, it seemed that the most fearful vision that ever startled human eye, would be less terrible than these embodied phantoms. I strove to break the spell. I called aloud, but the echoes of my own voice rang through the cavern like the shrieks of innumerable spirits. Then I felt the thin golden thread on my brow, and remembered all that had chanced since I clung to the saving hand of Sir Galahad, within sight of the island-shore. And while I pondered, it seemed as though my nature had become like that of the other dwellers in Avillion, and I had entered on a new sphere of being. In this sphere, my memory, alive to the past of others, was utterly dead to my own. From the golden thread a balmy influence passed into my brain, stilling all those pangs which in the human world so often teach us that to suffer needs but *to remember*.

My life seemed only to have begun from the moment when my feet touched the shore of Avillion. But from that time it was a full, real life, acute to enjoy, and as acute to endure. Kneeling on the floor of the cavern, the terror that convulsed me plainly showed that I was human still. And like the cry which weak humanity sends up to heaven, was that which, bursting from my shrinking soul, became a prayer to God.

"O Thou, who tookest me out of the deep waters, save me from this hell!"

I lifted up mine eyes, and saw standing beside one of the gigantic pillars, a form of flesh and blood. I knew it well—the dark, sombre face, in whose upper lineaments was stamped the impress of intellect and beauty, equally divine, while the lower features denoted stormy human passions—ambition, sensuality, and obstinate will—a mixture of the angel and the beast. It was Merlin the demonborn.

Still, to behold living and breathing man was bliss unutterable in this horrible place. I leaped forward and clasped the knees of the enchanter. He looked down upon me with contemptuous triumph.

"Weak child of the after ages, how thou quailest with fear at these poor shadows! With all the boasted glories of thy modern time, the magician of the elder world is greater than thou."

At this scornful speech, I arose, trembling still, but striving to answer him boldly. "Merlin, why comest thou to mock me, after affrighting me with thy horrible phantasms? What sent thee thither?"

"The merciful tenderness of Morgue la Faye, and mine own will. I desired to see if one of the vaunted later world was bolder than the greatest magician of ancient time. I am content: now let there be peace between us." He reached his hand; but I paused, irresolute. "Thou fearest to clasp the hand of Merlin, the demon-born!"

He had spoken aloud the words in my heart. I dared not deny them.

"Fool! I *am* the son of a demon—of a spirit great, strong—and good, because he *was* strong. What is virtue, but that power which is the mightiest? Therefore my demon sire was as worthy of worship as any of your angels."

I shrank aghast, and instinctively made the sign which was used as a symbol in those olden times to whose simplicity I had apparently returned—the sign of the holy cross. The magician made it likewise.

"Fear not," he said: "I, too, worship God. I, with men and spirits, must needs revere the one Omnipotent Spirit, the origin of all."

As he spoke I regarded him with less of dread; for upon his dark face had dawned something which made it like unto an angel's. Such a light might have irradiated the brow of the great Hierarch of heaven, before he rebelled and fell.

"Merlin, I fear thee not, nor hate thee: God made us all—men, angels, and demons (or, as thou callest them, spirits). We are alike His children, or may become such, one day. Give me thy hand, and guide me from this dreary cave once more into the fair valley of Avillion, if indeed I am still near there."

"This is Avillion. Thou art in the island of the blest," said the magician.

I marvelled greatly. "How can it be so, when I suffer trial, and terror, and pain? Dost thou call this happiness?"

Then Merlin answered, taking up his parable, like the prophets of olden time:—

"Can the day exist without the night, or the sunshine without the shade? Does not good itself need the opposition of evil? Far higher than a dull life of perpetual selfish bliss, is that state of being which consists of temptation and triumph, struggle and victory, endurance and repose. Thus, in our life here, is intermixed just so much of evil and of suffering as will purify and lift us one stage nearer to divine perfection."

"Then all suffer, and are tempted, and must be?"

"Thou scarce knowest which thy words imply," replied Merlin; and now his speech was soft, almost heavenly, so that I loved to listen to him. "Here, as on earth, temptation comes from man, suffering from God. One is a torturing flame, the other a refining fire. In Avillion, some have to struggle against the evil within themselves: some are ordained to suffer for, with, or from their brethren."

"Which, Merlin, is thy destiny?"

"It comes upon me now!" cried the enchanter, while the heavenly influence passed from his face, and it kindled with lurid fire. He gnashed his teeth, and his glaring eyes were fixed upon a dim alcove, where stood among the stalactite images one that was likest to humanity.

Horror! while we beheld—for my gaze was rivetted too—there was a change in the icy phantom. The indistinct thing took form like a statue; the statue seemed transforming into flesh; roundness and colour came into the transparent limbs; the rigid hair stirred with life. Momently the icy shape was becoming a beautiful woman.

Merlin looked, and his face was like one struggling with the death-agony.

"Vivienne! for whom I burned in such mad passion, art thou following me still? Look!" and he clutched my hand. "Dost thou not see her, with her bare, white-gleaming limbs; her floating, perfumed tresses, in every golden thread of which she netted my soul? Dost thou not feel her young breath, that once came upon my already wrinkled brow like the breath of spring? Vivienne—my love, my beautiful: it is she—it is she!"

He drew a long gasping sigh, and stretched out his arms with a gesture of incontrollable passion. But still his feet were steadfast: he approached no nearer to the alluring phantasm, which appeared continually changing from crystal to flesh, and then back again into crystal. Merlin's gleaming eyes drank in athirst every varying line of the lovely form.

"See!" he cried, "her brow unbends, she will smile soon; she who was so harsh, so cold! Her ripe lips part sunnily; she leans forward, her lithe form drooping like an aspen. Vivienne—Vivienne, come!"

But that instant, the cry of delirious joy became a shriek of horror. He pressed his hands upon his eyes.

"Temptress! fiend! nay, I mingle all foul names in one, and call thee *woman*. Begone!"

He clung to the basalt pillar against which he had leaned. His face was hidden, but I saw that in the stalwart arm every muscle and nerve was quivering.

"Still there? Is not the struggle ended yet? Be thyself, Merlin! Remember the time on earth: thy mad passion that counted a life's wisdom as nothing to one heartless woman's love. Think of the long wanderings after her fair, cursed foot-steps—cheated, befooled, mocked—think of her treachery at last. Ah, Vivienne, smilest thou still? So didst thou, luring me to enter the magic cave—so rung thy light laugh: I heard it as the spell-closed rock shut down upon me, writhing in a darkness that might have been eternal. Murderess, I defy thee! Thy tortured slave is thy victor now!"

He sprang away, and disappeared in the gloom. Immediately the woman's form became congealed once more into its semi-transparent substance. There was a sound like the roar of many floods, and the whole scene melted away.

I found myself on the margin of a lake, surrounded with mountains. Silvery mists hung over the water, and trembled on the hill sides:—all things looked pale, shadowy, and pure. At first, I seemed to be in a deep solitude; but presently I became aware of a boat gliding over the lake. There, reclining on a golden bed, even as that wherein he traversed the sea to the city of Sarras, I saw the form of him who alone was pure enough to behold the Sangreal—the virgin-knight, Sir Galahad.

Chapter VIII

As Sir Galahad neared the shore I saluted him with a reverent and joyful heart. In him seemed perpetually to abide the spirit of holiness, and that love of God which is the fountain from whence diverge wide streams of universal love. He was at once Galahad the Christian champion, before whose righteous arm fell alike the world's temptations and its opposing powers—Galahad, the pious knight who saw appear the goblet which held the Holy Greal, in the mystic covering of white samite—Galahad the youth, at once loving and pure; devoted to heaven, yet not free from human ties—witness his friends, Sir Bors and Sir Percival, and the holy self-devoted maid, Sir Percival's sister—Galahad, the tender son, who dying "kissed Sir Bors and Sir Percival, saying, 'Salute my father, Sir Launcelot, and bid him remember this unstable world,'" and then was borne upward by angels.

All these things, as I had read of them in old romaunt and history, returned vividly to my memory. I said unto him—

"O Galahad, knight beloved of God and man, is this indeed the form whose breath parted while yet in prayer before the holy table, in the sacred city of Sarras? Did the angel-hands then bear thee, not at once to heaven, but to this happy Island of Avillion?"

He smiled serenely, and answered—

"Yea! It was God's will that I should still serve him in the flesh, and so I dwell in Avillion, among those who have journeyed thither, like Arthur, without seeing death."

"And is thine, like theirs, an existence whose bliss consists in trial conquered?" I asked, remembering Merlin and the horrible cave.

A faint shade of sadness overspread the beautiful face:—

"Not for myself I suffer, but for my brethren. I minister here as angels do on earth. They weep over human sin and sorrow; but their tears are holy, and soon dried— they know that the All-wise and All-merciful cannot but make all clear at last."

"But, save thee, the dwellers in Avillion have each this mournful doom of trial?"

"Call it not *doom*," he answered gently, "since it is God's will, and therefore must be good.—Now, of all whom thou hast seen here, whose inner struggle wouldst thou behold? Desire, and the desire will be fulfilled—it is ever so in the Happy Isle of Avillion."

"I would see Arthur," I said.

The young knight lifted me by the hands, and instantly, with the speed of a winged thought, we stood unseen by the couch of the son of Uther Pendragon.

The King seemed to strive with troubled dreams. His huge limbs tossed restlessly, and his sleeping fingers ever sought blindly the renowned Excalibur, which lay beside him—at once his sceptre and his sword. He called oftentimes upon his good knights of the Round Table—Tristram, and Launcelot; also, Gawaine, his near kinsman, so well beloved, and by Sir Launcelot's fatal hand slain. Then, suddenly awaking, he lifted up his voice and cried—

"O valiant companions of old! O dear land of Britain! when will Arthur revisit ye once more? Why must this yearning never be allayed?—even in the happy vale of Avillion it brings perpetual pangs!"

And he smote upon his manly breast, that was long since healed of the "grievous wound," but rent with an inward struggle, harder perhaps to bear.

Galahad came and stood beside him. I wist not whether Arthur beheld the vision; but his countenance softened into peace—even as that of a sleeper when an unseen angel passes by. He took Excalibur once more, but used it neither as a sceptre nor a sword. Lifting up the hilt, which was made in the form of a cross, he kissed it with devotion.

"O Thou, for whose blood in the Sangreal my good knights spent so many years in a patient quest, give me patience too, that I may wait until Arthur be worthy of his kingdom, and his kingdom of him! Quell this impure earthly ambition, both in memory and in desire—let me grow meek, and pray, until the time comes when the son of Uther shall reign again in Britain."

He kissed once more the battle-cross formed by the elfin sword, and then lay down and slept like a little child.

As Galahad passed out, the whole chamber was lightened by the holy gladness of his smile. Truly it might be seen that he had been among the angels; that in the eyes which had beheld the shining of the Sangreal dwelt the reflection of its brightness evermore.

I followed after, traversing with him the blessed isle. For it was blessed, even though it was not a region of unmixed joy, or perfect repose. Each human soul was pressing onward, and on each brow was the divine light of Hope. They drew strength even from the trials endured—as he who pushes forward in a race feels his cheek fanned by the fresh breeze into health and beauty, while the listless lingerer on perfumed banks droops wearily, howsoever the sun may shine.

"But," I said to Sir Galahad, "when the trial is over rest comes? I would fain see this rest."

He took me to a bower where reclined two lovers in the cool of day—

"Enter, brother!" said Galahad, "my ministry is needless here."

So I passed, alone and still invisible, to the presence of Sir Launfal and Tryamour.

As grief grows keener from the memory of joy, so happiness is deepened by the remembrance of vanished sorrow. I felt this when I beheld Launfal and his beloved. He talked with her of the troublous time on earth; but he spoke even of suffering with a smile.

"Dost remember, love, the Forest of Carlyon: how I lay in poverty, despondency, and pain—when the three Faërie maids came riding by, and brought me unto a region of peace and beauty, even to thee? O dear eyes, that looked upon me in my darkness and my misery, and loved me amidst all!"

And, as he lay at her feet, he drew down to his own the lovely head, and kissed the drooping eyes—radiant as those of a princess of Faërie; but tender as those of a loving woman.

Then again spoke Launfal:—

"How hard it was, after that season of bliss, to mix once more with the vileness of earth—how bitter, save for those hours when a wish brought me the dear presence of my Faërie love. Then, when for that pure smile I had to endure the false queen Guinever's—more cursed in her love than in her hate—"

"O my faithful one! yet thou didst remember me!" And as Tryamour bent over him, her long locks, dropping immortal balm, fell in golden waves on the bosom of her knight and love.

"I remembered thee? Could I forget my life, my other soul? Yet in the dungeon and at the stake did I endure, nor implored thee to come and save me: I never asked of thee aught—not even love—yet thou gavest me all!"

She smiled upon him with her heavenly eyes, and bade him remember earth's sorrows no more.

"Nay, it is sweet to remember," answered Launfal. "Here, in this dear bower, let me think of the lonely dungeon where I lay in perpetual darkness, knowing that the first entering gleam of daylight would be a signal to guide me unto death. Let me call back the moment when dazzled, blinded, I staggered forth at last. By degrees, all grew clear: I heard the leafy rustling of the great pile formed of yet green trees—ah! cruel lengthening of torture, planned by that revengeful woman-fiend! I saw her sitting on the polluted throne, beside her deluded spouse, my dear lord King Arthur! He loved me once—even now he blenched at the sight of me, and turned away his troubled face; perchance, he could not yet believe that I had so wronged his honour. Then came the chains, the lighted torch, the approaching flame—"

"Speak no more!" shuddering said the Faërie lady—with the woman's heart.

"Yet a little; but only of thee—of thee, Tryamour!—as the steps of thy fair palfrey sounded musically along the palace terrace, and thou stoodest forth with thy immortal beauty to proclaim the honour of thy true knight. Oh! the rapture, when I felt the cool breeze wrapping my freed limbs as with a garment, and the swift steed bore me on, ever following thee, past the gleam of the now harmless pyre, past the shoutings of the multitude, far, far over forest, mountain, and sea, into the happy vale of Avillion."

He looked up; first heavenwards, and then into that earthly heaven, the eyes of her he loved. As I beheld him, it seemed that his face, sublimed by past suffering, was more beautiful even than hers, which bore the cloudless aspect of perpetual bliss. I saw how it was that, in some things, *a man* is greater than an angel.

As these two sat together, leaning cheek to cheek in the silence of perfect love, the birds in the linden-trees over-head broke forth into singing; and lo! amidst the marvels of the Happy Isle, I distinguished one more—that their very song was speech. Thus it ran:—

"But for the rain, the green earth would wither; without the evening gloom, man could not behold the stars. So, storm bringeth freshness; night, dawn; trial, peace; and death, immortality!"

I fell on my face, praying—nay, almost weeping, as one sometimes does in a heart-poured prayer such as was mine. When it ended, I arose; but the marriage-bower, and those happy ones who abode therein, I saw no more

Chapter VIII [sic]

I stood once more beside the lake amidst the hills. It was still veiled in that perpetual mist; and the solitary marge was dimly illumined by a light like that of a gray June midnight, when the pale half-moon has just set. There was no sound, not even of a stirring leaf; for the hills sloped down to the water-side, bare and treeless; lake, mountain, and sky—sky, lake, and mountain—reflected each other in ghost-like silence and repose.

At length, through the mist, I heard a sound of many footsteps. They came nearer; and I distinguished the form of Merlin, leading a mounted band of the dwellers in Avillion. Suddenly he paused, and the loud trumpet-tone of his voice rang over the still shore:—

"Who will go with me across the Lake of Shadows?"

There stepped forward the giant figure of King Arthur—Morgue la Faye following. Behind them Sir Galahad stood, meek, yet fearless; and these three alone answered Merlin's summons. But the King paused, and said,—

"How shall we cross the awful lake? Galahad, thou only among us who has known death, aid us now."

The young knight advanced to the margin, and stretched his arms out over the water that lay before him, solemn, soundless, unrippled by a single wave. Then I saw glide towards him the boat in which he had formerly reclined, with its purple sails shadowing the golden bed. It came on, impelled invisibly; for there was no man therein.

"Enter!" said Galahad, in his angel-voice; and immediately the vessel rocked beneath the great bulk of the two mightiest of Britain's ancient sons, Arthur and Merlin. "Enter thou, too, my brother," said they to me.

So I entered tremblingly, yet eagerly, after Morgue la Faye. Then Merlin uttered a spell, and the boat darted forward from the strand without either wind or tide.

Far out into the lake we sailed. The silvery vapours shut out from my vision alike shore and sky. I cast my eyes downwards; and lo! it seemed that, like a bird of the air sweeping over a city of earth, the boat glided over a new world lying beneath the waters. In its mysterious depths, I saw palaces, towers, tombs, outlined dimly through a gigantic shroud of mist, like that which hung above the surface. At times, stirring amidst this shroud, I distinguished denser vapours, which scarce bore airy form, but resembled the *cirri* that float in a summer evening sky.

Merlin arose. As the masses of his black robe fell heavily around him, he might have been likened to a thunder-cloud lifting itself slowly from the horizon. He wore no magic symbols; he held no books of power. In the strength of his soul alone lay the necromancer's might.

"Ye who desired to visit the Lake of Shadows—say, who among you seeks to call up the ghastly inhabitants of the City of the Dead?"

King Arthur spoke first:—

"I yearn for tidings of my kingdom on the earth. Therefore I would fain summon those who lie buried in Britain, and whose spirits may still hover round the spot where their bones repose. Which among them, deemest thou, is most able to answer my summons?"

"Love only has power over death," replied the enchanter. "Call one of those who were dearest to thee on earth."

"They were few indeed!" And a grim, almost scornful smile swept over Arthur's face. "Ambition was all to me. I loved my royal kingdom more than any of its subject dwellers—save, perhaps, Guinever and Gawaine."

"Choose between them!" said Merlin's stern voice.

The monarch paused, irresolute.

"Gawaine, thou wert a valiant knight; indeed I loved thee, my sister's son! But Guinever sat with me on that dear-prized throne. I summon her, not as the wife of Arthur, but the Queen of Britain."

Morgue la Faye's hand dropped from her brother's, and Merlin's dark brow was knitted in wrath. Nevertheless he leaned over the vessel's side, dipped his fingers in the lake, and uttered the spell:—

"Soul of Guinever Queen of Britain, arise!"

Slowly lifting itself out of the deep appeared one of the cloud-like vapours. Gradually it became a human form, wearing a nun's garb. Then I remembered the story of the death of her whose spirit parted ere Sir Launcelot came to Almesbury, over whom "he wept not greatly, but sighed." Perchance that one long tearless sigh followed the frail Guinever's fleeting soul even to its resting-place; for in the wail that arose from the waters, I heard evermore the words—

"Launcelot! Launcelot!"

"Peace, complaining spirit! False queen, false wife, false woman, answer thy lord!" cried the enchanter.

Arthur spoke—stern, cold, passionless. He thought neither of pity, anger, nor revenge—only of his Britain. But to all his questions came from the suffering soul no word, save the cry of "Mercy, mercy! I repent! Let me rest!" And ever and anon, in mournful plainings, was repeated the wail, "Launcelot! Launcelot!"

The king sat down wrathful and silent; and the phantom faded into a wreath of mist that seemed continually to hover round the vessel.

Then Sir Galahad arose, and stood before Arthur and Merlin, meek reproach, mingled with sorrow, clouding his eyes.

"Oh, men!" he said: "sinful yourselves, yet so harsh to judge the sinning—is there no pity in God's dear heaven for such as these? The convent-cell at Almesbury yet bears record of the tears, the sackcloth, the bloody scourge—sad portion of her who was once a queen! The aisles of Glastonbury yet ring with those funeral orisons wrung from the penitent despair of the knighted monk!"

And turning from where Arthur and Merlin sat together—both shrinking into silence before his words—Galahad dipped his hands in the lake, writing in the stirless waters the sign of the holy cross.

"Oh, dear father, my lord Sir Launcelot, whose sins may God pardon! no voice but mine shall summon thee here. Let me look on thy face once more!"

There was a pause; and then rising from the misty depth, I saw the mailed image of a knight. It was Guinever's lover—faithful in sin, but yet most faithful—the bravest of the champions of the Round Table—Sir Launcelot du Lac. Beneath the shadowy helmet were the features—still, and ashen gray—as they might have appeared to his brother monks who gazed down weepingly into the deep grave at Joyous Garde.

He spoke not, and none spoke with him. Only his son Galahad, with clasped hands, knelt and prayed.

Even while the spirit lingered, there came and hovered over his helm a cloud-like shadow; and through the silence was heard that continual wail—"Launcelot, Launcelot!" But it won no answer, either in word or look, from the pale spectre of Guinever's knight.

The phantoms both grew dimmer; and then I was aware of another sight coming near the vessel. It seemed an open boat; and therein, resting on a bed, was a woman dressed in fair array; and "*she lay as though she had smiled.*" By this, and by the writing in her hand, I knew the vision was she who had died for love of Sir Launcelot—Elaine, the fair maid of Astolat. I looked on the beautiful dead image, and thought of the time when the waters of Thames had floated up to the feet of Sir Launcelot this poor broken lily, that asked no guerdon for love faithful even unto death, but burial from his hand. And when I remembered this, my heart melted with pity, and I wept.

"Dost thou weep for me?" said a voice, sweet in its sadness, like a vesper-bell heard over the sea at night. I felt it came from the pale lips that looked "*as if they smiled.*" "Weepest thou for me, because I died? Nay: for love's bliss was greater than death's pain."

"How so—when the love proved vain?" I asked.

She did not answer my words; but went on murmuring softly, as one does in musing aloud:—

"Dear my lord Sir Launcelot! was it sin or shame that I should love thee, who came and stood before me like an angel in a dream? I never thought tenderly of living man, save thee. Thou wert the sun that unfolded my life's flower: when the sun set, it faded, and I died."

The voice was thrilled with a meek sorrow that roused my pity into wrath.

"Surely it was evil in the sun to scorch the poor flower," I cried, remembering how the concealed knight took and wore in the fray the token of Elaine la Blanche; and how, when she swooned at his wound, he, saying no word of any former love, prayed her brother, Sir Lavaine, to bring her to him, and took her in his arms and kissed her. Then I thought of all the days of fondest tendance which to the knight brought renewed life, to the fair maid death. And lastly, of the cruel scorn which, knowing her pure love, instead of requital offered pitiful gold. And my swelling heart told me that Sir Launcelot had done a grievous wrong.

But again the voice seemed to answer my thoughts, though it spoke not to me, but dreamily and vague:—

"Was it, then, so sorrowful to die for thee, my Launcelot? or did my death lay aught to thy charge? Nay: it was no sin of thine. I worshipped thee, as one should only worship Heaven; Heaven punished me—then pityingly took me home: I am content!"

Again my tears fell to hear that low, tender voice; and I marvelled in my heart whether on earth it had been ever thus uncomplaining. The spirit answered once more:—

"What was I, that I should murmur against thee, O my lord Sir Launcelot? Only once—when I lay in my tears, and darkness, and despair—I heard the blithe sound of thy trumpets, and saw thee going forth again into the fair world; while I—forgotten, forsaken—was to thee less than the grass under thy footsteps. Oh, forgive me, my lord and love, for that one cry of reproach against thee! I would have been—aye, ten thousand times—that trodden grass, if for a moment it gave freshness to thy feet!"

I looked on the calm features, where no movement of the lips gave token of the voice which spake. But the deep peace of the smile that sat on the dead face was an echo of the words which the spirit uttered. And when I thought of the pure soul which had departed in the tower of Astolat—praying and confessing meekly unto God, and remembering with tender and forgiving love Sir Launcelot—I said in my heart that unto such, against whom earth's hopes are closed, does the kingdom of heaven open.

While I watched this vision, Arthur, Merlin, and Sir Galahad sat at the vessel's prow, each absorbed in thought; little to them was maiden's love or maiden's woe. But Morgue la Faye came near with her woman's soul shining tearfully in her majestic eyes, and cried—

"Tell me—thou pure and meek spirit, whom I have summoned from thy rest—does the remembered love of earth wound thee even in Paradise?"

Elaine la Blanche answered:—

"I love still, but I suffer no more: God looked on me in mercy, and drew wholly unto Himself that love which in life was divided. I am happy—yet I forget thee not: I never could forget thee, my lord Sir Launcelot!"

While the voice yet spoke, there stood beside the bed another spirit—also in woman's form. Before its glory the mists dispersed, and light broke forth upon the waters. Soon another voice was heard, sweet as that which had murmured its patient sorrow; but clear and joyous as the angels' harping before the throne.

"Galahad, dear brother of my soul, say unto my brother in the flesh, Sir Percival—and to that true knight Sir Bors—that far exceeding the holy city of Sarras, to which we four journeyed together, is the Eternal city, New Jerusalem. Say, I rejoice that I died, a willing sacrifice, for the glory of God."

Galahad lifted his brow, radiant with exceeding joy.

"Maiden—through life pure and heaven-devoted, as was the virgin-mother of Nazareth—say, where does thy soul abide?"

"In Paradise; ministering there as many of God's servants do on earth, and as thou dost in Avillion. Therefore my spirit, inter-penetrated and made strong by its love of God—which in life was entire and undivided—is commanded to succour this soul, once tortured by earthly love. Sister, come!"

Over the bier she bent, lifting by the hand the pale form, even like Him who lifted the dead, and said, "Arise."

Elaine arose. To the opening eyes came a brightness, less of earth than heaven; to the lips came a voice—no mournful complainings, but melodious hallelujahs. And so, linked hand-in-hand, the sister-souls passed from sight, not sinking like the rest into the dim city of the dead, but soaring upwards unto the mount of God.

Chapter IX

As one who falls, flooded and dazzled by a sunshine cloud—or as Paul fell, blinded by the heavenly vision near Damascus—so sank I. Human eye and ear could not endure the glorious radiance, the angelic melody. Beneath them, my brain and sense seemed numbed—or rather exhaled into delicious death.

From this trance I awoke, feeling on my brow the light touch of a woman's hand. It brought strange, undefined remembrances. Wistfully I looked up.

I lay in the midst of the great hall, once filled with many knights and ladies. It now held only the fair presence of Queen Morgue la Faye. But she stood beside me less as a queen than a woman. Her gorgeous robes were thrown aside, and in her white garments she seemed a simple earthly maid, even resembling—I strove to remember what or who she resembled; but my thoughts fled away, like winged birds, ever fluttering on before, yet impossible to seize. Amidst them I heard continually the murmuring of the little fount which had sprung up at Morgue la Faye's bidding from the cloven marble floor. It seemed singing to me an olden song of some long-past existence; and yet, when I drew nearer, its waters were as smooth and as opaque as the marble which encircled them. But still, rising from their depths, came that mystic murmur, as it were a voice from the inner earth.

I leaned eagerly over the well, and my greedy ear drank in its musical whispers. Morgue la Faye said to me—

"Child of man, what dost thou hear?"

"I hear a sound, like the evening wind in the full-leafed linden-trees that grew—where was it they grew? Or like that Eolian harp we put between the ivied window, and listened—*who* listened, and *when?* Alas! alas! the thoughts slip from me; I cannot grasp them!"

"Bend down thy head again over the water."

"I feel—I feel a perfume; it comes from a violet-bank, the bank where—but no, all is gone. Again, it is like a rose-garden; I am walking there in sunshine and gladness; and now it changes to a sweet clematis-breath—wafted through that still autumn night, with the stars shining coldly overhead, and the waning crescent glimmering through the trees. Ah me! ah me! it is fled from me! No more! no more!" And uttering these mournful words, the perpetual dirge of life, I fell down weeping beside the mysterious spring.

Morgue la Faye stood on the other brink; for the well had grown wider and broader, and even now was swelling out into an infant stream. She stood, her falling hands meek-folded, her head half bent, watching me. A gleam of womanly pity softened the steel-like brightness of her eyes.

Perceiving it, I cried imploringly,—

"O Queen of Avillion, I am not of thy nature, but only mortal man! Why dost thou try me thus?"

"Because, as thou sayest, thou art not of our nature," she answered softly.

"Thou canst not stay in our happy isle; but I have no power, nor yet desire, to cast thee thence. Thou must depart of thine own will."

"Depart!" I echoed sorrowfully; for now that the spell had ceased, I felt no more the vague memories and wild longings which it had awakened. I thought with fear of quitting the beautiful island for some unknown region, perhaps of horror and woe.

"Poor mortal!" Morgue la Faye continued. "Art thou then so loath to depart? Do the sounds and sights of former times, which I have raised up before thee, fail to win thee back to earth?"

"I know not of what thou speakest," I answered, trembling. "True, I had a vision; but it is gone now. I would fain stay in Avillion."

"It cannot be," said the firm but still gentle voice of King Arthur's sister, as she crossed the spring, its waters sinking not beneath her airy footsteps. Then she bade me kneel, and took from my head the slender thread of gold which continually encircled it.

Instantly my brain reeled beneath the thronging memories with which it teemed. All came back to me—my land, my home, my Lilias—each thought piercing my soul like arrows tipped with that bitterest poison, the remembrance of eternally-lost joy.

I dashed myself on the ground at the feet of Morgue la Faye:—

"Cruel queen, why didst thou take from me that blessed spell of Oblivion? Why torture me with these memories of earth? O Lilias my wife! my love! my beautiful! would to Heaven that I might see thy face once more!"

Morgue la Faye lifted me from the earth, where I grovelled in mad despair, and led me to the brink of the magic well.

"Now, poor child of mortality, cast thine eyes down once more."

I did so. Oh marvel! As the clouds of oblivion had passed from my soul, so passed the dusky shadow from beneath the water, which became crystal clear. While I gazed, there grew defined from out its depths the image of a scene—an earth-landscape—one that I knew—oh how well! Blue and dim rose the mountains—those giant spectres of my childhood, which, night after night, enclosed the descending sun in their craggy, ghostly arms; beneath them lay the valley, and the broad river, and the woody slope, where stood— a Home.

We had chosen it as our home, our wedded home, when—the melancholy voyage ended—Lilias and I should return to our own land and our own people. There it stood, near the spot where we had both dwelt from childhood—a house reverend and beautiful with years. Over its brown walls climbed the ivy, min-

gling with the dear clematis, cherished of old; its painted gothic windows trans-
mitted every sunbeam in rainbow-tinted glory; and from its protecting eaves the
brooding swallows merrily flew—their cheerful homes without being meet em-
blems of that most blessed one within.

A moment, and the scene changed to the interior. I saw the quaint labyrin-
thine chambers, whose gloom was made beautiful by the presence of youth and
happiness. Pictures shone from the dark-panelled walls; in a recess, the ivory-keyed
instrument smiled over the soul of music shut up within it; above the green,
branch-adorned hearth, fresh-gathered flowers bent to their own fair images in
the mirror.

And near them, pure and lovely as they, was my own life's flower, whom I
had chosen to adorn and bless my home—my wife Lilias!

She sat droopingly, her cheek resting against the crimson chair—the
same where mine had rested in many an hour of mental and bodily suffering.
The remembrance seemed to strike her then; for suddenly she lifted her face,
wherein was love so intense that it almost became agony, and cried—aye, *I
heard the very tone*—

"Wilfred, beloved, come!"

I would have plunged into hell itself to answer that call! Hearing it, I sprang
madly into the waters, there to seek the vision and the voice.

In a moment, Avillion and its dwellers had vanished from me for ever.

Chapter X

Awaking, I found myself, not in the happy home—not in the dear arms of my
Lilias—but lying in the depth of a thick wood, which, though in all things resembling earth, was yet unknown to me.

I had gained a strange new land—but different from both those I had mysteriously traversed; it was neither Elysium nor Avillion. It was a human world. I
trod it with the body of a living man—a man of modern time. I repeated to myself the name I bore in my father's house, Wilfred Mayer. Another name, not less
familiar, I murmured, mingled with many tears; the name of my long-parted
wife—my dear Lilias. Every home-recollection came back to me, as to one who
after a season of madness is restored to health and reason. The intervening time
was dim; I could scarce tell whether it were vision or reality. But all seemed ended
now. I felt a real man, dwelling on a real earth.

I touched the moss whereon I lay—the same green carpet of which Lilias
and I had often heaped fairy-cushions in her childish days; when I, a sickly youth,

was glad to make myself a child for and with her. Thinking of this, I laid my cheek on the soft moss, kissed it, and wept.

Suddenly I heard a footstep passing by. It was a stranger—human like myself. The face was such a one as in this nineteenth century may be seen sometimes—nay, often—in street, or mart, or social dwelling; not radiant in superhuman beauty, nor yet devoid of an inward spiritual charm; the face neither of a god nor an angel, but of *a good man*. The moment I saw it, I acknowledged this; stretched out my hand to him, and called him "brother."

"You say right," he answered, smiling. "We are all brothers here, and though I cannot say I know your face, yet there is something in it which seems familiar to me. Therefore, welcome, brother!"

"Welcome to where? for indeed I know not."

"To a quiet spot on God's earth, which its inhabitants try to make as near as they can to Paradise. We call it Eden-land, or the Happy Isle."

"Another Happy Isle!" I cried, and again became bewildered. "Oh, friend! I have dreamed such wild dreams, if indeed they be dreams. Help me to clear my poor wandering brain. I desire nought but quiet, and home, and Lilias."

"Lilias? I knew the name once; it was a sorrowful name to me, but its memory is softened here. Come, stranger and brother, you shall speak no more, think no more, until you have rested and grown calm. Follow me to my home."

He took my hand and guided me through the wood. I noticed more closely his face, his bearing, even his garments. The latter were simple and manly; such as one in our century and our English clime might wear, consulting ease and grace rather than fantastic fashion. We entered his dwelling, which was characteristic as his dress—entered by an unlatched door. Then he began to fulfil the gentle precept which I saw written over his hearth. *"Feed the hungry, and clothe the naked."*

In a brief time I stood beside him, already feeling like a denizen of this new home and new world. Then we sat down together by that hospitable hearth, and he said to me—

"My brother—or rather my son, for you are a youth compared with these white hairs—will you now tell me by what name I shall call you?"

"Its sound will bring back mournful remembrances," said I. "It is mine, and my father's also,—Wilfred Mayer."

The stranger clasped my two hands in his, and then looked at me eagerly, fondly, parting back my hair as though I had been a little child. "I could weep now," he said, "save that in this happy place are no tears shed, not even for earth's memories. I rejoice, and thank Heaven, that I look in the face of my sister's son."

"You are then—"

"Ay, say the name, since it is not forgotten on earth," and he smiled with a calm pleasure; "the name I bore when we were all little children together—*Cyril*."

"I learned it when I was a child too," cried I, clasping his hand once more. "Well I remember how on many a stormy winter's night my mother would stand by my little bed, pale and grave, and teach me in my simple prayers to say, 'God preserve Uncle Cyril far over the seas.'"

"Did she so?—my dear Hester—my true sister!" murmured the old man with a tremulous lip. "Go on, tell me more."

"He was always a mystery to me, this Uncle Cyril, whom I had never seen, and of whom no one spoke without looking sorrowful. Once, too, when there came to us, with her babe in her arms, the mother of Lilias—"

"You mistake," cried Cyril. "The mother of Lilias died at birth. Nay, but I forget time's passing. Perhaps there was a second Lilias? Go on, Wilfred."

"I remember that day well: how I, a blithe schoolboy, was touched by her sweet, quiet face, and hearing she had come from abroad, asked her, as I did all strangers, if she brought news of Uncle Cyril; how she looked very mournful, and my mother took me away, telling me not to speak to her of Uncle Cyril more."

Cyril drooped his head lower on his hands, only saying softly, "Go on, my sister's child, go on."

"I remember also, though faintly, for I was still very young, how there used to come letters from abroad, over which my mother looked grave, nay, wept sometimes, and I knew they were from Uncle Cyril. Over the last she did not weep but smiled, took me on her knee, and told me that Uncle Cyril was coming home. Week after week passed, but he came not. My father sometimes hinted of ships that set sail for home, and vanished strangely on the wide deep, never reaching land. And day by day my mother's face grew sadder, and she started at every sound. When I asked her what had become of Uncle Cyril's ship, she would shudder and say that God alone knew—no living man could tell."

I paused, but he motioned me to continue.

"Month after month went by, and a strange awe came over me. All day I pondered about the missing vessel, whose fate no man knew. Sometimes at night I dreamed about it; I saw it on fire,—or becalmed until all the crew perished by slow famine or maddening thirst,—or striking on a rock, and sinking in a moment, as though some great demon from the world below had sucked it in with all its living freight. Every wild sea-tale that I had read—every wilder fancy that boyhood's dreamy brain could conceive—were gathered up to give form and shape to the story. Yet still it was there—a nameless horror—a mystery sealed, until the great day when the sea should give up her dead."

"Amen!" said my companion, solemnly. "But tell me still of that dear home."

"There, week by week, hope grew fainter—faded—died. At last my mother told me, sadly, but without weeping, to leave out one name in my childish prayers—for that Uncle Cyril was with God, and needed them no more. But the awe and expectation would not pass away; and many a night I started up in my little bed, dreaming that he was come."

I ceased, and a deep silence fell upon us both, as we sat by the red embers of the sinking fire—for the climate had changed in this new world, and I felt no longer the glow of perpetual summer, but the pleasant chill of autumn. I thought of the region, and of my companion, with a curiosity born scarce of fear but wonder. Had Cyril indeed passed through the awful gate, and did I stand in the Land of the Dead, with one of its unearthly inhabitants? He might have read my thoughts; for my hand was caressed once more by his hand of flesh and blood, as he said—

"My kinsman, Wilfred Mayer,—know that God's power and mysteries, even on earth, are greater than men dream of. Listen to the tale of one who, though he has seen strange things, and been led through strange paths, yet looks, like thee, to the same ending of the journey—death's calm sleep, and the waking unto an eternal morrow."

He lifted his eyes to heaven: I drew near and listened to his words.

"There was a boy once, born with every passion in his nature so vehement, that a feather's touch might turn him either to good or evil. It is so sometimes: Gabriel and Lucifer were both archangels, and the boldest of all the apostles was he who stood consenting unto the death of Stephen. We cannot fathom these mysteries.

"Well! the boy of whom I speak had two good angels ever at his side—his twin sister Hester, and one who was of distant kindred, though she had grown up with them, eating the same bread, and drinking of the same cup. Of these two the youth loved one dearly, as a brother should; the other—God alone knoweth how he loved *her!* In this love were mingled esteem, reverence, tenderness, passion. Every one of his heart's fibres clung around her, day by day. And because they had so twined—slowly, imperceptibly, like household links—she never felt or saw them; but when dearer bonds came, she untwined these, smilingly, unconsciously—slipped from them; they fell—and the boy's heart broke!

"I speak wildly: it did not break; but its softness became iron—its full, rich tide was turned to gall. She lived to weep a sister's tears—mark you, *only a sister's!*— over an outcast and a prodigal. She never knew the truth; if she had—why even then it would have been the same. She had done no wrong—she never loved him.

"He became a wanderer over the wide world. The face of God, which he had mocked in the glare of cities, he learned to see revealed in the terrible lone-liness of the desert—in the wonders of the mighty deep. Still he wandered on—God's mercy following him. Who could hide from the presence of the Eternal? In the grand mountain solitudes It came, bringing awful peace—It soothed him in the deep river-flow—It smiled upon him in the green, sunny savannah. So, through the wide arms of Nature—the Nature which He had made—God drew unto himself this erring soul; and it grew pure and calm.

"After many years, the man yearned to see the home whence the boy had fled with curses. He embarked for England—his heart's desire flying swifter than the vessel; but an unseen hand prevented both. Nor ship nor crew were ever heard of more."

"Tell me, O strange relater of this marvellous tale, whither sped the fated ship—or how?"

His voice changed, and his countenance likewise. He spoke now like one, who forgetting himself, had become a teacher among his brethren.

"I said before, in this world, concerning which proud man thinks he knows all, there are many mysteries of which he knows nothing. Who has ever found a path through the region of eternal ice? Whose daring bark has sailed over the mighty Antarctic Sea?"

"It is true! It is true! But my sense is bewildered; explain the mystery further."

He went on:—

"Men traverse the seas, year after year, safely; but then comes a tale of some ship which has vanished mysteriously from the face of the deep—how, or by what means, none can ever tell. In the thronged ocean-pathway no floating wreck, no glimpse of a flaming vessel, gives token how she perished: men shudder, marvel,—and forget, until they hear a like tale."

"It is even so!" I sighed.

"Now, listen! *The vessels perish not*: He to whom belong land and sea, hides them in the hollow of His hand, and brings them safe to a haven in the midst of the deep—an island-garden—the Eden whence Adam was driven. It is here!"

I started in trembling wonder:—

"This, then, is Paradise?"

"Not Paradise, such as when man needed continually the visible presence of angels; but an Eden suited for earth's late-born children—a land where men of this modern time may live in peace, and worship God."

He rose up, for while we talked night had fallen:—

"Now, my son—are you not even as my son?—go! Rest and sleep. To-morrow I will show the wonders of this land."

Chapter XI

I laid me down, and slept the deep sleep of healthful weariness. At dawn I awoke;—there was, then, night and day, sunrise and sunset, in this Eden-land? The golden darts fell on my eyelids, and slumber passed away. My mind was clear; I remembered all the past, even its sufferings; but suffering itself was calm. I waited meekly for the strange mysteries of my fate to work themselves out: they were a mingled and knotted web; but the beam was held by a Hand Divine.

I lay on my bed, my once-tortured heart beating peacefully beneath my folded hands. Ere the dawn-streaks had faded from the sky, Cyril stood beside me.

"My son, arise! He who loves not the early morning loves not the memory of his youth."

I arose, and clad myself in the simple garments of this land. As I felt my limbs free to bound, and the sweet morning air played round my bare throat, and tossed my long wavy hair, it seemed to me that even these little things influence man's character, and that he in whose soul dwells the love of the beautiful, will ever follow nature's most perfect Art, in order that in himself he may show, as far as he can, the image of that grace which he delights to behold in others.

We quitted Cyril's dwelling, and went out towards the forest.

"Whither do you lead me, my kind guide?" I said.

He answered, "To worship, with morning freshness, the God of the morning."

He walked along a little further, quite silent, and then stood still. We were in a narrow valley, lying east and west, enclosed on two sides by the gray mountains and purple woods, and between them, from out the sea which bounded the valley eastward, burst the sunrise. Oh! it was glorious!

"Beautiful! how beautiful is morning!" murmured Cyril. And turning round, he said, "It ever seems to me, dear kinsman, as though the earth at dawn recovers its Eden-freshness; or that when night, the shadow of God's protecting hand laid over it, is withdrawn, there comes a passing vision of the glory departing."

"It is so," I answered. "Nay, it seems as though He who called Himself the 'bright and morning star,' and 'the Sun of Righteousness arising,' had especially hallowed the dawn of day."

"And meant that man should hallow it too. Therefore, come and see how we hail the morning."

I followed him far in the forest to a great temple. Its strong tree-pillars had never been reared; they had risen of themselves through the mystic inward principle of life, which no human power can give to the meanest blade of grass. Its walls were formed of interlacing verdure, its pavement tessellated with flowers. Through its leafy arches rang the voices of innumerable choristers, invisible cherubs of the air, hymning continually. And its roof was the blue infinite ether, through which the moon climbed, and the stars wandered in their courses. Upwards rose the prayers and praises of the worshippers; there was not one human veil between them and heaven.

I heard from afar the loud song; I saw the multitude like that "which no man can number;" every age, sex, and rank, uniting the same solemn strain. There, for the first time *and the last*, I beheld a church on earth praising God with one voice.

"Is it the Sabbath?" I whispered.

"Every day is a Sabbath here."

"And the priest? I see none."

"Every man is a priest—a priest in his own household. Yet there are degrees of honour, men called on to be teachers among the flock; but none says to his brother, 'Stand aside, I am holier than thou;' none cries arrogantly, '*My* truth is the only truth, and thine a lie.' For we know that each flower may drink in the same sun, yet assume a different hue, and give forth a different perfume, according to its nature and clime. Forms are nothing: it is the spirit within which is the life."

"Still," I said, "there can be but one sun and one dew to give that life."

"Yes," he answered, "and if the flower grow strong and shed its odours, no matter what flower it be, doubt not but the true life is there. How else could the fruits exist? Yet these are mysteries amidst which the wisest among us can but grope blindly; only we know that one day all will be made plain."

"Amen!" said I, as the multitude arose from their knees, and their morning worship done, went about that which is also a kind of worship—daily toil for themselves and their dear households.

"But," said I unto Cyril, "I see here labour and endurance; Eden-land is then no place of continual rest."

"Rest!" cried Cyril, while his brow shone with a prophet-like radiance. "Does the Omnipotent rest, when He sends through the wide universe His love, which is Himself? Do the angels rest when they traverse infinite space to do his bidding? And think you that we shall rest when we become, like them, ministering spirits? No; in earth or heaven there is not, there ought not to be, any perpetual rest."

As he ceased, we came to a little hill which overlooked a wide champaign. There I saw the tokens of all necessary toil: the labourer delved the field, the woodman cleared the forest, the manufacturer and mechanic plied their handi-work, for ornament as well as use. I pondered awhile, and then said to my guide—

"Another mystery comes to me. In this land there are both rich and poor?"

"There are, because Eden-land is a reflex of the world—our modern world. Therein, while earth lasts, rich and poor *must* 'meet together.' Equality is but a fantastic dream. Until men's natures are made all similar, their outward lives and circumstances will vary. The oak and the bramble may spring from the same soil, but one crawls on the earth while the other tops the forest. Yet the same life-prin-ciple germinates in both."

We stood where we could see at once town and hamlet, cottage and lordly dwelling, the blue sky bending over all. And I began to moralize and think how Heaven had made every created thing for good. I wondered if the world of hu-man hearts were pure and peaceful as the outer world which I beheld. So, as we sat by the way-side, I spoke my thoughts to Cyril.

He smiled, and said my desire should be presently fulfilled. We reclined under a woodbine-hedge; I lay pulling garlands of white convolvulus, and think-ing how strange it was to see again all the flowers I loved—the flowers of earth, but far more beautiful. There came, rising and falling, the song of the reapers in the field, and against the horizon twined and curled in fairy wreaths, the smoke from the distant furnace where the metal-workers plied their trade. There was poetry and happiness even in labour and poverty.

As I mused there came past one of the gleaners; a girl—a very Ruth—laden with golden-eared wheat. She went along singing, tossing the wavy sheaf over her shoulder, and leading by the other hand an old man who crept feebly along.

While he tottered on, the echoes of his cumbrous staff kept time to the girl's light-hearted warble; and as they passed us by and wound down the hilly road, it seemed to me like the seraphs, Hope and Cheerfulness, making music to the sound of Poverty's heavy tread. And like a sweet poem accompanying the strain came Cyril's half-musing speech:—

"I do not believe that the All-merciful and Almighty ever created or per-mitted evil. That which we call so, can be only a mysteriously-disguised form of good. If want and sorrow were not, where then would be charity? If none suf-fered, who could show love, pity, and sympathy? If help were never needed, who could know the joy of gratitude? O man, canting of a sinful and miserable world! how darest thou to speak thus of that earth on which its Maker looked, 'and be-hold it was very good'?"

He sat, forgetting me and all else, in a reverie deep and calm. I looked on the face, where every mark of earthly pain was obliterated, and I could have knelt before him.

From our wayside-nook I marked many a passer-by. The poor man carolled gaily on foot, the rich man rolled in his gay equipage, serene yet thoughtful; for riches have many cares, and the great are Heaven's stewards upon earth. Then came a various multitude, their faces not disguised with false smiles; but each brow was clear as the day, each man's heart being written on his countenance. Here was the region where none dreaded Truth.

Yet there were as many varying shades of character as in the land from whence I had drawn my being. The wise man raised his thoughtful brow to heaven—that heaven which seemed nearer to him than earth. Yet he was not lifted up by pride, so as to scorn his brethren; but walked among them, humble as the most unlearned of them all. The unlettered man, without mocking or envying the gifts to which he could not aspire, moved on his lowly way, his diligence and benevolence strewing earth with flowers, though they could not make him wings to soar upward to the stars.

Women passed by, clad not in costly garments, but with that robe of meekness which is above all price. Wearing it, they appeared perpetually fair; for a beautiful soul makes a beautiful face, and she who is ever-loving, will surely be loved evermore. In Eden-land were no neglected daughters, estranged sisters, or forsaken wives; for each had learned that to love is to win love, and that while man's glory is in a wise and tender sway, woman's strength is often in her weakness; that from her cradle to her grave, no woman was ever truly happy, unless she could look up to man in some relation of life—either father, brother, husband, or friend, and say, humbly and lovingly, "I will obey thee, for thou art greater than I."

These scenes I beheld—these thoughts I pondered over; then I returned with Cyril to the little cottage in the forest, and the sun set upon my first day in Eden-land.

Chapter XII

It was again dawn in the forest-temple; the worshippers were departing, each his several way, to his home or to his merchandize. I noticed the various groups, and my mind was bewildered with many conjectures. Did there reign here, as in the olden world, the two mighty ones, Love and Death? How, then, could perfect happiness exist?

I uttered my thoughts aloud, but Cyril smiled serenely at my doubts. He answered them not, save by the meek and trusting speech—

"All that is, is good; we learn this lesson in Eden-land." And then he pointed to a train which had separated itself from the rest, and passed into a green alley of linden-trees.

"Let us follow them!"

We did so. There was in the midst an old man, gentle and saint-like in mien, to whom they all listened earnestly. He taught, not of religion, but of that which is next to it in holiness—Love. He spoke of all tender affection—of kindred, of friendship, and lastly of that mysterious bond between man and woman which heaven ordained to complete the being and fulfil the happiness of either—true and faithful wedded love.

Love, then, was known here. I marvelled, remembering all its miseries on earth: changed love—hopeless love—lost love. But as these doubts arose, they faded before the words of him who spake, answering as it were to my inward thought.

"Love that changes is not love—it is a dream, a delusion, an idol worshipped with the senses, not the heart. Pure love is rarely hopeless, save through wrong done each to the other, or evil coming from the world outside. And lost love— who shall call that *lost* which heaven takes? Therefore in this our happy dwelling, where there is no sin, there can be no sorrow; and love, given to be man's chief joy, and out of which his own erring will alone has created misery, is here no longer a curse but a blessing."

And as I looked around, on the faces of young and old there came a tender light, a blushing joy, which echoed his words in smiles. I thought of the world wherein I had once dwelt, and sighed to remember how man there made a hell of what should have been a heaven.

Again the pastor spoke of the sacredness of love; how that between two young hearts that leaned each to each like meeting flowers, no blast of human fate should be suffered to come. Then he spoke of two who loved one another— but worldly fortune stood between, and Poverty's iron arms tore them asunder.

"Shall this be, O my brothers?" he cried. "Come, ye childless ones! who have none to inherit your countless stores, give unto these, and babes' voices may yet rise up in prayer for you. Ye lonely ones—in whose heart love was a fresh fountain, until God sent the Angel of Death to seal the waters on earth, that they might spring forth purer and brighter in heaven—remember the time of youth, and make these blest with the blessedness to which ye yourselves once looked! All ye who know what love is, bid these love one another, and be happy!"

While he yet spake, many came and showered offerings at his feet: aged parents, whose children had gone away to be no longer supports on earth but watching angels in heaven, and who, clinging feebly to each other, went slowly following to their rest; women—to whom the name of wife was a long-vanished or never-fulfilled dream—who had learned to walk, meek and pale, over the grave of love, the treasures of their virgin hearts unknown, save to heaven and the unseen land of souls.

And then the whole multitude shouted and sang for joy, and went to seek the bridegroom and the bride.

It was a marriage—not like earthly marriages, celebrated in pomp and gay hypocrisy, but quiet, solemn—full of a happiness too deep for mirth. The young bride knelt, clothed in white, her head myrtle-garlanded. Few wedding guests were there, save those who loved them both: the mother who gave a daughter and received a son; and the sisters who took into their dear circle of affection one more, to whom "sister" had hitherto been an unuttered name. She murmured it now in a tone which foretold gentle yielding, and household peace between them all for evermore. Ruth-like, she had said in her heart, "Thy people shall be my people;" and in that spirit she came among them. Once she turned, and knelt with her bridegroom for the blessing of the mother whom she had made his mother also. Then she arose, left all, and followed him who was to her—

"Friend, father, brother, home, and universe!"

I stood with Cyril, and beheld this happy sight—this true *marriage*. In both our hearts was one thought; the same, and yet different; there came to our lips one name—"Lilias!" It was uttered with a sigh, which might have been mournful; but in this land of peace and holiness even the sting of sorrow was taken away. The regret for lost joy, and for joy never realized, had alike grown calm. We looked upon it as souls departed look back on their earth-sufferings, from whose immortal height of perfect knowledge and perfect peace, the deepest woe appears only a light cloud round the mountain's foot whose summit is in the skies.

Cyril and I grasped each other's hands, and left the scene.

The day fleeted like one of those quiet happy days of which every hour goes by, leaving some grateful odour of duties performed and pleasures enjoyed; and like this, Cyril said, passed every day in Eden-land. As we sat watching the sunset over the western hills, there came into my mind solemn thoughts of the closing of man's brief day. In the morning I had beheld the golden shadow of the angel of Love; now it seemed to me that in the soughing of the solemn trees, in the gathering clouds that darkened the sky, I felt the presence of the angel of Death. I spoke my thoughts to Cyril, and he answered—

"It may be so. Arise, and let us go forth to meet him."

We went forth, up the mountain, towards the cottages of the mountaineers; and as we climbed higher and higher, we seemed to follow the steps of the departing sun, and the eventide became clear and beautiful, though solemn still. It was a twilight less like the fading than the dawning day.

And like the twilight peace without was that which dwelt within the dwelling which Cyril entered. There lay—feebly fluttering within its prison, waiting the hour of its summons—an immortal soul. As I crossed the threshold, I seemed to feel the breath of the Death-angel who stood there, invisible, with folded wings, until those pinions should be lifted to bear away one more spirit to the unseen land.

"Hush! tread softly," said a young man's voice. He who spoke arose from the ground where he had been kneeling at the feet of two people, on whom he gazed with the tenderness of an only child. They were both old; but the woman's face, as it rested on her husband's breast, had a pallor deeper than that of age. From the path they had long trodden together her feet were now the first to glide. She knew it—he knew it—and yet both leaned calmly, heart to heart as ever, until the hour of parting should come. A brief parting it was—so brief, that they talked of it without a single tear.

She turned a little, and gave her hand to Cyril.

"I am going," she said, and smiled.

"The blessing of all whom thy pure life has blessed, go with thee, my sister," he answered.

We all echoed "Amen:" even the aged husband and the son. They never so much as said, "Beloved! stay with us a little longer;" for they knew that God had called her. Who should set himself, his human will and human love, against God's?

She spoke of many things—things of earth—life's joys and its sorrows. She was thankful for all, and showed how all had worked together for good. Much of her speech was a mystery to me; but thus far I understood—that these, like Cyril, had come through much affliction to the Happy Isle.

Then she laid her head closer to that true breast on which it had lain so many years, and her feeble fingers twined themselves amidst the shining curls of her tall son, who rested his cheek on her lap as though he were again a little child. Thus she reclined, silently enclasped until death by those whose love had brightened life. They waited with her: they went so near the dark portal as almost to hear the echo of the voice that called; and then they gave her from their tender arms, into those of God.

She was dead! No, not dead: she had only "gone away." *He* said so: the old man whose wife she had been; half of whose soul she had taken with her to the eternal land. There was no murmuring—no weeping: for here, they believed what the people of earth only *said*—that death, a righteous and peaceful death, is immortal gain. They knew that her spirit was now new-born into a diviner existence, thence to rise, sphere after sphere, until its pure essence became one with the All-Divine. So they laid her down—yet not *her*, but the likeness of her beloved form—and went out, father and son clasped in each other's arms. They stood looking upwards, following, as it were, her flight among the stars.

I watched them with a solemn wonder. It had troubled me at first to think that even in this happy place there was death—awful death—the great punishment of life. But now all was changed. I saw that nothing which God ordains is *punishment*; that greater, far greater than they who revelled in a perpetual Elysium of repose—greater than the many-centuried dwellers in Avillion, were these of Eden-land—who might pass through the gate of death into immortality.

After a space, I know not whether of hours or days—for the time seemed strange to me—I heard Cyril's voice saying—

"Come, my son, come with me into our garden!"

"Is it a fair garden?" I asked, as I walked with him.

"Very fair, in Heaven's sight!"

His words were strange; but I knew their import when he brought me to the spot: a little dell, sheltered among the hills, and planted all thick with flowers—at once an earthly and a heavenly garden. It was a place of graves.

Thither, while we entered, the son and the husband were bringing their beloved dead.

The burial was such as I had never seen in the former world. It was here no more than laying in the earth holy seed—sown for the resurrection. No black garments were allowed—no mock solemnities of crawling stranger-steps and muffled stranger-faces. A few prayers were said, less to hallow the rest of the dead—that needed no hallowing—than to speak peace and hope to the living. Then the soft earth fell, a kindly veil; and flowers were planted above, that no sign should be left of the mingling of dust with dust, save what was beautiful and dear.

Thus, in the summer twilight, we all stood around the new mound in that peaceful "garden;" and the little birds sang, and one pale, beautiful star came out in heaven, like the spirit of the departed watching us smilingly.

Then arose in the still air the voice of Cyril.

"We thank Thee, O Lord of life, that thou hast for a season sent death into Thy world, to make our faith eternal, and our love immortal as Thyself!"

Chapter XIII

Thus I dwelt with Cyril in Eden-land. Day by day we traversed it together, and I learned all things pertaining thereunto. After a space, my spirit began to turn within itself, and I pondered less over the marvellous things around me than over my own individual life. I tried to gather up the awful mysteries of my fate since the day when I had lain on the bosom of my Lilias, struggling with the horrible pain from which the German mystic had freed me, only to plunge me into worse horrors.

And when Cyril, watching my countenance, tried to read therein my thoughts, I opened my heart to him and related the fearful tale. As I went on, my passions rose; and the hatred and revenge with which the Mystic had inspired me, filled my soul once more.

Cyril looked upon me with his calm eyes.

"My son—my son! there is yet much alloy in that proud spirit. Know you not, that he who enters Eden-land must learn as his first lesson—to forgive?"

"I forgive? Oh, Cyril! I cannot. It is bitter—bitter! Was he not worse than a murderer? My own life was nothing: but Lilias—oh, Lilias!"

My heart melted within me: I could have wept!

He, too, was softened: he ever was at the sound of that name. But he gently reproved me.

"Wilfred, your fate is hard: but have you no pity for that miserable man? How know you what undeserved suffering he might have endured—what torments might have goaded him on to seek the Happy Isles. You are at peace—then pardon him."

"I know no peace," I cried. "My soul yearns even here for home and for Lilias. Oh, friend and kinsman, is there nothing to kill this worm that continually gnaws at my heart—the bitter memory of the past?"

Cyril answered solemnly—

"He who has pardoned, or will pardon, the sins of the whole world—the whole universe—forbids us to know peace, even here, until we too have pardoned all our enemies."

I sat speechless, in a dull despair.

"Then let me die!" was my thought; but I dared not breathe it. To die—to pass unforgiving into the presence of the All-Merciful!

"Come—go with me, my son, and I will show you it is not so hard to forgive."

I followed Cyril, even to the "garden." There, beside the little mound which his own hands had so lately raised, sat the husband of the dead. He was watering the flowers, and playing with them tenderly, as if they were his children.

"Herman," said Cyril, as the old man raised his meek and placid face, "tell this young passionate spirit that shrinks from forgiving wrong—tell my son Wilfred the story of thy life, and that of the pure soul who is now with God."

"She *was* a pure, beautiful soul, ever! And she suffered much wrong; but she forgave it all—all! Must I indeed recount these things again?" said the old man, dreamily.

There was no answer, and he continued—

"She was of your land, Cyril—the land which on earth is renowned for its wealth, its wisdom, and its just laws. Just laws? Merciful Heaven! is there justice beneath the sun?"

He paused a moment, and then went on—

"I was a stranger and a foreigner, and she an English girl, yet she loved me. I came of a wild, half-mad race (so men said), yet still she loved me. There was none to rule her except an old, rich, cruel woman, with whom she dwelt. This wretch turned me from the door, like a dog, and put me openly to shame. Then my gentle love arose—rose like a tigress bereft of her young; she said aloud—mark the words, for they *were* marked, ay, and for blood!—'*that retribution would follow.*'

"That night the wicked woman lay slain in her bed, and they snatched my newly-married wife from my arms, and accused her as a murderess.

"O evil, evil world! O horrible destiny which wrapped her round as with a coil! My pure innocence! To say that the little hand which I cherished like a bird in my bosom, bore on it the life-drops of a murdered human creature!

"Well, the bloodhounds of the law hunted her down: they made all clear, even to the mark of her fairy feet, that fled trembling to me when the house was still—she knowing not whence the awful stillness came. It was all plain—plain enough for the law to believe in; though some tender, merciful souls, who felt the responsibility of that accusation which can rarely be definitely proved, and on whose truth or falsehood hangs a human life—these still doubted of her guilt. But their few faint arguments were vain. Her doom was pronounced—the doom of DEATH!

"I dare not speak of myself or her: I speak of the world. I cry—as I had done then, but despair made me mad and dumb—'O man, how darest thou set thyself in the place of God, to judge life and death! How darest thou wrest His Word to sanction murder? When He said "blood for blood," He ruled His people with a visible sway: His eye inevitably marked the slayer. Can *thine*? Art thou omniscient too? Know that if one man perish innocent, it is enough to lay on thy head, and on the head of each administrator of a cursed law, the sin of Cain the murderer!'"

As he ceased, the old man sank on the grass exhausted; but his terrible words rang on my ear like a judgment. Oh, that through me they might pierce the world!

He spoke again, fainter:—

"Her doom approached. Pleadings for mercy came: 'She was so young! Even if guilty, it was hard to die!' But the law's iron tongue knelled, 'Let her die!' and man echoed it. One, a priest, even preached the justice of taking life for life— O God! and this man called himself a disciple of Him who was put to death at Calvary!

"Hour after hour fled; each tick of the clock falling on my ear like blood-drops. I sat beneath the dial, and as it moved I cursed Time—aye, almost Him who created Time—that it should be made the instrument of a slow death! Each man that passed me by, carelessly lounging through the brief hours on which hung another life, precious as his own, I yelled after him, 'Thou, too, art a murderer!'

"At last but one day came between her and death. Then, and not till then, they suffered me to feel the peace of her presence; for it was peace, even then. Her words fell on my burning heart like dew. Her meekness was beautiful, her forgiveness was sublime! She clung to my bosom; she knelt at my feet: she stopped my outcries of despair with embraces, my curses with prayers.

"Those who stood by melted into tears, and one who half-believed her guilty, went forth from the cell to spend his whole existence in striving to annul that terrible law of death by which man arrogates to himself the judgments of God.

"When the first paroxysm was over, her calmness made me calm. I entreated, and that good man who went from us entreated also, that we might have a brief space alone. The law which robs its victims of a whole precious lifetime of repentance or atonement might well grant the mercy of a few short minutes, whether to guilt or innocence: so it was permitted—to her.

"I took her in my arms and cradled her in my breast; my darling, on whose sinless brow lay the brand of murder! Suddenly the thought came,—that one day more—and the form I clasped, the fair neck whereon my kisses rained, would—

"My blood curdled into ice, and then a horrible determination entered my soul. I said, in a hissing whisper, 'Love, I will save thee!' and I showed her a ring I wore, small and beautiful, but which shut up within it poison—death. 'Sweetest, it is nothing; it will come in a moment, like sleep. My beloved, have pity on us both! let me save thee.'

"She looked amazed and doubting: 'How?'

"'Wilt thou, now, in my safe arms,—wilt thou *die*?'

"She drew herself from me—not in alarm, but in meek reproach:

"'No, love, not even for thee! I am in God's hands. I will not take the life He gave.'

"She snatched the ring from me, and trampled it under foot.

"We were to have one more interview—the last. But ere it came, a super-human energy and cunning had dawned within me, and taught me how to save her. My father, a German physician, was a man of wondrous knowledge. From him I had learned a secret which would make the frame as rigid as stone, so as to be for a time insensible to all assaults against life, while it preserved all the appearance of death, until suspended animation returned. I made the elixir: I calculated all—the time before it would take effect, and how long its power would last. I hid the tiny phial; fastening it by a hair among my long, thick curls; and then I went to the prison.

"When, human agony mastering all her strength, she lay fainting in my arms, I dropped on her lips the potion, death-bringing yet life-restoring, and then I went away, without a farewell.

"I heard the howl of the multitude, the thousands met to gloat over the sight of a slaughter according to law—a score of men formally destroying one helpless woman, who seemed already dead.

Not an hour after, the true murderer, conscience-stricken, gave himself up to justice, and the ministers of the law—ay, some of them honest men—found that on their heads and that of their children lay the guilt of innocent blood!

"I let them think so; I wished the curse to sink them to the lowest deep; and then I snatched from them my own pure dead, and fled. She woke to life and happiness upon her husband's breast!

"I wrote to my poor dream-haunted father, a German philosopher, whose worn brain was already half maddened with misery, and bade him seek us in the West, where human wickedness could trouble us no more. Then we two, my wife and I, sailed far away. But doom followed us still. The vessel never reached the land—at least, no earthly land. *That* happened—which I may not speak of to earthly ears—and we and all the ship's crew came hither to the island of peace. Thank God, bless God, for all!"

"And thy father?" I cried, while a sudden light darted through my mind; "tell me who was thy father?"

"We forget all such sorrows here; but his name on earth was Johann Foerster."

I fell on my knees:—

"Bear witness, heaven! that now at last from the bottom of my soul *I forgive!*"

Then I told him my story, and we embraced one another, and were at peace.

While we yet sat in the holy "garden" and talked, our speech was broken by a heavy thundering sound which came from the overhanging hills. I looked up, and saw that a portion of the rock had loosened from its place, and was falling, bringing death in its passage, to the plain beneath. A moment more, and, shuddering, I saw that right in the path of this avalanche of doom lay sleeping a young mountaineer. It was Herman Foerster's son!

With the speed of thought I sprang up the crags, my feet sinking at each step. I reached the spot; I shook him out of his sleep; but he clung to me, half bewildered still. It was too late. I heard the father's shriek; I saw Cyril's upturned face; and then the thunder rolled over us, stunning, deafening. It passed, and we were both alive.

Alive! but for how long? The ground had been torn from under us. We stood on a jutting precipice—a mere speck left between the perpendicular rock above and the yawning abyss below. Even this narrow spot of safety crumbled and quivered beneath our feet. We were two, and there was room but for one.

I paused. Revenge lay in my grasp. The grandson of Johann Foerster, the youth in whose veins ran my enemy's blood, was in my hands. Which should it be—life or death? vengeance or self-sacrifice? Life or death, revenge or sacrifice!

My choice was made. In one sigh of prayer I committed my soul to God; in one murmur I uttered the name of Lilias; then, with one farewell grasp of the boy's hand, I plunged into the awful void below.

*   *   *   *   *   *

I awoke. Oh, marvel beyond belief! I lay on the vessel's deck—I felt round my neck those dear soft arms. All had been a dream!

I heard the tender voice of my wife:—

"Wilfred, dearest, you have slept scarce an hour, and you wake, all calm, and so well!"

I leaned my head on her bosom, and our tears mingled together. Then I met the kind, half-melancholy gaze of the old German mystic. Lilias turned even from me to clasp his hand, and thank him.

He replied—

"Thank not me, but God!"

I spoke to him, the mistiness of my dream, which I knew was only a dream, struggling vainly with reality:—

"Dear friend, stay with us, and let us be to you in the stead of all you have lost!"

But he only shook his head, and said meekly—

"It is impossible! I have not yet found the Happy Isles!"

*   *   *   *   *   *

In our dear home—the home my wandering fancy pictured—I dwell with Lilias. The old house is musical with sweet young voices; baby footsteps patter, fairy-like, through its dim chambers. It is indeed a haunted house—haunted by all good spirits of peace, and happiness, and love. Lilias and I look towards the future and smile; the shadows of death, and sickness, and sorrow, have passed from us, and we shall grow old among our children's children.

Yet never, while life lasts, shall we altogether lose the memory of that strange dream of mine.

From *The Feasts of Camelot*

MRS. T. K. (ELEANORA LOUISA MONTAGU) HERVEY

Part I. Chapter III.
Sir Tristram's Tale of Mad King Mark

Never in all the world, I think, was there knight or king so mad as my uncle King Mark. While I was yet but a young squire I was sent into Cornwall to receive knighthood from my uncle; and sorry am I that I received it not rather from any man living; for there was neither honour nor courtesy to be learned from him. Though he calls himself King Mark he is really no king at all, save only by the sufferance of my lord King Arthur, who has forborne him these many years only for my sake, and because of his being kin also to dead Gorlois, Duke of Cornwall. Because of the mystery of King Arthur's early fostering, and the rebellion that came out of it, he seized that corner of land to himself, with all the estates thereto belonging, and would have all men call him king. And there he reigns and raves; and what he cannot do by the strong hand he will do by sleight and cunning; and for that cause has Sir Launcelot of the Lake ever called him "King Fox."

While I was yet but a new-made knight, my uncle's right of kingship was called in question by one Sir Maurice of Ireland, brother to the queen of that country. To end the dispute it was agreed that the matter should be decided by single combat, between Sir Maurice of Ireland and that knight of King Mark's court who should be of the best lineage. Thereupon, my uncle called me to him, and broke the affair to me.

"Fair nephew," said he, "this encounter falls to you by right of birth, and you must have to do with this knight of Ireland whether you be so minded or no."

"With your leave, Sir Mark," said I, for I never would call him king, "I must forbear to do battle in this cause."

Then my uncle looked at me askance from under his brows, and, said he, "Fair nephew, why so?"

"Because," I answered, "no true knight will fight but in a just cause; and well you know there is no king in all Logris but only my lord King Arthur."

"Say you so?" said King Mark; "we shall see!"

He said no more at that time; and I thought I was well out of the risk of shedding innocent blood in a wrong cause. But I was young then; and King Mark was more than a match for me.

It was soon spread abroad that I was afraid of Sir Maurice, who was a noble and approved knight; and that I had refused to meet him in single combat. For this cause Sir Maurice took occasion to taunt me as recreant from my vows of knighthood, perjured, and false. My blood was hot; and I threw down my glove, and dared him to meet me in mortal fight. So here were we two come to be deadly foes for no cause save an evil mind and a lying tongue.

We met full savagely. Twice I broke spear on Sir Maurice's hauberk, and twice he hurled at me, so that I had all but been unhorsed. But to make a long story short, I overcame him in the end; and though he never cried me mercy, yet I gave him his life; as Heaven forbid I should not, both because of the just cause he had come to do battle for, and because I began to see that I had been slandered to the knight. He now confessed me to be a worthy foe; and we embraced as friends and brothers, though we were both sorely wounded, and might not bear harness for many a day to come.

From that time my uncle seemed to grow all at once very kind to me. He gave it out that I had fought for his right of kingship; and made it be understood of all men that henceforward none should question it. It was in vain that I denied the tale; I was in the mesh, and I could not get out of it.

Disgusted and sick at heart, I resolved to leave Cornwall, and to set out, in company with Sir Maurice, for the court of King Anguish, of Ireland. My uncle did not oppose me; but as I was on the point of setting foot on shipboard, who should ride up to me, as I stood on the shore with Sir Maurice, but my uncle, mad King Mark!

"Fair nephew," said he, for so was ever his way of speech when he had some end of his own to serve, "I would that you should take this packet, bound with silken cord, to my brother-king, Anguish, of Ireland, and greet him well from me."

I took the packet, bound with silken cord, and making, as may be guessed, light leave-taking, went on shipboard with Sir Maurice. As I mounted to the deck I heard a low chuckle behind me, and, looking back, saw cunning King Mark go smiling away.

We made good voyage, and soon reached the domains of King Anguish. There I first saw the beautiful Isond. But little did I think what sorrow was in store for me through the crooked dealings of sly King Mark.

At first I was courteously received by all; and was especially happy in the kindness and favour of the beautiful Isond, to whom, the first day of my coming, I began to teach the music of the harp, in which from my earliest youth I had delighted, even more than in hunting. But full soon I saw and felt a change. King Anguish looked askance at me; even Sir Maurice began to slacken in his friendship; and it became clear that the letter I had borne from King Mark was at the root of it all.

Still, though all others looked coldly and suspiciously upon me, Isond remained kind and gentle as ever. So one day I thought I would take courage and ask her the cause why I had grown in such disfavour. Then she told me how King Mark had written to her father to bid him keep me closely watched that I should never return into his country of Cornwall, for that I had plotted to usurp from him his lawful lands; and that when I had pretended to do battle in his cause it was only done to prove his right to possess them, in order that I might, as his nephew, claim them in turn, as he had no sons to come after him. But this was not all. He had the cunning to give some colour to his falsehood by saying that my object in seeking the court of King Anguish was to ask the aid of that king to dispossess him at once of his crown.

For all this I cared little; the worst was to come. King Mark had asked for the hand of the beautiful Isond in marriage, and her father had consented to give her to the ruthless man. This was the greatest misfortune that could have happened to me, as I thought then,—for I was beginning to love, with all the devotion of knighthood, that gentle lady.

Sorrowfully did the beautiful Isond weep as she told me of her father's mistaken pledge to King Mark. But she was dutiful as she was fair; and I, as a good and true knight, was bound in honour henceforth to regard her as the promised wife of my uncle.

Bitterly grieving over her probable fate, I at once determined to depart from that court. By the advice of Isond I arranged to steal secretly from Ireland, lest, in any attempt to detain me, I might be forced to come to open war with her father; and this, with many tears, she earnestly entreated me by all means to avoid.

Just then it so happened that the distress I endured at hearing of my uncle's new treachery against me, together with the sorrow of losing Isond, caused an old wound to break out afresh. What gentle and good thoughts for my happiness were then in her mind I knew not at that time, though I did later; but the kind Isond, though skilled in surgery beyond most of her degree, yet said she was quite unable to attempt my cure.

"Sir Tristram," she said, "your wound has been made with a poisoned arrow; it can only be cured in that country where you received it. The shaft that struck you flew from the bow of one of a band of heathen marauders among the mountains of Wales; so at least a minstrel sang the tale to me. I pray you go now into that country, to the court of the good King Howell, who is my kinsman. His daughter, my cousin and namesake, the gracious Isond, is well skilled in leechcraft. Greet her well from me, and say I would that she would set herself to cure you of your wound. We two are so closely likened to each other, save that my cousin Isond is the fairer, that it may be you shall think the fair hands of Isond of Wales are the hands of the poor Isond which you have taught so well to draw forth the sweet music of the harp. Go now, Sir Tristram," she added, as I would fain have lingered over that sad leave-taking, "and God speed you for a good knight and true!"

Whether our secret talk had been overheard, I know not, but that very night I was seized while asleep, and hurried, bound, to a dungeon below the castle keep. There, for some days, I lay without hope of release; but the gentle Isond was busy devising means for my escape.

The first thing she did was to desire her damsels to spread abroad a report that I was greatly learned in magic arts, so as to put my gaolers in bodily fear of me. Next, she ordered that her harp should be wrapped in cloth of cloth, and borne with great care into my dungeon to while away the hours of my captivity.

There were at that time in Ireland, as there still are in this land, many people curiously fond of keeping dwarfs, who were brought over from the East. One of these frightful creatures, the smallest and most hideous of his kind, Isond procured. She caused him to coil himself up within the framework of the harp, for which purpose she took care to have the strings removed; that done, the harp, carefully swathed and bound, was brought into my cell, and there left; the dwarf having his orders what to do.

When next the gaoler brought me food and water for the night, I hid myself behind the harp; while the hideous dwarf rushed forward, and soundly rated the gaoler for coming so late with my supper, howling out in his ears, "If you do not go to the foul fiend for this, my name's not Sir Tristram!"

Horror-struck at what he conceived to be my abominable transforming of myself into an imp of Satan, the gaoler rushed out, at his wits' end, leaving the cell door open. Through it I slipped like lightning; and, aided by the dwarf who held the key of the postern gate, where my horse and good sword awaited me, I soon found myself in perfect safety.

Glad enough was I to reach the shores of Wales. There all fell out as I truly believe the virtuous Isond intended that it should. In the court of King Howell my happiest days were passed. His daughter, the gracious Isond, as she was called to distinguish her from her cousin and namesake of Ireland, was the sweetest lady in all the world. Under her loving care all my wounds, both of body and mind, were indeed cured; and here at my side she sits, King Howell's daughter, and the good wife of a poor knight, by name Sir Tristram.

"And now, Merlin," said Sir Tristram, when he had ended his tale, "I want to know why you smiled when I told of the poisoned arrow? I verily believe you put faith in nothing but God and knighthood."

"Truly," answered Merlin; "I am not so simple as to believe the story of a poisoned wound being only to be cured in the country where the wound was *dealt*; though there is a sort of truth at the bottom of that foolish saying, doubtless. Perhaps he might be nearer the mark who should say, that it would be most likely of cure in the land the poison came from; since it has been said that the wise men among the Saracens, which people make much use of such unknightly weapons, ceased not in their search till they had found out an antidote to the poison with which they tipped their arrows. Be that as it may; as to your bodily wound, Sir Tristram, depend on it there was no poison at all in the case, let the foolish minstrels sing what they may. Mischief take the bards! They will leave nothing as they find it; but are for ever stringing of rhymes and twanging of strings, to the utter confusion of all true history. It matters little that they have set me down for a wizard; but they have even dared to call our gracious lady Morgana, the 'Fay-lady.'"

"Nay, Merlin," said Queen Guenever, who was wife to King Arthur, "blame not the bards so greatly; you yourself are half the cause that my lord King Arthur's sister is accounted more than mortal wise. You found her apt, and taught her so many learned things that women seldom know of, that rumour has fixed upon her the blame of dealing with unlawful magic."

"Right, honoured lady," replied Merlin; "but that all men may know truly in the end, I keep the books of my uncle Bleise, as well as all that I have written down myself, fast locked in the great pyx in the church of St. Stephen. Heaven grant they never be lost; or a sorry history will be given of us all in the ages to come!"

Part II. Chapter XI.
Queen Isond's Tale of the One Good Deed.

In a castle, built on a strong rock looking over the broad waters that wash the Cornish shores, there lived an old knight who had two sons. When these two youths were yet but unbearded squires, not yet admitted into knighthood, there came to dwell there a young maiden passing fair, the orphan child of the old knight's brother, who had just then been newly slain in the wars. The old knight loved her as if she had been a child of his own; and secretly determined that he would in due time wed her to one or other of his two sons, if it should turn out that either of them grew into the young maid's liking.

The two youths were as different in all things as light is from dark. Bertrand, the elder, was bold and strong of limb, impatient of control, passionate and revengeful. Walter, the younger, was of a softer nature, reserved and quiet, but of deep affections; and he was, to the full, as brave as his brother, though few gave him credit for the force that was in him.

As time drew on, it happened that the liking of the young maid, Lenora, fell on the elder, Bertrand. And, as soon as the old knight noted that his elder son grew to be marvellously fond of the orphan child, he settled it all as he would have it, and the two were betrothed.

But when the two young squires had passed their noviciate, and came to receive knighthood at their father's hands, nothing would stay Bertrand, the elder, but he would away to the wars, where a neighbouring country was struggling to free itself from a foreign yoke. He could not rest, he said, in the old hall of his fathers, while the world's work was doing outside; but he would go forth and win for himself renown; and then he should come back more worthy of his betrothed lady, Lenora, and they would be wedded with great joy in the old castle of the rock.

With many tears Lenora parted with her lover; and, folding across his shoulders a scarf of blue samite, richly embroidered by her own hands, saw him mount and ride away.

Time went on. The wars were over. A year had passed by with lagging foot; and yet the bridegroom came not. When the autumn leaves began to fall, the old knight died. With his last breath he committed the young Lenora to the care of his son, Walter, till Bertrand, the elder, should return to claim his bride; appointing him guardian over her person and lands, and bidding him be a gentle and loving brother to one so forlorn. For, by this time, there had crept a misgiving into the knight's mind that all was not well with his son Bertrand, who came not home to the fulfilling of his pledge.

So the old knight died, and was buried by torchlight. And now, save for the ancient servitors and men-at-arms who had belonged to his following, there remained in the rock-castle only the youth, Walter, and Lenora the maiden betrothed.

As a miser guards his hoarded treasure, so did Walter guard the promised bride of his brother Bertrand. His task was a hard one. He loved the maid with a better love than his light-minded brother had done; and as time wore away, and he saw her deserted and drooping, his heart bled within him, and was sore for her sorrow. Yet he never spoke of his love to her; but held her in all honour, and kept his knightly faith unbroken.

At length, over the seas came Bertrand once more. But he came not alone. He brought with him a bride from a strange land, one light-minded like himself, who, in after days, brought a just retribution on his head; for she forsook him as he had forsaken his once love, Lenora, and broke her wedded vows to flee away in shameful flight with a knight of her own land.

Now, when Bertrand brought home his light lady, and set her in the home of his fathers, the just wrath of the good Walter was roused against him for Lenora's sake; and, mindless for the moment that he was of his own blood and kin, he challenged him to the combat as recreant and false, perjured lover and faithless knight.

The hot blood of Bertrand was up. He fell savagely on his brother; and, as he was the stronger and hardier of the two, it might have ended ill for the true Walter, but that the maid, Lenora, looking down from the rampart, saw the unnatural encounter, and came swiftly down to part the brothers. She rushed between the uplifted swords, and fell, wounded to death, beneath the stroke of Bertrand.

The sight of her innocent blood recalled them to themselves. Bertrand, aghast and bewildered at the issue of the foul wrong he had done, stood by, pale, and leaning on his sword; but Walter, all whose true soul was with the lost Lenora, knelt at her side, and strove in vain to stanch the wound dealt by the betrayer.

Her life was passing. To Bertrand she only said, "Be happy with your chosen bride." But to Walter she turned now with tender trust, crying, "Oh, true heart! well hast thou loved in silent love; and noble life hast thou lived. Live still, and remember me to the grave, where we two shall meet and go wedded souls to heaven. Bear with thy brother, for the sake of the old love that was between him and me. Never again, I charge you, cross sword with Bertrand, your brother. His I was once: yours am I now for ever." So saying, and yielding, for the first and last time, her dying lips to the pure kiss of Walter, Lenora quietly breathed away her life.

The brothers, mindful of her words, fell to battle no more. But the unruly spirit of Bertrand was hard to bear. He seemed now to hate his brother, whose virtues were a silent reproach to him. So Walter sorrowfully departed out of his old father's castle, and went forth to seek adventure wherein he might forget the tragic ending of his love. Many years he wandered, and many good deeds are recorded of him, in helping the oppressed, even to the shedding of his blood for them in numerous perilous encounters.

In one of his wanderings, it happened that he reached the skirts of a wood, near which many knights were gathered together, as if about to set out on some new quest. He turned his horse's head and joined them company, questioning them of their intent. They told him of a fierce combat which had just then come about, in which one knight had slain another unjustly, and against all fair and honourable laws of chivalry. By the account they gave of the slain knight and of the bearings on his shield, Sir Walter knew that it must be his brother Bertrand, who had fallen thus ingloriously; and he vowed to avenge his fall with the best might that he could. But when he came to put question as to the false knight he sought, it was told him that in those parts he was known as the Invisible Knight, because he ever wore his visor closed, so that no man knew his face. Out of this, strange tales had arisen of many having got hard blows at his hand, while none could see who dealt them. Sir Walter could sift the true from the false; and he well divined that he should not have far to seek.

Having parted company with the rest, he chose such a path through the wood as showed, by some broken branches strewed in the way, that a mounted knight had but newly cleft his way through the thick-grown trees. His course lay alone for some length; but at a clearing in the wood, he espied, resting beside a fountain, his arms soiled and stained with newly-shed blood, a knight of good stature, whose face he could not see. He doubted not that this was the Invisible Knight, since he answered in all points to the description that was given of him.

As the knight Walter looked on the supposed slayer of his brother Bertrand, the playmate of his youth, and the once-beloved of his own loved and lost Lenora, something of the fierce passion of his brother for a moment stirred his blood; and, hurling a bold defiance at the Invisible Knight, he challenged him to combat. Nothing loath, the latter mounted, and met his challenger in full career. Furious were the blows that hailed thick and fast on either helm. The Invisible Knight, especially, seemed moved by more than human hate, and fell upon Sir Walter like one possessed by a fiend.

Long and doubtful was the strife. And now, as both paused for one brief moment to gather breath to renew the fight, the Invisible Knight, forgetful of all disguise, raised has barred visor, and gazed fiercely on his foe.

Suddenly the sword dropped from Sir Walter's grasp. "Oh, Bertrand, my brother!" he cried, "stay thy hand. Pardon, oh pardon! I knew thee not. Oh my brother, how nearly had I slain thee, or thou me; and then would all the wide world have been a blank to one of us two for evermore!" But the frantic Bertrand fell on him once again. And, as Sir Walter would no more lift his sword against his brother's life, he fell, wounded, to the earth.

Then, first, a touch of remorse struck to the heart of the guilty Bertrand; and he repented him of the fatal disguise he had put on, in exchanging arms with the knight he had waylaid and slain in the wood.

Walter, seeing what was working in his brother's mind, gave him what comfort he could, saying, "Bertrand, my brother, if you were to know for a surety that I died by your own sword-stroke, you would find peace on this earth never more. See, then, I will wound myself with a stroke that shall go deeper than thine, that my blood may not be upon thy head." So speaking, he took his own sword and fell upon it; and spoke word never more.

Sir Bertrand, deserted by his evil wife, whose paramour he had set upon and slain in the wood, and now despoiled of his noble brother and sole of his kin, went mad, and lived but a short while after.

And now I come to the good deed of my lord King Mark. He caused the body of Sir Walter to be borne back to his own castle of the rock, and there to be buried in the chapel, beside the lady Lenora, in one grave with her. And he caused prayers and blessings and spousal rites to be read over them, that these two noble and true souls might go, as Lenora had said, "wedded souls to heaven." And my lord King Mark caused also to be raised over the sleeping dead a costly tomb of pure white marble, and on it were written these words:—

> "HERE LYETH THE NOBLE KNIGHT,
> WALTER OF THE ROCK:
> AND BESIDE HIM
> HIS SWEETEST LADY, LENORA;
> CRUELLY SLAIN ON EARTH,
> BUT WEDDED TO HIM IN HEAVEN."

When the tale was ended, King Arthur said, "Truly, fairest queen, your tale is a lovely tale; and though sad, yet full of such true nobleness as touches finer chords in the heart than tales of mirth and pleasantry, and leaves a sweeter ring in the soul. As for the good deed of your lord King Mark, it was well done, and showed indeed some ruth and pity, and a feeling for what is truly great; yet it could be wished that the living rather than the dead had been so humanely dealt with. But let us take the deed for what it is worth. Perhaps it may be yet further shown that some of his blood and race have done acts of nobleness and generosity, whence we may infer that nature is not all in fault, but that circumstance has wrought in him some of the ill that he has done. I would some innocent child, unmoved by passion, could speak for him. Young Alisaunder," continued the king, "among all the tales which children devour so eagerly, heard you ever a tale of one of King Mark's line, which might plead for your worst foe? King Mark has been your enemy more than any, for he forgot against your father Sir Baldwin the brother-ties and virtues which yet he honoured in Sir Walter of the Rock. Speak one good word for him, child, if thou canst."

"Gladly would I, my good lord King Arthur," answered the boy; "but indeed I never heard any tale that I remember about the false king's line.—Yet, stay, one strange tale I do remember; but that was not very long ago. Shall I tell it, King Arthur?"

"Do so, child," said the king. And Alisaunder began.

Part II. Chapter XII.
The Boy Alisaunder's Tale of the Forgiving Heart

I can't tell where it happened, nor what was the name of the king; but I remember that he had married a sister of King Mark's; and he had a little son who was born in a forest, and who grew up to be a great hunter of beasts, and a minstrel besides. People said it was because he had been born in a forest among the wild deer, and that the first music he ever heard was the loud wind playing amongst the branches of the huge forest trees. Do you think that was so, King Arthur? Ah! you smile: and I see Merlin lifts up his eyebrows and looks at Sir Tristram. But Sir Tristram looks grave, and does not laugh at me; so I will go on.

I don't know what was the name of the little son of the sister of King Mark; but I know his mother died, and his father took a new wife; and she was not like King Mark's sister, not by much so good and so true a lady. She treated her little stepson cruelly, and did him all the harm that she could. She had children of her own; and she hated him because his father loved him best, and often told her that his little son would inherit all his lands, and King Mark's besides; for the boy's uncle, King Mark, had no sons of his own.

One day she sent him out in a wild, wild storm, to gather herbs a long way off. When he came back he was weary and athirst; but she would let him have no drink; for she said he was hot, and he must wait till night, for it was better for him, and more wholesome, to drink the last thing before he lay down to sleep, as the cattle do.

Well, all that day she was brewing and brewing the herbs.—O, now I remember, the name of the king was Meliodus; yes, that was it, King Meliodus.

His little son, when night came, went into the sleeping-room where all the children lay. All were in bed and asleep but he. Before he lay down he bethought him of the drink he had been promised, for he was now more athirst than ever. He saw a cup standing on a settle beside his bed; but he could not believe that it was put there for him, for his stepmother was not used to be so careful of him, or so thoughtful of what he might want. So he said to himself,—"Perhaps it is not meant for me. I will go to bed and lie awake awhile, and see if my stepmother will come and give it me, as I know my own mother would have done if she had been living." With that he laid him down, and soon forgot all about the drink, and fell fast asleep,—he was so very, very weary.

Next day, one of the queen's own children, a little girl, fell sick; and do what the queen could, she might give her no ease. At last a sudden fear came into her mind, and she asked quickly,—"Child, did you take any drink last night?"

"Yes," said the little girl; "I woke up all hot and dry, and I got up and drank some of my brother's drink that stood by his bedside."

Then the queen fell down in a swoon; and before she could be got round again, her little girl was dead.

King Meliodus was away at this time. When he came home, he was sorely troubled at what had fallen out. Yet, whatever he might think, he said nothing. But one day, when again some drink was set near his little son, which he had seen the queen set there with her own hands, though she saw not that he was watching her, he went into the room where it stood, when the queen and his own little son were there, and none besides; and he took up the cup, and made believe as if he were going to drink; and he watched the queen's face all the while. Very white she grew, and whiter and whiter every moment, as he slowly raised the cup to drink from it. At last, just as it reached his mouth, she suddenly started forward with a great cry, and struck the cup out of his hand, so that it fell on the floor.

Then the king, without a word, took her by the hand and led her away. Across the great hall he led her, and right away to the castle-keep, where all the dungeons were. His little son followed, trembling and afraid, though he knew not what it meant; and begged the king to bring back his stepmother; or only to speak, and not to look so fearful and stern. But his father heeded nothing. Only, when he had gone down the great stone steps to the horrible prison beneath, dragging the queen after him,—and when he had thrust her into a stone cell, and locked and barred the door fast upon her,—then he came back and took his little son by the hand, just as he had taken the queen, speaking no word all the time, and so led him back into the castle, and left him alone.

After that King Meliodus summoned his men-at-arms, and all those that belonged to his following,—for he would do all openly; and he bade a great fire to be kindled with huge logs and hurdles in the middle of the courtyard for the burning of a wicked witch; for he told them how he had by chance found out that his little girl had died through evil practices, and that justice should be done at once, before the sun was two days older.

But the sun was only one day older when his little son came and knelt at his feet, and prayed of his father that he would give him the dungeon key; and let him go and take his stepmother out of the cold, damp stone cell, and bring her back into the hall to the warm log-fire. But his father would not hear him. Three times that day he prayed his father's mercy for the queen, though he knew not as yet the worse fate that was in store for her. But it was all no use.

The next day, when he came with the same pleading, that he might be let go and bring his stepmother indoors to the warm log-fire, his father, King Meliodus, answered him frightfully.

"She shall have logs enough and fire enough, child, be sure," said he. And as he said it the red blood mounted up into his face with fierce anger; and he looked again just as he had looked when the queen grew whiter and whiter, and struck the drinking-cup out of his hand.

Seeing the boy all amazed, he drew him to the window, and showed him where men were busy piling up great dry tree-branches, all in a wide circle round one long, stiff, upright stake that was set up in the midst, with a great iron ring in it, and a chain of iron fastened to the ring.

"See, boy!" said the stern king, "yonder is the fire to be kindled, and there stand the logs ready; think you there will be fire enough there to warm a cold heart—a heart cold and desperately wicked?"

The boy wrung his hands, for he had heard of such things, and he knew what was meant.

"Oh, father!" he cried, "dear father! you never will be so cruel. Forgive her—pray forgive her! What has she done?"

"I will tell you," said his father. "She made a hellish drink, and poisoned her own child with it."

"Oh! never," cried the boy; "never, never—it cannot be!"

"I tell thee, boy, it is so," said his father; "would you save her now?"

"Surely, father," he answered; "if she had killed me, too, she should not be burnt."

"Now, listen to me," said his fierce father; "it was you, boy, yourself that she meant to kill. She put the poison-cup at your own bedside; but my little girl drank of it, and she died."

The boy well remembered about the cup, and he was obliged to believe it now. But it made no difference to him. Still he said, "Spare her, dear father; she must be sorry!"

"Shall I tell you how she showed her sorrow?" said the king. "When her little girl was dead she brewed another hellish cup, and put it in your way. You saw me lift it to my lips; you saw the white witch strike it from my hand: would you spare her now?"

"She shall not suffer—indeed, indeed, she must not!" persisted the boy. "Why, dear, dear father, she saved your life—think how she loves you! Only spare her this once, and I will answer for it she will do this horrid thing never again."

While he spoke, a fearful shriek burst on their ears. Looking out, they saw the queen being led between two men, who were bringing her to the stake, to which they were just going to fasten her with the iron chain.

The boy said no more. He burst through the hall, and out away into the courtyard; and, clasping his arms round her, began to drag his stepmother away from the logs.

The king could resist no longer. He made a sign to the men, and they loosed their hold of her; and the boy, still clasping her closely round, dragged her safely away.

The king's little son was right. His stepmother never did him harm any more, but loved him tenderly ever after; and scourged herself and wore sackcloth for her sin.

————————

"That is all I know of the story," said Alisaunder. "The king's little son was right to do as he did,—was he not, King Arthur? I know I would have done the same, whatever had come of it. Would not you, Sir Tristram? I am sure you would.— Why, your eyes look as if there were tears in them! Oh, Sir Tristram, *you* are nephew to King Mark! Ah! I know now; it must be your story I have been telling."

King Arthur looked on the boy with a kindly smile. "Child," he said, "thou reprovest me. This story thou hast told so well is indeed the story of thy cousin's, Sir Tristram's, youth, though thou knewest it not. Methinks we have not far to seek for traits of nobleness and self-denial in the blood of King Mark's line, while we have before us this very Sir Tristram, and thy father, Sir Baldwin, that unhappy king's brother. Even in thee, too, my boy, young as thou art, I perceive a strain of true nobleness that will one day make the world ring with thy renown. Be the sins of King Mark, then, freely forgiven, for the virtues' sake of these that are of his kin. In good time, doubtless, we shall know how he has been beguiled to his undoing."

"I believe," said Merlin, "I hold the clue to some of his misdeeds. There went a rumour long ago that I, who—heaven only knows why!—am accounted a prophet, had foretold that one near akin to him should usurp his power, and hold him captive till his death-day. Thus, ever in dread, and knowing not from which hand his doom is to come, he wages an unnatural war with all his race."

"Merlin is ever wise and right," added Queen Isond. "No wonder that his study of the stars and planets has made people account him gifted beyond common men—as indeed he is, though neither wizard nor prophet. My lord King Mark has ever been kind and tender to me; and I think none can lay to his charge any act of cruelty or injustice where he has not been led to suspect treachery through a foolish rumour. When I protected and aided Angelides to withdraw her son from his pursuit, his anger against me was but for a time; and he told me afterwards that he thought it was womanly and well done."

"It is enough," said King Arthur. "When a good wife pleads for her erring lord, who shall deny her? Indeed, it seems to me that all are for him and none against him. Is there yet another voice to plead for King Mark?"

Then spoke the mother of King Arthur, the aged Igerna.

"There is mine, my son," she said. "King Mark is of kin to my first lord, Gorlois, the lover and wedded husband of my youth, before I was wife to Uther Pendragon, thy sire."

Thereupon, King Arthur said no more. But he rose up from his place, and slowly departed out of the hall.

After but a little delay, caused doubtless by a dislike to meet the many eyes that would be bent on him, at the lower end of the hall appeared King Mark: not as a captive, bound by chains; but led forward by no other hand than that of Arthur, the Most Christian King.

As soon as King Mark was seated in the place of greatest honour, next to Igerna, King Arthur spoke.

"In honour of our new guest," said he, "let the tale and the song go round."

Then the great beakers were filled anew: guest pledged guest as if a great conquest had been won in the land; and many a pleasant tale and touching song wiled away the last trace of care from the softened heart of King Mark.

But enough for the present hour. The chronicler of these will—God willing—at a fitting time record other tales of other Feasts of Camelot.

The King and the Bard

SALLIE BRIDGES

"Come, sing us a lay!" quoth Arthur,
   "My Bard of the Table Round!
Some ballad of lofty courage,
   That shall make our heart's-blood bound!"
And the monarch drain'd his goblet,
   While the minstrel tuned his lyre,
And fill'd it again, that the singer
   Might win from wine new fire.

"Now drink," said the generous sovereign,
   "That, when thy song shall be o'er,
We may fill with bright gold pieces
   And hand thee the cup once more."
But the minstrel's voice was silent,
   And the ruby wine undrain'd,
While Arthur, impatient, wondered
   Why the guerdon was not gain'd".

The bard from his seat rose slowly,
   And spoke to the waiting king:
"Sire, to-day my soul is tuneless,
   And no worthy lay can sing.
Not e'en for your tempting liquor,
   Not e'en for your promised gold,
Will my inner voice yield music;
   For true song cannot be sold!

"But when fitting words can utter
    Dreams that stir my own deep heart,
In thine shall the chords re-echo,
    Till it feels of mine a part.
Not till inspiration smiteth
    On the rock of silent Thought,
Can be welcome living waters
    To the king or people brought!"

"Thou art right!" the sovereign answer'd;
    "'Tis a lesson nobly told:
Monarchs cannot rule men's *spirits*
    By the might of law or gold!
Thou art first of all my minstrels,
    Thou art best of Britain's boast;
But take now my brimming goblet,
    And quaff it to Arthur's toast.

"Drink, gallant knights, to the minstrel
    Who dreads neither prince nor peer,—
Who can speak the truth to power,
    Nor flatters for price or fear,—
To the bard who freely renders
    The gift he has been given,
And sings but when his strain exalts
    His hearers nigher heaven!"

Avilion

SALLIE BRIDGES

"The island valley of Avilion,
　Where falls not hail, nor rain, nor any snow,
　Nor ever wind blows loudly; but it lies
　Deep-meadow'd, happy, fair with orchard lawns
　And bowery hollows crown'd with summer sea!"
　　　　　　　—Tennyson's "Morte d'Arthur"

"Arthur should come again!" the prophet said
The kingdom waited long, and each great soul
That star-like rose upon the nation's sky
Was watch'd for token of expected fate
That should achieve the change and good desired.
But never one fulfill'd the perfect dream
Of stainless character and lofty aim
That in tradition lived and hoping minds.
And, reading this, I murmur'd to myself,
"'Tis better so: the people must be great
That keep such standard of high excellence
Their best do never reach! So let me use
The gift the fairies gave me at my birth
To set in common view, with Saxon words,
A living image of the ideal knight,
Lest men forget, amid these restless times
Of hollow shows and worshipping of gold,
That truth and pureness once were in the world,
Nor lose their faith that they will come again!

And so I sang the songs of other days,—
Have ta'en to modern homes and modern hearts
The ghosts of ancient dead that lived their lives
As grandly or as weakly as their age
Or natures wrought on them! with my witch-wand
I open'd Fancy's portal, and led forth
In their own shapes, to breathe earth's air again,
The storied men who had become a name,
And group'd them all about the British king,
As once they circled him at Table Round,
And that fair queen, so frail because she loved,
That, false herself, kept her one lover true,
Whom Arthur trusted, blind to his great wrong,
Since his large, royal soul in others saw
Only the good and truth was in his own.

And then I said, with that vague, quenchless thirst
We dreamers know when mingles sorrow's shade
With discontent at our own labor done,
That seems so poor beside the vivid thought,
"And what reward is mine for this my work?
Men will forget it in a little while,
And when this brain is dust, how few will care
That once it throbb'd with Inspiration's heat!
Would I could go away from all the doubt,
The pain and turmoil of this weary life,
Into Avilion, where the good king went,
And rest me in the Happy Isle, like him!"
And so I closed my tired eyes, that press'd
Two tears between the lids, that, as they touch'd
The level ground, into a wonder grew;
For, lo! a lake that spread its waters up
Nigh to my feet, while through the sunset glow
A black barge hove in sight, like one that came
For wounded Arthur, only now it bore
No fair, crown'd queens, no hooded, weeping dames!
Only a pallid steersman stood at helm,
With white garb stirless as a statue's robe,

That seem'd to sweep adown o'er folded wings.
The boat came slowly to the coast, and paused.
I inland turn'd an instant's sight, and saw
That darkness gather'd o'er the fields, and light
Was all before, then stepp'd into the stern,
And o'er the rising tide the vessel moved.
We floated on; my comrade never spoke,
And I sat silent, with a lonely sense
Born from the far-off look in his sad eyes.
But once, remembering Charon, I arose
And laid a coin within his idle hand;
He gazed at it in wonder, curved his arm,
And dropp'd it in the waves; and, half abash'd,
I turn'd towards the glories of the sky.
The slanting rays shot up the azure arch
In silver streaks that waned in motes away,
Tinging the fleecy clouds with rainbow hues;
We sail'd on golden ripples, whose light foam
Died on th' horizon's verge, where, half in heaven,
A purple island hung with rosy shores;
While stretching off on either side there shone
White lustrous mountains edged with peaks of fire.
We came anear at last. Delicious airs
Play'd o'er my brow, that brought a faint, rare sound
Of distant harmony; while through my limbs
New vigor ran, that sent the dancing blood
Tingling in languid veins, as each heart-throb
More quick and eager with expectance grew.
In buoyant feelings I had long forgot,
My youth and hope came back to me once more;
And, like the slow uprising of a mist,
There roll'd away the darkness that was laid
Between my mind and things I strove to solve;
Deep, secret meanings dawn'd upon my brain,
That had been dull'd with dust, but in this clime
Saw clear the hidden truth. Sorrow and pain,
That woke such wild, blind prayers, look'd only now
As ministers to purify desire;

And e'en the earth's great riddle that we beat
Rebellious wills 'gainst,—ah! I may not show
What grand significance e'en evil took!
And, as I leap'd upon the shining beach,
I cried, "How few in that old world of woe
E'er dream'd the Happy Island lay so near!"
And such rich rapture stirr'd my grateful soul,
I bent my knee in worship's ecstasy,
Thanking my God that, after years of toil
To know the Truth, and fallings by the way,
My Faith in Him had stood the test of Thought!
But most my spirit thank'd Him that He is!
And, as I rose, one that I knew stood by,
And look'd in mine with eyes as tender, soft
As when we parted—ah! so long ago!
"I knew that you would come!" he said, when first
The bliss of meeting yielded feeling words;
"And I have waited here; for all the joys
Of this fair home were incomplete and poor
Till I had you once more, my life's beloved!
See these green lawns, these shaded, quiet woods,
Where we will walk together, as of yore,
And never change or part, or weep or yearn!
Was it not worth the tears we shed on earth
To love forever in Avilion thus?"
And so we talk'd a while, until I ask'd,
"I marvel that 'tis light here still! 'twas dusk
Beyond there when I started! Does the sun
Ne'er set on this bless'd land?" He gently said,
"At eventime there shall be light!" and then
I knew no night would e'er dispel the glow
That rested on this isle from unseen source.
And afterwards I question'd of the prince,
If yet he dwelt here while the nations wait;
And my dear comrade took my willing hand,
And led me through the shadowy lanes, wherein
He said we might meet Arthur and the queen.

I think mine eyes had glimpses of the views,
Through opening glades, that once my dreams believed
Were parts of all fair countries far away
That I had never seen,—green slopes and swells,
And high hills veil'd in floating, silver mists,
And countless waterfalls, and limpid streams
Where trees droop'd o'er and shaded lotus buds;
And 'neath our feet and all about us bloom'd
Rich, unknown blossoms, and the twining leaves
A dewy freshness bore; and in the midst
I walk'd in silent rapture, such as comes
To human hearts in love's divinest hour,
When speechless bliss o'erfloods the tender gaze
And lifts th' aspiring soul through joy to God!
And there was nothing of the sadness here
That stole through all the Nature I had known,
And made it ever seem like some vain show
In which a spirit grieves; but flowers and sky,
Meadow and stream, were freely, fully bright,
As if the soul of happiness inspired
Their life and beauty, where no sorrow came;
And all the higher pleasures of mere sense
Were so etherealized, we could but feel
A fine expansion, taintless of all flesh!
And, as we walk'd together as of yore,
Slow pacing mid the avenues of trees,
Then through an arching vista I beheld
A street of gold that ran 'twixt crystal domes,
And two that came adown its sparkling slope;
And, as we drew anear, I saw that one
Was grand in presence, kingly, and yet wore
Such courteous, kindly mien, that one who begg'd
Might call him "brother," though he graced a throne!
And clinging to his arm, with white hands link'd,
And small head thrown aback with all its wealth
Of flowing hair, that thus the loving eyes
Might seek the lofty face, was one that seem'd
The very fairest creature e'er I saw.

"Ah! see! they come!" my dear companion said,
"The king and Guinevere!" and, as he ceased,
We met them face to face, and Arthur spake
To one he knew a stranger, in sweet tones
Of simple welcome; and then, mid our talk,
He ask'd, at last, "Do those you left behind
Still keep a thought of me? Do men still hope
That I will come again, as Merlin told,
To do my best to win for them the right?"
And when I drew a picture of the times,
And how the nations groan'd because was found
No strong, true leader pure in life and aim,
He turn'd aside, as if to muse alone;
And one came slowly up between the glades,
On whose worn face there shone a holy smile,
That might have been a seraph's, and stood by
The while the queen ask'd, with a watchful glance
Towards the prince, "Do men on earth still love
As in the olden time? Do ladies keep
Their faith the same in spite of keen despair?"
I answer'd not, but fondly clasp'd the hand
That touch'd mine own, and something in our looks
Spoke more than words unto her woman-sense.
"Ah, well!" she said, without a sigh, or shade
On her smooth brow, "we too loved well as you
In years that are a dream, Isonde and I!
But then we loved with wrong, and pray'd to God,
Long ere we died, to wipe our deep sin out;
And when we came here, all our feelings clung
Whereto they ought, ere led astray by flesh!
See, now I stand by Launcelot, and no thrill
Stirs him or me: I love my lord the king!"
And I, remembering oft-repeated tales
Of their great passion, then towards Launcelot turn'd,
A sudden pity quivering on my mouth;
But he, with glowing brow and shining eyes,
Look'd up as if a vision met his view,
And murmur'd softly, through his parted lips,

"My God! my God! I love but Thee, my God!"
And just then Arthur came to me, and spoke
Like one whose mind has measured some resolve
And master'd it: "The time at last is ripe!
I will go back again! The people need
A chief whose soul knows glories that will lift
His deeds and motives o'er all petty price.
I wore a crown before, and felt its thorns;
And I have known since what it is to live
In heavens won by duty: so I go
To lead the way to truth through seas of blood!
Come with me, while I sit me down once more
Among the knights that shared my Table Round;
For who may tell if I can keep myself
Unscath'd by sin, and here return again?
My own dear queen! I never thought to see
A tear in sweet Avilion! Pray to God,
Who sends me on His errand, that His love
Shall compass me about until the end;
'Twill not be long to wait: you know, beloved,
A thousand years in His sight are a day!"

And so we went together to a vale
Bosom'd in verdant hills, where waters lay,
And round about, upon the lilied lawns,
A goodly company of noble men.
And Arthur sat him on a rising knoll,
With Guinevere's bow'd head upon his breast,
And told his high resolve, and ask'd of each
Some counsel of their wisdom, that his soul
Might carry back into the lives of men
The teachings won through death by heavenly thought.
And as they throng'd about him with deep words,
And deeper meanings, answering to his need
With wondrous axioms that each one had wrung
The pith of from a sharp experience,
I soon was 'ware that, mid the knightly shades
That once for right clash'd swords at Camelot,

Came large-brow'd, lifted heads, light-crown'd like kings;
And these with tuneful voices utter'd slow
Such music, knowledge, and prophetic sense,
I scarce knew which most marvellous seem'd to hear,
So blended with a simple, quiet ease
Was tone melodious and thought sublime.
And in a pause my comrade softly said,
"These are the poets, dear: before, we knew
Their minds by flashes; but from their own lips,
Oft wandering by these everlasting streams,
We now shall share the fulness of their growth,
And hear old strains completed that were left
With something wanting in our other sphere!"

The poets! O my poets! how I long'd
To see your faces once! How your sweet words
Have stirr'd the pulses of my hot young heart
Or still'd its fever! Masters, singers, skalds!
Ye were my friends that never play'd me false,
The teachers ever pointing to the True!
Your names lie gather'd in my inmost soul,
As cherish'd as the flowers that we keep
In token of great happiness and love!
O souls inspired, through whom amid my woe
I stretch'd my hands to God! I look'd on you,
Saw your grand foreheads, heard your voices clear,
And could not tell, for gazing in your eyes,
If white shapes hovering round your steps were they
Whose names your songs made glorious for aye,
The women ye had loved, or angels charm'd
From other heavens by the music here.
I saw ye all, my bards! ay, mine and earth's,
God's and eternity's! Albeit I saw
Where thorns had pierced your brows, and naked feet
Were scarr'd from treading ploughshares red with pain!

My stately Sophocles with Shakspeare walk'd,
Two royal natures mated, with a space

Betwixt their purple and the next who came;
Yet they were men too grand to look on men,
And blinded that they should but see the gods!
One sang to Grecian harp the world's child-faith,
And one its manhood's to a loftier lyre!
Homer and Milton, with majestic eyes,
That saw us tremble at their awful runes!
Then Sappho, with her hand in Tasso's twined,
Her fruitless passion spent in that wild leap
When flashing of her robe the ages thrill'd!
And he sublime through sorrow born of love,
Without a speck of prison-dust to float
'Twixt his fond hope and glories of his dream!
And crush'd Italia's boast, that sets her high
Above the thrones that cannot seize at least
Her great crown-gems, outshining all their power!
Virgil and Dante, with the sadness fled
Their human brows once caught among the lost!
Then Spenser, Chaucer, that had lived so near
To Nature's heart, they show'd us how our own
Throbb'd pulse to pulse with hers! While two grand forms
Came, with a prince between, who loved them well,
And made himself a prouder tomb than his
Of the same name who slept enthroned at Aix!
For, dropping out the sceptre from his hand,
He laid him down at last betwixt the dust
That bore eternal fames, and link'd his grave
On either side to sacred soil for aye!
The rare completed man of many lives,
Whose eager search strove ever towards the truth,
And sang the gleams he caught in deathless notes,
Great Goethe show'd in meanings of his speech
That earth's unquiet quest was found at last!
And that fine nature, brother of his mind,
True lover of the beautiful and free,
Schiller, who trod the highest paths of Art,
With Carl of Weimar looking upon both
As Saul might once have gazed upon the seer

That pour'd anointing oil upon his head!
Byron and Burns, those passionate, rich souls,
That here, unfetter'd from all scorn and ill
And weakness of the flesh, had grown sublime
By living purely out their higher selves;
Inspired of genius still, whose burning words
Startled a glance of fire to Arthur's eyes,
That faded into awe as solemn rose
The voice of one amid the moment's hush
That might have been a prophet of the Lord
To shake and gather spirits in the world,
If time and reason could have cast from life
The hot dreams of his youth ere death had led
His seeing mind unto the Fount of Light!
And after Shelley, with his trembling lips
Uttering low music into language breathed,
Endymion pass'd, who left to mark his rest
The record of a name in water writ,
And found his high thoughts known beyond the stars!
And as they moved aside, they group'd around
A fair, slight form but late come in their midst,
That stood within the circle of their tones
Calmly as one who long had known each soul,
Yet with a gladness shining on her face
Like to an exile's who is welcomed home
By old familiar voices, answering all
With some remember'd token of the past!
The mighty ancients spoke to her in words
As musical as choruses they sung;
The soul-blind minstrels of dim, distant days
Stood side by side with martyrs who had mix'd
The last triumphant strains of holy lives
With hatred's incense of ascending flames;
And all sublime and tender hearts that loved
And gave love language in their native tongues
That won new harmony from notes divine;
And they who play'd on lutes by sorrow tuned,
Or lifted nations, in a burst of song,

From deep despair to heights of conquering faith,—
These talk'd with her as one whom their blest sight
Saw worthy evermore to walk with them
In amaranthine fields 'neath trees that bear
The leaves of knowledge and the fruit of life!
And some there were that breathed in broken sounds
Such thrilling, earnest thoughts, I could but feel
That they had been the voiceless ones of earth,
Trying their new-won power with timid lips,
As children stammer ere they learn to speak!
Yet, as all cluster'd round the central shape,
As in the skies the constellations range
About a single star, ofttimes less bright
And smaller than the suns that orbit it,
She spoke some reverent word that drew reply,
Pointing her hands towards the far-off world,
Then towards the glowing beams of changeless light
Wherein the good king sat among his knights;
And all the streams and woods, and hills and vales,
Gave solemn echo to the glad refrain,
Suiting all time when wrong by right is slain,
Of "Pan, Great Pan is dead! Pan, Pan is dead!"

And, as the last note floated low away,
Arthur arose, and shoreward turn'd his steps,
And all the company went with him there;
Launcelot and Galahad on either side
Walk'd, with their lustrous faces, though one show'd
That pureness had belong'd to it from birth,
And to the other came through pain and death;
Then Bors and Bedivere, Sir Gareth, Kaye,
Tristan and Pellinore, Gawaine and Urre,
And all the other proud, familiar names
That shook the lists with shoutings in old days.
And the fair queen, after quick rain of tears,
With head uplifted like to one who sees
The bow of promise, all the storm forgot
In listening to the music of the bards.

And when we came upon the sparkling beach,
The barge was waiting, but the helmsman now
Was a great seraph, crown'd, with wings outspread,
Whose glory circled him as rays the sun.
And Arthur enter'd in, and round his form
The angel's radiance made wondrous light.
And some would fain have shared with him again
This new adventure; but he simply said,
"'Twas written I should go alone! my work
Needs not that more be banish'd from their heaven!
Nay, nay, dear friends! It is the will of God!"
And at the sacred Name all bow'd their heads
And let him pass, and, as the vessel heaved
On waves of golden light, the air seem'd full
Of glorious faces and of snowy plumes,
And over us unnumber'd voices join'd
In such sweet harmony, it swell'd the tears
In speechless ecstasy from my touch'd heart.
And then—and then—was it the stirring sail
Or sudden silence broke the marvellous spell?
Alas! I know not! only, in a flash,
I found myself once more within this world,
On which the shades had gather'd into night,
And mid the throng that wait the Coming King!

The Christmas of Sir Galahad

Elizabeth Stuart Phelps

When a fancy, fashioned neither after the inductive nor the deductive methods, attributable neither to natural selection nor to protoplasm, definable by no law of contradiction nor of excluded middle, presents itself to the public acquaintance nowadays, it is apt, as we all know, to receive rather a sorry welcome. And when, after the sadly tardy discovery of the Lady of Shalott, in South Street, one of those remarkable rumors, credence to which is at once a danger and a delight, stole about town, it stole on tiptoe, looking over its shoulder meanwhile at corners with one soft sly eye on the police and another on the daily press, and a startled glance at the fashionable churches, and a tender shudder at the shadow of the "Institute," and its beautiful finger at its lips—making thus slow progress, and, for every warmhearted faith which it shook by the outstretched hand, leaving two doubts to close ranks behind it.

Such as it is, however, and for what it may mean, this is the whisper. It would be found, so it is said, had we the eyes that see or the ears that hear either signs or sounds of such a matter, that certain of the old romances which we have been accustomed to regard as finished and fated for all time are, in fact, re-enacting and repeating themselves, with a timidity amounting almost to stealth, in the chilling and alien climate of our modern civilization: that steam has not scorched out valor, nor the telegraph overtaken chivalry, nor universal suffrage extinguished loyalty; that the golden years did not go dumbly to their graves, as we are wont to think; that they have arisen, like Lazarus, with their chin-cloths on, acquainted with things unlawful to utter—reserved, still visitors, shunned and strange. It is breathed that there somewhere walks the earth to-day the Blameless King; it is hinted that there somewhere hides the Mismated Queen; it has been said that at times the Vanished Knights of the Round Table gather together in strange guise, to stranger conclave; that a student familiar with their story would be well puzzled should he stumble upon them; that Sir Percivale has been seen in a Pennsylvania coal-mine; that Bohort was discovered in New York one day, in a bricklayer's apron, with a trowel in his hand; that Isoude the Fair was all but identified in a hospital at Washington during the War of the Rebellion; that Launcelot, penitent and pale, may be heard, if one is so fortunate as to trace him, in the form of a certain street preacher, but little known, who gathers ill-favored men and women about him in an unsavory part of the town at the decline of the Sunday afternoon; that Guinevere is rumored to spend much time alone in a chamber looking toward the west, engaged in keeping a certain watch which has been set her, for a peril and a promise which no man knows; that Arthur himself filled a post of high official importance at Washington not long ago, and, escaping identification through two terms' service, disappeared suddenly and mysteriously from public life; that, in short, a Romance never died, nor ever will, but is adjudged to be the only immortal thing on earth, save the soul of man.

As much as this, in common with a few others, so far favored, I had heard and forgotten, till chance threw the whole chain of pretty dreams before me, by lassooing one link around my very hands. As much as this I found myself compelled to recall with more than common thoughtfulness when I came face to face with Sir Galahad at a butcher's stall, last Christmas morning.

Did you ever know a lost knight to be found until a woman tracked him? Is it, therefore, surprising that if it had not been for Rebecca Rock, Sir Galahad Holt would have escaped recognition completely, and the modest number of men and women now admitted to the secret of the discovery have gone the hungrier and the sadder for the loss?

It was always a matter of deep scientific speculation to Rebecca Rock why, when she came to town to find work in the neck-tie factory, she should have chosen lodgings in the second back corner of 16½ Primrose Court. She would say: "If I had hit on the western side!" or, "If I had been able to pay the rent of that room opposite the factory!" or, "How near I came to settling on the little south attic of 17!"

And she sat and mused upon it with a puzzled face. If, indeed! What an "If" it was! Such an If as there would have been in the world if that other Rebecca had taken the wrong road and missed of meeting Isaac in the desert at the set of the sun; or if Eve had lost her way in the shrubbery of Eden, and just happened not to find Adam till nobody knows when!

Perhaps, too, such an If as there would have been if Heloise had never gone to school to Abelard, or Di Rimini had never seen her lover's face? The world would have lost a grand temptation. So much as that, Rebecca Rock, cutting "foundation" into strips for the public neck, eleven hours a day, confusedly felt; but she had never heard of Heloise, and if she had been obliged to sit beside Francesca Di Rimini in the necktie factory she would have shrunk in the wounded wonder of a snow-drift from a foot-mark.

How long it was before Galahad Holt, coming home from the organ factory at seven o'clock to his solitary ground-floor lodging at 16½, noticed the tall woman in the blanket shawl, who came a little later and passed his door in going up-stairs; how long before a sense of anything more than tallness and a shawl occurred to him; how soon he noticed the outline of her arm when the shawl fell from it, as she laid her large, strong hand upon the banisters; when he first observed the regular, calm echo which her step left upon the croaking stairs; when first he met her carrying a pail of water from the Court, and instead of feeling moved to carry it for her, only thought how evenly she carried it for herself; when first she smiled at suddenly observing him; when first he gravely said good-morning; when first he gravely joined her if they chanced upon the same side of the street in passing to and fro from work; how first he gravely learned to discuss with her the fall in wages, and the wind we had on Saturday, the rise in coal, and the sunset there would be to-night; and when first he gravely came to feel that wind, and fuel, sun and pay-day were no longer common matters for the common world in consequence, but a heritage of his and her discovery, ownership, and wealth, is not accurately known.

Strictly speaking, he himself knew accurately nothing. He worked, he ate, he slept; he shut himself into his lonely lodging (it was so singular, said all the Court, in Sir Galahad to board himself!); suns rose and set; she smiled and came and went; but he knew distinctly nothing. Nothing till, once upon a Sunday afternoon, he followed her to a little mission church they knew, sat on a wooden bench and watched her sing; but left in the middle of the chorus, and went abruptly home. He shut and locked the door; he stood still in the middle of the room.

"God bless her!" he said aloud. But he sat down and covered his face with his grimy, princely hands, and flushed as if he had done her a deadly wrong.

Had he the right to take a woman into his swept and garnished heart, even long enough to bless her in God's name and let her go? "It would turn to curses," said Sir Galahad, "upon us both. I will not bless her." Now he turned his head, at this, and saw her coming up the Court. "I will not, will not!" said Sir Galahad. But all his soul rose up and went to meet her, and laid its hands upon her head in benediction. And when Sir Galahad felt within himself that this was so, he fell upon his knees, and there remained till midnight. And in the morning he arose with a countenance as calm as ever knight wore in love or death or victory, and went away in his blue overalls to work, with his dinner-pail upon his arm, and nodded gravely to Rebecca; but smiled little and spoke less.

And so the Lady Rebecca, grieved and puzzled in her heart, would have dropped a tear or two upon her foundation strips, but for a heat upon her cheeks that burned and dried them all the day; and so at night, being feverish and wakeful, and, stepping down into the Court at an early hour for fresh water, she came suddenly upon a woman clambering into Sir Galahad's low window.

So she dropped her pail, and, in the icy swash that fell about her feet, sat down to catch her breath.

There, in the mud-puddle which the chilly water made, Sir Galahad found her sitting, when he had shut his window, had turned the key in his door, had come out, and had stopped and stood beside her.

"That's my wife, Rebecca, I've just locked in, in there," said Sir Galahad, standing in the starlight. "Will you come to the window and take a look at her?"

"I'd rather not," said Rebecca from her mud-puddle; but she rose, and shook the spatter from her clothes.

"Very well," said Galahad.

"You never told me," said Rebecca, picking up her pail, "that you had a wife, Sir Galahad!"

"I never thought of it till yesterday," said Galahad. "I ought to have. I ask your pardon, Miss Rebecca. She's crazy."

"Oh!" said the Lady Rebecca, stretching out her strong, large hand; but she drew it back, and hid it in her shawl.

"And takes opium," said Galahad Holt, patiently, "and is up to pretty much everything. It's going on six year now sence she left me. But she keeps a coming on me unexpected. The ground floor's saved a deal of talk and shame, I think; don't you? I thought I'd best keep house for her, all things taken in't the count, don't you? Sometimes I think she'll slick herself up a little and stay. But in a day or two she's off. She's got the Old Un in her head to-night," said Galahad.

"It's very hard; it's very, very hard!" Rebecca moaned.

"Rebecca Rock," said Sir Galahad, solemnly, "it's a curious place and time to say it; but I think there'll never come a better—"

"Oh! no," said Rebecca.

"And I may as well out with it, my girl, first as last, and once for all, and tell you how, if *you'd* been my wife, instead of her, I couldn't have loved you truer nor more single in my heart than I love you in the sight of God and these here stars this wretched night. And I'm a married man!"

"Oh! yes, yes!" said Rebecca.

"But I'm a married man," said he.

"People unmarry," said she.

She looked in a frightened way about the Court, at the stars, at the pump, at the mud-puddle; she gasped and thrust her hand out, but drew it back within her shawl. Sir Galahad did not touch it.

"I suppose," said Sir Galahad, very slowly, "as I could get divorced from Merry Ann. I've thought o't. I thought o't yesterday a long while. But it seems to me as if I'd better not. She'd be a coming back, ye see. Anyways, she'd be a living on this living arth. We might be meeting her face to face most any day. It seems to me, Rebecca, as if it was agin Natur for me to marry any woman while Merry Ann's a living creetur. How does it seem to you?"

"Galahad Holt," said Rebecca, "I'm not so good as you, and I'm very fond of you."

"For God's sake, don't tell me o't!" cried Sir Galahad.

"Well, I won't," said Rebecca.

"For, if it's agin Natur," said Sir Galahad, lifting his face to the stars above Primrose Court, "it's agin God. And rather than *be* agin them two I'd be on't the safe side, it seems to me."

"Very well," said Rebecca.

"So I think we'll wait," said Sir Galahad, taking off his hat and holding out his hand.

"Is the safe side always the right side, Galahad?" asked Rebecca.

"I don't exactly know," said Sir Galahad, with a puzzled face.

"Nor I," said Rebecca; "but I think we'll wait."

"Some folks wouldn't," said Sir Galahad. "But I don't see as that makes any odds."

"No," said Rebecca. So they shook hands, while Sir Galahad stood with his hat off beneath the stars; and the Lady Rebecca picked up her pail from the mud-puddle, and went up-stairs; and Sir Galahad went to the grocer's to get a little tea for his wife; and the world ran on as if nothing had happened.

Now the world had been running on quite as if nothing would ever happen again for four years, when Sir Galahad's Christmas came. And the Lady Rebecca had walked alone to the neck-tie factory; and Galahad had kept house on the ground floor; and Rebecca had lain sick of a deadly fever, and Sir Galahad had lost six months' wages in a strike; and the man's face had grown gaunt, and the woman's old, and his had pinched and hers had paled:—yet their hands had never met since they stood by the pump in the starlight; nor had Sir Galahad's knightly foot once crossed the croaking stairs which bore the regular, calm feet of the Lady

Rebecca to the solitary second back corner of 16½; nor had he said, God bless her! when she sung at the little church, lest, indeed, his whole soul should rise up perforce, and choose cursing for blessing and death for life.

And if Di Rimini had worked beside Rebecca at the neck-tie factory, she would have learned a royal lesson. And Abelard might well have sat at the feet of Galahad, making organs with his grimy hands. And if Eve or Isaac had wandered into the first floor front, or second back corner of 16½, on a lonesome, rainy evening, they would have wept for pity, and smiled for blessing, and mused much.

Now, it was on a rainy evening, with melting snow upon the ground and melting chills upon the wind, that the Lady Rebecca, crooked and crouching by her little lamp, sat darning stockings for Sir Galahad—a questionable exercise of taste, we must admit. She had not even offered to embroider him a banner, nor to net him a silken favor, nor to fringe so much as a scarf for the next tourna-ment to be held in Primrose Court. She had only said: "Will it be proper?" And he said: "Ask the landlady." And the landlady had said: "Law, yes!" And the Lady Rebecca had said: "Bring all you have." And Sir Galahad said: "I haven't got but two pairs to my name." And so here she was, crouching and darning and crooked, by her little lamp, when a knock startled the door of the second back corner of 16½ till it shook for fright to its sunken hinges, and the Lady Rebecca shook for sympathy till she opened the door, and shook on her own account when she had.

For Sir Galahad Holt stood in the door, erect and pale.

"I did not hear you on the stairs!" gasped the Lady Rebecca.

"I couldn't come up them stairs in my boots someway," said Sir Galahad, very huskily. Now the Lady Rebecca did not altogether understand in her own mind what Sir Galahad meant; but she saw that his feet lay bare and white upon her threshold—since, indeed, poor man! she had his stockings—and a fancy as of patient pilgrims came to her, and a dream of holy ground. But she said:

"Did you come to get the stockings?" But Sir Galahad answered solemnly:

"Did you think I'd cross the stairway till I came for you? Merry Ann's down below, Rebecca. Will you be afraid to step down with me?"

Where would Rebecca have been afraid to step with him? She followed him down the stairs, which would have croaked, it seemed, but could not, beneath Sir Galahad's solemn, shining feet.

Merry Ann was below, indeed—at length upon Sir Galahad's floor, before the cook-stove, a sickening, silent heap. A little shawl was tied about her head, and her face was hidden by her arm.

"I but just come in and found her," said Sir Galahad, in his commonplace, unromantic way; "and I thought I'd tell you what had happened, Rebecca, before the coroner was called. I don't think it was a fit. She'd walked a distance, I can't but think, and hoped to have catched a look at me. Poor Merry Ann!"

"Poor Merry Ann!" said Rebecca Rock, with all her heart. She had fallen on her knees beside the dead, and had dropped her face into her hands.

"And now, Rebecca," said Sir Galahad. "Now, Rebecca—" But when he saw her on her knees he dropped beside her and said no more. And when the landlady came in they did not ask her if it were proper; but she said "Law, yes!" as if they had, and turned her face away.

"And now, Rebecca," said Sir Galahad again—"now the grave is covered decent, and the room is swept, and the storm is over, and I've waited four years for you honest, in the sight of God and the stars o' Heaven, and Christmas comes o' Monday—"

"Very well," said Rebecca.

"I don't seem," said Sir Galahad, "to have the words I thought I had to say, my girl. I'd got so used waiting; hadn't you? I do not rightly see my way to take it natural and safe. I think I'd not like, nor dare, my dear, to have it any other day than Christmas Day; would you?"

I was glad there was no wind on Christmas, and that the snow lay drifted over from a little, laughing storm; and that the sun brooded with golden wings in the Primrose Court; and that the town was full of holly; and that the Lady Rebecca had a spray of myrtle in her large, firm hand, when she walked with Sir Galahad to the minister's front door.

And when I met Sir Galahad at the meat-stall, buying steak for dinner, and saw the eyes and smile he carried in the sight of God and Christmas Day, I bethought me of the records of the Spotless Knight; how he—tried, stainless, and alone—was found worthy to be the guardian ("pure in thought and word and deed") of the blessed cup from which our Lord drank the last wine which should touch his lips till he drank it new in the kingdom of the Father; how his mortal eyes beheld it, palled in red samite, treasured by "a great fellowship of angels"; how his mortal hand laid hold of it and Heaven, and his mortal name grew to be a holy thing upon the lips of men forever; and how since then "was there never one so hardy as to say that he had seen the Sangreal on earth any more."

"Sir Galahad," said I, "you have found the Sangreal, and I have found you!"

But he, smiling, shook his head.

"I don't feel altogether sure. It seems to me a man don't know what he's found till he's learned to bear his happiness as he bore his longing for't, and his waiting, and his loss. But I can't help hoping, somehow, that I'm fit to be married on a Christmas Day."

Elaine and Elaine

Elizabeth Stuart Phelps

I.

Dead, she drifted to his feet.
Tell us, Love, is Death so sweet?

Oh! the river floweth deep.
Fathoms deeper is her sleep.

Oh! the current driveth strong.
Wilder tides drive souls along.

Drifting, though he loved her not,
To the heart of Launcelot,

Let her pass; it is her place.
Death hath given her this grace.

Let her pass; she resteth well.
What her dreams are, who can tell?

Mute the steersman; why, if he
Speaketh not a word, should we?

II.

Dead, she drifteth to his feet.
Close, her eyes keep secrets sweet.

Living, he had loved her well.
High as Heaven and deep as Hell.

Yet that voyage she stayeth not.
Wait you for her, Launcelot?

Oh! the river floweth fast.
Who is justified at last?

Locked her lips are. Hush! If she
Sayeth nothing, how should we?

The Lady of Shalott

ELIZABETH STUART PHELPS

It is not generally known that the Lady of Shalott lived last summer in an attic, at the east end of South Street.

The wee-est, thinnest, whitest little lady! And yet the brightest, stillest, and ah, such a smiling little lady!

If you had held her up by the window—for she could not hold up herself— she would have hung like a porcelain transparency in your hands. And if you had said, laying her gently down, and giving the tears a smart dash, that they should not fall on her lifted face, "Poor child!" the Lady of Shalott would have said, "Oh, don't!" and smiled. And you would have smiled yourself, for very surprise that she should outdo you; and between the two there would have been so much smiling done that one would have fairly thought that it was a delightful thing to live last summer in an attic at the east end of South Street.

This, perhaps, was the more natural in the Lady of Shalott because she had never lived anywhere else.

When the Lady of Shalott was five years old, her mother threw her downstairs one day, by mistake, instead of the whiskey-jug.

This is a fact which I think Mr. Tennyson has omitted to mention in his poem.

They picked the Lady of Shalott up and put her on the bed; and there she lay from that day until last summer, unless, as I said, somebody had occasion to use her for a transparency.

The mother and the jug both went down the stairs together a few years after, and never came up at all; and that was a great convenience, for the Lady of Shalott's palace in the attic was not large, and they took up much unnecessary room.

Since that the Lady of Shalott had lived with her sister, Sary Jane.

Sary Jane made nankeen vests, at sixteen and three-quarter cents a dozen.

Sary Jane had red hair, and crooked shoulders, and a voice so much like the snap of a rat-trap which she sometimes set on the stairs, that the Lady of Shalott could seldom tell which was which until she had thought about it a little while. When there was a rat caught, she was apt to ask, "What?" and when Sary Jane spoke she more often than not said, "There's another!"

Her crooked shoulders Sary Jane had acquired from sitting under the eaves of the palace to sew. That physiological problem was simple. There was not room enough under the eaves to sit straight.

Sary Jane's red hair was the result of sitting in the sun on July noons under those eaves, to see to thread her needle. There was no question about that. The Lady of Shalott had settled it in her own mind, past dispute. Sary Jane's hair had been—what was it? brown? once. Sary Jane was slowly taking fire. Who would not, to sit in the sun in that palace? The only matter of surprise to the Lady of Shalott was that the palace itself did not smoke. Sometimes, when Sary Jane hit the rafters, she was sure that she saw sparks.

As for Sary Jane's voice, when one knew that she made nankeen vests at sixteen and three-quarter cents a dozen, *that* was a matter of no surprise. It never surprised the Lady of Shalott.

But Sary Jane was very cross; there was no denying that; very cross.

And the palace. Let me tell you about the palace. It measured just twelve by nine feet. It would have been seven feet post—if there had been a post in the middle of it. From the centre it sloped away to the windows, where Sary Jane had just room enough to sit crooked under the eaves at work. There were two windows and a loose scuttle to the palace. The scuttle let in the snow in winter and the sun in summer, and the rain and wind at all times. It was quite a diversion to the Lady of Shalott to see how many different ways of doing a disagreeable thing seemed to be practicable to that scuttle. Besides the bed on which the Lady of Shalott lay, there was a stove in the palace, two chairs, a very ragged rag-mat, a shelf, with two notched cups and plates upon it, one pewter teaspoon, and a looking-glass. On washing-days Sary Jane climbed upon the chair and hung her clothes out through the scuttle on the roof; or else she ran a little rope from one of the windows to the other for a drying-rope. It would have been more exact to have said on washing-nights; for Sary Jane always did her washing after dark. The reason was evident. If the rest of us were in the habit of wearing all the clothes we had, like Sary Jane, I have little doubt that we should do the same.

I should mention that there was no sink in the Lady of Shalott's palace; no water. There was a dirty hydrant in the yard, four flights below, which supplied the Lady of Shalott and all her neighbors. The Lady of Shalott kept her coal under the bed; her flour, a pound at a time, in a paper parcel, on the shelf, with the tea-cups and the pewter spoon. If she had anything else to keep, it went out through the palace scuttle and lay on the roof. The Lady of Shalott's palace opened directly upon a precipice. The lessor of the house called it a flight of stairs. When Sary Jane went up and down, she went sideways to preserve her balance. There were no banisters to the precipice. The entry was dark. Some dozen or twenty of the Lady of Shalott's neighbors patronized the precipice, and about once a week a baby patronized the rat-trap, instead. Once, when there was a fire-alarm, the preci-pice was very serviceable. Four women and an old man went over. With one ex-ception (she was eighteen, and could bear a broken collar-bone), they will not, I am informed, go over again.

The Lady of Shalott paid one dollar a week for the rent of her palace.

But then there was a looking-glass in the palace. I think I noticed it. It hung on the slope of the rafters, just opposite the Lady of Shalott's window,—for she considered that her window at which Sary Jane did not make nankeen vests at sixteen and three-quarter cents a dozen.

Now, because the looking-glass was opposite the window at which Sary Jane did *not* make vests, and because the rafters sloped, and because the bed lay al-most between the looking-glass and the window, the Lady of Shalott was happy. And because, to the patient heart that is a seeker after happiness "the little more, and how much it is!" (and the little less, what worlds away!) the Lady of Shalott was proud as well as happy. The looking-glass measured in inches ten by six. I think that the Lady of Shalott would have experienced rather a touch of mortification than of envy if she had known that there was a mirror in a house just around the corner measuring almost as many feet. But that was one of the advantages of be-ing the Lady of Shalott. She never parsed life in the comparative degree.

I suppose that one must go through a process of education to understand what comfort there may be in a ten by six inch looking-glass. All the world came for the Lady of Shalott into her little looking-glass,—the joy of it, the anguish of it, the hope and fear of it, the health and hurt,—ten by six inches of it exactly.

"It is next best to not having been thrown down-stairs yourself!" said the Lady of Shalott.

To tell the truth, it sometimes occurred to her that there was a monotony about the world. A garret window like her own, for instance, would fill her sight if she did not tip the glass a little. Children sat in it, and did not play. They made lean faces at her. They were locked in for the day, and were hungry. She could not help knowing how hungry they were, and so tipped the glass. Then there was the trap-door in the sidewalk. She became occasionally tired of that trap-door. Seven people lived under the sidewalk; and when they lifted and slammed the trap, coming in and out, they reminded her of something which Sary Jane bought her once, when she was a very little child, at Christmas time,—long ago, when rents were cheaper and flour low. It was a monkey, with whiskers and a calico jacket, who jumped out of a box when the cover was lifted; and then you crushed him down and hasped him in. Sometimes she wished she had never had that monkey, he was so much like the people coming out of the sidewalk.

In fact, there was a monotony about all the people in the Lady of Shalott's looking-glass. If their faces were not dirty, their hands were. It they had hats they went without shoes. If they did not sit in the sun with their heads on their knees, they lay in the mud with their heads on a jug.

"Their faces look blue!" she said to Sary Jane.

"No wonder!" snapped Sary Jane.

"Why?" asked the Lady of Shalott.

"Wonder is we ain't all dead!" barked Sary Jane.

"But we ain't, you know," said the Lady of Shalott, after some thought.

The people in the Lady of Shalott's glass died, however, sometimes,—often in the summer; more often last summer, when the attic smoked continually, and she mistook Sary Jane's voice for the rat-trap every day.

The people were jostled into pine boxes (in the glass), and carried away (in the glass) by twilight, in a cart. Three of the monkeys from the spring-box in the sidewalk went, in one week, out into foul, purple twilight, away from the looking-glass, in carts.

"I'm glad of that, poor things!" said the Lady of Shalott, for she had always felt a kind of sorrow for the monkeys. Principally, I think, because they had no glass.

When the monkeys had gone, the sickly twilight folded itself up, over the spring-box, into great feathers, like the feathers of a wing. That was pleasant. The Lady of Shalott could almost put out her fingers and stroke it, it hung so near, and was so clear, and brought such a peacefulness into the looking glass.

"Sary Jane, dear, it's very pleasant," said the Lady of Shalott. Sary Jane said, it was very dangerous, the Lord knew, and bit her threads off.

"And Sary Jane, dear!" added the Lady of Shalott, "I see so many other pleasant things."

"The more fool you!" said Sary Jane.

But she wondered about it that day over her tenth nankeen vest. What, for example, *could* the Lady of Shalott see?

"Waves!" said the Lady of Shalott, suddenly, as if she had been asked the question. Sary Jane jumped. She said, "Nonsense!" For the Lady of Shalott had only seen the little wash-tub full of dingy water on Sunday nights, and the dirty little hydrant (in the glass) spouting dingy jets. She would not have known a wave if she had seen it.

"But I see waves," said the Lady of Shalott. She felt sure of it. They ran up and down across the glass. They had green faces and gray hair. They threw back their hands, like cool people resting, and it seemed unaccountable, at the east end of South Street last summer, that anything, anywhere, if only a wave in a looking-glass, could be cool or at rest. Besides this, they kept their faces clean. Therefore the Lady of Shalott took pleasure in watching them run up and down across the glass. That a thing could be clean, and green, and white, was only less a wonder than cool and rest last summer in South Street.

"Sary Jane, dear," said the Lady of Shalott, one day, "how hot *is* it up here?"

"Hot as Hell!" said Sary Jane.

"I thought it was a little warm," said the Lady of Shalott. "Sary Jane, dear? Isn't the yard down there a little—dirty?"

Sary Jane put down her needles and looked out of the blazing, blindless window. It had always been a subject of satisfaction, to Sary Jane somewhere down below her lean shoulders and in the very teeth of the rat-trap, that the Lady of Shalott could not see out of that window. So she winked at the window, as if she would caution it to hold its burning tongue, and said never a word.

"Sary Jane, dear," said the Lady of Shalott, once more, "had you ever thought that perhaps I was a little—weaker—than I was—once?"

"I guess you can stand it if I can!" said the rat-trap.

"Oh, yes, dear," said the Lady of Shalott. "I can stand it if you can."

"Well, then!" said Sary Jane. But she sat and winked at the bald window, and the window held its burning tongue.

It grew hot in South Street. It grew very hot in South Street. The lean children, in the attic opposite, fell sick, and sat no longer in the window making faces, in the Lady of Shalott's glass.

Two more monkeys from the spring-box were carried away one ugly twilight in a cart. The purple wing that hung over the spring-box lifted to let them pass; and then fell, as if it had brushed them away.

"It has such a soft color!" said the Lady of Shalott, smiling.

"So has nightshade!" said Sary Jane.

One day a beautiful thing happened. One could scarcely understand how a beautiful thing *could* happen at the east end of South Street. The Lady of Shalott herself did not entirely understand.

"It is all the glass," she said.

She was lying very still when she said it. She had folded her hands, which were hot, to keep them quiet, too. She had closed her eyes, which ached, to close away the glare of the noon. At once she opened them, and said:—

"It is the glass."

Sary Jane stood in the glass. Now Sary Jane, she well knew, was not in the room that noon. She had gone out to see what she could find for dinner. She had five cents to spend on dinner. Yet Sary Jane stood in the glass. And in the glass, ah! what a beautiful thing!

"Flowers!" cried the Lady of Shalott aloud. But she had never seen flowers. But neither had she seen waves. So she said, "They come as the waves come;" and knew them, and lay smiling. Ah! what a beautiful, beautiful thing!

Sary Jane's hair was fiery and tumbled (in the glass), as if she had walked fast and far. Sary Jane (in the glass) was winking, as she had winked at the blazing window; as if she said to what she held in her arms, Don't tell! And in her arms (in the glass), where the waves were—oh! beautiful, beautiful! The Lady of Shalott lay whispering: "Beautiful, beautiful!" She did not know what else to do. She dared not stir. Sary Jane's lean arms (in the glass) were full of silver bells; they hung out of a soft green shadow, like a church tower; they nodded to and fro: when they shook, they shook out sweetness.

"Will they ring?" asked the Lady of Shalott of the little glass.

I doubt, in my own mind, if you or I, being in South Street, and seeing a lily of the valley (in a ten by six inch looking-glass) for the very first time, would have asked so sensible a question.

"Try 'em and see," said the looking-glass. Was it the looking-glass? Or the rat-trap? Or was it—

Oh, the beautiful thing! That the glass should have nothing to do with it, after all! That Sary Jane, in flesh and blood, and tumbled hair, and trembling, lean arms, should stand and shake an armful of church towers and silver bells down into the Lady of Shalott's little puzzled face and burning hands!

And that the Lady of Shalott should think that she must have got into the glass herself, by a blunder,—as the only explanation possible of such a beautiful thing!

"No, it isn't glass-dreams," said Sary Jane, winking at the church towers, where they made a solemn green shadow against the Lady of Shalott's poor cheek. "Smell 'em, and see! You can 'most stand the yard with them round. Smell 'em and see! It ain't the glass; it's the Flower Charity."

"The what?" asked the Lady of Shalott, slowly.

"The Flower Charity. Heaven bless it!"

"Heaven bless it!" said the Lady of Shalott. But she said nothing more.

She laid her cheek over into the shadow of the leaves. "And there'll be more," said Sary Jane, hunting for her wax. "There'll be more, whenever I can call for 'em—bless it!"

"Heaven bless it!" said the Lady of Shalott again.

"But I only got a lemon for dinner," said Sary Jane.

"Heaven bless it!" said the Lady of Shalott, with her face hidden under the leaves. But I don't think that she meant the lemon, though Sary Jane did.

"They *do* ring," said the Lady of Shalott, by and by. She drew the tip of her thin fingers across the tip of the tiny bells. "I thought they would."

"Humph!" said Sary Jane, squeezing her lemon under her work-box. "I never see your beat for glass-dreams. What do they say? Come, now!"

Now the Lady of Shalott knew very well what they said. Very well! But she only drew the tips of her poor fingers over the tips of the silver bells. Never mind! It was not necessary to tell Sary Jane.

But it grew hot in South Street. It grew very hot in South Street. Even the Flower Charity (bless it!) could not sweeten the dreadfulness of that yard. Even the purple wing above the spring-box fell heavily upon the Lady of Shalott's strained eyes, across the glass. Even the gray-haired waves ceased running up and down and throwing back their hands before her; they sat still, in heaps upon a blistering beach, and gasped for breath. The Lady of Shalott herself gasped sometimes, in watching them.

One day she said: "There's a man in them."

"A *what* in *which?*" buzzed Sary Jane. "Oh! There's a man across the yard, I suppose you mean. Among them young ones, yonder. I wish he'd stop 'em throwing stones, plague on 'em! See him, don't you?"

"I don't see the children," said the Lady of Shalott, a little troubled. Her glass had shown her so many things strangely since the days grew hot. "But I see a man, and he walks upon the waves. See, see!"

The Lady of Shalott tried to pull herself up on the elbow of her calico nightdress, to see.

"That's one of them Hospital doctors," said Sary Jane, looking out of the blazing window. "I've seen him round before. Don't know what business he's got down here; but I've seen him. He's talking to them boys now, about the stones. There! He'd better! If they don't look out, they'll hit"—

"*Oh the glass! the glass!*"

The Hospital Doctor stood still, so did Sary Jane, half risen from her chair;

so did the very South Street boys, gaping in the gutter, with their hands full of stones,—such a cry rang out from the palace window.

"*Oh, the glass! the glass! the glass!*"

In a twinkling the South Street boys were at the mercy of the South Street police; and the Hospital Doctor, bounding over a beachful of shattered, scattered waves, stood, out of breath, beside the Lady of Shalott's bed.

"Oh the little less and what worlds away."

The Lady of Shalott lay quite still in her brown calico night-gown [I cannot learn, by the way, that Bulfinch's studious and in general trustworthy researches have put him in possession of this point. Indeed, I feel justified in asserting that Mr. Bulfinch never so much as *intimated* that the Lady of Shalott wore a brown calico night-dress]—the Lady of Shalott lay quite still, and her lips turned blue.

"Are you very much hurt? Where were you struck? I heard the cry, and came. Can you tell me where the blow was?"

But then the Doctor saw the glass, broken and blown in a thousand glittering sparks across the palace floor: and then the Lady of Shalott gave him a little blue smile.

"It's not me. Never mind, I wish it was. I'd rather it was me than the glass. Oh, my glass! My glass! But never mind. I suppose there'll be some other—pleasant thing."

"Were you so fond of the glass?" asked the Doctor, taking one of the two chairs that Sary Jane brought him, and looking sorrowfully about the room. What other "pleasant thing" could even the Lady of Shalott discover in that room last summer, at the east end of South Street?

"How long have you lain here?" asked the sorrowful Doctor, suddenly.

"Since I can remember, sir," said the Lady of Shalott, with that blue smile. "But then I have always had my glass."

"Ah!" said the Doctor, "the Lady of Shalott!"

"Sir?" said the Lady of Shalott.

"Where is the pain?" asked the Doctor, gently, with his finger on the Lady of Shalott's pulse.

The Lady of Shalott touched the shoulders of her brown calico night-dress, smiling.

"And what did you see in your glass?" asked the Doctor, once more, stooping to examine "the pain."

The Lady of Shalott tried to tell him, but felt confused. So she only said that there were waves and a purple wing, and that they were broken now, and lay upon the floor.

"Purple wings?" asked the Doctor.

"Over the sidewalk," nodded the Lady of Shalott. "It comes up at night."

"Oh!" said the Doctor, "the malaria. No wonder!"

"And what about the waves?" asked the Doctor, talking while he touched and tried the little brown calico shoulders. "I have a little girl of my own down by the waves this summer. She—I suppose she is no older than you!"

"I am seventeen, sir," said the Lady of Shalott. "Do they have green faces and white hair? Does she see them run up and down? I never saw any waves, sir, but those in my glass. I am very glad to know your little girl is by the waves."

"Where *you* ought to be," said the Doctor, half under his breath. "It is cruel, cruel!"

"What is cruel?" asked the Lady of Shalott, looking up into the Doctor's face.

The little brown calico night-dress swam suddenly before the Doctor's eyes. He got up and walked across the room. As he walked he stepped upon the pieces of the broken glass.

"Oh, don't!" cried the Lady of Shalott. But then she thought that perhaps she had hurt the Doctor's feelings; so she smiled, and said, "Never mind."

"Her case could be cured," said the Doctor, still under his breath, to Sary Jane. "The case could be cured yet. It is cruel!"

"Sir," said Sary Jane,—she lifted her sharp face sharply out of billows of nankeen vests,—"it may be because I make vests at sixteen and three-quarter cents a dozen, sir: but I say before God there's *something* cruel *somewhere*. Look at her. Look at me. Look at them stairs. Just see that scuttle, will you? Just feel the sun in t' these windows. Look at the rent we pay for this 'ere oven. What do you s'pose the merkiry is up here? Look at them pisen fogs arisin' out over the sidewalk. Look at the dead as have died in the Devil in this street this week. Then look out here!"

Sary Jane drew the Doctor to the blazing, blindless window, out of which the Lady of Shalott had never looked.

"Now talk of curin' *her*!" said Sary Jane.

The Doctor turned away from the window, with a sudden white face.

"The Board of Health"—

"Don't talk to *me* about the Board of Health!" said Sary Jane.

"I'll talk to *them*," said the Doctor. "I did not know matters were so bad. They shall be attended to directly. To-morrow I leave town"—He stopped, looking down at the Lady of Shalott, thinking of the little lady by the waves, whom he would see to-morrow, hardly knowing what to say. "But something shall be done at once. Meantime, there's the Hospital."

"She tried Horspital long ago," said Sary Jane. "They said they couldn't do nothing. What's the use? Don't bother her. Let her be."

"Yes, let me be," said the Lady of Shalott, faintly. "The glass is broken."

"But something must be done!" urged the Doctor, hurrying away. "I will attend to the matter directly, directly."

He spoke in a busy doctor's busy way. Undoubtedly he thought that he should attend to the matter directly.

"You have flowers here, I see." He lifted, in hurrying away, a spray of lilies that lay upon the bed, freshly sent to the Lady of Shalott that morning.

"They ring," said the Lady of Shalott, softly. "Can you hear? 'Bless—it! Bless—it!' Ah, yes, they ring!"

"Bless what?" asked the Doctor, half out of the door.

"The Flower Charity," said the Lady of Shalott.

"*Amen!*" said the Doctor. "But I'll attend to it directly." And he was quite out of the door, and the door was shut.

"Sary Jane, dear?" said the Lady of Shalott, a few minutes after.

"Well!" said Sary Jane.

"The glass is broken," said the Lady of Shalott.

"Should think I might know that!" said Sary Jane, who was down upon her knees sweeping shining pieces away into a pasteboard dust-pan.

"Sary Jane, dear?" said the Lady of Shalott again.

"Dear, dear!" echoed Sary Jane, tossing purple feathers out of the window and seeming, to the eyes of the Lady of Shalott, to have the spray of green waves upon her hands. "There they go!"

"Yes, there they go," said the Lady of Shalott. But she said no more till night.

It was a hot night for South Street. It was a very hot night for even South Street. The lean children in the attic opposite cried savagely, like lean cubs. The monkeys from the spring-box came out and sat upon the lid for air. Dirty people lay around the dirty hydrant; and the purple wing stretched itself a little in a quiet way to cover them.

"Sary Jane, dear?" said the Lady of Shalott, at night. "The glass is broken. And, Sary Jane, dear, I am afraid I *can't* stand it as well as you can."

Sary Jane gave the Lady of Shalott a sharp look, and put away her nankeen vests. She came to the bed.

"It isn't time to stop sewing, is it?" asked the Lady of Shalott, in faint surprise. Sary Jane only said:—

"Nonsense!" That man will be back again yet. He'll look after ye, maybe. Nonsense!"

"Yes," said the Lady of Shalott, "he will come back again. But my glass is broken."

"Nonsense!" said Sary Jane. But she did not go back to her sewing. She sat down on the edge of the bed, by the Lady of Shalott; and it grew dark.

"Perhaps they'll do something about the yards; who knows?" said Sary Jane.

"But my glass is broken," said the Lady of Shalott.

"Sary Jane, dear!" said the Lady of Shalott. "He is walking on the waves."

"Nonsense!" said Sary Jane. For it was quite, quite dark.

"Sary Jane, dear!" said the Lady of Shalott. "Not that man. But there *is* a Man, and he is walking on the waves."

The Lady of Shalott raised herself upon her calico night-dress sleeve. She looked at the wall where the ten by six inch looking-glass had hung.

"Sary Jane, dear!" said the Lady of Shalott. "I am glad that girl is down by the waves. I am very glad. But the glass is broken."

Two days after, the Board of Health at the foot of the precipice which the lessor called a flight of stairs, the one which led into the Lady of Shalott's palace, were met and stopped by another board.

"*This* one's got the right of way, gentlemen!" said something at the brink of the precipice, which sounded so much like a rat-trap that the Board of Health looked down by instinct at its individual and collective feet, to see if they were in danger, and dared not by instinct stir a step.

The board which had the right of way was a pine board, and the Lady of Shalott lay on it, in her brown calico night-dress, with Sary Jane's old shawl across her feet. The Flower Charity (Heaven bless it!) had half-covered the old shawl with silver bells, and solemn green shadows, like the shadows of church towers. And it was a comfort to Sary Jane to know that these were the only bells which tolled for the Lady of Shalott, and that no other church shadow fell upon her burial.

"Gentlemen," said the Hospital Doctor, "we're too late, I see. But you'd better go on."

The gentlemen of the Board of Health went on; and the Lady of Shalott went on.

The Lady of Shalott went out into the cart that had carried away the monkeys from the spring-box, and the purple wing lifted to let her pass; then fell again, as if it had brushed her away.

The Board of Health went up the precipice, and stood by the window out of which the Lady of Shalott had never looked.

They sent orders to the scavenger, and orders to the Water Board, and how many other orders nobody knows; and they sprinkled themselves with camphor, and they went their ways.

And the board that had the Right of Way went its way, too. And Sary Jane folded up the shawl, which she could not afford to lose, and came home, and made nankeen vests at sixteen and three-quarter cents a dozen in the window out of which the Lady of Shalott had never looked.

The True Story of Guenever

Elizabeth Stuart Phelps

In all the wide, dead, old world of story, there is to me no wraith more piteously pursuant than the wraith of Guenever. No other voice has in it the ring of sweet harmonies so intricately bejangled; no other face turns to us eyes of such luminous entreaty from slow descents of despair; no other figure, majestic though in ruins, carries through every strained muscle and tense nerve and full artery so magnetic a consciousness of the deeps of its deserved humiliation and the height of its lost privilege. One pauses as before an awful problem, before the nature of this miserable lady. A nature wrought, it is plain, of the finer tissues, since it not only won but returned the love of the blameless king. One follows her young years with bated breath. We see a delicate, high-strung, impulsive creature, a trifle mismated to a faultless, unimpulsive man. We shudder to discover in her, before she discovers it for or in herself, that, having given herself to Arthur, she yet has not given all; that there arises now another self, an existence hitherto unknown, unsuspected,—a character groping, unstable, unable, a wandering wind, a mist of darkness, a chaos, over which Arthur has no empire, of which he has no comprehension, and of which she—whether of Nature or of training who shall judge?—has long since discrowned herself the Queen. Guenever is unbalanced, crude, primeval woman. She must be at once passionately wooed and peremptorily ruled; and in wooing or in ruling there must be no despondencies or declines. There are no soundings to be found in her capacities of loving, as long as the mariner cares to go on striking for them. At his peril let him hold his plummet lightly or weary of the sweet toil taken in the measure of it; at his peril, and at hers.

To Arthur love is a state, not a process; an atmosphere, not a study; an assurance, not a hope; a fact, not an ideal. He is serene, reflective, a statesman. The Queen is intense, ill-educated, idle. Undreamed of by the one, unsuspected by the other, they grow apart. Ungoverned, how shall Guenever govern herself?

Misinterpreted, value herself? Far upon the sunlit moor, a speck against the pure horizon, Launcelot rides,—silent, subtle, swift, as Fate rides ever. . . .

Poor Guenever! After all, poor Guenever! Song and story, life and death are so cruel to a woman. To Launcelot, repentant, is given in later life the best thing left upon earth for a penitent man—a spotless son. To Launcelot is reserved the aureola of that blessed fatherhood from which sprang the finder of the Holy Grael, "pure in thought and word and deed." To Guenever is given the convent and solitary expiation; to Guenever disgrace, exile, and despair. Prone upon the convent floor, our fancy leaves her, kissing Arthur's kingly and forgiving, but departing feet, half dead for joy because he bids her hope that in some other world— in which she has not sinned—those spotless feet may yet return to her, her true and stronger soul return to him; but neither in this world—never in this. Poor soul! Erring, weak, unclean; but for that, and that, and that, poor soul! Poor soul! I can never bear to leave her there upon the convent floor. I rebel against the story. I am sure the half of it was never told us. It must be that Arthur went back some autumn day and brought her gravely home. It *must* be that penitence and patience and acquired purity shall sometime win the respect and confidence of men, as they receive the respect and confidence of God. It must be that at some distant but approaching day *something* of the tenderness of divine stainlessness shall creep into the instinct of human imperfection, and a repentant sinner become to human estimates an object sorrowful, appalling, but appealing, sacred, and sweet.

Who can capture the where, the how, the wherefore of a train of fancy? Was it because I thought of Guenever that I heard the story? Or because I heard the story that I thought of Guenever? My washwoman told it, coming in that bitter day at twilight and sitting by the open fire, as I had bidden her, for rest and warmth. What should *she* know of the Bulfinch and Ellis and Tennyson and Dunlop, that had fallen from my lap upon the cricket at her feet, that she should sit, with hands across her draggled knees, and tell me such a story? Or were Dunlop and the rest untouched upon the library shelves till after she had told it? Whether the legend drew me to the fact, or the fact impelled me to the legend? Indeed, why should I know? It is enough that I heard the story. She told it in her way. I, for lack of her fine, realistic manner, must tell it in my own.

Queen Guenever had the toothache. Few people can look pretty with the toothache. The cheeks of royalty itself will swell, and princely eyelids redden, and queenly lips assume contours as unæsthetic as the kitchen-maids', beneath affliction so plebeian. But Guenever looked pretty.

She abandoned herself to misery, to begin with, in such a royal fashion. And, by the way, we may notice that in nothing does blood "tell" more sharply than in the endurance of suffering. There is a vague monotony in the processes of wearing pleasure. Happy people are very much alike. In the great republic of joy we find tremendous and humiliating levels. When we lift our heads to bear the great crown of pain, all the "points" of the soul begin to make themselves manifest at once.

Guenever yielded herself to this vulgar agony with a beautiful protest. She had protested, indeed, all winter, for that tooth had ached all winter; had never even told her husband of it till yesterday. She had flung herself upon the little cro-cheted cricket by the sitting-room fire, with her slender, tightly-sleeved arm upon the chintz-covered rocking-chair, and her erect, firm head upon her arm. Into the palm of the other hand the offending cheek crept, like a bird into its nest; with a caressing, nestling movement, as if that tiny hand of hers were the only object in the world to which Guenever did not scorn to say how sorry she was for herself. The color of her cheeks was high but fine. Her eyes—Guenever, as we all know, had brown eyes, more soft than dark—were as dry as they were iri-descent. Other women might cry for the toothache! All the curves of the ex-hausted attitude she had chosen, had in them the bewitching defiance of a hard surrender to a power stronger than herself, with which certain women meet ev-ery alien influence, from a needle-prick to a heartbreak. She wore a white apron and a white ribbon against a dress of a soft dark brown color; and the chintz of the happy chair, whose stiff old elbows held her beautiful outline, was of black and gold, with birds of paradise in the pattern. There was a stove, with little slid-ing doors, in Guenever's sitting-room. Arthur thought it did not use so very much more wood to open the doors, and was far healthier. Secretly he liked to see Guenever in the bird-of-paradise chair, with the moody firelight upon her; but he had never said so—it was not Arthur's "way." Launcelot, now, for instance had said something to that effect several times.

Launcelot, as all scholars of romantic fiction know, was the young brick-layer to whom Arthur and Guenever had rented the spare room when the hard times came on,—a good-natured, inoffensive lodger as one could ask for, and quite an addition, now and then, before the little sliding doors of the open stove, on a sober evening, when she and Arthur were dull, as Guenever had said. To tell the truth, Arthur was often dull of late, what with being out of work so much, and the foot he lamed with a rusty nail. King Arthur, it is unnecessary to add, was a master carpenter.

King Arthur came limping in that evening, and found the beautiful, protesting, yielding, figure in the black and golden chair. The Queen did not turn as he came in. One gets so used to one's husband! And the heavy, uneven step he left upon the floor jarred upon her aching nerves. Launcelot, when he had come, about an hour since, to inquire how she was, had bounded down the stairs as merrily as a school-boy, as lightly as a hare, and turned his knightly feet a-tip-toe as he crossed the room to say how sorry he felt for her; to stand beside her in the moody light, to gaze intently down upon her, then to ask why Arthur was not yet at home; to wonder were she lonely; to say he liked her ribbon at her throat; to say he liked a hundred things; to say it quite unmanned him when he saw her suffer; to start as if he would say more to her, and turn as if he would have touched her, and fly as if he dared not, and out into the contending, mad March night. For the wind blew that night! To the last night of her life Queen Guenever will not forget the way it blew!

"Take some Drops," said Arthur. What a tiresome manner Arthur had of putting things! Some Drops, indeed! There was nothing Guenever wanted to take. She wanted, in fact, to *be* taken; to be caught and gathered to her husband's safe, broad breast; to be held against his faithful heart; to be fondled and crooned over and cuddled. She would have her aching head imprisoned in his healthy hands. And if he should think to kiss the agonizing cheek, as *she* would kiss a woman's cheek if she loved her and she had the toothache? But Arthur never thought! Men were so dull at things. Only women knew how to take care of one another. Only women knew the infinite fine languages of love. A man was tender when he thought of it, in a blunt, broad way.

There might be men— One judged somewhat from voices; and a tender voice— Heaven forgive her! Though he spoke with the tongues of all angels, and the music of all spheres, and the tenderness of all loves, what was any man's mortal voice to her—a queen, the wife of Arthur, blameless king of men?

The wife of Arthur started from the old chair whereon the birds of paradise seemed in the uneven firelight to be fluttering to and fro. The color on her cheeks had deepened painfully, and she lifted her crowned head with a haughty motion towards her husband's face.

"I'm sure I'd try the Drops," repeated Arthur.

"I'll have it out!" snapped Guenever. "I don't believe a word of its being neuralgia. I'll have them all out, despite him!"

Guenever referred to the court dentist.

"I'll have them out and make a fright of myself once for all, and go mumbling round. I doubt if anybody would find it made any difference to anybody how anybody looked."

It cannot be denied that there was a certain remote vagueness in this re-
mark. King Arthur, who was of a metaphysical temperament, sighed. He was sorry
for the Queen—so sorry that he went and set the supper-table, to save her from
the draughts that lurked even in the royal pantry that mad March night. He loved
the Queen—so much that he would have been a happy man to sit in the bird-of-
paradise rocking-chair and kiss that aching, sweet cheek of hers till supper-time
to-morrow, if that would help her. But he supposed, if she had the toothache, she
wouldn't want to be touched. He knew he shouldn't. So, not knowing what else
to do, he just limped royally about and got the supper, like a dear old dull king as
he was.

If Queen Guenever appreciated this little kingly attention, who can say? She
yielded herself with a heavy sigh once more to the arms of the chintz rocking-
chair, and ached in silence. Her face throbbed in time to the pulses of the wind.
What a wind it was! It seemed to come from immense and awful distances, gathering slow forces as it fled, but fleeing with a compressed, rebellious roar, like
quick blood chained within the tissues of a mighty artery, beating to and fro as it
rushed to fill the heart of the black and lawless night.

It throbbed so resoundingly against the palace windows that the steps of
Launcelot, blending with it, did not strike the Queen's ears till he stood beside
her, in the firelight. Arthur, setting the supper-table, had heard the knightly knock,
and bidden their friend and lodger enter (as King Arthur bade him always) with
radiant, guileless eyes.

Sir Launcelot had a little bottle in his hand. He had been to the druggist's.
There was a druggist to the king just around the corner from the palace.

"It's laudanum," said Launcelot. "I got it for your tooth. I wish you'd try it.
I couldn't bear to see you suffer."

"I'm half afraid to have Guenever take laudanum," said Arthur, coming up.
"It takes such a mite of anything to influence my wife. The doctor says it is her
nerves. I know he wouldn't give her laudanum when her arm was hurt. But it's
just as good in you, Sir Launcelot."

Guenever thought it very good in him. She lifted her flushed and throb-
bing face to tell him so; but, in point of fact, she told him nothing. For something
in Sir Launcelot's eyes, the wife of Arthur could not speak.

She motioned him to put the bottle on the shelf, and signified by a slight
gesture peculiar to herself—a little motion of the shoulders, as tender as it was
imperious—her will that he should leave her.

Now Launcelot, we see, was plainly sorry for Guenever. Was it then a flitting tenderer than sorrow that she had seen within his knightly eyes? Only

Guenever will ever know; for Arthur, on his knees upon the crocheted cricket before the palace fire, was toasting graham bread.

Guenever, on her knees before the rocking-chair, sat very still. Her soft brown eyes, wide open, almost touched the cool, smooth chintz where the birds of paradise were flying on a pall-black sky. It seemed to her strained vision, sitting so, that the birds flew from her as she looked at them, and vanished; and that the black sky alone was left. The eyes that watched the golden birds departing were fair and still, like the eyes of children just awake. It was a child's mouth, as innocent and fair, that Guenever lifted just that minute suddenly to Arthur, with a quick, unqueenly, appealing smile.

"Kiss me, dear?" said Guenever, somewhat disconnectedly.

"Why, yes!" said Arthur.

He wasn't able to follow the train of thought exactly. It was never clear to him why Guenever should want to be kissed precisely in the *middle* of a slice of toast. And the graham bread was burned. But he kissed the Queen, and they had supper; and he eat the burnt slice himself, and said nothing about it. That, too, was one of Arthur's "ways."

"Only," said Guenever, as the King contentedly finished the last black crust, "I wish the wind would stop."

"What's the trouble with the wind?" asked Arthur. "I thought it was well enough."

"It must be well enough," said the Queen, and she shook her little white fist at the window. "It *shall* be well enough!"

For the pulse of the wind ran wildly against the palace and Guenever was speaking, and throbbed and bounded and beat, as if the heart of the March night would break.

All this was long, long, long ago. How long Guenever can never tell. Days, weeks, months,—few or many, swift or slow,—of that she cannot answer. Passion takes no count of time; peril marks no hours or minutes; wrong makes its own calendar; and misery has solar systems peculiar to itself. It seemed to her years, it seemed to her days, according to her tossed, tormented mood.

It is in the nature of all passionate and uncontrolled emotion to prey upon and weaken the forces of reflective power, as much as it is in the nature of controlled emotion to strengthen them. Guenever found in herself a marked instance of this law. It seemed to her sometimes that she knew as little of her own story as she did of that of any erring soul at the world's width from her. It seemed to her that her very memory had yielded in the living of it, like the memory of a person in whose brain insidious disease had begun to fasten itself. So subtle and so sure had been the disease which gnawed at the Queen's heart, that she discovered with a helpless terror—not unlike that one might feel in whom a cancerous process had been long and undetected working—that her whole nature was lowering its tone in sympathy with her special weakness. She seemed suddenly to have become, or to feel herself become, a poisoned thing.

We may wonder, does not the sense of guilt—not the sensitiveness to, but the *sense* of guilt—come often as a sharp and sudden experience? Queen Guenever, at least, felt stunned by it. Distinctly, as if it and she were alone in the universe, she could mark the awful moment when it came to her. Vivid as a blood-red rocket shot against her stormy sky, that moment whirred and glared before her.

It was a fierce and windy night, like that in which she had the toothache, when she and the King had eaten such a happy supper of burnt toast (for *hers* was burnt, too, although she wouldn't have said so for the world, since the King had got so tired and warm about it). How happy they had been that night! Sir Launcelot did not come again after supper, dimly feeling, despite the laudanum, that the Queen had dismissed him for the evening. She and Arthur had the evening to themselves. It was the first evening they had been alone together for a long time. Arthur sat in the chintz rocking-chair. He held her in his lap. He comforted her poor cheek with his huge, warm hand. His shining, kingly eyes looked down on her like stars from Heaven. He said:—

"If it wasn't for your tooth, little woman, how happy we would be."

And Guenever had laughed and said: "What's a toothache? I'm content, if you are." And then they laughed together, and the golden birds upon the old chair had seemed to flit and sing before her; and brighter and sweeter, as they watched her, glimmered Arthur's guileless eyes.

The stars were fallen now; the heavens were black; the birds of paradise had flown; the wind was abroad mightily and cold; there was snow upon the ground; and she and Launcelot were fleeing through it and weeping as they fled.

Guenever, at least, was weeping. All the confusion of the miserable states and processes which had led her to this hour had cleared away, murky clouds from a lurid sky. Suddenly, by a revelation awful as some that might shock a soul upon the day of doom, she knew that she was no longer a bewildered or a pitiable, but an evil creature.

A gossip in the street, an old neighbor who used to borrow eggs of her, had spoken in her hearing, as she and Launcelot passed swiftly through the dark, unrecognized, at the corner of the Palace Court, and had said:—

"Guenever has fled with Launcelot. The Queen has left the King. All the world will know it by to-morrow."

These words fell upon the Queen's ear distinctly. They tolled after her through the bitter air. She fled a few steps, and stopped.

"Launcelot!" she cried, "what have we done? Why are we here? Let me go home! Oh! what have I done?"

She threw out her arms with that tender, imperious gesture of hers—more imperious than tender now—which Launcelot knew so well.

Strange! Oh! strange and horrible! How came it to be thus with her? How came she to be alone with Launcelot in the blinding night? *The Queen fled from the King? Guenever false to Arthur?*

Guenever, pausing in the cruel storm, looked backward at her footsteps in the falling snow. Her look was fixed and frightened as a child's. Her memory seemed to her like snow of all that must have led her to this hour.

She knew not what had brought her hither, nor the way by which she came. She was a creature awakened from a moral catalepsy. With the blessed impulse of the Prodigal, old as Earth's error, sweet as Heaven's forgiveness, she turned and cried: "I repent! I repent! I will go home to my husband, before it is too late!"

"It is too late!" said a bitter voice beside her. "It is too late already for repentance, Guenever."

Was it Launcelot who spoke, or the deadly wind that shrieked in passing her? Guenever could never say. A sickening terror took possession of her. She felt her very heart grow cold, as she stood and watched her foot-prints, on which the snow was falling wild and fast.

It was a desolate spot in which she and Launcelot stood. They had left the safe, sweet signs of holy human lives and loves behind them. They were quite alone. A wide and windy moor stretched from them to a forest, on which a horror of great darkness seemed to hang. Behind them, in the deserted distance, gleamed the palace lights. Within these the Queen saw, or fancied that she saw, the shadow of the King, moving sadly to and fro, against the drawn curtain, from behind which the birds of paradise had fled forever.

From palace to wilderness her footsteps lay black in the falling snow. As she gazed, the increasing storm drifted, and here and there they blurred and whitened over and were lost to sight.

So she, too, would whiten over her erring way. Man was not more merciless than Nature.

"I will retrace them all!" cried Guenever.

"You can never retrace the first of them," said again bitterly beside her Launcelot or the deathly wind. "Man is more merciless than Nature. There is no way back for you to the palace steps. In all the kingdom, there is no soul to bid you welcome, should you dare return. The Queen can never come to her throne again."

"I seek no throne!" wailed Guenever. "I ask for no crown! All I want is to go back and to be clean. I'll crawl on my knees to the palace, if I may be clean."

But again said sneeringly to her that voice, which was either of Launcelot or of the wind:—

"Too late! too late! too late! You can never be clean! You can never be clean!"

"Launcelot," said Guenever, rallying sharply and making as it seemed, a mighty effort to collect control over the emotion which was mastering her, "Launcelot, there is some mistake about this. I never meant to do wrong. I never said I would leave the King. There is some mistake. Perhaps I have been dreaming or have been ill. Let me go home at once to the King!"

"There is no mistake," said once more the voice, which seemed neither of Launcelot nor of the wind, but yet akin to both; "and you are not dreaming and you can never return to the King. The thing that is done is done. Sorrow and longing are dead to help you. Agony and repentance are feeble friends. Neither man nor Nature can wash away a stain."

"God is more merciful!" cried Guenever, in the tense, shrill voice of agony, stung beyond endurance. It seemed to her that nature could bear no more. It seemed to her that she had never before this moment received so much as an intellectual perception of the guiltiness of guilt. Now mind and heart, soul and body throbbed with the throes of it. She quivered, she struggled, she rebelled with the accumulated fervors and horrors of years of innocence. But it seemed to her as if the soil of sin eat into her like caustic, before whose effects the most compassionate or skillful surgeon is powerless. She writhed with her recoil from it. She shrank from it with terror proportioned to her sense of helplessness and stain.

"They who are only afflicted know nothing of misery!" moaned Guenever. "There *is* no misery but guilt!"

She flung herself down in the storm upon the snow.

"God loves!" cried Guenever. "Christ died! I *will* be clean!"

It seemed then suddenly to the kneeling woman, that He whose body and blood were broken for tempted souls appeared to seek her out across the desolated moor. The Man whose stainless lips were first to touch the cup of the Holy Grael, which all poor souls should after Him go seeking up and down upon the earth, stood in the pure white snow, and, smiling, spoke to her.

"*Though your sins,*" he said, "*are scarlet, they shall be white.*"

He pointed, as he spoke, across the distance; past the safe, sweet homes of men and women, toward the palace gates. It seemed to Guenever that he spoke again and said:—

"Return!"

"Through those black footsteps?" sobbed the Queen.

But when she looked again, behold! each black and bitter trace was gone. Smooth across them all, fair, pure, still, reposed the stainless snow. She could not find them, though she would. They were blotted out by Nature, as they were forgiven of God. Alas! alas! if man were but half as compassionate or kind. If Arthur—

She groveled on the ground where the sacred Feet had stood, which now were vanished from her. Wretched woman that she was! Who should deliver her from this bondage to her life's great holy love? If Arthur would but open the door for her in the fair distance, where the palace windows shone; if he would take a single step toward her where she kneeled within the wilderness; if he would but loiter toward her where that Other had run swiftly, and speak one word of quiet to her where He had sung her songs of joy! But the palace door was shut. The King took no step toward the wilderness. The King was mute as death and cold as his own white soul. On Arthur's throne was never more a place for Guenever.

Guenever, in the desert, stretched her arms out blindly across the blotted footprints to the palace lights.

Oh! Arthur. Oh! Arthur, Arthur, *Arthur* . . .

"Why, Pussy!" said Arthur. "What's the matter?"

However unqueenly, Pussy was one of the royal pet names.

"My little woman! Guenever! My darling! Why do you call me so?"

Why did she call him indeed? Why call for anything? Why ask or need or long? In his great arms he held her. To his true breast he folded her. Safe in his love he sheltered her. From heaven the stars of his eyes looked down on her. As those may look who wake in heaven, whose anguished soul had thought to wake in hell, looked Guenever. She was his honored wife. There was no Launcelot, no wilderness. The soul which the King had crowned with his royal love was clean, was clean, was clean!

She hid her scarlet face upon his honest heart and seemed to mutter something about "dreams." It was all that she could say. There are dreams that are epochs in life.

"But it wasn't a dream, you see," said Arthur. "We've had a scare over you, Guenever. You took the laudanum, after all."

"Launcelot's laudanum! Indeed, no! I took the drops, as I told you, Arthur."

"The bottles stood together on the shelf, and you made the blunder," said Arthur, anxiously. "We think you must have taken a tremendous dose. I've sent Launcelot for the Doctor. And Nabby Jones, she was in to borrow eggs, and she said a little camphire would be good for you. She just went home to get it. But I've been frightened about you, Guenever," said Arthur. Arthur spoke in his own grave and repressed manner. But he was very pale. His lips, as the Queen crept, sobbing, up to touch them, trembled.

"Well, well," he said, "we won't talk about it now." Guenever did not want to talk. She wished Nabby Jones would stay away, with her camphire. She wished Launcelot would never come. Upon her husband's heart she lay. Within her husband's eyes the safe, home fire-light shone. Across the old chintz chair the birds of paradise were fluttering like birds gone wild with joy.

Without, the wind had lulled, the storm had ceased, and through the crevices in the windows had sifted tiny drifts of cool, clean snow.

And this, know all men henceforth by these presents, is the true story of Guenever the Queen.

The Cross and the Grail

Lucy Larcom

Arthur's knight had trials long,
Going forth to right the wrong:
Arthur's knight had perils great,
On the moorlands desolate,
In the dungeon and the fen,
Slaying dragons, rescuing men.

Knightly souls must needs be true:
Arthur's knight had work to do,
Vows to keep and quests to make,
Such as heroes undertake:
Tokens in the earth and sky
Led him on to victory.

Visions of the Holy Cup
Shone before him, gazing up
Where, upon some peak remote
Morning's sudden sword-flash smote,
Or where pilgrim-pathways steep
Rose, and sank in sunsets deep.

Sometimes, tinged with radiance strange,
Would the beaker seem to change
To the outline of a cross—
Emblem of life's gain in loss—
Glimpsing, fading like a cloud,
As he stood, with forehead bowed.

'Twas the cup the Master drank;
Veiled to those who weakly shrank
From His awful sacrifice;
Only shown to faithful eyes
Turned in steadfast prayer to Him:
Only pure lips touched its brim.

Only knightly purity
Could the glorious vision see:—
But if once his longing sight
Drank its overflow of light,
Soul of Arthur's knight grew strong
For the unending strife with wrong.

*   *   *

On a mountain in the West
Hangs a snowy cross impressed,
Melted not by summer's heat,
Undefiled by careless feet,
Gleaming through the clouds, a sign
Of the Sacrifice Divine.

That white cross is lifted up
Like an overbrimming cup:
Downward from its stainless snow
Rills of limpid crystal flow;
And the traveler at their brink
May of heaven's refreshment drink.

Say not that by accident
Those gray crags were seamed and rent!
God can write upon His hills
Any message that He wills.
Glad the mountains are, to bear
Christ's dear sign aloft in air.

Holy Cross and Holy Grail!

Hold them not an idle tale
Of the dead crusader's years!
They are for the ear that hears,
For the open eyes, that see:
Man, the vision is for thee!

Wear the white cross on thy heart,
For Christ's messenger thou art.
From His love's great overflow,
Love divine shalt thou bestow;
Thou, a stream of life, shalt bless
Souls that thirst for righteousness.

Only manhood that is pure
Work achieves that shall endure:
Manhood like the Master's, brave
With His strength, His world to save
From the curse that sin has wrought;—
Brave and pure, in deed and thought.

Subtler wrongs than Arthur's knight
Ever faced, are thine to fight.
In thine own heart, at the board
Where the dizzying wine is poured;—
Foes in thine own household stay:
Gird thee! shrink not from the fray!

Go thou forth, the knight of Christ;—
Him, whose perfectness sufficed
To make men and angels see
God in our humanity.
Lo! His Cup, His Cross divine!
Conquer by each holy sign!

Thou, if pure in heart, shalt see
God in all things, close to thee;—
In each drop of water quaffed,
Taste a sacramental draught;—

Feel, in every breeze, the breath
Of His life, who vanquished death.

Purity and sacrifice!
Lo! the Christ, before thine eyes!
Unto mortal vision given,
Yet receding into heaven,
That thy human soul may climb
After Him, to heights sublime!

Bear His Cross, receive His Cup!
Be thy whole life offered up
For thy brethren, in His name
Who to save our lost world came!
Never lower standard can
Shape thee to a perfect man.

Kathanal

KATRINA TRASK

The sky was one unbroken pall of gray,
Casting a gloom upon the restless sea,
Dulling her sapphire splendour to a dark
And minor beauty. All the rock-bound shore
Was silent, save a widowed song-bird sang
Far off at intervals a mournful note,
And on the broken crags of dark gray rock
The waves dashed ceaselessly. Sir Kathanal
Stood with uncovered head and folded arms,
His soul as restless as the surging sea
Lashed into passion by the coming storm.
His helmet lay upon the sand; its crest,
A floating plume of deep-hued violet,
Was tossed and torn in fury by the wind
Until it seemed a thing of life. He stood
And watched it, only half aware at first
That it was there, then scarce aware of aught
Besides the plume. As in the room of death
Some iterated sound or motion holds
Attent the stricken mind, benumbed, and keeps
The horror of its grief awhile at bay
As by a spell, so now, though Kathanal
Had sought the sea-shore to be free of men
Because of his sore agony of heart,
And all the passion of his daring soul
Was tossing like the sea in fierce revolt,

His thoughts and gaze were centred on his crest.
Before the gray of sea and sky he saw
Naught but the waving, waving of the plume;
Before the vision of his love, Leorre,
Her tender eyes aglow with changeless light,
The golden splendour of her sunny hair,
Her winning smiles of grace and sweetness blent,
There came the waving, waving, of the plume;
Between his sorrow and his weary soul,
Between his trouble and his clear-eyed self,
There came the waving, waving of the plume;
Until he felt, in some half-conscious way,
It was his heart, and he a stranger there
That looked down, from a height, indifferent
Upon it at the mercy of the wind.

Sudden, with that long lingering trace of youth
That gave to him the fascinating charm
Which other men were fain to emulate,
He quickly stooped, and tore it from his helm,
And cast it far out on the tossing sea.
It lighted on the waves a purple bird,
Floating with swan-like grace before the wind.
The action quenched impatience. Kathanal,
Impulsive, passionate and sensitive,
In moods was ever ready with response
To omen and to change of circumstance.
He stood a moment, and then forward sprang
To catch it ere it vanished out of reach.
It was too late—the outward-flowing tide
Bore it from wave to wave beyond his sight.

"Ah, God!" he cried aloud, "what have I done?
It is the omen of a curse to me;
My crest is gone, my knightly symbol lost,
My helm dishonoured through an act of mine."

Then came the memory of early youth,
The recollection of a high resolve

To keep his manhood free from touch of stain,
To be a knight like Galahad, pure and true.
So few short years had passed since that resolve,
And yet he had forgotten loyalty
And truth and honour for the fair Leorre,
The wife of Reginault, his patron knight,—
The brave old man who treated him as son.
Long had he loved her with a knightly love,
And fought for her, and chosen her the queen
Of many a tournament. She still was young,
Fairer than morning in the early spring.
When she had come, a gladsome bride, to grace
The castle of old Reginault, and warm
His grand old spirit into youth again,
Sir Kathanal had bowed before her, saying,
"My gracious lady, take me as your knight";
And she had answered, with her winning smile,
"You are Sir Reginault's, and therefore mine."
Well had he loved her from that very hour,
Giving her honour as his old friend's bride,
Making the castle ring with merriment
To do her service, and fulfil the hest
Of Reginault, who bade him use his grace
To make her life a round of holidays.
But day by day his selfish love had grown
From friendly service to a lover's claim,
Until he had forgotten Reginault
In her fair eyes, and all things else but her,
Who granted him no boon, no smallest act
Of love or tenderness.

                    At last the strife
Between deep yearning for some touch of love,
And brave endeavour for self-mastery,
Had driven him to madness and despair.
To the lone sea he brought his agony
To face it boldly, and his spirit, quick
To wear new moods, caught a despondent gloom
From the dark omen that oppressed his soul.

"Love is divine," he said, "and it is well
To love Leorre, wife though she be, for love
Is free to noble natures; but at last,
When in her shining eyes I see response,
Albeit unconscious, to my longing pain,
I cannot rest content with boonless love,
Although divine. I fear me, if I stay
Within the circle of her tempting charm,
I shall, through some wild impulse, wantonly
Fling my unsullied knighthood to the winds,
As now I flung the plume from out my helm."

He went at even-song time to Leorre,
And told her of his struggle by the sea,
Of his determined purpose and resolve.

"Leorre, I love you with a love unsung
By poets, and unknown by other men,
Undreamed by women; I must leave you, dear;
I cannot see you fair for Reginault,
I cannot watch your sweetness not for me.
I will go far upon some distant quest
Until this frenzy ceases, and the quest
Shall be for you, my love, for you alone.

"Dear, sunny head that lights my darkened way
With its bright, golden glory, let me seek
A crown that well befits it for my quest.
Fair waist that curves beneath the heart I love,
I shall engirdle you with priceless gems
Won by my prowess for your perfect grace.
O wondrous neck! great lustrous, flawless pearls,
That shall be royal in their worth, to match
The white enchantment of your beauty fair,
Shall be my quest for you.

                    "I will not come
Back to the court of Constantine, Leorre,
Until I bring that which shall honour you,

And winning which, I shall have cooled my pain."

She came and knelt beside him, took his hand,
Looked deep into his ardent eyes,—her own
Like stars that shone into his inmost soul.

"Will you, indeed, go forth," she answered low,
"Across the world upon a quest for me?
And will you falter not, nor swerve, nor fail,
Nor turn aside from seeking, night nor day,
Until you conquer with your prowess rare
The prize for me? And may I choose the quest
I most desire?"

       "Ah! surely, what you will,"
Said Kathanal, as echo to his eyes,
Which answered ere the words could form themselves.

She waited, silently; the room was still;
Sir Kathanal was faint from drinking deep,
With thirsty eyes, the beauty of her face.

At last she spoke, almost inaudibly,
But evermore the thought of her low speech
Made melody within his memory.

"Go forth, my knight of love, o'er land and sea,
And purify your spirit and your life,
And seek until you find the Holy Grail,
Keeping the vision ever in your thought,
The inspiration ever in your soul.
Let Tristram yield his loyalty and honour
For fair Isoud, and die inglorious,—
Let Launcelot in Guenever's embrace
Forget the consecrated vows he swore,
And bring dark desolation on the land,—
My knight must grow the greater through his love,
The better for my favour, the more pure!

More than all gifts, or wealth of royal dower,
I want, I crave, I claim this boon of thee."

Between the bronze-brown of his eyes and her,
There sudden came a faint and misty veil;
Through the wide-open window a sun's beam
Flashed on it, making o'er her bowèd head
A halo from his own unfallen tears.
He rose and lifted her, loosed her sweet hands,
And fell upon his knees low at her feet.

"Leorre, my love, my queen, my woman-saint,
I am not worthy, but I take your quest;
I will not falter and I will not swerve
Until I see the Grail, or pass to where
I see the glory it but symbols here,
In Paradise. Beloved, all the world
Is better for your living, all the air
Is sweeter for your breathing, and all love
Is holier, purer, that you may be loved."

"Rise, Kathanal, stand still and let me gaze
Upon you with that purpose in your face!
So brave, so resolute! I love you Kathanal!
Nay! do not touch me, listen to my words!
Surely it cannot be a sin to speak,
Perchance it is a debt I owe my knight
For his life's consecration, once to say
To him, as I have said to my own heart,
Just how I love him.

                    "I would follow you
Across the world, if it might be, a slave,
To serve you at your bidding night and day;
Or I would rouse me to my highest pride
That I might be your queen, and lead you on
To glory. I am strong to do and bear
The uttermost my mind can think, for you,
To cheer you, help you, strengthen you; and yet—

I am a woman, and my senses thrill
If you but touch the border of my robe,
And if you take my hand, before the court,
And raise it to your lips, I faint, I die,
With the vast tide of my unconquered love."

"Great Christ! how can I hear you and depart?
I did not know you loved me. O my sweet,
Here by your side I stay; my quest shall be
The love-light dawning in your shining eyes."

"Is this your answer, Kathanal," she sighed,
"To the unveiling of my heart of hearts?
No! now, if ever, you will surely go
On the sole quest that makes that action right."

"Leorre, come once to me!" he said with arms
Outstretched to her. Quickly she backward drew
With one swift whispered "Kathanal!"

                     "Leorre,
You cannot love and be so calm and still;
My soul would sacrifice both earth and heaven
For one full, rapturous kiss from those sweet lips
That lure me on to madness by their spell."

"It is my love that keeps me calm," she said;
"Love makes us strong for what is bitterest;
Were we faint-hearted through imperfect love
We could not part; but loving perfectly
We are full strong for that, and all things else.

"Farewell, my Kathanal, take as you go
This spotless scarf, the girdle from my robe,
And put it where the purple plume has been,
And wear it as my favour in your helm.
If that lost plume was darksome omen ill,
Let this defy it with an omen fair,

A prophecy to spur you on your quest.
My heart says it is better as it is;
I joy me that you flung into the sea
That purple plume my loving, longing gaze
Has often followed in the tournament.
Remember, purple doth betoken pain,
And white betokens conquest, purity;
Look, Kathanal, beloved, in my eyes!
I *know* that you will find the Holy Grail."

She stood immaculate, and from those eyes
That oft had kindled passionate desire
He drew an inspiration high and pure,
A prescient sense of victory and peace;
And falling on his knees once more, he bowed,
Kissed her white robe, and left her standing there.

Then followed days of struggle and dark gloom.
Far from the court he found a lonely cell,
Where morn and night he prayed, and, praying, wrought
A score of earnest, unrecorded deeds
To purify and cleanse himself from sin.

Oft the old passion would arise and sweep
His spirit bare of every conquest. Once
The longing and the yearning were so great,
So strong beyond all thought of holiness,
He sprang up from his bed at dead of night
And stopped not, night nor day, until he reached
His old home by the sea, and saw Leorre.
Her hair had its untarnished golden glow,
Her beauty was unchanged, but her sweet mouth
Had caught a touch of pathos in its smile;
She wore a purple robe, and stood in state
Beside Sir Reginault,—who greeted him
With tender, grave, and kind solicitude,—
And lifted eyes that smote upon his heart
With a long gaze of passionate appeal

That held a pain at bay deep in their depths.

"So weak," he whispered to his heart, "for self,
I will be strong for her; she needs my strength."

Again he hurried from her sight, half glad
For the remembered pain within her eyes;
Ashamed of his own soul that it was glad.

For years he struggled, prayed, and fought his fight;
And sometimes when his soul was desolate
And he was weary from his eager quest,
When such a sense of deep humility
Would fall upon his praying, watching heart
That he would fain forego all in despair,
A marvellous ray of light, mysterious,
Would slant athwart the darkness of his cell,
Then he would rouse him to his quest once more
And say, "Perchance the Holy Grail is near!"

One night at midnight came the ray again,
And with it came a strange expectancy
Of spirit as the light waxed radiant.
The cell was filled with spicy odours sweet,
And on the midnight stillness song was borne
As sweet as heaven's harmony—the words,—
The same Sir Launcelot had heard of old,—
"Honour and joy be to the Father of Heaven."
With wide eyes searching his lone cell for cause
He waited: as the ray became more clear
And more effulgent than the mid-day sun,
He trembled with that chill of mortal flesh
Beholding spiritual things. At last—
Now vaguely as though veiled by light, and then
With shining clearness, perfectly—he saw
The sight unspeakable, transcending words.

Forth from his barren cell came Kathanal,

Strong and inspired, born anew for deeds.
Straightway he grew to be the bravest knight
Under King Constantine, since Sir Sanpeur;[1]
The boldest in the battles for the right;
The kindest in his judgment of the wrong.
His eyes that held the vision of the Grail
Were ever clear to see and know the truth;
His lips that had been touched by holy chrism
Were strong to utter holy living words;
He sang of life in life, and life in death,
And taught the lesson that his heart had learned—
All love should be a glory, not a doom;
Love for love's sake, albeit bliss-denied.

To his old home beside the sapphire sea
Floated his songs and his far-reaching fame;
For in the land no name was loved so well
As Kathanal the peerless Minstrel Knight.

Lone in her chamber sat Leorre, and heard
The songs of Kathanal by courtiers sung—
Arousing words, like a clear clarion call
To truth and virtue, purity and faith.
She clasped her hands and bent her head, and wept
In silent passion pent-up tears, for joy;
For now she knew—far off, beyond her sight—
Her love had seen the sacred Holy Grail.
And as she listened, inspiration came,
Irradiating all her spirit, lifting it
Beyond her sorrow and her daily want
Of Kathanal. Soft through her soul there crept
The echo of a benedicite,
Enwrapping her in calm, triumphant peace.

Then she arose, put on her whitest robe,
And went out radiant, strong, and full of joy.

---

1. Sanpeur, the hero of the first and longest of the three narrative poems in Trask's volume, is the greatest of the knights of Constantine's court.

Guinevere in Almesbury Convent

LIZETTE WOODWORTH REESE

She pores the missal on her knee,
Or, haply as she climbs the stair,
Some sound, some odor sets her free,
From the long days of fast and prayer;
And all about comes Camelot.

At dusk she walks her garden gray,
And hears the nightingales without,
Maddening the marsh with Yesterday;
And straight—an alien dusk about,
And a hoarse word the king is not!

Clamor and dusk in Camelot!
She speeding from the palace forth,
By river-path and orchard plot,
Toward the tall convent in the north,
Set in its apple-trees apart.

She paces thus, and starts to find
Her Almesbury lilies at her feet,
Her nuns grown shadowy behind,
And nightingales that sing so sweet
The marsh is fain to break its heart!

From Avalon

EMILY HUNTINGTON MILLER

I know it well, that green and tranquil isle,
Encircled by the arms of summer tides
That sway and smile, and whisper of the sea.
Not far away it lies; its fragrant shades
Shot through by golden lances of the sun,
And stirred by gentle airs that wander still,
On noiseless feet, to find the chamber fair
Where, couched on mystic herbs and asphodel,
Healed of his hurts, King Arthur lies asleep.
Oft have I found its shelter. When the stress
Of warring winds, and sharp tumultuous storms
Have left me spent and breathless on the field,
Then my swift thoughts, for healing and for rest,
Bear me away to peaceful Avalon.
The sweet enchantments of the bounteous queen
Have changed the shifting waves to fields of rye,
And seas of meadow-grass, that softly break
Against the low-browed wall that shuts about
The blessed trees, veiled in eternal bloom.
The bees make happy tumult, and the air
Quivers with gauzy, bright-winged, dancing motes,
And small white butterflies go shimmering by,
Silent as souls amid the scented boughs.
The skies bend low; the pale moon idly drifts,
A phantom ship, to some celestial port,
And night and day flow on in still content,
Through blissful years in changeless Avalon.

Knights of King Arthur's Court

JESSIE WESTON

The scent of the may is in the air,
　　And its stars on each bough are hung,
With largesse of blossom and perfume rare
　　To the wandering breezes flung,
And the fairies tread a measure fair
　　To the chime by the blue-bells rung.

And the wood-birds carol unafraid,
　　For no man hath done them wrong,
While King Arthur's knights pass adown the glade,
　　And each, as he rides along,
Wending his way by sun and shade,
　　Beguileth the hour with song.

Sir Gawayne

"A song, a song for the springtide,
　　A song for the golden days,
For the lovelit eyes of the maidens,
　　And the knight whom their lips shall praise
And who but I should sing it,
　　Who was ever the Maidens' Knight?
Such honour hath been my guerdon
　　For many a fair-fought fight.

"Oh, my heart is fain for the clamour
 And cry of the battle-field,
For the crash of the splintered spear-shaft,
 And the clang of the smitten shield.
But 'tis sweeter when toil is over
 To lay me a while to rest
In the arms that so soft enfold me,
 And for pillow a snow-white breast.

"And what if such joys be fleeting?
 Ah, little I reck the while
I ride adown thro' the sunlight,
 With ever a song and a smile!
For when my last fight is foughten
 I know that a white-robed band
Of maidens shall bid me greeting
 On the shores of a sunlit land!"

Sir Tristan

"Tho' the springtide sun be fair,
Brighter far beyond compare
Shineth Iseult's golden hair!

"Springtide hours pass all too fleet,
Haste, my steed, on flying feet,
Ah, but Iseult's lips are sweet!

"Iseult, lily, Iseult, rose,
At my heart the love-drink glows,
Thro' my veins like fire it flows!

"Iseult, Iseult, when the light
Fadeth, clasp me, hold me tight,
Kiss me, dearest, into night!"

Sir Lancelot

"Art thou waiting for me, my Lady,
Alone in thy royal bower?
Dost thou send a word thro' the silence
To hasten the passing hour,
'Hath he ever a thought for me, my knight?
Will he come to my arms with the fading light?'

"I am coming, love, I am coming—
Breathe soft, O wind of Spring,
Sail fast, O fleecy cloudlet,
Speed, bird, on glancing wing,
Whisper a word in my Lady's ear,
Tell her the sound of my feet ye hear!

"Ah, never had knight a lady
Fair as my queen is fair;
On a golden throne she sitteth,
In the blaze of her red-gold hair—
And little he dreams, my lord the king,
Of the secret that maketh her heart to sing.

"Are we false? are we true? I know not,
The twain are so wrought in one;
But whether for joy or for sorrow,
The sands of our fate must run—
And what matter if men condemn us quite,
Since all the world shall be ours to-night?"

Sir Perceval

"I ride adown the forest aisles
   From morn till evening shade,
Beneath the stars of heaven my head,
   At fall of night, is laid.

No comrade wendeth at my side,
  No voice bids me God-speed,
Alone by hill and vale I ride,
  Alone by wood and mead.

"For somewhere, near, or far away,
  One waiteth long mine aid,
I may not rest, by night or day,
  Until his grief be stayed.
For many a year, with prayer and tear,
  I've sought to find the way,
But rough or smooth, the path I choose
  Still leadeth me astray.

"I may not rest from off my quest,
  I may not stay my hand,
Tho' Life and Love be waiting me,
  Far in a distant land.
I may not see my wife's fair face,
  I may not faint nor fail,
Till I have won Anfortas grace,
  And found the Holy Grail."

*   *   *   *   *

Sir Gawayne hath sought the isles of light
  Beyond the shores of day,
Where morn never waneth to shades of night,
  And the silver fountains play;
There he holdeth high court as the Maidens' Knight,
  In the Maidens' Isle, for aye.

And Tristan sleeps by his lady's side,

  To the dirge of the sounding sea;
And the foaming wave and the flowing tide
  Hide the twain, that no man may see
Where they take their rest, and their fate abide,
  Till the dawn of Eternity.

But Lancelot wrought a penance hard
    To win from his sin release,
And his face was by fast and vigil marred
    Or ever his pain might cease.
Now his body lieth in Joyous Gard,
    And his soul hath gotten peace.

And Perceval, doth he wake or sleep?
    Ah, no man shall tell that tale—
Perchance he lieth in slumber deep
    With the Eastern sands for veil;
Or perchance, in a distant land, doth keep
    Watch and ward o'er the Holy Grail.

But when the archangel trump shall call,
    And the Heavenly Feast be spread,
Say, which of those heroes, among them all,
    Shall lift up a fearless head,
And walk the pavement of Heaven's high Hall
    With unashamèd tread?

Sir Gawayne, methinks, shall hide his face,
    Abashed and overawed,
And the lovers twain, by Jesu's grace,
    Sit low at the Heavenly board;
But the King of Heaven shall rise from His place
    When He seeth Monsalväsch' lord—

"Welcome, O Brother, who bare thy part
    In the travail of My soul,
Who knew no rest of hand or heart
    Till thy brother might be made whole;
Come thou, and sit at My side, apart,
    While the stars 'neath our footstool roll."

An Iseult Idyll

G[RACE] CONSTANT LOUNSBERY

Part I

Throughout the ambiguous April day
The skylark wings his singing way,
And trills a rhapsody of May.

The wind that sweetens earth with spring
Falls on the ocean, wakening
The rising waves beneath his wing.

While swiftly from her native lea
A Cornish bark, rejoicingly,
Bears Iseult o'er the Irish sea.

With eyes reverted toward the land
Dimly she sees the paling strand
Diminish to a silvery band.

But, as a carrier pigeon springs
Homeward on strong, exulting wings,
The alien ship glides on, and flings

The waters green to gleaming spray,
Threading its pathless southward way,
While shine and shower cross the day.

And where the ripples bud and break
The sea mews drift along its wake,
Like boats the tide at will may take.

Then landward o'er the glistering main
Fair Iseult flings her song. In vain!
The wind beats back the sad refrain,—

Song

Farewell, farewell, a long farewell to thee,
O happy isle, blue girdled of the sea!
Fair are thy fields of green that fade to grey,
And dim mine eyes, with watching wistfully
The lengthening of the endless watery way.
Farewell, farewell, a long farewell to thee.

Farewell, farewell, a long farewell to thee!
Thine is my love, and thine the heart of me,
Through all the widening of the alien years
My hopes be thine, and thine the memory
That brightens through the bitterness of tears.
Farewell, farewell, a long farewell to thee!

Farewell, farewell, a long farewell to thee!
Thou art the world, what other world could be?
Lo! I had hoped, when life was o'er, to die
Upon thy breast, and smiling peacefully
To whisper, ere words falter to a sigh,
Farewell, farewell, a long farewell to thee!

Part II

As clouds obscure the April skies,
The overwhelming tears arise,
And tremble in her baffled eyes.

The gleeful breezes pluck and woo

Her kirtle, where the crocus' hue
Flames up a robe of violet blue.

Hers is a face whose beauty seen
Makes one forget what life has been,
And own her, henceforth, utter queen.

Thus Tristram, dreaming, lingers there
Unknown, perplexed of her despair,
And timid, seeing grief so fair.

"I would not anger thee, by Heaven,
Yet let my presence be forgiven
For all the joy that thine has given!

"Sorrow, methinks, has wearied thee,
And weariness comes over me
From battling with the wind and sea.

"Behold a goblet rich with gold,
And mellow wine, matured of old,
A luscious draught of heat and cold!

"Nay, cheer thy heart, and pledge me then,
As in those hours of anguish, when
Wounded I lay among thy men."

So pleads he, till she smiles again,
And, drinking, feels through every vein
A joy that trembles into pain.

He raises high the bowl with half
The dancing poison, sweet to quaff,
And drains its sweetness with a laugh.

And, in a trenchant stroke of light,
Love cleaves the darkness of their night,
And puts the fading world to flight.

As one who knows not Life from Death,
Nor yet what power Love's language hath,
He calls with half-abated breath,—

Iseult! One wild, unmated word,
Iseult! No sound so sweet is heard
In all the lyric speech of bird.

But, softer than a startled sigh,
Her voice reluctant, breathes reply,
Tristram!—a tender, summoning cry.

And all is silent save alone
The sea's reverberate monotone,
With Love's own voice in unison.

The Dwarf's Quest

A Ballad

SOPHIE JEWETT

Sir Dagonet was sad of heart;
   Beneath the city gate
He watched King Arthur's knights depart;
   He watched in love and hate.

He saw great tears fall from the eyes
   Of Lancelot and the King;
He thought: "Apart the sweet Queen lies,
   And knows no comforting."

Sir Percivale and Galahad
   Rode by in shining mail;
He marked their eyes, assured and glad,
   And cursed the Holy Grail.

Though many passed and saw him not,
   He hoarded, in his pain,
A smile from sad Sir Lancelot,
   Three sweet words from Gawain.

King Arthur's fool was Dagonet,
   An impish, mocking thing;
His wont by day to carp and fret,
   At night to dance and sing.

The foot and fist of rude Sir Kay

He bore with jest and sneer;
But wept to meet on any day
    The eyes of Guinevere.

That night he sat without the gate,
    Close by the city wall,
Till King and court, returning late,
    Climbed sadly toward the Hall.

He thought of all the good knights bent
    On unknown, wandering ways;
He thought of feast and tournament,
    And laughter of old days.

He would not enter with his King;
    He heard the warder call,
Yet waited, crouched and shivering,
    Beside the city wall.

Crooked and weak was Dagonet,
    What might to him avail
The hope whereon high hearts were set,
    To find the Holy Grail?

Yet ice and flame were in his breast;
    He hid his curling lip,
And wept for fierce desire to quest
    With the great Fellowship.

On nameless, shining paths afar,
    Where'er the vision bade,
He saw them ride,—saw like a star
    The face of Galahad.

Then on his heart fell unforgot,
    More soft than April rain,
The smile of sad Sir Lancelot,
    The sweet words of Gawain.

And Dagonet the jester laid
   His face against the stone,
And prayed to Him who once had prayed
   In blood and tears alone;

And lo! a strange voice reached his ears,
   Borne on soft-drifting wings;
'Twas gentler than Queen Guinevere's,
   'Twas kinglier than the King's.

It spake: "Thou foolish one, look up!
   Believe, and be thou glad;
There waits one vision of the Cup
   For thee and Galahad."

But Dagonet cried: "Lord, to me
   What may thy grace avail,
Since, late, in wrath and misery,
   I cursed the Holy Grail?"

Low in the dust knelt Dagonet;
   The sweet voice filled the air:
"Thy cursing lips I do forget,
   Because of thy heart's prayer."

Next day 'twas told through Camelot,
   With pity or with jest,
That Dagonet the dwarf came not
   Because he rode the Quest.

Next day and next, for many a day,
   Sir Dagonet rode hard;
Sometimes deep forest blurred his way,
   Or swollen torrent barred;

But everywhere the bright spring laid
   Her gold about his feet;
And every hour the high Quest made

Hope at his heart stir sweet.

At hermitage and castle gate
    He asked, alway in vain:
Nor Lancelot had passed of late,
    Nor Bors, nor good Gawain.

Now once it chanced that his path ran
    Along a riverside,
Till, where a chestnut wood began,
    He saw the ways divide.

And close beneath the roadside cross
    There lay a wounded knight;
His blood was black upon the moss,
    And dimmed his armor bright.

Sir Dagonet bent low and gazed
    In eyes that knew him not;
Then, weeping, to his heart he raised
    The head of Lancelot.

. . . .

Past midnight, when the moon was set,
    And utter dark the night,
Round Lancelot and Dagonet
    There shone a sudden light.

And in the light, soft-footing came,
    Four maidens grave and pale;
In lifted hands that burned like flame,
    One bore the Holy Grail.

Unveiled the Holy Chalice gleamed;
    Sweet odors filled the air;
The roadside cross an altar seemed,
    The winds were chant and prayer.

The dwarf knelt low in that blest place,
    Adored, and trembled not;
Then, with swift sorrow on his face,
    He turned to Lancelot.

He cried: "My lord, awake and see!
    Methinks thy quest is done!
The Holy Grail doth shine on thee
    More bright than moon or sun!"

Sir Lancelot groaned, but spake no word;
    He had nor voice, nor will;
Perchance the heavy eyelids stirred
    One moment, and were still.

Swift as it came the vision went;
    The dwarf moaned bitterly:
"My answered prayer is punishment
    Since my lord might not see!"

He groped to find where the cross stood,
    There was no ray of light;
He prayed: "Thou to the fool art good,
    Be gracious to the knight."

He cried and prayed beneath the cross,
    With foolish words and wild;
But Lancelot upon the moss
    Slept like a little child.

And in the dawning of the day
    The dwarf forgot to weep,
Seeing how fair Sir Lancelot lay,
    A-smiling in his sleep.

Sir Dagonet fell on his knee;
    He fingered head and limb;
And said: "The Grail was shown to me,

Its healing was for him.

"He will awaken whole and strong
    As ever he hath been;
He need not know his trance was long,
    Nor what the fool hath seen."

He sprang to horse: "Farewell, Sir Knight,
    Thy high vow shall not fail;
Some happier day thou shalt alight
    Upon the Holy Grail."

When birds from sky and tree and ground
    Sang loud and broke his rest,
Sir Lancelot rose blithe and sound
    To fare upon his quest.

But fast while morning hours were cool,
    And slow when noon waxed hot,
Sir Dagonet, King Arthur's fool,
    Rode back to Camelot.

At Camelot, with boisterous cries,
    Men asked him of his quest,
Till something in the rider's eyes
    Silenced the merry jest.

Sir Dagonet dwelt with the court;
    He mused on what had been;
By night he made them goodly sport;
    By day he served the Queen.

.   .   .   .

One slow, still morn of summer's prime,
    Through fields of yellow grain,
With saddened brow, before his time,
    Rode back the good Gawain.

But when the long nights of the year
    Darkened, and word came not,
Sir Dagonet and Guinevere
    Prayed for Sir Lancelot.

. . . .

Like swallows when winds first blow sweet,
    The knights came one by one;
Each told of travail and defeat,
    And how his quest was done.

Till, when the third bright June befell,
    And nightingales were glad,
From out the east came Bors to tell
    Of young Sir Galahad,

How won was the most Holy Quest:
    How Percivale and he
Were laid 'neath sacred earth to rest
    In Sarras over sea.

For Galahad brave eyes were wet,
    And gentle Percivale;
None ever heard how Dagonet
    Achieved the Holy Grail.

Keeping Tryst

A Tale of King Arthur's Time

ANNIE FELLOWS JOHNSTON

Now there was a troubadour in the kingdom of Arthur, who, strolling through the land with only his minstrelsy to win him a way, found in every baron's hall and cotter's hut a ready welcome. And while the boar's head sputtered on the spit, or the ale sparkled in the shining tankards, he told such tales of joust and journey, and feats of brave knight errantry, that even the scullions left their kitchen tasks, and, creeping near, stood round the door with mouths agape to listen.

Then with his harp-strings tuned to echoes of the wind on winter moors, he sang of death and valour on the field, of love and fealty in the hall, till those who listened forgot all save his singing and the noble knights whereof he sang.

One winter night, as thus he carolled in a great earl's hall, a little page crept nearer to his bench beside the fire, and, with his blue eyes fixed in wonderment upon the graybeard's face, stood spellbound. Now Ederyn was the page's name, an orphan lad whose lineage no man knew, but that he came of gentle blood all eyes could see, although as vassal 'twas his lot to wait upon the great earl's squire.

It was the Yule-tide, and the wassail-bowl passed round till boisterous mirth drowned oftentimes the minstrel's song, but Ederyn missed no word. Scarce knowing what he did, he crept so close he found himself with upturned face against the old man's knee.

"How now, thou flaxen-haired," the minstrel said, with kindly smile. "Dost like my song?"

"Oh, sire," the youth made answer, "methinks on such a wing the soul could well take flight to Paradise. But tell me, prithee, is it possible for such as *I* to gain the title of a knight? How doth one win such honours and acclaim and reach the high estate that thou dost laud?"

The minstrel gazed a little space into the Yule log's flame, and stroked his long hoar beard. Then made he answer:

"Some win their spurs and earn the royal accolade because the blood of dragons stains their hands. From mighty combat with these terrors they come victorious to their king's reward. And some there be sore scarred with conquest of the giants that ever prey upon the borders of our fair domain. Some, who have gone on far crusades to alien lands, and there with heart of gold and iron hand have proved their fealty to the Crown."

Then Ederyn sighed, for well he knew his stripling form could never wage fierce combat with a dragon. His hands could never meet the brawny grip of giants. "Is there no other way?" he faltered.

"I wot not," was the answer. "But take an old man's counsel. Forget thy dreams of glory, and be content to serve thy squire. For what hast such as thou to do with great ambitions? They'd prove but flames to burn away thy daily peace."

With that he turned to quaff the proffered bowl and add his voice to those whose mirth already shook the rafters. Nor had he any further speech with Ederyn. But afterward the pretty lad was often in his thoughts, and in his wanderings about the land he mused upon the question he had asked.

Another twelvemonth sped its way, and once again the Yule log burned within the hall, and once again the troubadour knocked at the gate, all in the night and falling snow. And as before, with merry jests they led him in and made him welcome. And as before, was every mouth agape from squire's to scullion's, as he sang.

Once more he sang of knights and ladies fair, of love and death and valour; and Ederyn, the page, crept nearer to him till the harpstrings ceased to thrill. With head upon his hands, he sat and sighed. Not even when the wassail-bowl was passed with mirth and laughter did he look up. And when the graybeard minstrel saw his grief, he thought upon his question of the Yule-tide gone.

"Ah, now, thou flaxen-haired," he whispered in his ear. "I bear thee tidings which should make thee sing with joy. There *is* a way for even such as thou to win the honours thou dost covet. I heard it in the royal court when last I sang there at the king's behest."

Then all aquiver with his eagerness did Ederyn kneel, with face alight, beside the minstrel's knee to hear.

"Know this," began the graybeard. "'Tis the king's desire to 'stablish round him at his court a chosen circle whose fidelity hath stood the utmost test. Not deeds of prowess are required of these true followers, with no great conquests doth he tax them, but they must prove themselves trustworthy, until on hand and heart it may be graven large, '*In all things faithful.*'

"To Merlin, the enchanter, he hath left the choice, who by some strange spell

I wot not of will send an eerie call through all the kingdom. And only those will hear who wake at dawn to listen in high places. And only those will heed who keep the compass needles of their souls true to the north star of a great ambition. The time of testing will be long, the summons many. To duty and to sorrow, to disappointment and defeat, thou may'st be called. No matter what the tryst, there is but one reply if thou wouldst win thy knighthood. Give heed and I will teach thee now that answer."

Then smiting on his harp, the minstrel sang, so softly under cover of the noise, that only Ederyn heard. Through all the song ran ever this refrain. It seemed a brooklet winding in and out through some fair meadow:

"'Tis the king's call. O list!
Thou heart and hand of mine, keep tryst—
　　Keep tryst or die!"

Then Ederyn, with his hand upon his heart, made solemn oath. "Awake at dawn and listening in high places will I await that call. With the compass needle of my soul true to the north star of a great ambition will I follow where it leads, and though through fire and flood it take me, I'll make but this reply:

"'Tis the king's call. O list!
Thou heart and hand of mine, keep tryst—
　　Keep tryst or die!'"

Pressing the old man's hand in gratitude (he could say no word for the strange fulness in his throat that well-nigh choked him), he rose from his knees and left the hall to muse on what had passed.

That night he climbed into the tower, and, with his face turned to the east, kept vigil all alone. Below, the rioters waxed louder in their mirth. The knife was in the meat, the drink was in the horn. But he would not join their revels, lest morning find him sunk in sodden sleep, heavy with feasting and witless from wine.

As gray dawn trailed across the hills, he started to his feet, for far away sounded the call for which he had been waiting. It was like the faint blowing of an elfin horn, but the words came clearly.

"Ederyn! Ederyn! One awaits thee at nightfall in the shade of the yew-tree by the abbey tower! Keep tryst!"

Now the abbey tower was the space of forty furlongs from the domain of the earl, and full well Ederyn knew that only by especial favour of his squire could he gain leave of absence for this jaunt. So, from sunrise until dusk, he worked with will, to gain the wished-for leave. Never before did buckles shine as did the buckles of the squire entrusted to his polishing. Never did menial tasks cease sooner to be drudgery, because of the good-will with which he worked. And when the day was done, so well had every duty been performed, right willingly the squire did grant him grace, and forthwith Ederyn sped upon his mission.

The way was long, and, when he reached the abbey tree, he fell a-trembling, for there a tall wraith stood within the shadows of the yew. No face had it that he could see, its hands no substance, but he met it bravely, saying: "I am Ederyn, come to keep the king's tryst."

And then the spectre's voice replied: "Well hast thou kept it, for 'tis known to me the menial tasks thou didst perform ere thou couldst come upon thy quest. In token that we two have met, here is my pledge that thou may'st keep to show the king."

He felt a light touch on the bosom of his inner vestment, and suddenly he stood alone beside the gruesome abbey. Clammy with fear, he knew not why, he drew his mantle round him and sped home as one speeds in a fearsome dream. And that it was a dream he half-believed, when later, in the hall, he served at meat those gathered round the old earl's board. But when he sought his bed, and threw aside his outer garment, there on his coarse, rough shirt of hodden gray a pearl gleamed white above his heart, where the wraith's cold hand had touched him. It was the token to the king that he had answered faithfully his call.

Again before the dawn he climbed into the tower, and, listening when the voices of the world were still, heard clear and sweet, like far-blown elfin horn, another summons.

"Ederyn! Ederyn! One awaits thee at the midnight hour beside black Kilgore's water. Keep tryst!"

Again to gain his squire's permission he toiled with double care. This time his task was counting all the spears and halberds, the battle-axes and the coats of mail that filled the earl's great armament. And o'er and o'er he counted, keeping careful tally with a bit of keel upon the iron-banded door, till the red lines that he marked there made his eyes ache and his head swim. At last the task was finished, and so well the squire praised him, and for his faithfulness again was fain to speed him on his way.

It was a woful journey to the waters of Kilgore. Sleep weighed on Ederyn's eyelids, and haltingly he went the weary miles, footsore and worn. But midnight found him on the spot where one awaited him, another wraith-like envoy of the king, and it, too, left a touch upon his heart in token he had kept the tryst. And when he looked, another pearl gleamed there beside the first.

So many a day went by, and Ederyn failed not in his homely tasks, but carried to his common round of duties all his might, as if they were great feats of prowess. Thus gained he liberty to keep the tryst with every messenger the king did send.

Once he fared forth along a dangerous road that led he knew not where, and, when he found it crossed a loathly swamp all filled with slime and creeping things, fain would he have fled. But, pushing on for sake of his brave oath, although with fainting heart, he reached the goal at last. This time his token made him wonder much. For when he wakened from his swoon, a shining star lay on his heart above the pearls.

Now it fell out the squire to whom this Ederyn was page was killed in conflict with a robber band, and Ederyn, for his faithfulness, was taken by the earl to fill that squire's place. Soon after that, they left the hall, and journeyed on a visit to a distant lord. 'Twas to the Castle of Content they came, where was a joyous garden. And now no menial tasks employed the new squire's time. Here was he free to wander all the day through vistas of the joyous garden, or loiter by the fountain in the courtyard and watch the maidens at their tasks, having fair speech with them among the flowers. And one there was among them, so lily-like in face, so gentle-voiced and fair, that Ederyn well-nigh forgot his oath, and felt full glad when for a space the king's call ceased to sound. And gladder was he still, when, later on, the earl's long visit done, he left young Ederyn behind to serve the great lord of the castle, for so the two friends had agreed, since Ederyn had pleased the old lord's fancy.

Yet was he faithful to his vow, and failed not every dawn to mount to some high place, when all the voices of the world were still, and listen for the sound of Merlin's horn. One morn it came:

"Ederyn! Ederyn! One waits thee far away. By the black cave of Atropos, when the moon fulls, keep thy tryst!"

Now 'twas a seven days' journey to that cave, and Ederyn, thinking of the lily maid, was loath to leave the garden. He lingered by the fountain until nightfall, saying to himself: "Why should I go on longer in these foolish quests, keeping tryst with shadows that vanish at the touch? No nearer am I to a knight's estate than when, a stripling page, I listened to the minstrel's tales."

The fountain softly splashed within the garden. From out the banquet-hall there stole the sound of tinkling lutes, and then the lily maiden sang. Her siren voice filled all his heart, and he forgot his oath to duty. But presently a star reflected in the fountain made him look up into the jewelled sky, where shone the polar constellation. And there he read the oath he had forgotten: "With the compass needle of my soul true to the north star of my great ambition, I will follow where it leads."

Thrusting his fingers in his ears to silence the beloved voice of her who sang, he madly rushed from out the garden into the blackness of the night. The Castle of Content clanged its great gate behind him. He shivered as he felt the jar through all his frame, but, never taking out his fingers, on he ran, till scores of furlongs lay between him and the tempting of that siren voice.

It was a strange and fearsome wood that lay between him and the cave. All things seemed moaning and afraid. He saw no forms, but everywhere the shadows shuddered, and moans and groans pursued him till nameless fears clutched at his heart with icy chill. Then suddenly the earth slipped way beneath his feet, and cold waves closed above his head. He knew now he had fallen in the pool that lies upon the far edge of the fearsome wood,—a pool so deep and of such whirling motion that only by the fiercest struggle may one escape. Gladly he would have allowed the waters to close over him, such cold pains smote his heart, had he not seemed to hear the old minstrel's song. It aroused him to a final effort, and he gasped between his teeth:

> "'Tis the king's call! O list!
> Thou heart and hand of mine, keep tryst—
> Keep tryst or die!'"

With that, in one mighty struggle he dragged himself to land. A bow-shot farther on he saw the cave, and by sheer force of will crept toward it. What happened then he knew not till the moon rose full and high above him. A form swathed all in black bowed over him.

"Ederyn," she sighed, "here is thy token that the king may know that thou hast met me face to face."

He thought it was a diamond at first, that sparkled there beside the star, but when he looked again, lo, nothing but a tear.

Then went he back unto the joyous garden by slow degrees, for he was now sore spent. And after that the summons came full often. Whenever all the world seemed loveliest and life most sweet, then was the call most sure to come. But never once he faltered. Never was he faithless to the king's behest. Up weary mountain steps he toiled to find the sombre face of Disappointment there in waiting, and Suffering and Pain were often at his journey's end, and once a sore Defeat. But bravely as the months went by he learned to smile into their eyes, no matter which one handed out to him the pledge of Duty well performed.

One day, when he no longer was a beardless youth, but grown to pleasing stature and of great brawn, he heard the hoped-for call of which he long had dreamed: "Ederyn! Ederyn! The king himself awaits thee. Midsummer morn at larksong, keep tryst beside the palace gate."

As travellers on the desert, spent and worn, see far across the sand the palm-tree's green that marks life-giving wells, so Ederyn hailed this summons to the king. The soul-consuming thirst that long had urged him on grew fiercer as the well of consummation came in sight. Hope shod his feet with wings, as thus with every nerve a-strain he pushed toward the final tryst. So fearful was he some mishap might snatch the cup away ere it had touched his thirsty lips, that three full days before the time he reached the Vale of Avalon, and sat him down outside the entrance to the palace.

Now there came prowling through the wood that edged the fair domain the gnarled dwarfs that do the will of Shudderwain. And Shudderwain, of all the giants thereabouts, most cruel was and to be feared. Knowing full well what pleasure it would give the bloody monster, these dwarfs laid evil hands on Ederyn. Sleeping they found him, and bound him with hard leathern thongs, and then with gibes and impish laughter dragged him into a dungeon past the help of man.

Two days and nights he lay there, raging at fate and at his helplessness, till he was well-nigh mad, bethinking him of all his baffled hopes. And like a madman gnawed he on the leathern thongs till he was free, and beat his hands against the stubborn rock that would not yield, and threw himself against the walls that held him in.

The dwarfs from time to time peered through the slatted window overhead and mocked him, pointing with their crooked thumbs.

"Ha! ha! Thou'lt keep no tryst," they chattered. "But if thou'lt swear upon thy oath to go back to the joyous garden, and hark no more for Merlin's call, we'll let thee loose from out this Dungeon of thy Disappointment."

Then was Ederyn tempted, for the dungeon was foul indeed, and his heart cried out to go back to the lily maiden. But once more in his ears he thrust his fingers and cried:

> "'To the king's call alone I'll list!
> Oh, heart and hand of mine, keep tryst—
> Keep tryst or die!'"

On the third night, with the quiet of despair he threw him prone upon the dungeon floor and held his peace, no longer gnawing on his thongs or beating on the rock. A single moonbeam straggled through the slatted window, and by its light he saw a spider spinning out a web. Then, looking dully around, he saw the dungeon was hung thick with other webs, foul with the dust of years. Great festoons of the cobweb film shrouded his prison walls. As up and down the hairy creature swung itself upon its thread, the hopeless eyes of Ederyn followed it.

All in a twinkling he saw how he might profit by the spider's teaching, and clapped his hand across his mouth to keep from shouting out his joy so that the dwarfs could hear. Now once more like a madman rushing at the walls, he tore down all the dusty webs, and twisted them together in long strands. These strands he braided in thick ropes and tied them, knotting them and twisting and doubling once again. All the while he kept bewailing the stupid way in which he wasted time. "Three days ago I might have quit this den," he sighed, "had I but used the means that lay at hand. Full well I knew that heaven always finds a way to help the man who helps himself. No creature lives too mean to be of service, and even dungeon walls must harbour help for him who boldly grasps the first thing that he sees and makes it serve him."

So fast and furiously he worked that, long before the moonbeam faded, his cobweb rope was strong enough to bear his weight, and long enough to reach twice over to the slatted window overhead. By many trials he at last succeeded in throwing it around a spike that barred the window, and, climbing up, he forced the slats apart and clambered through. Then tying the rope's end to the window, he slid down all the dizzy cliffside in which the dwarfs had dug the dungeon, and dropped into the stream that ran below.

Lo, when he looked around him it was dawn. Midsummer morn it was, and, plunging through the wood, he heard the lark's song rise, and reached the palace gate just as it opened to the blare of trumpets for the king's train to ride forth. When Ederyn saw the royal cavalcade, he shrunk back into the wayside bushes, so ill-befitting did it seem that he should come before the king in tattered garments, with blood upon his hands where the sharp rocks had cut, and with foul dungeon stains.

But that the king might know he'd ever proven faithful, he sank upon his knees and bared his breast at his approach. There all the pledges glistened in the sunlight, in rainbow hues. There Pain had dropped her heart's blood in a glittering ruby, and Honour set her seal upon him in a golden star. A diamond gleamed where Sorrow's tear had fallen, and amethysts glowed now with purple splendour to mark his patient meeting with Defeat. But mostly were the pledges little pearls for little duties faithfully performed; and there they shone, and, as the people gazed, they saw the jewels take the shape of letters, so that the king read out before them all, "*Semper fidelis.*"

Then drew the king his royal sword and lightly smote on Ederyn's shoulder, and cried: "Arise, Sir Knight, Sir Ederyn the Trusty. Since I may trust thee to the utmost in little things as well as great, since thou of all men art most worthy, henceforth by thy king's heart thou shalt ride, ever to be his faithful guard and comrade."

So there before them all he did him honour, and ordered that a prancing steed be brought and a good sword buckled on his side.

Thus Ederyn won his sovereign's favour. Soon, by his sovereign's grace permitted, he went back to the joyous garden to woo the lily maiden. When he had won his bride and borne her to the palace, then was his great reward complete for all his years of fealty to his vow. Then out into the world he went to guard his king. Henceforth blazoned on his shield and helmet he bore the crest—a heart with hand that grasped a spear, and, underneath, these words:

"*I keep the tryst!*"

When Tristan Sailed

Helen Hay Whitney

When Tristan sailed from Ireland
   Across the summer sea,
How young he was, how debonnaire,
   How glad he was and free.
Why should he know the gales would blow,
   The skies be black above,
How should he dream his port was Death,
   And Doom, whose name is Love?

The Lady Iseult, sweet as prayer,
   We hardly dare to pray,
Pearl-pale beneath her shadow hair,
   Grows fairer day by day,
The ichor gains her spring-kissed veins,
   Her skies the eyes of youth.
How should she dream the ichor Love,
   Was hellebore in truth?

So Tristan sailed from Ireland
   As youth must always sail;
He quaffed the cup, nor asked the wine;
   He dared, nor feared to fail.
And be it poison, be it life,
   Or wrecks that strew the shore,
Tristan set forth! nor ask the end,
   Else youth shall sail no more.

Songs of Tristram & Yseult

ELIZABETH COLWELL

Tristram Sings

I

Yseult, my breast is stricken
With a more deadly dart,
Than that the Giant Morholt
Aimed at my knightly heart.

I linger and I languish
From sufferings far more
Than those which held me, helpless,
On thy White-haven shore.

Ah, canst thou not sustain me!
Lean down thy lips and bless.
Heal thou once more in pity,
Tristram of Lyonesse.

II

I drank the proffered potion,
But as a cooling draught;
Ah, from the Cup of Silver
'Twas madness that I quaffed.

Quick thro' my lithesome body
There ran a thread of fire;
It touched my heart to rapture,
And kindled my desire.

Now, all that mighty prowess
Which made Tintagel's fame
Is but a slender reed stem,
Swayed by swift passion's flame.

III

Thy body is a rose-jar—
A cup of fragrance, blown
In some remoter cycle,
When Beauty claimed her own.

Thy lingering caresses,
And thy white hands' delight,
Are like the slender jonquils,
Pure in the pale moonlight.

The wind that stirs the Poppies,
The warm wind from the South,
Makes no more subtle music,
Than whisperings of thy mouth.

Thy breasts are two white lilies,
Faint rose-red at the heart,
Where hidden sweetness lingers
And quick, shy tremors start.

O let me be the sunshine,
Here in this silent room,
To lift the tender petals,
And share the bowls of bloom!

Thy lips are two red berries;
I crush them, and the stain
Of their ripe sweets is memory
Of mingled joy and pain.

Twin stars in a fair heaven—
The lights of summer skies—
Deep azure of the ocean;
Like these thy lustrous eyes.

The white of the white sea-spray,
When sky and sea-spray meet,
Is not so light a wonder,
As whiteness of thy feet.

I would my Harp were stringed
With threads of thy Golden Hair:
Then might I sing more seemly
My Love and my Despair.

Yseult Sings

I

A queen am I, in title,
With vassals at my call;
Brave Knights and lovely Ladies
Make pleasure in my Hall.

While sparkling wine is circled
With quip and idle jest;
And while the King his favor
Bestows upon some guest,

I seek my silent chamber
That overlooks the sea,
And with my Harp, sing softly,
Some sad, sweet melody.

II

All day I feign light laughter,
All night my loosened hair
I gather close to smother
My sobs and my despair.

I burn with a bright fever;
I droop—I drown—I die;
At night my lonely pillow
Is lonelier than when I

Lay lone in distant Ireland,
Within that Castle, steep,
That sheltered my young girlhood,
And held my virgin sleep.

III

Without, a bird is singing;
That mellow, liquid note
Came with a flash of crimson,
Across the Castle moat.

The roses, too, are climbing
Up to my window-sill,
And tulips and white lilies
Are opening, until

It seems that Nature, spendthrift,
Is lavish with her Art.
And Spring—sweet Spring—is here—
But not within my heart.

IV

Where lombardies lean seaward,
And white waves wash the cliff;

Where wild flowers bloom and wither,
I walk, and wonder if

Of all the ships a-sailing
Upon the restless sea,
There will not come one, bringing
My happiness to me.

Galahad in the Castle of the Maidens

SARA TEASDALE

(To the maiden with the hidden face in Abbey's painting)

The other maidens raised their eyes to him
Who stumbled in before them when the fight
Had left him victor, with a victor's right.
I think his eyes with quick hot tears grew dim;
He scarcely saw her swaying white and slim,
And trembling slightly, dreaming of his might,
Nor knew he touched her hand, as cool and light
As a wan wraith's beside a river's rim.
The other maidens raised their eyes to see
And only she has hid her face away,
And yet I think she loved him more than they,
And very fairly fashioned was her face.
Yet for Love's shame and sweet humility,
She could not meet him with their queenlike grace.

Guenevere

SARA TEASDALE

I was a queen, and I have lost my crown;
A wife, and I have broken all my vows;
A lover, and I ruined him I loved:—
There is no other havoc left to do.
A little month ago I was a queen,
And mothers held their babies up to see
When I came riding out of Camelot.
The women smiled, and all the world smiled too.
And now, what woman's eyes would smile on me?
I am still beautiful, and yet what child
Would think of me as some high, heaven-sent thing,
An angel, clad in gold and miniver?
The world would run from me, and yet I am
No different from the queen they used to love.
If water, flowing silver over stones,
Is forded, and beneath the horses' feet
Grows turbid suddenly, it clears again,
And men will drink it with no thought of harm.
Yet I am branded for a single fault.

I was the flower amid a toiling world,
Where people smiled to see one happy thing,
And they were proud and glad to raise me high;
They only asked that I should be right fair,
A little kind, and gownèd wondrously,
And surely it were little praise to me
If I had pleased them well throughout my life.

I was a queen, the daughter of a king.
The crown was never heavy on my head,
It was my right, and was a part of me.
The women thought me proud, the men were kind,
And bowed down gallantly to kiss my hand,
And watched me as I passed them calmly by,
Along the halls I shall not tread again.
What if, to-night, I should revisit them?
The warders at the gates, the kitchen-maids,
The very beggars would stand off from me,
And I, their queen, would climb the stairs alone,
Pass through the banquet-hall, a hated thing,
And seek my chambers for a hiding-place,
And I should find them but a sepulchre,
The very rushes rotted on the floors,
The fire in ashes on the freezing hearth.

I was a queen, and he who loved me best
Made me a woman for a night and day,
And now I go unqueened forevermore.

A queen should never dream on summer nights,
When hovering spells are heavy in the dusk:—
I think no night was ever quite so still,
So smoothly lit with red along the west,
So deeply hushed with quiet through and through.
And strangely clear, and sharply dyed with light,
The trees stood straight against a paling sky,
With Venus burning lamp-like in the west.
I walked alone among a thousand flowers,
That drooped their heads and drowsed beneath the dew,
And all my thoughts were quieted to sleep.
Behind me, on the walk, I heard a step—
I did not know my heart could tell his tread,
I did not know I loved him till that hour.
The garden reeled a little, I was weak,
And in my breast I felt a wild, sick pain.
Quickly he came behind me, caught my arms,

That ached beneath his touch; and then I swayed,
My head fell backward and I saw his face.

All this grows bitter that was once so sweet,
And many mouths must drain the dregs of it,
But none will pity me, nor pity him
Whom Love so lashed, and with such cruel thongs.

Tristram and Isoult

MARTHA KINROSS

Characters

KING ARTHUR OF BRITAIN

KING MARK OF CORNWALL

SIR TRISTRAM OF LYONESSE

SIR LAUNCELOT DU LAC

SIR ANDRED

SIR DINAS THE SENESCHAL

SIR SADOK

QUEEN GUINEVERE

QUEEN ISOULT, CALLED LA BELLE

ISOULT BLANCHE MAINS OF BRITTANY

BRANGWANE

BLANCHELYS

YGRAINE

LAUREL

COLOMBE

KNIGHTS, LADIES, PAGES AND SERVING-WOMEN

Part I

SCENE.—*A hall in the castle of Camelot, hung with tapestries worked with events in the life of Arthur: the drawing of the sword from the stone; the crowning of Arthur; the battle with the eleven kings and their host; the wedding with Guinevere; the Lady of the Lake and the sword Excalibur. The furnishing of the hall is several great settles of oak with carven backs, a king's chair of cedar with dragons for arms, the dragon's claws and crowns of gold;*

*and a queen's chair, smaller and less rich. Also there is a couch; and a table made of black
and white marble on top to form a chess-board, with chessmen of silver. The deep casements
at the back look into the great court of the castle, from which the noise of a tourney—
clashing of steel and cries and trumpets blown—rises faintly into the chamber. The ledges
of the casements are spread with cloths and cushions, and therefrom Queen Guinevere and
Queen Isoult of Cornwall have watched the joust.*

GUINEVERE. Jesu! how he doth smite! The brittle spears
      Shatter before him as when winter breathes
      Hard on the mailéd boughs.
ISOULT.   He ever jousts
      As is our fancy—best beneath mine eyes.
GUINEVERE. Thy fancy held this day, though he knew not
      What eyes this lattice hid.
ISOULT.   The man in me—
      That every woman that is fathered hath—
      Leaps out to arm him with the secret wrath:
      The hate I must keep sheathed, or bare
      In the mere bloodless pass of look and word;
      The scorn I cover with submission; all
      The woman's forced endurance, strike through him
      When I do watch him, doubling his great strokes
      Wherein I taste of battle.
GUINEVERE.   It is long
      Since he hath fired our lists.
ISOULT.   "Too long," I urged,
      "Men say thou hast begun to slack in deeds,
      To dull in fame; thy days passed in the hunt,
      Or idler yet, aharping at my side.
      Go to this joust. I will not go with thee,
      For fear that thou be known, and many knights
      Be keen for winning glory at a thrust
      In Tristram overborne." . . . When he was gone
      Brangwane and I took horse, with Dinadin.
      We three rode softly, following in his track
      A league or two behind.
GUINEVERE.   The horn is straked!
      The tilts are done—and the king blows to lodging.

Brangwane runs in.

BRANGWANE. The black knight wins the day! The black knight wins!
　　The cry is cried for him throughout the field.
　　But he, as by a magic, vanished away!
　　The king is vexed to lose him. All the knights,
　　With Launcelot, are in quest.

ISOULT.　　　　　　　　　Hark, hark, how loud!
　　He rides to Joyous Gard and to Isoult.
　　Go, Brangwane, go and seek Sir Launcelot.
　　Tell him the stranger knight that won the day
　　Is Tristram. Pray him send a messenger
　　To turn my lord, with knowledge I am here,—
　　Am with the queen. Make haste, make haste!

Brangwane goes.

GUINEVERE.　　　　　　　　Isoult,
　　Isoult the fearless, I have envied thee
　　Thy Joyous Gard, and the avowéd years
　　Lived open to King Mark and to the world.
　　A flame too great to cover, as to quench;
　　A wind-blown beacon shaming secret love,
　　Our cautious smoulder eating in the dark.
　　And if, as yet men have not seen our fire,
　　It seems they feel the heat. There have been hints.
　　Always some mockery on Gawaine's lips,—
　　Mordred suspects. When Launcelot is here,
　　I feel them watching us. And if I turn
　　Full shortly, I surprise the meaning glance
　　That's sped 'twixt eye and eye, and see it sink,
　　Downcast in a feigned sleekness, to the floor.
　　All eyes are watchmen, all tongues witnesses.
　　For we above the people lift tall heads,
　　And every rumour blowing over us,
　　Scattereth our seeds of action through the land.
　　And I, rank weed, oh, what an evil crop,
　　Throughout the king's good acres have I sown!
　　But I was born a woman,—not a queen.
　　When that state fell to me, with Arthur's choice,
　　One older, colder, wise in tutory,

They should have sent to bring me to the throne.
Instead they sent me Launcelot,—my Launcelot!
Together we rode o'er the missal-page
Of the green April earth—love's Book of Hours,
Blazoned with Spring—whose every word was love.
'Twas in the flowers I smelled, the air I breathed,
The birds I hearkened, and in mine own heart.
And then, ah, then, I came to Arthur. . . . Him,
I scarce do ever think on as a man;
One shaped to fit his destiny—as they say
The bee is,—in the birth-call of the womb.
And Merlin fed him with a wisdom sealed
Out of the kingly past—to perfect kingship.
Old shadowy prophecies did point to him.
But not to me—ah, not to me—to match
That royal front of Arthur's with a brow
Calm as the orbéd forehead of some saint—
The altar's moon that shineth candle-starred.
None are deceived in me: this crown I wear
Is like the bale-fire set upon the hill;
Or penance pressing on my aching head;
Its jewels, eyes that never shut, but spy
Into my guilty thought.

ISOULT.   So God me help,
I sin not, for my husband is my shame.
I put on Tristram's love, a crown to wear
In all men's sight. 'Tis Tristram makes me queen.
Not Cornish Mark.

GUINEVERE.   And yet hadst thou been wed
To one like Arthur—

ISOULT.   Aye, the cause lieth there.
And hadst thou wedded been to one like Mark!
Yet is there other difference of our fates;
For unwithholden I loved Tristram first.
With a false name for shield, he came to us,
Wounded and weak, to ask my mother's skill.
I did not know him for my uncle's slayer;
I must have held him blameless had I known,

Since he for Cornwall fought, to serve his king,
His country, as our Marhaus fought for Ireland.
I deemed not then the stream of kinsman's blood
That flowed betwixt us. . . . Strength came slow to him.
In the long twilights, on the castle walls,
As all the littler stars do drop away
To leave the heavens hallowed to the moon,
So lesser thoughts went from us, and our hearts
Were left for love to fill. Then he would string
His harp, and sing me those brave songs he made,
Or tell the happenings of King Arthur's court.
And time went softly, till one doomful day,
My mother, seeking, found his broken sword,
And struck by the strange work, all diapered,
Pieced to the rough edge of the ragged blade
The splintered steel she took from Marhaus' wound—
Whereof he died—and for a vengeance kept.
Keener than if the sword itself had turned
Its point upon her, passed the sudden truth
Into her breast. Clamorous for her revenge
She sped unto my father: "Knowest thou,
King Anguish, whom thou harbourest? Knowest thou,
Tristram is he who took my brother's life,
And cometh here for leech-craft, as the bitten
Desireth the dog's hair unto the bite,
Or as we bind the adder on the part
Its fang hath venomed?"
                              Brangwane heard the words—
And I being warned, got Tristram safely thence.
Thus was the end—thus knew we that we loved.
By peril hastened, ere its hour had come,
Was passion brought to birth. And travailing died
The joy that Love is born of, with one look
Upon Love's new-born face. But Love—Love lived!
GUINEVERE. And whither, then, went Tristram?
ISOULT.   To Cornwall.
GUINEVERE. Time passed ere ye did meet?
ISOULT.   Three years. Three years

Ere he to Ireland came again, to beg
A bride for Tristram's uncle, Cornish Mark.
A bride to close the breach between two kings,
And range her with the marble women who
For ever prop the roofs of palaces
With their numbed arms. . . . I went—and all the rest
Is known to thee.

GUINEVERE.   Thou hast not wronged the highest,
Nor daily undermined his builded hope;
Nor known thyself the worm that eats the heart
Of a whole realm, and leaves it at the core
But rottenness. Would I were dead! I weary
Of love's unrest. I long for convent walls,
The prayer-paved cloisters paced by quiet feet,
Preparedly, to death. Love hath no peace.
I dread that Launcelot may tire with straining
To reach the happiness beyond his reach,
And end with taking lesser happiness
That is not noble, but is near.

ISOULT.   Ah, bitter,
Bitter doubt that Isoult knows!

GUINEVERE.   When Tristram wedded
Isoult Blanche Mains of Brittany?

ISOULT.   Aye, then.
And night and day I maddened with my doubt.
The past was done: like tapestry from the wall,
I tore away the past, and faced the blank.
But then did fancy weave with burning thread,
Out of a brain of fire, the pictures new.
A woman's face, from bowers that were mine,
Looked on me; white and tall she stood, this maid,
Amid the green, with lily-pointed hands
That Tristram loved. And like a dreadful Fate,
I wove them curses,—imaged doom on doom—
My life-thread wrought into that weaving, dyed
With mine own heart. I prayed that it might snap.
For I was mad—yea, mad with jealousy!
But then came Tristram's letter, telling all,

And with it—peace.

GUINEVERE.   King Howell made that marriage.
A slack knot tied by Age's trembling hands,
And never for Love's binding. . . . Ah, Isoult,
There is a worser thief than the soft eyes
To steal love from us,—Time, that changeth Love,
Himself, into a ghost with faded lips
Too cold for kisses, and with cheeks whereon
Is withered all the blossom of the blood.
Then will regret pursue us like remorse!
I fear to keep this love of Launcelot's—
And fear yet more to lose it. If thou thinkest
Of Arthur's goodness as my great reproof,
I say it doth absolve me,—aye, in part,—
And with the chapel chills the marriage-bed.
Had I met Arthur ere he was the king—
Or ere he was my husband—then, perchance,
What is, had never been. For who would wish—
Without the checks and starts of wind-rocked March,
The sharp-shod runners of the April rain,
And swelling buds,—the sudden summer blown?
And much that day is robbed that hath no dawn
To lift the slumber from earth's widowed lids,
Dim with the dews of solitary sleep,
And turn her waking wonder on the sun.

  She pauses, listening.

ISOULT. Sir Truant comes.

  Enter Tristram. He is in armour, but has laid aside his shield, his helmet,
  and steel gauntlets.

TRISTRAM.   My Queens,—the world's two queens—
How dare I break upon their converse, thus,
Were I not summoned? Launcelot's messenger
Did bid me back, with tidings of one here
Whose eyes would know me when I should be hid
From the high God.

  He kisses the hand, first of Guinevere, then of Isoult.

GUINEVERE. [*With reproach.*] And thou wouldst ride away,
And not divulge thee, even to Launcelot?

Fie! Was this brotherly done?

TRISTRAM.   Then, Madam, blame
My vow; my vow was secrecy.

GUINEVERE.   This vow,
Doth it embrace the king? Thou has not spoke
With Arthur?

TRISTRAM. Nay, not yet; but now I go.
He hath had news of late, as Launcelot telleth,
Which touches me so closely that the king
Had mind to send for me to Camelot.

ISOULT. 'Tis no ill tidings, prithee?

GUINEVERE.   Thou speakest as I,—
Even as I that have a fearful heart.
Never a shadow falleth round my feet,
But I look up to see Fate swoop and strike:
I live beneath its wing. . . . I'll be thy herald,
And tell the king thou art already come.
And if I leave thee with this lady here,
Thou wilt not quarrel with my courtesy,
Methinks, Sir Tristram?

                    Guinevere goes out.

ISOULT.   What took thee from the lists
In such hot haste?

TRISTRAM. [*Taking her in his arms.*] Thou knowest, ah, thou knowest!
I thought thee far away at Joyous Gard.
How come ye to be here?

ISOULT.   We followed thee,
Brangwane and I, and Dinadin rode with us.
I must be here to take thee in my arms
Ere thou cool from the anvil of the strife—
Hammered red-hot with ringing stroke on stroke—
The ardour on thee, and the glow undimmed.
For I, the woman, catch a fire from thee,
As doth some little cloud that flieth far,
Aflame upon the edges of the dusk.
Yea, would I were; to clothe me with thy glory;
High in the heavens and in all men's sight
Ablaze with thee,—my wings with victory burning—

Thy triumph on my breast!

    He draws a carcanet of rubies from under his mail and clasps it on her throat.

TRISTRAM.   Behold it there!

My triumph on thy breast,—behold it blaze.

These be the fires of glory—these my fame,

Wherewith I clothe thee.

ISOULT.   Ah, the carcanet!

The tourney's prize of rubies, won by thee!

Now shall I never envy Guinevere

Her diamonds, more.

TRISTRAM.   What, thou to envy

Her jewels, thou!

ISOULT.   For every diamond there

Stands for a joust, and flasheth unto fame

The name of Launcelot.

TRISTRAM.   Her diamonds semble

The April colours of that shaken queen;

Like purity a-pulse with hotter fires

That come and go within the fitful soul,

Against its will. Thine are these steadfast stones.

    Isoult takes off the necklace and holds it in her hands.

ISOULT. Heart-shaped, heart-tinctured, 'tis the rosary

Of lovers' hearts, whereon we'll tell the names

Of those who for love's sake have lived and died.

This, constant Hero's heart; and this the heart

Of that Egyptian Queen—

TRISTRAM.   And this, congealed

Of some dark passion, is Morgan la Fay's.

Now come we to the greatest, to Isoult—

ISOULT. Nay, this for Guinevere. Thou knowest her not—

Her love for Launcelot.

TRISTRAM.   Methinks I do:

Queen first, and lover last. I named her April,

A changeful April; thou to Autumn belongest,

Rare Autumn with the ever-deepening heart

That death doth hardly chill; with her last leaf

Still giving to the asking of the wind:

A fear, a fate, inwoven with thy spell.

Thy dark eyes are the doors of mystery;
The shadow of the forests is thy hair;
Thy whiteness hath been washed in the sea-depths
And glimmers with their pearl. And oh, my Queen,
Thy spirit shakes me as the blast the wood;
Thy beauty stirreth with a wild unrest.
Thou art the thirst between fulfilling draughts!
A hunger in me that cries out for more!
A hunger as one hath for scented fruit,
That ever as it feeds the grosser want,
Stingeth the finer, more insatiate sense,
With somewhat yet unseized!

ISOULT.   Yea, but the sweet,
    Is it not worth the pain that we have dured?
TRISTRAM. And that which is to come.
ISOULT.   What meanest thou?
    What pain that is to come? Ah, wilt thou go
    Upon this quest, this new quest of the Grail?
TRISTRAM. That is for Galahad and the others; I
    Have found my Grail,—the cup from Brangwane's bosom
    We drew the while she slept, upon the ship
    I drank of it; the magic-mingled wine
    Shot through my body like the Northern fire,
    And all the streaming banners of my blood
    Moved to the sound of music in my veins.
ISOULT. Not then for the first time—
TRISTRAM.   But long before,—
    I loved thee in the king thy father's hall,
    The day thy healing fingers searched my wound.
    My life hung like a dying candle-smoke;
    A fume, a vapour, was the fading sense
    A touch had snuffed, a touch less sure than thine,
    Less learned in all leech-craft.
ISOULT.   The years did wait,
    Until that day of Mark's great hunt. All day
    They hunted, till the moon was in the sky,
    But thou unseen hadst stolen from the chase.
    The ancient forest stood above our heads,

Its arches loftier risen with the dusk;
We heard the distant summons of the horns
That wove their thin, sweet silver through the brake,
Even as the moonlight chequering the shades.
The Hunt of Life swept by—the baying pack—
The tongues so loud in cry that found us not.
So seemed it as a faint, far dream that passed.
Unreal life, unreal death, unreal
All things, save only love!

TRISTRAM.   Oh, night of nights,
That from mid-heaven plucked our topmost star,
Yet left a shining host.

ISOULT.   Put me not off,
Even with these memories. Put me not off!
Tell me what meant thy words.

TRISTRAM.   What words, Isoult?

ISOULT. "And all that is to come."

TRISTRAM.   If we must part—

ISOULT. Must part? Who hath the power to part us?

TRISTRAM.   Cornwall.
Sessoynes invades the realm; and him our Mark
Dare not encounter with, as Arthur fears.

ISOULT. 'Tis Arthur, then, that sets thee to this task?
I would be sworn!

TRISTRAM.   Not Arthur,—Cornwall, Cornwall.
All that I am is thine, but I was hers
In those old years in which she was the mother
Of my fore-running race.

ISOULT.   I see the end!
Thus ends the life together, ends my peace.
Hast thou no thought of me? Do I not weigh
'Gainst Cornwall?

TRISTRAM.   Thine by all I am. But Cornwall—
By that which was, and will be, am I hers.
For stronger than ourselves this love of the birth-land,
In which I hear, like the voices of the leaves,
The tree of all my line that whispereth
To me, its living root in Cornish soil,

The loyalties of countless lives and deaths.

Guinevere enters with Arthur and Launcelot.

GUINEVERE. Who talks of death? A happier theme we bring,
When the king comes, as now, to speak thine Isoult's praise.

Arthur kisses Isoult on the brow, Launcelot salutes her hand.

ARTHUR. Ah, Madam, Queen, and loyalest of lovers,
No praise o'errateth thy true counselling
That spurred Sir Tristram hither to our lists,
When he, content with courage hardily proven
Upon a hundred helms, had lagged at home,
Leaving to maiden spears the prize at arms.
And wisely hast thou thought to spare him labour,
And come unknown. Our knights grow envious
Of his great fortune both in love and war.
Would that all women were as thou, more jealous
For worship than for love!

ISOULT.   Methinks the sun
Must cool a little, and the earth likewise,
Ere that time come.

LAUNCELOT.   Thine act doth bring it nearer.

ISOULT. So sayest *thou*, Launcelot?

ARTHUR.   So say we all.
So saith, I am sure, mine own Queen here.

ISOULT. Wilt thou not take some shorter way, my lord,
Unto thy meaning,—speak the matter out?
The curtain of these broidered courtesies
Scarce hides that arméd sense that stands in wait
To strike my heart.

ARTHUR.   What meaning should I have
But good towards thee, and Tristram whom I hold
Above all knights of mine save one,—save only
My Launcelot.

Lays his hand on Launcelot's shoulder.

ISOULT. What meaning? Cornwall's peril.
Cornwall invaded.

ARTHUR.   And King Mark—

ISOULT.   My husband.
Why say ye not my husband Mark, my lord?

What should we care for peril to King Mark,
 For peril to our peril?
ARTHUR.   Cornwall, say.
ISOULT. And Cornwall a grim trap a-gape for us.
 One good it hath, that the green Irish sea
 Washes its shores.
ARTHUR.   'Tis Tristram's land. To his
 Deliverance doth threated Cornwall look:
 Her right to find a rescue in that race
 That hath undone her with a coward king.
 Out of the same blood bane and antibane.
ISOULT. There's bane, in sooth. Ye put me well in mind
 Of that fell cup King Mark once brewed for us,
 And would again.
TRISTRAM.   No tricks now, never dread.
 For he hath need; one doth not lop the arm
 That fends him.
ISOULT.   Ye are against me—all!
ARTHUR.   None is
 Against Isoult, save Isoult's nobler self.
 What, wast thou eager for a tourney's honour,
 To have him false unto the greater thing?
 Thou say'st King Mark is false? If so he be,
 Doth that absolve the true man from his truth?
 Mark cannot shrink the measure of a king
 By his shortcoming.
ISOULT.   Nature should make us kings
 That gather up her force, as a great wave
 Thundering upon the shore, and leave their mark
 High-measuring o'er the rest.
TRISTRAM. It is enough.
 No words more. All is said.
ARTHUR.   At Camelot,
 Whiles he is gone, lodge you with Guinevere.
GUINEVERE. I pray you stay with me.
ISOULT.   And he with Mark?
 Oh fool, to think I had found rest! Such rest
 The sea-bird hath upon the straining mast.

Now must I forth into the wind again.

GUINEVERE. Why heart, dear heart, why dost thou fret at this,—
　　'Twill not endure.

ISOULT. 　　　　　　'Twill not endure, nor I,
　　Nor thou, nor life, nor love, nor anything—
　　But it will make the time too brief, more briefer.
　　　　Takes up her cloak from the couch.
　　Gramercy, Launcelot, for Joyous Gard.
　　My day now set lays golden on its towers
　　A last, reluctant light.

LAUNCELOT. 　　　　　Be comforted.
　　Thou wilt return.

ISOULT. 　　　　　　I will return no more!
　　The joy was lended me as was the castle;
　　I was the guest of Joy and take my leave.
　　Anguish of Ireland is my father, Tristram
　　My love,—I that am Anguish born, and wed
　　To Sorrow, dwell but passingly with Joy.
　　Ah, Launcelot, a mockery that name!
　　For who shall put a guard round joy to keep it,
　　Or who shall house joy 'neath the daily roof?
　　Joy is a wayfarer that pitches tent
　　Now here, now there—his roof the summer's leaf,
　　The green pavilion of a sunny hour.
　　But Dolorous Gard stands sure, fixed as despair,
　　And gray as grief, and moated with our tears.
　　There have I leave to bide till my life's end.
　　There shall no envy turn me from the doors.
　　　　Queen Isoult goes out.

Part II

SCENE I

SCENE.—*A tower of Tintagil Castle. The sea smokes on the crags at its base, the din of surf and sea-birds besets its battlements. It looks upon a round of waters, and in the west the sunset is spread in splendour. Queen Isoult works at one side of a tapestry frame, Brangwane at the other. The damsel Blanchelys, seated on a cushion at Isoult's feet, gives her yarns as she requires them.The damsel Laurel sits on another cushion, a lute idle in her hands, while Ygraine, a third damsel, kneeling, leans on the parapet.The parapet is low, and broad on top, and in one place, for near the length of a man's body, the stones of it are broken and crumbled away, and a few grasses have found hold in this breach. A small door leads into the higher, closed part of the tower, in which is the turret stair.*

ISOULT. What dost thou watch, Ygraine?

YGRAINE.   Madam, the sea.

BRANGWANE. I know not why it fumes—the airs are still.

        Laurel moves her cushion nearer the parapet.

LAUREL. Look where the sea is held a prisoner
        Amid the rocks, and like a baited beast
        Turns, snapping with bared fangs.

YGRAINE.   Nay, yonder wave,
        Pursued by one that runneth hard behind,
        Flings up her wild white arms, beseeching help.
        Ah, now he seizeth her!

ISOULT.   The sea's a book,
        A many-linéd book, wherein to read
        Vexed histories. . . . The red yarn, Blanchelys.

BRANGWANE. Methinks that this old tower likes you best
        Of bleak Tintagil's bounds.

ISOULT.   It hath outwatched
        So oft my vigil, as myself it grows,
        In fantasy, to seem. About my feet
        The spume and strife, the ceaseless petty surge
        That spends on me in vain—from which I rise
        To my high loneliness and the wide dark,
        At war with God's strong winds. And thoughts like birds
        That whirl for ever, crying bitterness,
        Around my head.

YGRAINE.   As sea-birds, not as swallows,
        The merry swallows that like children play,
        Circle on circle skimming round the tower,
        Till my head swims to watch.

BRANGWANE.   Sooth, hold it fast,
        Else it may fly away, thou feather-brain!

YGRAINE. Backs purple as a dark, wind-labouring sea,

And tails as forkéd as the lightning flash,
And breasts as white as ever shone a sail.
Oh, swallow, swallow, flitting, gurgling swallow,
To live as thou dost live 'twixt sea and sky!
Even thy nest a cradle o'er the foam,
Hung from the battlements.

ISOULT.   It was the name—
Sea Swallow—of that ship whereon we sailed
From Ireland, once.

BLANCHELYS.   Madam, please you to tell
The story of the voyage and the storm.

ISOULT. Nay, ye have heard that story many a time.

BLANCHELYS. We never tire to hear it o'er again.

ISOULT. No, no, my heart is heavy; 'tis an hour
Sets memory chiming with the vesper-bell.

            Lets fall the tapestry from her hands.

The hour I was wont to wait his coming
From the day's hunt; to mount the turret wall
And lift the bugle to my lips, and wind,
And hear the wraith of errant sound a-seeking—
A question blown adrift about the wood,
A want forlorn, grown faint with wandering,—
Till far away, as if the west found voice
Of clearest gold, a sunset-clarion voice—
Came answer—Tristram's horn.

LAUREL.   Sir Tristram's horn!
Oh, the good days at Joyous Gard! Dear Madam,
Then knew we happiness.

BLANCHELYS.   Would we were there.

ISOULT. Aye, would we were.

BRANGWANE.   'Tis time Sir Tristram came.
We know the battle hath been fought and won
And worsted Sessoyne's forces on the way
To make their homage to King Mark.

LAUREL.   Ha, Sessoynes,
Ye little thought when Cornwall ye invaded,
To match with Lyonesse!

            Enter Colombe.

COLOMBE.   Madam, I bring thee warning,—

    King Mark comes up the stair.

ISOULT.   He cometh here?

COLOMBE. He would have speech with thee.

ISOULT.   Upon what matter?

    It boots not—let him come.

BRANGWANE.   We'll not all leave thee.

ISOULT. Think ye I fear him? Yea.

        Signs them to leave her. They go, all but Brangwane, who lingers.

    I bade thee go.

        Brangwane goes.

        Isoult takes up the tapestry. Mark enters.

MARK. My feet oft stumbled at this stranger stair.

    Me needeth Tristram's guidance—he who knows

    Blind worm-ways of this castle, as the maggot,

    That works to eat the kernel, knows the nut.

        Isoult plies her needle.

    What, like ye not my likening? Silent still?

    Thy tower keepeth count of yonder road.

    Here canst thou watch the winking sun-speck grow

    League after league, into the rider mailed.

    The rider that ye wait,—nor wait not long.

    Tristram returns.

ISOULT.   So I do know, my lord.

MARK. I know thou knowest. Did I lack the news

    For its procurance would I send to thee.

    I used it but to bring me into favour;

    A phrase, methought, that needs must stand my friend.

    My tongue hath tainted it.

ISOULT.   The tongue will taint

    If that the tongue be false.

MARK.   My tidings false?

ISOULT. Nay, even thou must sometime speak the truth,

    When truth confirms itself, as Tristram comes.

    Once more redeemed from servage thine estate.

    Three times for Cornwall he hath done great battle:

    With Marhaus—out of that our story grew—

MARK. A blameless tale, in sooth.

ISOULT.   He is the sword
    Thou drawest on thy foes, yet hadst thou liefer
    He broke, than conquered.

MARK.   The battle being done,
    Let him unto his scabbard till our need.
    Let him unto his wife—he hath a wife.
    Small good she gets of him. . . . 'Tis strange her name
    Should be Isoult—even as thine—Isoult
    Of Brittany. I do not grudge the name—
    So he content himself with that.

ISOULT.   A man
    Clean and straight-dealing as the tempered sword.
    The dagger is the weapon to thy choice:
    The secret tool of household treacheries,
    The stabber in the dark.

MARK.   What, dost thou fear it?

ISOULT. I never fear. [*She rises.*]

MARK.   Almost I believe thy vaunt,
    Thou never fearest. Once I saw the stag
    Bay, when thou hadst outridden all the hunt.
    The tempest-shaken forest of his head
    Threw off the dogs like leaves—thy best hounds ripped.
    The sharp tines turned on thee, but with a thrust
    Thy knife sank home and carved him to the morte.
    To make thee fear—the end I set my life. [*He draws closer.*]
    Before I die to make thee fear, albeit
    Thou'rt panoplied in some immortal stuff
    That turns the edge of death.

ISOULT.   To end with life
    It were to end with thee.

MARK.   Nay, not to end,
    For thou forgettest Hell that is to come.

ISOULT. Brave spirits burn a fire against the fire;
    The coward hath some terror to himself,
    Some terror that he sputtereth, half brent,
    Like the green log whereof the heart is water.

MARK. Well canst thou taunt! But I'll no more endure.
    I'll have thee not in Hell? Then on this earth

I'll have thee, by God's blood, in Tristram's spite,
With Tristram banished!

ISOULT.   Banished again, Sir King?
Hast thou forgot when thy knights rose as one
To bring him back?

MARK.   Now hath he fewer friends;
Some slain, some follow quests. Of his sworn fellows,
Lamorak is dead, Blamore de Ganis hurt,
Palomides doth chase the glatissant beast,
And Gareth hath green wounds.

ISOULT.   But Launcelot
Is left, and Arthur.

MARK.   Aye, the king is his,
The king who keepeth Launcelot in hall.
And she, the royal strumpet, the crowned Lie,
Doth friend thee.

ISOULT.   Foul mouth, speak you
Of Guinevere?

MARK.   'Tis known the Queen is Launcelot's paramour;
Yet hath she shame to hide it,—thou dost flaunt.
Didst thou not send Palomides with word:
"There be four lovers in the world—Launcelot
And Guinevere, and Tristram and Isoult?"

ISOULT. "There be four lovers in the world"—Aye, true.
This tale thy spies have brought. Thou takest pains
To gather tales that put thee from thine ease,
Dog-like to sit and scratch a flea-bit ear.
And like a dog thou sniffest at the thresholds
Of doors are shut to thee.

MARK.   Each dog his day
As the old saw saith. Mark you that.

ISOULT.   Oh, wherefore,
And wherefore, waste thyself with hate of Tristram?
Thou covetest his courage? Canst thou heir it,
If that he die, as 'twere a coat of mail
To steel thy fearfuller flesh?

MARK.   The day is come,
The day of the dog, Isoult, and from this turret

Thou shalt not go alive.

He seizes her. They struggle.

ISOULT.   Wilt *thou* kill *me*?

Not even with thy sword!

He forces her towards the broken parapet.

MARK.   Look down, look down!

ISOULT. I am undizzied.

MARK.   Upon the edge of death?

ISOULT. Thou shalt not cast me down into the depths.

I step from hence into the nearer heaven.

Or if I fall, 'tis as the burning brand

God hurls from his high ramparts, through the skies,

To fire the world! Take off thy hands! Take off!

With a swift movement she frees the dagger hidden in her girdle
and strikes at him.

MARK. The dagger is *thy* weapon!

ISOULT.   Against thee!

Mark wrests the dagger from her and flings it over the parapet.
They stand farther from the verge. He grips her by the wrists.

MARK. Thy blood yet sits its throne; the furtherest drop

Doth feel the central power; sovereign still

This pulse that beats unstarted, keeping tune.

Thy white face looks no whiter than its wont

Beneath thy midnight hair. Thy lips are red

As if his kiss were fresh on them. Isoult!

Shall I not break thy body's vase and spill

Its royal wine ere he may drink again?

Why, thou wert crushed as is the gannet's egg,

Or unfledged young. This beauty then a thing

To shudder at; this flesh a bleeding pulp

Thy lover would abhor to take in his arms.

How would I gloat upon that ruinage—gloat!

This delicate body I may never touch

For love,—bebroken by my hate—hate—hate!

Grips her more fiercely, and sways her to and fro.

ISOULT. Even though thy valiance be against a woman,

I never heard thee speak so like a man.

MARK. Thou wouldst look up out of the flames of Hell

And smile defiance in the face of God.
How white thou'lt look in Hell!
White as the evening's large, unstinted star
Looks in the fiery west.

He forces her backward upon the brink.
    Thou pliant weed
That keepest root-hold, bending to the wind,
Now shalt thou—out!

    Cry, cry upon God's help!
Or on thy Tristram, aye, or on thy Mark!

Brangwane's voice heard without.

BRANGWANE. I come, my lady—Queen Isoult—I come!

MARK. What noise?

   Enter Brangwane running.

BRANGWANE. Thou villain—coward—stay thy hands!

MARK. Thou darest berate *me*?

BRANGWANE.   Who, who, but thou,
 Would lay rude hands on thy royal queen?
 How fare you, Madam? When I sat at work
 Upon the bastion, thy small girdle-knife
 Thou wearest in the knowledge of thy Mark,
 Came hurtling to my feet, and struck, point-fast,
 Betwixt the stones. And I that know him likewise,
 Ran, raising such alarm, Sir Fergus comes
 And Dinas.

ISOULT.   'Twas a feint,—to teach me fear,
 Wherein our Mark doth teach his very master.
 I must conceive with cowardice by him,
 Who never on this body fathered aught,
 No, nor is like!

   Enter Sir Fergus and Sir Dinas the Seneschal.

SIR FERGUS.   How is it with the Queen?

ISOULT. 'Tis well, good Sirs. My Brangwane is too hasty.
 As I leaned o'er to see a swallow's nest
 This dagger, lodging in my girdle, dropped.
 There have you all the matter. But my thanks
 Are for your care.

   A horn is wound, far off.

Hearken, 'tis he! 'Tis Tristram,
    As I do know that horn!
Sir Dinas.   Then God be praised!
Mark. We'll to the outer gates to wait my nephew.
    Come, Sirs, and go with us to meet him.

            Mark goes out, followed by Sir Fergus and Sir Dinas.

Isoult. Still am I standing, though but now death's sickle
    Lay sharp upon life's root. A little while,
    A little while withdrawn—but yet there runs
    That shiver through me that the barley knows
    When in its golden hour the whole field shakes
    With sudden prophecy of the reaper's scythe.
    The time is ripe—is ripe.

            With a swift change, she runs to the parapet.

                        Look, where he comes!
    See, Brangwane, yonder, canst thou make him out?

            Waves her scarf—the wind takes it from her hand.

    My very scarf flies to him on the wind.
    Oh, would I were as light upon the air!

SCENE II

Scene.—*A great hall in the castle of Tintagil. On either side long settles against the wall. At one end of the hall three or four steps mount to a platform which forms a dais; on this platform a smaller table with three chairs placed, two side by side, another at the right end of the table; all three chairs face the hall. From the dais, in turn, two other short flights of stairs, right and left, lead up to the arched doorways of other apartments of the castle, the space at the back of the platform between these two abutments being filled by an oriel. Above the dais is the minstrels' gallery. From the mighty beams of the roof hang faded banners and pennants, and cressets swung by chains; while a row of tall silver standards bearing tapers flanks the tables. The boards are covered with cloths of fair damask and dressed with flagons and goblets, dishes of gold and silver, fruits piled in pyramids, cold viands and great pasties made like castles. The king's board on the dais is richest of all. Pages go to and fro strewing the floor with rushes from baskets which they carry on their arms. Several serving-women are putting the last touches to their task of binding the silver standards with garlands festooned from standard to standard. Besides the pages and serving-women, Brangwane, Blanchelys, Laurel, and Ygraine are in the hall.*

LAUREL. [*To one of the women.*] This garland wanteth trimming.

BRANGWANE. [*To one of the pages.*] Sirrah, not there!
    Not rushes there upon the dais,—roses,
    Those that I gave thee. Thick-pate, not to know
    What's fittest for the queen!

YGRAINE.   Were I a rose
    I'd give the dearest petals of my heart
    For strowings to her feet.

BRANGWANE.   Hark to Ygraine
    That favoureth no knight. Her love o' the Queen
    Is maid-love for a man, nun-love for a saint,
    And child-love for a mother, all in one.

YGRAINE. I never had a mother.

       They all laugh.

BRANGWANE.   What, hast thou found
    A new way to be born? This is great tidings,
    And maybe thou wilt earn all women's thanks—
    And yet I have my doubt.

BLANCHELYS.   Oh, she was made
    Of moonshine by a frost-fairy in Spring,—
    She dreams white dreams that are afeared to melt,
    And hides them glimmering in the lap of dawn
    From men's eyes and the day.

YGRAINE.   Ah, do not laugh.
    I never had a mother in remembrance.
    That should not move your mirth.

BRANGWANE.   Nay, if we laugh
    It is because we snatch at any chance
    Of laughter till Mark come. For in his presence
    Laughter is never free. He spins a web
    That binds the moth-wings of our pleasures fast.
    A spinner of the fine-drawn web of guile
    Is subtle Mark.

BLANCHELYS. This is the spider's lair,
    This hall so dark and full of wandering airs.
    And all those banners whispering in the roof,
    That talk of battles, blood, and woeful deeds;
    That seem as if they wave farewells, and stir

With dead men's sighs.

YGRAINE. A forest of old pennants,
    An autumn wood of history o'erhead
    That shaketh its sad leaves.

LAUREL.   Time-worn tongues
    That speak of kinglier days, and kinglier men
    Than this same Mark.

BRANGWANE.   And he is deaf to them.
    How dim these cressets burn!

      Enter Andred.

ANDRED.   Fair damsels all,
    What do ye here?

BRANGWANE. At the queen's bidding, see
    This hall is dressed.

ANDRED.   We make a feast to-night
    To show mine uncle's love—mine uncle Mark,
    That rules, and fights, and *wives*,—by proxy.

LAUREL.   Fie,
    Fie on you, Andred! Mark hates the Queen. I've watched
    And have made sure.

BLANCHELYS.   Why would he keep her, then?

ANDRED. Hate is the itch love getteth when ahealing,
    A fiery itch that cannot hold hands off.
    That woman,—to have that woman near, yet scorned,
    Scorned from the touch of her! To sit anhungered
    And see another feast!

BRANGWANE.   The varlets hear thee.

      Signs the Pages to go.

    Thou hast an evil tongue for Queen Isoult.
    She likes thee not, and never hides her heart.
    As Martin's summertide, her hot is hot,
    Her cold is cold.

ANDRED.   Hot day with Tristram makes
    Cold night for Mark. Is't that ye mean?

BRANGWANE. [*In anger.*] Thou knowest
    My meaning runneth clear of all such slime;
    Thine is the scum that grows on stinking wits!

YGRAINE. [*Who has moved away from them, not heeding, as she turns.*]

I hear a noise this way.

BRANGWANE.   'Tis they, they come.

> *Enter, by a door in the left, in the abutting wall, Mark, followed by his knights.*
> *By a like door on the right enters Isoult with her train of ladies. Mark, meeting*
> *her, leads her up the steps to the dais, where they sit in the two chairs side*
> *by side and Tristram in the third chair. The knights and ladies sit on the*
> *settles at the long tables. Brangwane takes her place behind the queen's*
> *chair.*

YGRAINE. All beauty comes with her: beauty of earth
    And spring-flecked meadows, in her mantle flowered;
    Beauty of seas in frozen spray of pearls;
    And of the under-earth in minéd gems.
    Beauty of night in her dark hair thick-starred;
    And of the day in her gold-tissued robe
    That clothes her with the shining of the sun.

BLANCHELYS. She is all golden,—studded like a sceptre.

LAUREL. She wears the carcanet Sir Tristram gave.

> *A Harper sings from the gallery.*

HARPER.
    His falcon stoops upon the herne;
    His greyhound courseth through the fern;
    His dogs make music bold and clear,
    A-hunting of the fleet-foot deer.
    His horn is master of the call;
    His harp delighteth bower and hall.
    His no is no, his yes is yes.
        Tristram of Lyonesse!
        Tristram of Lyonesse!

    His good sword never tasted rust,
    His lance thrusts caitiffs in the dust.
    Keen is his lance, and keen his blade,
    For battle in his country's aid.
    And ne'er shall king or country fall,
    While still he fighteth for Cornwall.
    Who doth our wrong redress?
        Tristram of Lyonesse!
        Tristram of Lyonesse!

MARK. A song made in thine honour, that usurps
    Thine office. None do sweep the strings like thee.
    Fetch us the harp,—let Tristram sing.
TRISTRAM.   Uncle,
    Hold me excused to-night. My voice is husked
    With battle cries. I should be hoarser than
    The raven o'er the field.
MARK.   No more than meet.
    The raven is the warrior's fitting songster.
    We care not for thy hoarseness; that might roughen
    A love-tale, but not this of victory
    Over Sessoynes.
TRISTRAM.   Hold me excused, I pray,
    For when I feast I fain would wash the taste
    Of battle from my lips.

          Mark signs a page, who pours wine into a goblet and gives to Tristram.
          Tristram drinks, having first lifted the cup to the king and queen.
MARK.   Thou dost not like
    The taste of blood, then, and the work of Cain?
TRISTRAM. I am not Bersark as the Northmen are.
    Thou talkest of Cain, but in all nobler battle
    The brotherhood is branded with the blood
    Upon man's brow.
MARK.   God wot, this is the note
    Of Arthur, new to thee. If not of battle,
    Then let us have a ballad of the chase,
    Or a sea-chanty; thou hast sung the sea
    As 'twere thy mistress.
TRISTRAM.   Nay, it is my master.
    The sea hath here beneath these very floors,
    Builded himself a house that beggars thine.
    Unnumbered palaces throughout the world
    Are his, to take the rest he never taketh.
    He is the king of warriors. He breathes
    In battle, and he walks in conflict.
    Unceasingly the squadrons of his hosts
    Storm on the shrinking coasts of all this land,
    And win new empire for him, inch by inch.

My childhood years were rocked by that vast wrath,
And slumbered to the thunder of that charge.
If still I move from conquering act to act,
It is the sea's great voice that captains me—
The strife that salteth sea-born blood like mine,
Sharp with the sword-edge of the wind and wave.

ISOULT. My childhood was as thine,—the sea did fill it.
The sea is my land's lover: not as Cornwall's
Stern-bosomed, rock-faced coast, but woman-like,
She lieth in his arms, upon his breast.
And in her colour lives her constancy:
Green Ireland is his own, his wedded land.
Thou dost remember it.

MARK.   In Brittany
Thou hast the sea?

TRISTRAM.   'Tis much as Cornwall is.

MARK. In Brittany,—the word doth bring to mind
The one thing wanting to our cheer to-night.
The hero of the feast here widowed sits.
The toasted draught were richer did it come
Chaliced in those fair hands, so praised, so famed,
That men have named Isoult of the White Hands—
Isoult thy wife.

TRISTRAM. I scarce do know my wife.
I wedded at the king her father's wish
Isoult of Brittany. 'Twas known to him
That on the morrow of our marriage day,
My ship that felt the tide, must lift her sail.
Our marriage was a gleam of winter sun,
Too brief to work the earliest sign of change.
Unthawed the crystal seals of that young spirit;
For all desire of mine, her virgin snow
Unbreathed upon.

MARK.   Doth she not fret for this?

TRISTRAM. She dwells with quiet: mine were a rude life
To share.

MARK. Upon ourselves doth rest, too much,
The blame of this, to lean our burdens on thee.

But thou dost never spare thyself, forswearing
No stubborn quest, nor lost, despairful cause.
We know no way but to enforce thy good.
To banish thee to house and wife and ease.
Banish, I say? I banish thee our cares,
Our quarrels, our ungrateful realm of Cornwall—
Worn with an outward and an inward strife.
To Brittany and get us twain an heir!
So my accompt with thee shall be expunged,
And thy long serving will have served thyself.
Cornwall is sterile; Life hath spent her all
To make one perfect thing. Had she saved aught,—
Sown in less splendour from the future's store—
Aye, had she made one woman less supreme,
And kept the stuff to shape a line of kings,
I had not laid this crowning charge on thee
To get thyself a son, Cornwall an heir.

      A murmur of approval runs round the hall.

TRISTRAM. [*Rising.*] Doth it please ye to see me banished, Sirs?
SIR SADOK. A son of thine should rule us.
MARK.   Hast thou no will

To be the source unto a stream of kings?

      Rises and holds forth his sceptre.

I do decree thee banished.
Witness all, I here decree him banishment,
Until such time as he shall send an heir
To be his warrant.

      Taking the wine-cup from his flagon-bearer.

                  Take ye for a pledge,
Two names like jewels in the solvent cup,
That they may merge and mingle to a third:
Tristram of Lyonesse, of Knighthood peerless,
And his Isoult—Isoult of the White Hands.

      As the pages pass to and fro filling the cups, some men turn upon each other
      looks confused and amazed; some steal glances at the frozen anger of the queen;
      and one or two drink boldly "Tristram of Lyonesse and his Isoult" and name not
      the White Hands.

TRISTRAM. Sir knights, what say ye? Ye have heard the King?

DINAS THE SENESCHAL. What need we Tristram's son with Tristram's self?
>Is Tristram not thine heir?
SEVERAL VOICES SPEAKING TOGETHER. Tristram is heir.
ANDRED. Give Tristram leave to stay in Cornwall, Sire,
>And get an heir for thee. 'Twere speedily done,
>Methinks, and with good will.
TRISTRAM.   Silence, thou knave!
>[*To Mark.*] And thou that pratest of thy throne. Thy throne!
>'Tis on my back—I shrug, thy kingdom quakes.
>Long have I carried thee; even such a load
>As yonder thy humped dwarf doth bend beneath;
>Thou that hast neither hands to fend thee with,
>Nor feet on which to stand and walk upright,
>That art but cunning brain and crafty heart.
>Our blood is in thee but our blood gone foul.
>Stagnation of our truer-running race,
>False hast thou ever been, and false wilt be!
>I've served thee, stooped to take thy burden, till
>Thou thinkest me thy beast to breed for thee.
>Thou to beget a king? Thou couldst not get
>A trullion knave; for Nature will not suffer
>Another of thy kind usurp a throne.
>   *Unsheathes his sword.*
>This that bought Cornwall from the Irish truage,
>And from Blamore freed Ireland in turn;
>That wrought deliverance for the Woeful Isle
>Of Servage, and hath Sessoynes beaten back;
>That none hath bettered,—no, not Launcelot!
>Proved manhood of a score of splendid lists,
>And like a child thou biddest it to bed.
>Look well upon this sword! Ha! Never start!
>Thy kingship is so shamed that I must spare it.
>I'll not pluck down what I have builded up.
>But when thou fallest, as the juggled ball
>Wanting the point that stayeth it in air—
>To me 'tis naught. Here have I done with thee.
>I'll never draw this more in cause of thine.
>And ye that look on it have looked your last.

*The sword rings home into the scabbard. Tristram leaps down the dais-steps
and passes from the hall. Isoult rises.*

Scene III

SCENE.—*The same hall later. The long tables disordered as with feasting: the table on the
dais has been removed. The torches have burned out, but the setting moon streams through
the mullion and the open casement where Tristram and Isoult stand. None beside themselves
are in the hall, but in the minstrels' gallery Brangwane keeps watch. After a time, weary
with vigil, her head droops upon the baluster and she sleeps.*

TRISTRAM. Look yonder where too long the unsleeping sea
  In a vain anguish for the moon hath tossed.
  All night the hope of her hath burned his breast;
  All night hath her white promise on the wave
  Lain unredeemed; but now at last she cometh,
  Stooping unto her rest within his arms,
  As thou to me.
ISOULT.   The tapers, one by one,
  Have sighed their passing spirits to the air;
  The garlands droop, and ghosts of roses breathe
  A perfume made more poignant by their pain.
  Joy, as it withers, pierceth all the sense
  With its remembered sweet. . . . The wind-stripped stalk,
  I stand above the ruin of life's rose,
  The petals of these last hours round my feet.
  Ah, fool was I to come again to Cornwall,
  And fool wert thou to hearken to his need!
  Fools, fools, we twain, to the oft-broken snare
  Of Mark's fair words!
TRISTRAM.   I'll take thee hence, my queen.
  I'll find a way. We must endure our time
  Until Mark's vigilance doth sleep. Or else,
  The true lovers of the world I'll draw to me,
  And come and take thee from him with my might.
  So fret thee not.
ISOULT.   Tristram, I fear—I fear!
TRISTRAM. That word upon these lips for the first time

And for the last. [*Kisses her.*]

ISOULT.   That being far away,
  Thou wilt forget.

TRISTRAM.   Forgetfulness of thee!
  I go from thee into the absent void,
  As doth the star, new-shaken from his sphere,
  That spills his heart in fire along the way
  Till none of him be left. Yea, all the way
  Leading from thee is backward paved with fire
  Out of my burning heart.

ISOULT.   It is not all
  My fear.

TRISTRAM. What more?

ISOULT.   That she—that white Isoult
  Whom thou hast wedded—

TRISTRAM.   Is that doubt not laid?
  Lost in thy sunlight is that small, pale face,
  Lost as the moon at mid-day in the sky.
  A ghost—a wraith.

ISOULT.   My very name she taketh.

TRISTRAM. Oh, jealous of a name? This is unworthy
  Mine utter loyalty in thought and flesh.
  For thy sake is she left her maidenhood;
  And on our marriage night the faith to thee
  Was laid between us as a naked blade.
  Some find the wife a sword, but then I took
  The sword to wife, begetting battle, strife,
  And bloody issue. I might have turned to peace;
  Part of thy fever in me being bled
  Out of the wound Mark's ambushed hirelings made
  That set upon my life. She tended me,
  King Howell's daughter. Gentle was the leech,
  And in my ravings ever heard her name—
  "Isoult—Isoult"—and knowing not of thee,
  What should she think but that she was desired?
  And so, in sooth, she was, for bottomless hunger
  Can feed upon the stones and name them bread;
  Or as the shipwrecked sucks his parchéd veins,

The blood of mine own fancy fed my heart.
She was the mirror where I made thy face.
What serveth not to make it? Shadows, sun,
Earth, air, and water, everything!
The summer cloud, in white processional
Of softly changing shapes, thy mimicry,—
Here shines thy silver shoulder, there thy face.
God made thee once: I've made thee o'er and o'er
From head to foot—as the first woman was
Out of man's side—out of my living breath.

ISOULT. And she? Doth she love thee?

TRISTRAM.   Jesu defend!
Yet few men hath she known. And so—belike—
Silent she is: her heart hath built its nest,
As the wild sea-bird, in the sheer cliff's edge,
And there beyond our reach the white thing broods,
And lives the life of lonely rock and wave.
Bretagne hath mothered her (whose mother died)
Till she hath grown the daughter of Bretagne,
Made in her likeness,—even to the depth
Of strange sea-water eyes.

ISOULT.   I had not heard
Of these strange eyes, but alway of her hands.
Are they, in truth, so beautiful, her hands,
Or overpraised?

TRISTRAM. Isoult of the White Hands,
With finger-tips that taper as to prayer,
Like those, palm-joined, of saints petitioning.
Ah, lilies of the Virgin's garden, they,
And meant for telling o'er the rosary beads,
And holding tapers waxen as themselves.
Not as these buds upon thy body-stem
That thy face as the perfect flower crowneth;
Not made for love as these warm, living hands
That quiver with the lightnings of thy blood.
The touch of her cold hands had chilled my heart,
Even could it spare a drop not pledged to thee.
Frost lies on them although they be so fair.

But thine—but thine—that flutter at the wrist—
A lesser beating heart—are they so quick,
Or is it they conceive beneath my touch
With two-fold life? . . .

        How picture we the Grail?
An angel tall the thrice veiled chalice bears
Of vermeil tinct; a mystic rose of light,
A streaming splendour men may not behold?
Thou art my Grail, all roseate with love's wine,
Thy heart, thy body as a chalice filled;
My cup of Life that makes the angel's wan.
My sacring cup, my very Grail, my—

ISOULT.   Silence!

Oh say no more, for thou blasphemest thus.
And with the morrow, cold, these hands, as *hers*,
Will mate each other in their emptiness.
Ah, God, why hast thou made so vain this love
Thou didst foredoom to us? Was it our will
Or Thine, Thy wind of destiny, that drove
Across life's main, where Thou didst fix the course,
Our blinded way that brought us each to each
And to our fate?

TRISTRAM. For that let Him be thanked.

But rather doth it seem to me God made
Us parts of the one barque—the barque of Cornwall.
Thou wert the queenly figure of the prow
Treading the heads that dared thee into foam:
I kept the hard-cramped helm and steered the course;
And ever held we the ship's length between.
So was it first, and had been, save for Mark.
Save I must see thee,—see thy womanhood
Shamed in such mating, shamed in thine own eyes,
In all men's shamed, and crying to be matched!
And I that asked thee for the craven's wife
Had put this scorn on thee,—my work it was!
I took the place by Nature to me belongeth,
And men looked up to me and over Mark.

ISOULT. The place beside me—be thou ever there!

Wilt thou be blown from me by the mere gust
And flaw of kingship so unsteady? Take me,
This night, this hour, take me hence with thee!
Thou shalt not leave me!

TRISTRAM.   Take thee hence this night?

ISOULT. Aye, canst thou not?

TRISTRAM.   Then must it be by force,—
The issue I have shirked. The gates are guarded.
Ye may be sure no friends are on the watch.
And Brangwane goes with us and Gouvernail.
Four horses 'neath Mark's nose? Nay, there's no way,
Except here, now, I pull him from his throne.
God knows I do not lust to fill his place.
What light he showeth, I have held aloft,
Whiles he dripped fire on me for my pains.
I fling him down to smoulder: I'd not set
My foot on him to quench; for he's enkindled
From that same vital heat my mother was.
I would not kill him.
When I am gone, ride forth as to the hunt,
Thy maidens with thee, and those knights we trust—
Fergus, Dinas, Lambegus, and Sentraille—
Past Adtherpe's castle, to the forest manor
Where erst we lodged,—

ISOULT.   Yea, with my warder's leave?
He hath me once again and means to keep me.
Doubt not I'll be well watched when thou art gone,—
And that the least!

TRISTRAM.   He would not touch—
God's name, he would not dare to lay a hand
On thee!

ISOULT. What, would he not? Look here and here,—
Nay, 'tis too dark for thee to see, my lord,
The pattern of my fetters, in the flesh
Mark's hands have gyved.

TRISTRAM.   When? When?

ISOULT.   'Twas ere ye came.

TRISTRAM. God, he shall answer this! Ye go with me

To-morrow morn, and openly we go.
What, shall I skulk from Mark and his poor caitiffs,
I that have had to do with Northgalis—
With Northgalis and his proved hundred knights.
Half Mark's are tainted, and the best with me.
'Tis I have kept them his; while Tristram bent
The hardiest might bow.

ISOULT.   To Camelot,
    Or whither, do we go?

TRISTRAM.   To Lyonesse.
    Let Mark come take thee there! Ah, there beginneth
    The old life that we knew at Joyous Gard.

ISOULT. Nay, never, nevermore to dream that dream!
    Not twice do we surprise Fate unawares.
    And could we come again to Joyous Gard,
    We need not think to find a tenderer spring
    In the sad rustle of remembered hours,
    Long sere, long dead, round our reëntering feet
    That last year trod the May.

TRISTRAM.   Love, thou art wearied.
    To-morrow wilt thou see with happier eyes,—
    To-morrow with the morn.

ISOULT.   I see no morrow,
    Methinks. To-day is dead without an heir.
        Slowly and prophetically.
    I prayed thee take me hence—hence with the hour.
    The hour waited: thou hast made the choice.
    The hour waited, and the hour hath flown.
    I heard it fly away. And now there comes
    One with a darker plume.

TRISTRAM.   What meanest thou?

ISOULT. And we are hovered with its awful wings.

TRISTRAM. Art thou afeared?

ISOULT.   Afeared. Lay thy hand here.
    Feel how this riderless runaway doth pound,
    Trailing the reins of reason at his heels.
    What is there in the world to work this change,
    To work Queen Isoult's fear?

TRISTRAM.   Aye, what indeed?

ISOULT. I never feared to die: to have thee die
  I have faced many times. But this Unknown—
  This fog of fear in which I grope to find
  Myself—and cannot find—

TRISTRAM. [*Lightly, as he draws her down to him in the king's chair.*] I banish it,
  Even as I am banished—with a breath.

   Kisses her.

   Mark creeps down the stairs that lead to the dais from the archway at left.
   He crouches behind the chair.

  Fear of Mark? Of the arch craven? Let him shake
  His aspen life out. But for us—we laugh
  At him—at fear—at fate—at death—

   Mark's sword passes through Tristram's body.

MARK.   Yea, now!

  Laugh now! No laughter? Then I laugh for thee.
  Ha! ha!

   With the stroke Tristram leaps like the struck hart, and falls in front of the
   king's chair. Isoult stands stiffened. Brangwane, starting up, hangs over the
   railing of the minstrels' gallery.

BRANGWANE. I heard a laugh! A devil laughed!
  King-devil Mark, what hast thou done? Oh, God!
  I slept that should have watched! I slept, I slept!

   Sinks down, sobbing, against the railing.

  Isoult, my queen, forgive—forgive—forgive!

Part III

SCENE.—*A tower-chamber in King Howell's castle in Brittany. Double doors at back stand*
open into a second and larger apartment. On the right a chimney-piece; on the left case-
ments looking on the sea. Near the middle of the chamber a couch, covered with a bearskin,
on which the wounded Tristram, clad in a loose, furred robe, is lying. At the side of the couch,
on another bearskin spread upon the floor, a stool with flagon and goblet; at the foot a harp.
The fire smouldering in the chimney strikes gleams from a stand of arms holding Tristram's
armour. The couch faces the casement and the western light. Behind the head of the couch,
in the shadows, where Tristram cannot see her, Isoult Blanche Mains, seated on a low stool,
her chin upon her hand.

TRISTRAM. Isoult! Isoult!

ISOULT BLANCHE MAINS. How should I know if I
    Be summoned?

TRISTRAM. Not Mark's Isoult, but mine.

ISOULT BLANCHE MAINS. "Not Mark's Isoult," he saith. Oft, so oft,
    He calls on her, my name I have relinquished
    To one that long since took from me all else.

TRISTRAM. Not ever Mark's but mine, mine from the first,
    Mine alway to the end.

ISOULT BLANCHE MAINS. I might have known!
    My wifehood is a name—my name is wife.
    And my sole portion is to sit and hear
    It crushed with hungered mouth, as if it had
    A body like God's wafer, 'twixt his lips.
        She rises and goes to the head of the couch.
    Doth the wound burn? How may I ease my lord?

TRISTRAM. [*Starting.*] Ha, is it thou? What other should it be?
    Putting out his hand to her.
    I wander, and I give thee pain, my child.
    So flawed a vessel that the sense doth leak.
    'Twas like our Mark to set Death's door ajar
    And turn and flee affrighted at first peep.
    Ah, would that he had finished—flung it wide!
    What time hath passed since I came here? I lose
    The count.

ISOULT BLANCHE MAINS. A sennight since ye came, my lord.
    Five days thou didst lie hid in Cornwall,—five,
    With perverse winds, upon the ship.

TRISTRAM.   Too long,
    Too long it taketh life to burn in twain.
    I am a stubborn brand. . . . Come close, White Hands,
    As snow upon the fire of my wound,
    Kneel here beside me, I am failed of breath.
    And when ye saw the sail ye knew it mine?

ISOULT BLANCHE MAINS. I knew it well, my lord.

TRISTRAM.   Didst thou not think,
    In bitterness,—"Ah never the whole man:
    When he is broken, he doth come to me

    For healing?"

ISOULT BLANCHE MAINS. Nay, I had much grief, much grief,

    To see thee as thou art,——no bitterness.

    And the queen's letter praying for my skill,

    And blotted with her tears——

TRISTRAM.   And on the queen,

    On her, too, is thy pity?

ISOULT BLANCHE MAINS. Am I not

    The shadow to the light of thy great love?

    Queen Isoult's shadow, that is moved by her,

    And lives the shadow's life?

     The sunset shoots its far, spent glory through the tower. Tristram raises him-
     self upon his arm.

TRISTRAM.   'Tis the last light.

    And all the heaven waxeth crystal-thin

    About to break upon another world

    And let us through the walls. Thinner, finer glows

    Yon further bound of crystal. . . . Ah, a sail,

    And look how fast it comes!

ISOULT BLANCHE MAINS. [*Eager, and going to the casement.*] It cannot be,

    There is not time,——and yet——

TRISTRAM.   What sayest thou?

    The cupped sail holdeth the last lees of light,

    As wine within the hollow of the hand,

    Ere night shall drink it. . . . Daughters of the sea,

    That take the salutation of the sun

    At morn and eve on thy white, swelling breasts

    The light doth flush to beauty as a rose,——

    Swift-speeding sails, doth one now come for me?

    To bear me where the bed is ready made,

    Wind-digged and deep betwixt green crest and crest.

    Hither it bears! Look, look!

ISOULT BLANCHE MAINS. Nay, calm thyself.

TRISTRAM. Wouldst thou not say it had a purpose, now,

    A living will that leans not on the wind,

    Nor heedeth not the wave? . . . Alas, alas,

    I mock myself with fancy. [*He sinks back.*]

ISOULT BLANCHE MAINS. Rest, my lord,

And drink of this.

      Offers the cup; he puts it by.

TRISTRAM.   Nay, take the harp and sing

    The latest song I made.

ISOULT BLANCHE MAINS. I cannot sing;

    There are no wings of music on my heart

    To lift the burden up.

TRISTRAM.   Then canst thou speak it.

    For I would have her hear it when I die—

    A thing to keep by her when music strokes

    The heavy head of sorrow. Set it down.

    But let me hear thee speak it first, I pray.

    ISOULT BLANCHE MAINS speaks.

    Sea Swallow that didst bear her on thy wings

    To old Tintagil, home of Cornish kings,

    Sea Swallow bring her thence again to me.

    We will take refuge, we storm-driven three,

    We will take refuge with the friendly sea.

    Sea Swallow, bear us from the servile earth

    To those wild realms unruled that gave us birth,

    To the waste reaches of the restless brine

    Whose life and freedom still I take for mine,

    Whose life and freedom long thou hast made thine.

    Sea Swallow, her sole throne shall be thy prow,

    The flashing spray shall crown Queen Isoult's brow.

    The waking East shall greet her morning's guest,

    The sunset lead her through the lingering west,

    The sunset lead thee to thy starry quest.

    Sea Swallow, hasten ere it be too late;

    The queen is wearied of her empty state.

    Come let us lay our lives in the wind's hand,

    For mine is wasting in the woeful land,

    For thine is wasting on the idle strand,

        Sea Swallow.

TRISTRAM. Thou hast the words. . . . What is that music, hark!
>   Do I not hear a strain? 'Tis passing faint.

ISOULT BLANCHE MAINS. 'Tis but the sea wind humming on this castle
>   As 'twere a harp.

TRISTRAM.   'Tis the great Harper—He
>   I once did think made melody of our lives.
>   'Tis Chance, but Chance, that breatheth through our strings.
>   The tune is in ourselves, not in the wind.
>   God draws us from the welter, as the sun
>   Buildeth his pillared house upon the wave,
>   And with a sweep of cloudy sleeve wipes out.
>   Weaker than water, stablished as the dust,
>   So are we.

ISOULT BLANCHE MAINS. Nay, forbear from speech, my lord,
>   That wastes thy breath.

TRISTRAM.   What, shall I hoard the last?
>   When I am beggared, save a gasp or two?
>   The road of life begins to rise uphill
>   So steep I pant. When I have reached the top
>   What lies Beyond? What think ye? . . . I shall prove.
>   My horn here—wynd for Gouvernail—my men
>   To bear me out upon the battlements.
>   There shall I have the uttermost round of air
>   That rings the earth and sea. Sound ye the morte!
>   Sound, for the hunt is done.
>   And when in the dark wood the morte is blown—
>   The lonely blast that questioneth of God—
>   The little echo of man's self comes back
>   To him for answer!

>   *Isoult Blanche Mains takes the horn from his hand and blows a call.*
>   *Gouvernail enters.*

ISOULT BLANCHE MAINS. The litter let them bring,
>   Brian and Boris, Uwaine, Meliot.

>   *Tristram lies with his eyes closed, Isoult Blanche Mains watching him.*
>   *So still he lies, doubt seizes her. She goes to the stand of arms and uncovers his*
>   *shield. With all the strength of her two arms she carries it and holds it before*
>   *his face to catch the misting of his breath. He opens his eyes.*

TRISTRAM. I ever hoped to die with shield unstained.

Enter four retainers with a litter; they kneel, bringing it level with the couch. Gouvernail and Isoult Blanche Mains help Tristram to rise and lie upon the litter.

TRISTRAM. Lift me, my men.

ISOULT BLANCHE MAINS. See that ye leave him not.

    If there be change let Gouvernail bring me word.

        Tristram is carried out by his bearers. Isoult Blanche Mains, kindling a waxed rush at the fire, lights the tapers in the sconces. She goes to the casement and stands. The light changes from rose to silver.

ISOULT BLANCHE MAINS. The ship hath passed from sight. With twilight merged,

A dream in sleep, it threadeth through the gray.

Her ship it scarce could be; there is scant time

Since I did send the messenger. Pray God,

She speedily come, for shortening of his pain.

Look where the moon is rising like a saint

And all the waves press up as worshippers

To touch her garment's hem. She mounts, she soars,

But lays her absolution on the earth.

        Kneeling at the casement.

Oh, shining virgin, steep my heart for me

In thy white peace and in thy frozen calm,

And let me be as thou, and hope no more.

        While she speaks Queen Isoult enters, hooded and wrapped in a long cloak. Isoult Blanche Mains turns and sees her.

Who art thou? Art thou she?

QUEEN ISOULT.   Yea, I am she

Ye sent for. Speak, and say he lives.

ISOULT BLANCHE MAINS. He lives,

Though anguished. Flesh to such a spirit cleaveth

Closer than spirit to the flesh; for life,

Full loth to lose his pattern, needeth him

More than he needeth life. One need is left.

QUEEN ISOULT. What is that need?

ISOULT BLANCHE MAINS.   To see thee ere he die.

QUEEN ISOULT. Bring me to him.

ISOULT BLANCHE MAINS.   With that he passeth. . . . Soft!

Full weak is he for joy. . . . And ere thou goest,

Beseech thee, for a grace, that thou wilt stand
And let me look on thee. For I would see
What is this power that eateth out men's hearts.
So my young brother died for love of thee,
Kehydius, when with my lord he went
To Cornwall; came too close unto that fire
That withered his green youth and scorched its sap,
With knowledge all too fierce.
                                        Beautiful!
More beautiful than I had dreamed, thou art.
Not my poor fancy fashions such a face,
But God, that at the last hath breathed on it
His own regret at having made a thing
Too fair for death. I see the veils of sorrow
Upon thy beauty, as the autumn fields.
And I that have much cause, as I stand here
And read thee, cannot hate.

QUEEN ISOULT.   Nay, those unhappy,
    The noble never hate.

ISOULT BLANCHE MAINS. Unhappy? Thou?

QUEEN ISOULT. God knoweth that I am, and with a grief
    Too cruel for thy years.

ISOULT BLANCHE MAINS. Too cruel? Ah,
    More cruel than the grief that gnaweth me?
    Until it seemeth I must pluck my heart
    Out of my breast, and hold it in my hand
    To soothe its crying,—give my bosom respite,
    An hour's respite from unceasing ache.

QUEEN ISOULT. Alas, my child, have we done this to thee?
    Hapless ye came betwixt us and the Fate
    That drew on us, and took this hurt, Isoult.
    What blight upon the name that it should bring
    The circle of my sorrow in thine arms,
    Young crescent spirit, in thy tender hold?
    Isoult, Isoult, but bring me to him quick!
    We know not when the little moment falls,
    The Now into the Never bottomless.

ISOULT BLANCHE MAINS. He is upon the battlements.

Goes toward the doors, then stops and listens.
                    But stay,
I hear the shuffle of his bearers' feet
That bring him in.
                    Queen Isoult withdraws into the dusk, dropping the hood upon her head, gath-
                    ering the gray cloak about her. The litter is brought in and laid upon the couch.
                    Isoult Blanche Mains bends over Tristram.
                    My lord? How fares my lord?
TRISTRAM. Where's Gouvernail?
                    He sees La Belle Isoult.
                    Who's there? Thou—thou, my queen!
Nay, I that saw thee in all shining life
Must make thee of the shadows gathering.
Dear Shadow, I am bound unto thy House.
Go with me the dim road I travel on,
Go with me, shade from that pale orb that sits
In old Tintagil, fixed above the feast.
Queen Isoult sits with gaze all wide and dark,
Dark and deserted of the errant soul.
Mark holdeth a high revel,—see the lights,
And hear the music—
                    More and more eager in his vision, he raises himself from his elbow until he
                    sits upright.
QUEEN ISOULT.   Tristram, 'tis Isoult,
That kneeleth at thy couch—that claspeth thee.
My flesh and blood.
TRISTRAM.   Art thou indeed the flesh?
I have had dreams that had these hands—this hair—
                    Isoult Blanche Mains goes out, softly, unnoted.
Dreams, dreams and dreams! Was it thy ship we saw?
I said it came for me.
QUEEN ISOULT.   Yea, Isoult sent,
Isoult of the White Hands and whiter thoughts.
Where is she? She hath gone.
TRISTRAM.   Her small white spirit
Swept with the stress of thee, as the sea-bird
Before a great surge bursting full and strong.
The storm is on us—let her flee inshore

To safer pastures,—but come thou, my sea!

QUEEN ISOULT. Am I the sea?

TRISTRAM.   Thou art the sea at flood

That lifts my drifting soul against the stars.

I sink, I am dashed down, dazed—dizzied—lost—

And darkened! [*He falls back.*]

QUEEN ISOULT. [*Wildly.*] Tristram, I am with thee, stay!

Oh, stay for me!

            Snatching the flagon she pours out a draught.

The cordial, drink it—drink!

            *He dies. A pause. Then slowly from her bosom she takes a small gold vial
            on a chain.*

Then must I mix with this my stirrup-cup.

So with a draught let it begin and end.

For first that potion by my mother mingled—

The magic should have bound my love to Mark—

By chance I found, and all amazed we stood,

Turning the flacket curiously wrought,

Poring upon its depths, nor dreamed the flame,

That leapt there, Love, death-tinged with darker drops.

It was the sunset hour; the sea was wine,

And purple-brimming to its far gold edge,

Where at the rim Night met Day's warmer lips,

Even as thy mouth did meet and close with mine.

            She kisses him.

Farewell,—this last cup sealéd with a kiss,

As was the first. Oh come, most cordial death,

I drink thee; thou, the wine of love distilled

Too sweet, its ruby waxed too red, its rapture

An ecstasy too strong. What other end

Than this, with hearts strained past the bounds of speech

To enter on that silence more supreme.

Send thine assuaging coolness through these veins,

And quench the thirst that life could never fill.

Yea, Tristram, in my hands the Grail upraised

As thou didst say: the blood our passion bled,

The destined cup that moved athwart our lives

In mystery and splendour. Lo, again,

My heart I plunge with thine into the bowl.

I drink the marriage of immortal fates.

The cup is emptied!

> *The chalice falls from her hand. She throws herself on Tristram's body. Enter Isoult Blanche Mains, running. She grasps the heavy doors, striving to close them.*

ISOULT BLANCHE MAINS. Help me! They come—they come!

Mark and his men! Help me to bar the doors!

Queen Isoult dost thou hear? The doors—the doors,

And ere it be too late!

> *Isoult Blanche Mains sees the bodies of Tristram and Isoult, and stands looking on them. Mark appears in the door; he is in armour, with his vizard raised. His followers, some holding a torch in one hand, a sword in the other, crowd behind him, with the flickering of light on steel.*

ISOULT BLANCHE MAINS. [*Pointing to the dead.*] We had no power,

Nor I, nor thou. Love such as theirs, it seems,

That God Himself doth scarcely dare to touch.

THE END

For All Ladies of Shalott

ALINE KILMER

The web flew out and floated wide.
  Poor lady! I was with her then.
She gathered up her piteous pride,
  But she could never weave again.

The mirror cracked from side to side;
  I saw its silver shadows go.
"The curse has come on me!" she cried.
  Poor lady! I had told her so.

She was so proud: she would not hide.
  She only laughed and tried to sing.
But singing, in her song she died.
  She did not profit anything.

Elaine

EDNA ST. VINCENT MILLAY

Oh, come again to Astolat!
  I will not ask you to be kind.
And you may go when you will go,
  And I will stay behind.

I will not say how dear you are,
  Or ask you if you hold me dear,
Or trouble you with things for you
  The way I did last year.

So still the orchard, Lancelot,
  So very still the lake shall be,
You could not guess—though you should guess—
  What is become of me.

So wide shall be the garden-walk,
  The garden-seat so very wide,
You needs must think—if you should think—
  The lily maid had died.

Save that, a little way away,
  I'd watch you for a little while,
To see you speak, the way you speak,
  And smile,—if you should smile.

Guinevere at Her Fireside

DOROTHY PARKER

A nobler king had never breath—
　　I say it now, and said it then.
Who weds with such is wed till death
　　And wedded stays in Heaven. Amen.

(And oh, the shirts of linen-lawn,
　　And all the armor, tagged and tied,
And church on Sundays, dusk and dawn,
　　And bed a thing to kneel beside!)

The bravest one stood tall above
　　The rest, and watched me as a light.
I heard and heard them talk of love;
　　I'd naught to do but think, at night.

The bravest man has littlest brains;
　　That chalky fool from Astolat
With all her dying and her pains!—
　　Thank God, I helped him over that.

I found him not unfair to see—
　　I like a man with peppered hair!
And thus it came about. Ah, me,
　　Tristram was busied otherwhere. . . .

A nobler king had never breath—
I say it now, and said it then.
Who weds with such is wed till death
And wedded stays in Heaven. Amen.

Iseult of Brittany

DOROTHY PARKER

So delicate my hands, and long,
   They might have been my pride.
And there were those to make them song
   Who for their touch had died.

Too frail to cup a heart within,
   Too soft to hold the free—
How long these lovely hands have been
   A bitterness to me!

The Naming of the Lost

Valerie Nieman

". . . so by her subtle working she made Merlin to go under that
stone to let her wit of the marvels there. . . . And so she departed
and left Merlin."

—*Le Morte D'Arthur*

I call myself the lost one. I walk the rails
below the mountain, above the water's curve,
companioned only by my steady breath.
I, I—there is no soul behind that word,
a cry against a time which even my flesh
and hidden bones cannot recall to me.
My face is the one which I saw reflected,
without a name. And it may be this day
that I will walk myself down, or tomorrow.

The rails are rusted, brown as the hillside,
but the sun strikes an echo from the steel,
keen of ten thousand steps of stretched metal,
twisting upon its spikes. My ear against
the rail, I hear distance, distance, distance.

This dress, lilac flowers now stained by sweat,
I took from a woman's line of drying clothes.
I took it the way I'll take a name. Perhaps
the place I walk to, Catawba, that will be
my name. On the beating under-skin of my wrist

I taste the day. I am river water
which flows swift deep and green, carrying more
than itself, secrets, not knowing more
than tangled currents and the rub of the banks.
I feel pregnant, as if a river's child
were growing hidden by this borrowed skirt,
but I remember no lust, and no man's arms.

In the heat of the late of summer, cool on my back
a shadow's thrown. An edge of an echo, steps.
"Is someone there?" I call. The shade moves on,
slowly passing like the shadow of a cloud
that is not there. The sky is hot, hazy.
I look back, to find no one behind. Again,
without a reason, I had thought that one
for whom I seem to wait was following me.
But there's no one, not least myself, who has
the name by which to spin me clear around,
to make my feet daintily dance, my hands
weave gold from the summer-straw air. My path
follows along the steps that I have found.

The land broadens, mountains rise on the smell
of sassafras, of tree bark spice, green juice
sweet in the stems of rock maples and beech.
I feel the sandstone ribs of the country like
the bones of a lover. I, the nameless one,
will love only one sure as rock in himself,
his name pressed in every cell. When he
dies, his bones will cry his name in the wind
that lifts the tipping wings of the red-tailed hawk.

Upon my left there widens a bay of land,
a green lawn down from the tracks to the river bank,
and sunk to its rungs in the meadow soil, a chair,
alone, with neither house nor barn nearby.
The chair looks out across the flowing stream.
I go down, stepping from cinders to grass and mounds

of starry flowers foaming here, and here.

A kitchen chair, and turned from oak—one rung
is broken where a farmer's foot would rest.
Seven rods support the rounded back, the gray
wood carved to show an open pair of hands.
I rest my hands upon the back and watch
the river flowing north, nestling against
the near bank, gnawing it from beneath. One day
it will devour the meadow, this chair, and all.

I lift my feet from broken shoes and stand,
the grass blades bend, soft edges unblooded
against my ankles. The heat goes from my skin.
Ahead, Catawba lies, and they say there
that white and glistening salt is hilled beside
the tracks, burning under the sun, waiting
for rain to run it into sterile earth.
A long walk, yet, and so I sit and rest,
my shoulder-blades within the back's embrace.

In the river's deepest bend, I see bottom,
and broken hulls of sunken barges finned
with heavy carp upon the bows. Silt stirs.
Quickened with the raw Appalachian earth
which ran down red in spring rain, three dragons rise,
their wings unfurling, up from the barges' depth.
The dragons rest suspended in the stream,
great fish with golden scales. Watching, I scarcely
hear the tread of feet on the railroad ties.

"Good day."
        I turn. An old man stands where I
had left the tracks; he holds one hand above
his eyes, blocking the river's reflected light.
"Who are you?" I call. He cocks his head.
"A farmer here. My name is Merle." He waits
for mine. I fold my hands on emptiness.

He takes long strides in high, brown boots, pushing
aside the grass and starlike flowers, the steps
of a younger man. White hair hangs collar-long
on his blue-sky shirt of faded plaid, and white
his beard as well, but streaks with black. "My chair,"
he says, a resonant voice. "D'ye like it, girl?"

What can I say but that I do? He kneels
beside me. "And what d'ye see from sitting there?"
I motion, nothing, and the old man steadies
himself with a hand on the seat and gazes out
across the water. My lips, my throat grow cold,
as after chewing mint. "I see dragons,
their scales like light, all golden in the stream."
"A good eye, girl—your name?"
                                    "The lost one," I say.
"I've found a name in every place I've been,
where the pale moon has faded flowers, where
the sun is old and copper-dark. And now
I walk to Catawba landing, and that, perhaps,
will be my name, or hold a name for me."

And though his years lie worn and plain on him
he rises smoothly, and kneels before my feet.
He clasps my hand in his. "Welcome," he says,
"my Nimue, after a long and barren time."
I try to rise, but feel my shoulders held
firmly within the chair. "I say again,
welcome. A new Siege Perilous, I made
this to wait until you'd stray across the world."

I struggle, cry, "I wish to leave!" Then feel
myself untutored, rude. "You left before,"
he says, "and then I could not follow you.
But came the time appointed for the spell
to end—a water spell which found an end
as water must. And since, I ever watched
your path. For you, like all who spurn their hearts,

have lost yourself."
               "And where have you followed?"
"I have been many places behind you. Steps,
and half-heard sounds, and shadows that soon passed."

I find some corner of myself within
that name, Nimue, Nimue, a place dusty
and cool with shadows lying thick at noon.
It may be I recall a long night's dream,
or a name I once had taken, or refused.

The weight of his hands on mine is warm as summer
in my lap, his dark eyes deep as August shade.
"Remember, then"——a distant image flares
of a slow stream, green banks, and two riders,
their horses gray. "Oh!"
               "Remember, then."

The riders halt beside a waiting cave,
ragged darkness guarded by an unshaped stone.
The woman slips to the dark man's arms, and she
is robed in green. Her hair, all free, is gold.
The woman waits; the man goes forward. Dark
around him closes as she sings of sleep
flowing north, weaves a spell of stream and brook.
The stone rolls closed to seal away the cave.
She smiles, a secret warm beneath her ribs
as a child not born. I push the memory
away——a vision, no more. "It is not I,
this water-singer, green-eyed maker of spells."
His hands are firm. "Nimue," he says,
"it was a far time away."
               "I won't believe."

But light ebbs from white, to gold, to red,
and merciful tears arise from a hollow place,
and I can cry for days from dawn to dust
and each relinquished past, long slipped away.

"You knew me as Merlin, then, and you were mine,
as Arthur was who passed to Avalon,
noble still. But you were dangerous,
a lake reflecting fair, bright skies while all
below is rocks and shards. And so I fell,
knowing that time must wear away that taint
before our stricken lives could be renewed."
His fingers touch my cheek and gather there
the tears. "River-child, my Nimue, look."

A teardrop rests, silver, in the palm of his hand:
he breathes upon it, speaks familiar slow
commanding words. And where the tear had been,
a green pearl-gem appears, faintly glowing
with evening light. "Take it, an orient
layered of long forgetting." He lets go
my hands. "Is it some spell to bind me, now,
within a flowered meadow? Do you give
me sleep as I awake to myself?"
                                "Would I,
who have so long followed all your paths?"

I take the tear-jewel in my lips, perfect
roundness. Layer by layer it dissolves,
the sharp of anguish, bitter salt of remorse,
at center, sweet. And memory speaks as reeds
at water's edge and water tumbling down
to green and silent pools. I see, I see
the ageless through the old, Merlin, ancient
Myrddin who wears no more a farmer's face.

I learn again the names of things, the words
to free the winter's ice-bound streams, and warm
them clear, and freshening. My beating flesh
recalls a thousand thousand paths I walked
alone, and each a long night's longest dream.

"Ah, Nimue, this time we'll thread the nighting

stars upon our chains. This time we shall
become the rulers of all powers, of earth
and air, and fire, water, since we at last
have come to rule ourselves."
                            "But I remain
the water-flow, and you the lasting stone.
Can you embrace, and not be worn away?
Can I be held and not break free to foam,
or chafe myself, confined, to stagnancy?"

"In time that was, my river-child, in time
when Camelot burned, new-pulled from imagining's
flame. But there are times between the stars
when all the elements are joined." A light
wind comes between us, lifts his hair, and falls,
is gone. "Yet if a teacher may regain
an erring student," I ask, "can a lover forgive
such a betrayal?"
                            "Have you not lost yourself
and found yourself again?" He lifts me from
the charmed chair by his hand's warm touch on mine.
"We'll sing together a song, and arches raise
of a new Camelot which shall not fall."

The chair crumbles, falls fine to ash and sifts
upon the flowered lawn. A new wind bears
the ash across the slow, north-flowing stream.
Three dragons wing from their water-nest to fly
in patterns tangled as ancient auguries.
The stars come out like salt, strewn, and fill
the night from north to south. I match my heart
to his, his breath to mine.
                            Soft-bladed grass
closes above the place our feet had been.

Guenever Prays for a Child

WENDY MNOOKIN

St. Anne.
You knew emptiness,
            the years
of hollow longing.
Your prayers were answered.
Answer mine now.

Let it be tonight.

            Arthur.
            Our people marvel
            at your strength in battle.
            They travel far
            to seek your wisdom in court.
            You've performed miracles.
            Do this for me.

            Let it be tonight.

Guenever Listens to a Minstrel Sing of Love

WENDY MNOOKIN

At ten, sewing,
pushing the needle in and out,
I looped the threads
    just so
and pulled them through:
    a petal.

Amazed, I tried again,
and again a petal,
raised and distinct,
    beautiful.
I did more and more,
    a field of petals.

"Mother!" I cried,
"look what I've done!
A new stitch—
    petals—"
I thrust the sewing at her
    for her praise.

She looked.
She smiled her grown-up smile
and bent her head towards me.
    "Petals.
How clever you are!

But Guenever,

this isn't new.
It's called the *petal stitch*."
She kissed my head
   and walked away.
Others were in the room,
   witnesses.

I didn't cry.
Careful not to run
I left the room,
   no sorceress
of stitchery, just a girl
   who skipped one lesson.

Guenever Loses Her Baby

WENDY MNOOKIN

3 days late

Is it possible
after all the years
of filling space

with emptiness
that a child
latches on

and grows
stretching the shell
of my body

around her
molding me
to mother?

5 days late

I'll have a feast
light all the candles
drape the banners

serve sixteen courses
and a board of pastries
minstrels will play

acrobats tumble
and at the end
a horn will sound

"The Queen's with child!"

8 days late

Those who hate
Arthur and me
will watch her closely.

Green eyes or grey?
Red hair or brown?
Which one does she resemble?

Maybe me—
her mother's child
exposing no one

leaving me
always uncertain
whose child she is.

9 days late

I can't bear
the days of waiting
not knowing.

What if
   she looks like Lancelot?
      I must find out

what to do
   how to shake her
      loose.

No!

10 days late

I dream
   I'm a wild duck
      flying

Arthur
   sends his hawk
      to bring me down

I'm grabbed
   by the neck
      twisted

a whistle
   I fall down
      and down

I can't fly
   I drop
      to the ground

broken
   the dog's mouth
      closes on me

he brings me
to his master
Lancelot

I wake to blood

Guenever Retreats to Almesbury After Arthur's Death

WENDY MNOOKIN

The sisters say walk,
walk in the garden.
So I do. I work in the garden,
raking fingers through thick blankets of thyme,
pinching off tops of basil. Smell
makes me dizzy. I hold my head.
Fingers smell rich.

spice fingers
unsullied with food
saved for dipping
in cinnamon
       sweet basil
          honey
but I don't dip
I save the smell of you
on fingers

I thin the sage and tie up mint.

fresh rushes
on the floors
at festivals
   roses
      lilies
         mint

but the soft crush
turns brittle
         filthy

There are weeds,
more weeds than I can pull.
And I am late for prayers.

        The sisters say read,
why don't you read?

        I have your letter
in the pages of my Bible.

        Guenever
        in you I have my earthly joy
        leave Almesbury now
        and be with me

The words tilt on the page.
I turn my head, follow them
up
    down.
I snap the book shut
to keep the words still.

        do not write
        no use in sending letters
        I cannot read them

        I will not read your letters

        The sisters say rest,
get some sleep.
I lie awake and wait for Matins.

        awake
        I do not see

Gaheris and Gareth
unarmed
    slain
by you in my rescue

The nuns return from morning prayers
to sleep. Three hours until Prime.
Three hours to lie awake.

    entombed
    a stone house built around her:
    Crazy Anne: killed her husband

    eyes closed
    I see you
    fighting Arthur lying dead

Air cuts my eyes
like broken glass.
I will not close my eyes.

    The sisters say eat,
you must eat to stay well.
I move the food around and smile.

Yesterday I swooned at Vespers.
I must eat some bread.
A little bread
so I won't swoon.
So I can stay awake.

    lying in bed
    hip bones push
    against skin

    it is my time
    I bleed

Guenever Returns from the Garden

WENDY MNOOKIN

Sister Margaret and I
walk with Caroline
back from the garden.

We walk in silence,
although now I speak.
There is little need

for talk,
and the sisters observe
silence.

Caroline skips ahead.
Her hair floats
up

   and down

      until she's lost
in leaves
as she rounds
a tree
  my eyes strain
to find her
I see the bough

that closed
around her
        leaves
orange
     gold

but Caroline is gone

leaves
where hair should be
I see red
       black

Sister Margaret eases me
down
I breathe
in gasps
      a voice
from far away
a voice
I do not recognize
          my voice
speaks
of things I have not said before

Margaret listens.
It grows late, and cold,
and still she listens.

My voice comes back
from far away.
My breath comes easy.

When I'm done speaking
we sit in silence
for a long time.

Then I say,

just under the quiet,
"I will stay at Almesbury

until I die.
I cannot look
at Lancelot's face

again.
I cannot lose him
again."

Bibliography of
Arthurian Fiction by Women

Ahern, Jerry and Sharon Ahern. "Siege Perilous." In *Grails: Quests, Visitations, and Other Occurrences*. Ed. Richard Gilliam, Martin H. Greenberg, and Edward E. Kramer. Atlanta: Unnameable Press, 1992. 389–414. (Reprinted in *Grails: Visitations of the Night*. Ed. Richard Gilliam, Martin H. Greenberg, and Edward E. Kramer. New York: ROC, 1994. 191–212.)

Aiken, Joan. *The Stolen Lake*. Ill. Pat Marriott. London: Jonathan Cape, 1981.

Ashby, Ruth. *Quest for King Arthur*. Time Machine 23. Ill. Scott Caple. New York: A Byron Preiss Book/Bantam, 1988.

Baldry, Cherith. "Hunt of the Hart Royal." In *The Chronicles of the Holy Grail*. Ed. Mike Ashley. New York: Carroll & Graf, 1996. 94–108.

————. *Sir Kay's Quest*. Rochester, NY: Round Table Publications, 1996.

Bevan, Clare. *Mightier Than the Sword*. London: Puffin Books, 1991.

Bingham, Jennie M. *Annals of the Round Table and Other Stories*. New York: Phillips & Hunt, 1886.

Bowers, Gwendolyn. *Brother to Galahad*. New York: Henry Z. Walck, 1963.

Bond, Nancy. *A String in the Harp*. New York: Atheneum, 1976.

Bradley, Marion Zimmer. "Chalice of Tears, or I Didn't Want That Damned Grail Anyway." In *Grails: Quests, Visitations, and Other Occurrences*. Ed. Richard Gilliam, Martin H. Greenberg, and Edward E. Kramer. Atlanta: Unnameable Press, 1992. 43–52. (Reprinted in *Grails: Quests of the Dawn*. Ed. Richard Gilliam, Martin H. Greenberg, and Edward E. Kramer. New York: ROC, 1994. 27–35.)

————. *The Forest House*. New York: ROC, 1995.

————. "Here There Be Dragons?" In *Excalibur*. Ed. Richard Gilliam, Martin H. Greenberg, and Edward E. Kramer. New York: Warner Books, 1995. 183–92.

———. *The House Between the Worlds*. New York: Del Rey/Ballantine, 1982.

———. *The Mists of Avalon*. New York: Alfred A. Knopf, 1982.

———. "The Pledged Word." In *The Merlin Chronicles*. Ed. Mike Ashley. New York: Carroll & Graf. 130–36.

Bradshaw, Gillian. *Hawk of May*. New York: Simon and Schuster, 1980.

———. *In Winter's Shadow*. New York: Simon and Schuster, 1982.

———. *Kingdom of Summer*. New York: Simon and Schuster, 1981.

Caldecott, Moyra. *Crystal Legends*. Ill. Anthea Toorchen. Wellingborough, Northamptonshire: Aquarian Press, 1990.

———. *The Green Lady and the King of Shadows: A Glastonbury Legend*. Glastonbury: Gothic Image Publications, 1989.

Caldecott, Moyra and Lynette Gusman. *Taliesin & Avagddu*. Somerset: Bran's Head Books, 1985.

Cameron, Anne. *Stubby Amberchuck & the Holy Grail*. Madeira Park, BC, Canada: Harbour Publishing, 1987.

Cameron, Eleanor. *Time and Mr. Bass: A Mushroom Planet Book*. Ill. Fred H. Meise. Boston: An Atlantic Monthly Press Book, 1967. (Only a few pages of Arthurian material.)

Chadwick, Elizabeth. *First Knight*. Story by Lorne Cameron, David Hoselton, and William Nicholson. Screenplay by William Nicholson. New York: Pocket Books, 1995.

Chant, Joy. *The High Kings*. Ill. George Sharp. Designed by David Larkin. Toronto, New York, etc.: Bantam, 1983.

Chapman, Vera. "Belle Dame, sans Merci." In *The Camelot Chronicles: Heroic Adventures from the Time of King Arthur*. Ed. Mike Ashley. New York: Wing Books, 1995. 10–26.

———. *The Enchantresses*. London: Victor Gollancz, 1998.

———. *The Green Knight*. London: Rex Collings, 1975.

———. *King Arthur's Daughter*. London: Rex Collings, 1976.

———. *The King's Damosel*. London: Rex Collings, 1976.

———. "A Sword for Arthur." In *The Merlin Chronicles*. Ed. Mike Ashley. New York: Carroll & Graf, 1995. 155–64.

———. *The Three Damosels*. London: Magnum Books, 1978. (Combines *The Green Knight*, *The King's Damosel*, and *King Arthur's Daughter*.)

Chase, Beatrice. *A Dartmoor Galahad*. New York: Longmans, Green and Co., 1923. (Has a character named after the Galahad of Arthurian legend.)

Chase, Mary Ellen. "A Candle at Night." *Collier's* (9 May 1942): 17, 74–77.

———. *Dawn in Lyonesse*. New York: Macmillan, 1938.

Cherryh, C. J. *Port Eternity*. New York: DAW, 1982.

Chetwin, Grace. *On All Hallows' Eve*. New York: Lothrop, Lee & Shepard Books, 1984.

Christian, Catherine. *The Sword and the Flame: Variations on a Theme of Sir Thomas Malory*. London: Macmillan, 1978. (Published in the U.S. as *The Pendragon*. New York: Alfred A. Knopf, 1979.)

Clare, Helen [pseudonym of Pauline Hunter Blair]. *Merlin's Magic*. London: John Lane, 1953.

Closs, Hannah. *Tristan*. London: Andrew Dakers Ltd., 1940.

Cochran, Molly, and Warren Murphy. *The Forever King*. New York: TOR, 1992.

———. *The Broken Sword*. New York: TOR, 1997.

Collins, Joan. *King Arthur and the Knights of the Round Table*. Ill. Malcolm Stokes. Loughborough, Leicestershire: Ladybird Books, 1986. (Original children's story about Bran, a falconer's son, who is taken to Camelot by Lancelot.)

Cooper, Susan. *The Dark Is Rising*. New York: Atheneum, 1973.

———. *Greenwitch*. New York: Atheneum, 1974.

———. *The Grey King*. New York: Atheneum, 1975.

———. *Over Sea, Under Stone*. New York: Harcourt, Brace & World, Inc., 1965.

———. *Silver on the Tree*. New York: Atheneum, 1977.

Craik, Dinah Maria Mulock. "Avillion; or, The Happy Isles. A Fireside Fancy." In *Avillion and Other Tales*. 3 vols. London: Smith, Elder and Co., 1853. I:1–115.

———. "Jack the Giant-Killer." In *The Fairy Book: The Best Popular Fairy Stories Selected and Rendered Anew*. London: Macmillan, 1863. 68–82.

———. "Tom Thumb." In *The Fairy Book: The Best Popular Fairy Stories Selected and Rendered Anew*. London: Macmillan, 1863. 83–89. (Reprinted as "Merlin and Tom Thumb" in *The Merlin Chronicles*. Ed. Mike Ashley. New York: Carroll & Graf, 1995. 223–30.)

Crompton, Anne Eliot. "Excalibur." In *Camelot*. Ed. Jane Yolen. Ill. Winslow Pels. New York: Philomel Books, 1995. 79–90.

———. *Gawain and Lady Green*. New York: Donald I. Fine Books, 1997.

———. *Merlin's Harp*. New York: Donald I. Fine, 1995

Curry, Jane Louise. *The Sleepers*. Ill. Gareth Floyd. New York: Harcourt, Brace & World, 1968.

Darby, Catherine. *A Dream of Fair Serpents*. New York: Popular Library, 1979.

Deal, Babs H. *The Grail*. New York: David McKay, 1963.

Dexter, Susan. "Where Bestowed." In *Excalibur*. Ed. Richard Gilliam, Martin H. Greenberg, and Edward E. Kramer. New York: Warner Books, 1995. 363–75.

Doyle, Debra, and James D. Macdonald. "Stealing God." In *Tales of the Knights Templar*. Ed. Katherine Kurtz. New York: Warner Books, 1995. 248–72. (A Grail story.)

Elliott, Janice. *The Empty Throne*. Ill. Grahame Baker. London: Walker Books, 1989. (1st was 1988.)

———. *The King Awakes*. London: Walker Books, 1989.

Evans, Quinn Taylor. *Merlin's Legacy: Daughter of Fire*. New York: Zebra Books, 1996. (Book 1 of Merlin's Legacy.)

———. *Merlin's Legacy: Daughter of Light*. New York: Zebra Books, 1997. (Book 3 of Merlin's Legacy.)

———. *Merlin's Legacy: Daughter of the Mist*. New York: Zebra Books, 1996. (Book 2 of Merlin's Legacy.)

———. *Merlin's Legacy: Shadows of Camelot*. New York: Zebra Books, 1997. (Book 4 of Merlin's Legacy.)

Farmer, Penelope. *The Magic Stone*. Ill. John Kaufmann. New York: Harcourt Brace, 1964.

Fleischer, Leonore. *The Fisher King*. A novel based on the motion picture written by Richard LaGravenese. New York: Signet, 1991.

Ford, Williston Merrick. *Grail: An Agelong Romance*. Boston: The Christopher Publishing House, 1961.

Fortune, Dion. "The Death of Vivien Le Fay Morgan" [an epilogue to Fortune's novel *Moon Magic*, alleged to have been received mediumistically after Dion Fortune's death]. In *Aspects of Occultism*. London: The Aquarian Press, 1962. 78–87.

———. *Moon Magic*. London: Aquarian Press, 1956.

———. *The Sea Priestess*. London: Published by the author, 1938.

Friesner, Esther M. "The Death of Nimue." In *Fantasy Book* (June 1985), 59–60. (Reprinted in *The Merlin Chronicles*. Ed. Mike Ashley. New York: Carroll & Graf, 1995. 386–90.)

———. *Druid's Blood*. New York: Signet/New American Library, 1988.

———. "Goldie, Lox, and the Three Excalibearers." In *Excalibur*. Ed. Richard Gilliam, Martin H. Greenberg, and Edward E. Kramer. New York: Warner Books, 1995. 193–225.

———. "Sparrow." In *Return to Avalon: A Celebration of Marion Zimmer Bradley*. New York: DAW Books, 1996. 218–50.

Gabaldon, Diana. "Surgeon's Steel." In *Excalibur*. Ed. Richard Gilliam, Martin H. Greenberg, and Edward E. Kramer. New York: Warner Books, 1995. 67–90.

NY: The Authors' Press Publishers, 1913.
ley Young. Boston: Small, Maynard & Co.,

. Ill. Norman Green. New York: Step-Up
35.
rlds." In *Return to Avalon: A Celebration of*
: DAW Books, 1996. 251–74.
ood. Garden City, NY: Doubleday, 1978.
York: M. Evans & Co., 1990.
ondon: The Bodley Head, 1988
The Bodley Head, 1986.
e, Somerset: Bran's Head Books, 1982.
n: The Bodley Head, 1983.
ontagu). *The Feasts of Camelot, with the Tales*
and Daldy, 1863.

Hildebrandt, Rita. *Merlin and the Dragons of Atlantis*. Ill. Tim Hildebrandt. India-
napolis: Bobbs Merrill, 1983.

Hirsch, Connie. "Judas." In *Grails: Visitations of the Night*. Ed. Richard Gilliam,
Martin H. Greenberg, and Edward E. Kramer. New York: ROC, 1994. 275–
99.

Hodges, Margaret. *Knight Prisoner: The Tale of Sir Thomas Malory and His King Arthur*.
Decorations by Don Bolognese and Elaine Raphael. New York: Farrar, Straus
and Giroux, 1976.

Holder, Nancy. "To Leave If You Can." In *Grails: Quests, Visitations, and Other Occurrences*. Ed. Richard Gilliam, Martin H. Greenberg, and Edward E. Kramer.
Atlanta: Unnameable Press, 1992. 605–20. (Reprinted in *Grails: Visitations
of the Night*. Ed. Richard Gilliam, Martin H. Greenberg, and Edward E.
Kramer. New York: ROC, 1994. 416–29.)

———. "Prayer of the Knight of the Sword." In *Excalibur*. Ed. Richard Gilliam,
Martin H. Greenberg, and Edward E. Kramer. New York: Warner Books,
1995. 91–105.

Hollick, Helen. *The Kingmaking*. Book One of Pendragon's Banner. London:
Heinemann, 1994.

———. *The Pendragon's Banner*. Book Two of Pendragon's Banner. London:
Heinemann, 1995.

———. *Shadow of the King*. Book Three of Pendragon's Banner. London:
Heinemann, 1996.

Holmes, Lillian. *Little Sir Galahad*. Chicago: David C. Cook Publishing Co., 1904.

Janey, Rebecca Price. *The Eerie Echo*. The Heather Reed Mystery Series #3. Dallas: Word Publishing, 1993. (Young adult novel about a sixteen-year-old detective and a mystery surrounding the Grail.)

Jewett, Eleanore M. *The Hidden Treasure of Glaston*. Ill. Frederick T. Chapman. New York: Viking, 1946.

Johnson, Barbara Ferry. *Lionors*. New York: Avon, 1975.

Johnston, Annie Fellows. *Keeping Tryst: A Tale of King Arthur's Time*. Boston: L. C. Page & Co., 1905.

————. *The Little Colonel's Knight Comes Riding*. Boston: The Page Co., 1907.

————. *Two Little Knights of Kentucky; Who Were the "Little Colonel's" Neighbours*. Boston: L. C. Page and Co., 1899.

Johnston, Velda. "Stranger on the Beach." *Good Housekeeping* (Nov. 1987): 211–14, 222, 224–37, 258–78. (Romance set in a town called Camelot; no other Arthurian content.)

Jones, Heather Rose. "The Treasures of Britain." In *The Chronicles of the Holy Grail*. Ed. Mike Ashley. New York: Carroll & Graf, 1996. 208–17

Jones, Mary J. *Avalon*. Tallahassee, FL: Naiad Press, 1991.

Karr, Phyllis Ann. "The Coming of the Light." In *The Camelot Chronicles: Heroic Adventures from the Time of King Arthur*. Ed. Mike Ashley. New York: Wing Books, 1995. 360–73.

————. "Galahad's Lady." In *The Chronicles of the Holy Grail*. Ed. Mike Ashley. New York: Carroll & Graf, 1996. 151–77.

————. *The Idylls of the Queen*. New York: Ace, 1982.

————. "Merlin's Dark Mirror." In *The Merlin Chronicles*. Ed. Mike Ashley. New York: Carroll & Graf, 1995. 199–208.

————. "Mordred and the Dragon." In *The Ultimate Dragon*. Ed. Byron Preiss, John Betancourt, & Keith R. A. DeCandido. New York: Dell, 1995. 207–15.

————. "The Truth About the Lady of the Lake." *Fantasy Magazine* 9 (Summer 1990): 47.

————. "Two Bits of Embroidery." In *Invitation to Camelot: An Arthurian Anthology of Short Stories*. Ed. Parke Godwin. New York: Ace Books, 1988. 31–45.

Katz, Welwyn Wilton. *The Third Magic*. Vancouver/Toronto: A Groundwood Book/ Douglas & McIntyre, 1988.

Kennealy, Patricia. *The Hawk's Gray Feather: A Book of the Keltiad*. New York: ROC, 1990. (Vol. 1 of The Tales of Arthur.)

————. *The Copper Crown: A Novel of the Keltiad*. New York: Bluejay, 1984.

————. *The Silver Branch: A Novel of the Keltiad*. New York: New American Library, 1988.

————. *The Throne of Scone: A Book of the Keltiad*. New York: Bluejay, 1986.

Kennealy-Morrison, Patricia. *The Hedge of Mist*. New York: HarperPrism, 1996. (Vol. 3 of The Tales of Arthur.)

————. *The Oak Above the Kings*. New York: ROC, 1995. (Vol. 2 of The Tales of Arthur.)

Kudlinski, Kathleen. "The Changing of the Shrew." In *Camelot*. Ed. Jane Yolen. Ill. Winslow Pels. New York: Philomel Books, 1995. 5–15.

Kuncewicz, Maria. *Tristan*. New York: George Braziller, 1974.

Kushner, Ellen. *Knights of the Round Table*. Ill. Judith Mitchell. Choose Your Own Adventure, 86. New York: An Edward Packard Book/Bantam Books, 1988.

Lackey, Mercedes. "The Cup and the Grail." In *Grails: Quests, Visitations, and Other Occurrences*. Ed. Richard Gilliam, Martin H. Greenberg, and Edward E. Kramer. Atlanta: Unnameable Press, 1992. 15–34. (Reprinted in *Grails: Quests of the Dawn*. Ed. Richard Gilliam, Martin H. Greenberg, and Edward E. Kramer. New York: ROC, 1994. 2–19.)

————. "Once and Future." In *Excalibur*. Ed. Richard Gilliam, Martin H. Greenberg, and Edward E. Kramer. New York: Warner Books, 1995. 327–38.

Laubenthal, Sanders Anne. *Excalibur*. Introduction by Lin Carter. New York: Ballantine, 1973.

Leader, Mary. *Triad*. New York: Coward, McCann & Geoghegan, 1973.

Lee, Tanith. "Exalted Hearts." In *Grails: Quests, Visitations, and Other Occurrences*. Ed. Richard Gilliam, Martin H. Greenberg, and Edward E. Kramer. Atlanta: Unnameable Press, 1992. 53–60. (Reprinted in *Grails: Visitations of the Night*. Ed. Richard Gilliam, Martin H. Greenberg, and Edward E. Kramer. New York: ROC, 1994. 2–7.)

————. "The Kingdoms of the Air." In *The Chronicles of the Holy Grail*. Ed. Mike Ashley. New York: Carroll & Graf, 1996. 228–63.

————. "King's Mage." In *The Merlin Chronicles*. Ed. Mike Ashley. New York: Carroll & Graf, 1995. 255–64.

————. "The Minstrel's Tale." In *Invitation to Camelot: An Arthurian Anthology of Short Stories*. Ed. Parke Godwin. New York: Ace Books, 1988. 19–29.

Le Feuvre, Amy. *Legend Led*. London: The Religious Tract Society, n.d.

Linwood, Mary. *The House of Camelot: A Tale of the Olden Time*. London: J. F. Hope, 1858.

Lively, Penelope. *The Whispering Knight*. Ill. Gareth Floyd. New York: E. P. Dutton, 1971.

Llywelyn, Morgan. "Their Son." In *Invitation to Camelot: An Arthurian Anthology of Short Stories*. Ed. Parke Godwin. New York: Ace Books, 1988. 2–17.

Macdonald, James D., and Debra Doyle. "Holly and Ivy." In *Camelot*. Ed. Jane Yolen. Ill. Winslow Pels. New York: Philomel Books, 1995. 125–35.

Manning, Rosemary. *The Dragon's Quest*. Ill. Constance Marshall. Garden City, NY: Doubleday, 1962.

———. *Greensmoke*. Ill. Constance Marshall. Garden City, NY: Doubleday, 1957.

Mason, Bobbie Ann. *In Country*. New York: Harper & Row, 1985. (Set in modern times but contains a Grail motif.)

Mazer, Anne. *A Kid in King Arthur's Court*. New York: Disney, 1995.

McCaffrey, Anne. "Black Horses for a King." In *Camelot*. Ed. Jane Yolen. Ill. Winslow Pels. New York: Philomel Books, 1995. 93–123.

McGraw, Eloise Jarvis. *Joel and the Great Merlini*. Ill. Jim Arnosky. Columbus, Ohio: Pantheon Books/Weekly Reader Books, 1979.

McKenzie, Nancy. *The Child Queen: The Tale of Guinevere and King Arthur*. New York: Del Rey, 1994.

———. *The High Queen: The Tale of Guinevere and King Arthur Continues*. New York: Del Rey, 1995.

Meaney, Dee Morrison. *Iseult*. New York: Ace, 1985.

Meigs, Elizabeth Bleecker. *The Crusade and the Cup*. Ill. Edward and Stephani Godwin. New York: E. P. Dutton and Co., 1952.

Mitchell, Mary. *Birth of a Legend*. London: Methuen, 1956.

Mitchison, Naomi. *To the Chapel Perilous*. London: George Allen and Unwin, 1955.

Murdoch, Iris. *The Green Knight*. London: Chatto & Windus, 1993.

Neville, Mary. *King Arthur or a Knight of Our Day*. London: Chapman and Hall, 1876.

Newman, Sharan. *The Chessboard Queen*. New York: St. Martin's, 1983.

———. *Guinevere*. New York: St. Martin's, 1981.

———. *Guinevere Evermore*. New York: St. Martin's, 1985.

———. "The Palace by Moonlight." In *Invitation to Camelot: An Arthurian Anthology of Short Stories*. Ed. Parke Godwin. New York: Ace Books, 1988. 201–21.

Norman, Diana. *King of the Last Days*. London: Hodder and Stoughton, 1981.

Norton, Andre [name changed from Alice Mary Norton]. "Pendragon." In *Dragon Magic*. New York: Ace Books, 1972. 103–40.

———. *Merlin's Mirror*. New York: DAW, 1975.

———. *Steel Magic*. Ill. Robin Jacques. Cleveland: The World Publishing Co., 1965.

———. "That Which Overfloweth." In *Grails: Quests, Visitations, and Other Occurrences*. Ed. Richard Gilliam, Martin H. Greenberg, and Edward E. Kramer. Atlanta: Unnameable Press, 1992. 35–42. (Reprinted in *Grails: Quests of the*

Dawn. Ed. Richard Gilliam, Martin H. Greenberg, and Edward E. Kramer. New York: ROC, 1994. 20–26.)

———. *WitchWorld.* New York: Ace Books, 1963.

Nye, Jody Lynn. "Sword Practice." In *Excalibur.* Ed. Richard Gilliam, Martin H. Greenberg, and Edward E. Kramer. New York: Warner Books, 1995. 339–61.

Ouspenskya, Ilona. "The Curse of the Romany." In *Grails: Quests of the Dawn.* Ed. Richard Gilliam, Martin H. Greenberg, and Edward E. Kramer. New York: ROC, 1994. 74–89.

Paterson, Katherine. *Park's Quest.* New York: Lodestar Books/E. P. Dutton, 1988. (A young boy muses about the Arthurian legends as he quests for knowledge about his father who died in Vietnam.)

Paxson, Diana L. "The God-Sword." In *Excalibur.* Ed. Richard Gilliam, Martin H. Greenberg, and Edward E. Kramer. New York: Warner Books, 1995. 3–28.

———. "Lady of Avalon." In *Return to Avalon: A Celebration of Marion Zimmer Bradley.* New York: DAW Books, 1996. 58–79.

———. *The White Raven.* New York: William Morrow, 1988.

———. "Wild Man." In *Camelot.* Ed. Jane Yolen. Ill. Winslow Pels. New York: Philomel Books, 1995. 17–38.

Peare, Catherine Owens. *Melor, King Arthur's Page.* New York: Putnam's, 1963.

Peters, Elizabeth [pseudonym of Barbara Gross Mertz]. *The Camelot Caper.* New York: Meredith Press, 1969.

Phelps, Elizabeth Stuart. "The Christmas of Sir Galahad." *Independent* 23 (7 Dec. 1871): 1.

———. "The Lady of Shalott." *Independent* 23 (6 July 1871): 1. (Reprinted in *Sealed Orders* 48–64.)

———. *Sealed Orders.* 1879; rpt. New York: Garret Press, 1969.

———. "The True Story of Guenever." *Independent* 28 (15 June 1876): 2–4. (Reprinted in *Sealed Orders* 65–80. Also reprinted in *The Camelot Chronicles: Heroic Adventures from the Time of King Arthur.* Ed. Mike Ashley. New York: Wing Books, 1995. 261–72.)

Phillips, Teresa Hyde. "King Arthur." In *Collier's* 26 Aug. 1933: 7–9, 37–38. (A short story about a doctor named Arthur who is called "King Arthur" but who doesn't live up to the name.)

Pledger, Lynne. "Gwenhwyfar." In *Camelot.* Ed. Jane Yolen. Ill. Winslow Pels. New York: Philomel Books, 1995. 63–76.

Proud, Linda. *Knights of the Grail: Based on the Legend of King Arthur.* London: The Good Company for Children Co., 1995.

Quiller-Couch, Sir Arthur and Daphne du Maurier. *Castle Dor*. London: J. M. Dent, 1962.

Resnick, Gloria. "The Lily Maid of Astolat." In *Return to Avalon: A Celebration of Marion Zimmer Bradley*. New York: DAW Books, 1996. 369–91.

Resnick, Mike and Linda Dunn. "Merdinus." In *Castle Fantastic*. Ed. John DeChancie and Martin H. Greenberg. New York: DAW Books, 1996. 226–46.

Richardson, Marjorie. "Launcelot's Tower." In *St. Nicholas: An Illustrated Magazine for Young Folks*, 19.1 (Nov. 1891–April 1892): 56–59.

Robbins, Ruth. *Taliesin and King Arthur*. Berkeley, CA: Parnassus Press, 1970.

Roberson, Jennifer. "Guinevere's Truth." In *Return to Avalon: A Celebration of Marion Zimmer Bradley*. New York: DAW Books, 1996. 395–98.

———. "The Horse Who Would Be King." In *The Merlin Chronicles*. Ed. Mike Ashley. New York: Carroll & Graf. 137–54.

Roberts, Dorothy James. *The Enchanted Cup*. New York: Appleton-Century-Crofts, 1953.

———. *Kinsmen of the Grail*. Boston: Little, Brown and Co., 1963.

———. *Launcelot, My Brother*. New York: Appleton-Century-Crofts, 1954.

Robins, Madeline E. "Nimuë's Tale." In *Invitation to Camelot: An Arthurian Anthology of Short Stories*. Ed. Parke Godwin. New York: Ace Books, 1988. 145–64.

Rofheart, Martha. *Glendower Country*. New York: G.P. Putnam's Sons, 1973. (Not specifically Arthurian, but contains many Arthurian allusions and references.)

Rosen, Winifred. "What Do Women Want?" In *McCall's* 8 May 1980: 110–111, 170–72.

Rusch, Kristine Kathryn. "Controlling the Sword." In *Excalibur*. Ed. Richard Gilliam, Martin H. Greenberg, and Edward E. Kramer. New York: Warner Books, 1995. 47–65

Rush, Alison. *The Last of Danu's Children*. New York: A Tom Doherty Associate Book, 1984.

St. John, Nicole [pseudonym of Norma Johnston]. *Guinever's Gift*. New York: Random House, 1977.

Salmonson, Jessica Amanda. "Namer of Beasts, Maker of Souls: The Romance of Sylvester and Nimuë." In *The Merlin Chronicles*. Ed. Mike Ashley. New York: Carroll & Graf, 1995. 322–59.

Sampson, Fay. *Black Smith's Telling*. Book Three in the sequence Daughter of Tintagel. London: Headline, 1990.

———. *Daughter of Tintagel: Comprising Wise Woman's Telling, White Nun's Telling, Black Smith's Telling, Taliesin's Telling, Herself*. London: Headline, 1992.

―――. *Herself.* Book Five in the sequence Daughter of Tintagel. London: Headline, 1992.

―――. *Taliessin's Telling.* Book Four in the sequence Daughter of Tintagel. London: Headline, 1991.

―――. *White Nun's Telling.* Book Two in the sequence Daughter of Tintagel. London: Headline, 1989.

―――. *Wise Woman's Telling.* Book One in the sequence Daughter of Tintagel. London: Headline, 1989.

Scarborough, Elizabeth Ann. "The Camelot Connection." In *Invitation to Camelot: An Arthurian Anthology of Short Stories.* Ed. Parke Godwin. New York: Ace Books, 1988. 47–82.

Schiller, Barbara. *The Kitchen Knight.* Ill. Nonny Hogrogian. New York: Holt, Rinehart and Winston, 1965.

Schwartz, Susan. "Count of the Saxon Shore" (a short story). In *Alternatives.* Ed. Robert Adams with Pamela Crippen Adams. New York: Baen Publishing Enterprises, 1989.

―――. *Grail of Hearts.* New York: TOR, 1991.

―――. "Seven from Caer Sidi." In *Invitation to Camelot: An Arthurian Anthology of Short Stories.* Ed. Parke Godwin. New York: Ace Books, 1988. 109–30.

―――. "Troubled Waters." In *Excalibur.* Ed. Richard Gilliam, Martin H. Greenberg, and Edward E. Kramer. New York: Warner Books, 1995. 399–425.

Seaman, Hollis Rowan. "Colors 1994." *The Round Table,* 4.1 & 2 (1987): 36–37.

Senior, Dorothy. *The Clutch of Circumstance or the Gates of Dawn.* London: Adam and Charles Black, 1908.

Service, Pamela F. *Tomorrow's Magic.* New York: Atheneum, 1987.

―――. *Winter of Magic's Return.* New York: Atheneum, 1985.

Seton, Anya. *Avalon.* Boston: Houghton Mifflin, 1965.

Sharmat, Marjorie Weinman. *The Lancelot Closes at Five.* New York: Scholastic, Inc. / An Apple Paperback, 1976. (Children's story that takes place in a housing complex called Camelot, with houses that have names like Lancelot, Excalibur, etc.)

Sharpe, Ruth Collier. *Tristram of Lyonesse: The Story of an Immortal Love.* Illustrations from original paintings by Richard Sharpe. New York: Greenberg, 1949.

Simon, Heather. *The Spaceman and King Arthur.* Adapted from Walt Disney Productions' Screen Presentation. London: New English Library / Times Mirror, 1979.

Spiller, Anne. *The Cartomancer.* New York: St. Martin's, 1987.

Spirn, Michele. *In Search of the Ruby Sword*. N.p.: January Productions, 1984.

Springer, Nancy. "The Raven." In *Camelot*. Ed. Jane Yolen. Ill. Winslow Pels. New York: Philomel Books, 1995. 137–51.

Stang, Jo Anne. *Shadows on the Sceptered Isle*. New York: Crown, 1980.

Starr, Kara. *Merlin's Journal of Time: The Camelot Adventure*. Solana Beach, CA: Ravenstarr Publications, 1989. (Purports to be the results of communing with Merlin. Not presented as fiction, but it seems kindest to the book to take it as such.)

Sterling, Sara Hawks. *A Lady of King Arthur's Court: Being a Romance of the Holy Grail*. Pictured by Clara Elsene Peck. Philadelphia: George W. Jacobs, 1907.

Stewart, Mary. *The Crystal Cave*. London: Hodder and Stoughton, 1970.

———. *The Hollow Hills*. London: Hodder and Stoughton, 1973.

———. *The Last Enchantment*. London: Hodder and Stoughton, 1979.

———. *Mary Stewart's Merlin Trilogy*. New York: William Morrow, 1980. (Combines *The Crystal Cave, The Hollow Hills*, and *The Last Enchantment*.)

———. *The Prince and the Pilgrim*. New York: William Morrow and Co., 1995.

———. *The Wicked Day*. London: Hodder and Stoughton, 1983.

Stone, Eugenia. *Page Boy for King Arthur*. Ill. Rafaello Busoni. Chicago: Wilcox and Follett, 1949.

———. *Squire for King Arthur*. Ill. Rafaello Busoni. Chicago: Follett Publishing Co., 1955.

Sutcliff, Rosemary. *The Lantern Bearers*. Oxford: Oxford University Press, 1959.

———. *The Light Beyond the Forest: The Quest for the Holy Grail*. Decorations by Shirley Felts. London: The Bodley Head, 1979.

———. *The Road to Camlann*. Decorations by Shirley Felts. London: The Bodley Head, 1981.

———. *The Sword and the Circle: King Arthur and the Knights of the Round Table*. Decorations by Shirley Felts. London: The Bodley Head, 1981.

———. *Sword at Sunset*. London: Hodder and Stoughton, 1963.

———. *Tristan and Iseult*. London: The Bodley Head, 1971.

Tarr, Judith. "The Grail of Heart's Desire." In *Return to Avalon: A Celebration of Marion Zimmer Bradley*. New York: DAW Books, 1996. 29–57.

———. "Silver, Stone, and Steel." In *Excalibur*. Ed. Richard Gilliam, Martin H. Greenberg, and Edward E. Kramer. New York: Warner Books, 1995. 227–39.

Tattersall, Jill. *Lyonesse Abbey*. New York: William Morrow, 1968.

Taylor, Anna. *Drustan the Wanderer: A Historical Novel Based on the Legend of Tristan and Isolde*. London: Longman, 1971.

Thomas, Frances. *A Knot of Spells*. Port Talbot, West Glamorgan: Barn Owl Press, 1983.

Thomas, Frances. *The Region of the Summer Stars*. Port Talbot, West Glamorgan: Barn Owl Press, 1985.

Trevor, [Lucy] Meriol. *Merlin's Ring*. London: Collins, 1957.

Tyler, Therese. *In the Shadow of the Sangreal*. Philadelphia: Campion and Co., 1911.

Unerman, Sandra. *Trial of Three*. London: Dennis Dobson, 1979.

Van Asten, Gail. *The Blind Knight*. New York: Ace, 1988.

Vandercook, Margaret. *The Girl Scouts of the Round Table*. Philadelphia: John C. Winston, 1921.

Viney, Jane. *The Bright-Helmed One*. London: Robert Hale, 1975.

Ward, Cynthia. "When the Summons Came from Camelot." In *The Ultimate Dragon*. Ed. Byron Preiss, John Betancourt, & Keith R. A. DeCandido. New York: Dell, 1995. 233–42.

Waters, Elisabeth. "Trees of Avalon." In *Return to Avalon: A Celebration of Marion Zimmer Bradley*. New York: DAW Books, 1996. 209–17.

Wein, Elizabeth E. *The Winter Prince*. New York: Atheneum, 1993.

Wilmot-Buxton, E. M. "The Seven Champions." In *The Merlin Chronicles*. Ed. Mike Ashley. New York: Carroll & Graf. 231–47.

Wolf, Amy. "The Hour of Their Need." *Realms of Fantasy* (April 1995): 40–47.

Wolf, Joan. *Born of the Sun*. New York: New American Library, 1989.

———. *The Road to Avalon*. New York: New American Library, 1988.

Woolley, Persia. *Child of the Northern Spring*. New York: Poseidon Press, 1987.

———. *Guinevere: The Legend in Autumn*. New York: Poseidon Press, 1991.

———. *Queen of the Summer Stars*. New York: Poseidon Press, 1990.

Wurts, Janny. *That Way Lies Camelot*. New York: HarperPrism, 1996.

———. "That Way Lies Camelot." In *Grails: Quests, Visitations, and Other Occurrences*. Ed. Richard Gilliam, Martin H. Greenberg, and Edward E. Kramer. Atlanta: Unnameable Press, 1992. 461–88. (Reprinted in *Grails: Quests of the Dawn*. Ed. Richard Gilliam, Martin H. Greenberg, and Edward E. Kramer. New York: ROC, 1994. 264–88.)

Yarbro, Chelsea Quinn. "Night Mare." In *Invitation to Camelot: An Arthurian Anthology of Short Stories*. Ed. Parke Godwin. New York: Ace Books, 1988. 166–99.

Yolen, Jane. *The Acorn Quest*. Ill. Susanna Natti. New York: Thomas Y. Crowell, 1981.

———. *The Dragon's Boy*. New York: Harper and Row, 1990.

———. "The Dragon's Boy." In *Fantasy & Science Fiction* (Sept. 1985): 91–106.

———. "Dream Reader." In *The Merlin Chronicles*. Ed. Mike Ashley. New York: Carroll & Graf, 1995. 16–35.

———. "The Gwynhfar." In *Tales of Wonder*. New York: Schocken Books, 1983. 26–32.

———. *Hobby*. The Young Merlin Trilogy, Book Two. San Diego: Harcourt Brace & Co, 1996.

———. "Meditation in a Whitethorn Tree." In *Invitation to Camelot: An Arthurian Anthology of Short Stories*. Ed. Parke Godwin. New York: Ace Books, 1988. 223–42.

———. *Merlin*. The Young Merlin Trilogy, Book Three. San Diego: Harcourt Brace & Co, 1997.

———. *Merlin's Booke*. Ill. Thomas Canty. Minneapolis: Steel Dragon Press, 1986.

———. *Passager*. The Young Merlin Trilogy, Book Three. San Diego: Harcourt Brace & Co, 1996.

———. "The Quiet Monk." In *Isaac Asimov's Science Fiction*, March 1988. 60–71. (Reprinted in *The Camelot Chronicles: Heroic Adventures from the Time of King Arthur*. Ed. Mike Ashley. New York: Wing Books, 1995. 380–92.)

———. "The Sword and the Stone." In *Fantasy and Science Fiction*, Dec. 1985. 87–104.

[Yonge, Charlotte.] *The History of the Life and Death of the Good Knight Sir Thomas Thumb: With Divers Other Matters Concerning the Court of Good King Arthur of Britain*. Ill. J. B. [Jane Blackburne]. Edinburgh: Thomas Constable, 1855.

Yorgason, Brenton and Margaret. *Family Knights*. Salt Lake City: Bookcraft, 1986.

Yunge-Bateman, Elizabeth. *The Flowering Thorn*. Privately printed by the author, 1961.

Bibliography of
Arthurian Poetry and Drama by Women

Alama, Pauline. "Muirgan, the 'Sea-Born.'" In *A Round Table of Contemporary Arthurian Poetry*. Ed. Barbara Tepa Lupack and Alan Lupack. Rochester, NY: Round Table Publications, 1993. 29.

Anderson, Colleen. "Parsival's Remorse." *The Round Table* 5 (1989): 35.

———. "A Question of the Grail." *The Round Table* 4.1&2 (1987): 31.

———. "The Turning." *The Round Table* 4.1&2 (1987): 60. (Arthur contemplates and resists his return.)

Arden, John and Margaretta D'Arcy. *The Island of the Mighty: A Play on a Traditional British Theme in Three Parts*. London: Eyre Methuen, 1974.

Atwood, M[argaret] E. "Avalon Revisited." *The Fiddlehead* 55 (Winter 1963): 10–13. (A sequence of Arthurian poems.)

Austin, Martha W. *Tristram and Isoult*. Boston: The Poet Lore Co., 1905.

Bartlett, Gertrude. "Ballade of Tristram's Last Harping." In *Canadian Poets and Poetry*. Ed. John W. Garvin. New York: Frederick A. Stokes Co., 1916. 398.

Benson, Jean. "The Guardian." *Pendragon* 27.1 (Spring 1998): 39.

———. "Pendragon." *Pendragon* 27.1 (Spring 1998): 39.

Bickley, Beulah Vick. "The Grail of Spring." In *The Grail of Spring*. Cedar Falls, IA: Holst Printing Co., 1934. 14.

Bostock, Carol J. "Pendragon." In *A Round Table of Contemporary Arthurian Poetry*. Ed. Barbara Tepa Lupack and Alan Lupack. Rochester, NY: Round Table Publications, 1993. 33–34.

Boyle, Marian. "Artorius, Rex Invictus." *The Round Table* 4.1&2 (1987): 56.

Bradbury, Audrey. *"The Vision of Sir Launfal": A Choric Drama*. Boston: Expression Co., n.d.

[Brereton, Jane H., writing under the pseudonym "Melissa."] "Merlin: A Poem Humbly Inscrib'd to Her Majesty." In *Merlin: A Poem, Humbly Inscrib'd to Her*

Majesty. To Which Is Added, The Royal Hermitage: A Poem. Both by a Lady. London: Edward Cave, 1735. 3–9. [Reprinted in *Poems on Several Occasions: by Mrs. Jane Brereton. With Letters to Her Friends, and an Account of Her Life.* London: Edw. Cave, 1744. 181–87.]

———. "Merlin's Prophecy. Humbly Inscrib'd to his R. H. the Prince of Wales." In *Merlin: A Poem Humbly Inscrib'd to Her Majesty. To Which Is Added, The Royal Hermitage: A Poem. Both by a Lady.* London: Edward Cave, 1735. 11–12. [Reprinted in *Poems on Several Occasions: by Mrs. Jane Brereton. With Letters to Her Friends, and an Account of Her Life.* London: Edw. Cave, 1744. 189–91.]

Bridges, Sallie. "Legends of the Round Table" (a sequence of 14 poems). In *Marble Isle, Legends of the Round Table and Other Poems.* Philadelphia: J. Lippincott, 1864.

Budzisz, Annette M. "Contrapletes." *The Round Table* 1.1 (Spring 1984): 18. (The poem contains allusions to Amfortas and Tristan.)

Cartier, Marie. "The Naturopath." *The Round Table* 4.1&2 (1987): 16. (Refers to Morgan le Fay.)

Chesterton, Frances. *Sir Cleges.* In *Three Plays for Children.* New York: French, 1924.

Colander, Valerie Nieman. (See Nieman, Valerie.)

Colwell, Elizabeth. *Songs of Tristram & Yseult: Quatrains.* Chicago: n.p. [privately printed], 1907. Limited to 100 copies.

Constantine, Pamela. "Conjuration." In *A Round Table of Contemporary Arthurian Poetry.* Ed. Barbara Tepa Lupack and Alan Lupack. Rochester, NY: Round Table Publications, 1993. 1. (A Merlin poem.)

———. "The Land Is Empty Now." In *A Round Table of Contemporary Arthurian Poetry.* Ed. Barbara Tepa Lupack and Alan Lupack. Rochester, NY: Round Table Publications, 1993. 48.

Cooke, Rose Terry. "The New Sangreal." In *Poems.* New York: William S. Gottsberger, 1888. 268–71.

Cooney, Ellen. "Guenevere Grown Old." *The Round Table* 4.1&2 (1987): 55.

———. *The Quest for the Holy Grail.* San Francisco: Duir Press, 1981.

Costello, Louisa Stuart. "A Dream." In *The Maid of Cyprus Isle and Other Poems.* London: Sherwood, Neely, and Jones, 1815. 56–58.

———. "The Funeral Boat: A Legend." *Forget Me Not* (1829): 185–92.

———. "The Legend." In *Summer Amongst the Bocages and the Vines.* 2 vols. London: Bentley, 1840. 1:297–301.

Dalkeith, Lena [pseudonym of Jeanne Cherry]. *Sir Gareth of Orkney.* In *Little Plays.* London: T. & E. C. Jack, 1907.

Dane, Clemence [pseudonym of Winifred Ashton]. *The Saviours: Seven Plays on One Theme*. With music by Richard Addinsell. London: Heinemann, 1942.

Davis, Georgene. *The Round Table: A History Drawn from Unreliable Chronicles*. Rutland: The Tory Press, 1930.

Demetrick, Mary. "The Lady of the Lake Goes to Paris to Get Away from It All." *The Round Table* 4.1&2 (1987): 61–62.

Doughty, Maryellen. "King Arthur's Eyes." *The Round Table* 4.1&2 (1987): 57–58.

Field, Michael [pseudonym of Katherine Harris Bradley and Edith Emma Cooper]. *The Tragedy of Pardon*. London: Sidgwick and Jackson, 1911.

Flood, Julie B. "Merlin." In *A Round Table of Contemporary Arthurian Poetry*. Ed. Barbara Tepa Lupack and Alan Lupack. Rochester, NY: Round Table Publications, 1993. 2–3.

Footman, Jennifer. "Creator." *The Round Table* 4.1&2 (1987): 15. (A Merlin poem.)

Freeman, Keller Cushing. "The Death of Arthur: A Requiem for Six Voices." *The Round Table* 4.1&2 (1987): 38–45.

Goldowsky, Barbara. "Lancelot." *The Round Table* 5 (1989): 22–23.

———. "The Love Letter." *The Round Table* 5 (1989): 21. (References to Lancelot and Guinevere.)

Gray, Frances Angevine. "Comrade to Galahad" and "Glastonbury Abbey." In *Signature of Time*. Portland, Maine: House of Falmouth, 1968. 19 & 23.

Hare, Amory [pseudonym of Mrs. James Pemberton Hutchinson]. *Tristram and Iseult: A Play by Amory Hare with Scenes by Wharton Esherick*. Gaylordsville, CT: The Slide Mountain Press, 1930.

Haywood, Eliza, and William Hatchett. *The Opera of Operas; or, Tom Thumb the Great. Alter'd from the Life and Death of Tom Thumb the Great and Set to Music after the Italian Manner*. London: William Rayner, 1733. (An adaptation of Henry Fielding's *Tragedy of Tragedies*.) Reprinted in *the Plays of Eliza Haywood*. Ed. Valerie C. Rudolph. New York: Garland Publishing, 1983.

Hearne, Isabel. *Queen Herzeleid, or Sorrow-of-Heart: An Episode in the Boyhood of the Hero Parzival: Poetic Play in Three Acts*. London: Nutt, 1911.

Hemans, Mrs. [Felicia]. "Taliessin's Prophesy." In *A Selection of Welsh Melodies with Symphonies and Accompaniments by John Parry and Characteristic Words by Mrs. Hemans*. London: J. Power, 1822. 37. (Music appears on 35–36.)

Hollins, Dorothea. *The Quest: A Drama of Deliverance—In Seven Scenes and a Vision*. London: Williams & Norgate, 1910.

Jackson, Myrna. "Lancelot Interrupts the Performance." In *An Arthurian Miscellany*. Ed. Barbara Tepa Lupack and Alan Lupack. Rochester, NY: Round Table Publications, 1998. 9–12.

Jacobs, Maria. "Discrepancy." *The Round Table* 4.1&2 (1987): 35. (Mark observing Isolt's love for Tristan.)

————. *Iseult, We Are Barren*. Windsor, Ontario: Netherlandic Press, 1987.

Jewett, Sophie. "The Dwarf's Quest: A Ballad." In *Persephone and Other Poems: By Members of the English Literature Department, Wellesley College, for the Benefit of the Wellesley Library Fund*. Boston: The Fort Hill Press, 1905. Reprinted in *The Poems of Sophie Jewett*. 2d ed. Ed. Louise Rogers Jewett and Mary Whiton Calkins. New York: Thomas Y. Crowell, 1910. 169–78.

Johnson, Melissa. "Arthur Dreaming in the Castle Hall." In *An Arthurian Miscellany*. Ed. Barbara Tepa Lupack and Alan Lupack. Rochester, NY: Round Table Publications, 1998. 8.

————. "Guinevere Dreaming, Alone in Bed." In *An Arthurian Miscellany*. Ed. Barbara Tepa Lupack and Alan Lupack. Rochester, NY: Round Table Publications, 1998. 8.

————. "Lancelot Dreaming in the Wild." In *An Arthurian Miscellany*. Ed. Barbara Tepa Lupack and Alan Lupack. Rochester, NY: Round Table Publications, 1998. 7.

Karr, Phyllis Ann. "An Idyll of the Grail." In *The Chronicles of the Holy Grail*. Ed. Mike Ashley. New York: Carroll & Graf, 1996. 287–91.

Kernaghan, Eileen. "The Chalice Well, Glastonbury." In *A Round Table of Contemporary Arthurian Poetry*. Ed. Barbara Tepa Lupack and Alan Lupack. Rochester, NY: Round Table Publications, 1993. 17.

Kilmer, Aline. "For All Ladies of Shalott." In *Vigils*. New York: George H. Doran Co., 1921. 37.

Kimball, Hannah Parker. "Merlin Revivified and the Hermit." *Poet-Lore* 12.4 (1900): 537–540. (A brief dialogue between Merlin and a hermit.)

King, Vivian Smallwood. "Merlin to Vivien." In *Contemporary American Women Poets*. Ed. Tooni Gordi. New York: Henry Harrison, 1936. 269.

Kinross, Martha. *Tristram & Isoult*. London: Macmillan, 1913.

LaBombard, Joan. "The Magician." *The Round Table* 4.1&2 (1987): 13–14.

Landon, Letitia Elizabeth. " A Legend of Tintagel Castle." *Fisher's Drawing Room Scrapbook* (1833): 8–9.

Landgraf, Susan. "Tree Temple." In *An Arthurian Miscellany*. Ed. Barbara Tepa Lupack and Alan Lupack. Rochester, NY: Round Table Publications, 1998. 5–6

Larcom, Lucy. "The Cross and the Grail." In *The Cross and the Grail. By Lucy Larcom. With Selections from the Poets Shakespeare, Longfellow, Whittier and Phoebe and Alice Cary*. Ill. Dora Wheeler. Chicago: Woman's Temperance Pub'n Association, 1887. 1–5 [unnumbered].

Leitch, Mary Sinton. "Tintagel." In *Contemporary American Women Poets*. Ed. Tooni Gordi. New York: Henry Harrison, 1936. 281.

Lepovetsky, Lisa. "Somewhere in Her Dying Heart." In *Grails: Quests, Visitations, and Other Occurrences*. Ed. Richard Gilliam, Martin H. Greenberg, and Edward E. Kramer. Atlanta: Unnameable Press, 1992. 154. (Reprinted in *Grails: Quests of the Dawn*. Ed. Richard Gilliam, Martin H. Greenberg, and Edward E. Kramer. New York: ROC, 1994. 171–72.)

Lewis, Anne-Marie. "Barter." *Pendragon* 27.1 (Spring 1998): 41.

————. "Guinevere." *Pendragon* 27.1 (Spring 1998): 41.

Lounsbery, G[race] Constant. "An Iseult Idyll." In *An Iseult Idyll and Other Poems*. London: John Lane, 1901.

Lucas, Barbara. "Guinevere's Farewell." In *A Round Table of Contemporary Arthurian Poetry*. Ed. Barbara Tepa Lupack and Alan Lupack. Rochester, NY: Round Table Publications, 1993. 9.

————. "Lancelot's Farewell." In *A Round Table of Contemporary Arthurian Poetry*. Ed. Barbara Tepa Lupack and Alan Lupack. Rochester, NY: Round Table Publications, 1993. 8.

Lunn, Jean. "Elegy for Camelot." *The Round Table* 5 (1989): 54–55.

Mackinstry, Elizabeth. "Merlin." In *Puck in Pasture*. Garden City, New York: Doubleday, Page and Co. at their Country Life Press, 1925. 61–67.

McCann, Janet. "Merlin." In *CEA Critic* 43.4 (May 1981): 15.

McGarvey, Margaret. "At Astolat." In *D*Dawn and Other Poems*. Darien, GA: The Ashantilly Press, 1964. 28–29.

McLanathan, Mary Leland. *Three Kings: A Christmas Legend of Long Ago*. Ill. Rosina Emmet. New York: Anson D. F. Randolph and Co., 1886.

Merington, Marguerite. *The Testing of Sir Gawayne: All Hallowe'en*. In *A Treasury of Plays for Children*. Ed. Montrose J. Moses. Ill. Tony Sarg. Boston: Little, Brown, and Co., 1926. 107–36.

Millay, Edna St. Vincent. "Elaine." In *Second April*. New York: Mitchell Kennerley, 1921. 56–57.

Miller, Emily Huntington. "From Avalon." In *From Avalon and Other Poems*. Chicago: A. C. McClurg and Co., 1896. 7–8.

Mnookin, Wendy. *Guenever Speaks*. Ill. Deborah Davidson. Rochester, NY: Round Table Publications, 1991. (A sequence of poems in Guenever's voice.) (The poems "Guenever Plots Against Elaine" and "Guenever Views the Corpse of Elaine" first appeared in *The Round Table* 5 [1989]: 19 & 20. The poem "Guenever Speaks" appeared in *The Round Table* 4.1&2 [1987]: 46–51. This poem becomes "Guenever Retreats to Almesbury after Arthur's Death,"

"Guenever Returns from the Garden," and the "Epilogue" in the volume *Guenever Speaks*.)

Mumford, Ethel Watts. *Merlin and Vivian: A Lyrical Drama*. Music by Henry Kimball Hadley. New York: Schirmer, 1907.

Nesbitt, Patricia. "He Rides Out." *The Round Table* 4.1&2 (1987): 17.

Nieman, Valerie. "The Naming of the Lost." *The Round Table* 5 (1989): 4–10. (A Merlin and Nimue poem.)

Palfrey, Sara Hammond. "King Arthur in Avalon." In *King Arthur in Avalon and Other Poems*. Boston: W. B. Clarke Co., 1900. 1–15.

Parker, Dorothy. "Guinevere at Her Fireside." In *Death and Taxes*. New York: Viking, 1931. 42–43.

———. "Iseult of Brittany." In *Death and Taxes*. New York: Viking, 1931. 39.

Paxson, Diana L. "The Feast of the Fisher King: A Masque in Verse (with Narrative Inclusions)." In *Grails: Quests, Visitations, and Other Occurrences*. Ed. Richard Gilliam, Martin H. Greenberg, and Edward E. Kramer. Atlanta: Unnameable Press, 1992. 61–83. (Reprinted in *Grails: Quests of the Dawn*. Ed. Richard Gilliam, Martin H. Greenberg, and Edward E. Kramer. New York: ROC, 1994. 36–59.)

Phelps, Elizabeth Stuart. "Afterward." *Independent* 32 (22 July 1880): 1. (Reprinted as "Guinevere" in *Songs of the Silent World*. Boston: Houghton Mifflin, 1891. 59–63.)

———. "Elaine and Elaine." *Independent* 35 (7 June 1883): 35. (Reprinted in *Songs of the Silent World*. Boston: Houghton Mifflin, 1891. 77–78.)

———. "The Terrible Test." *Sunday Afternoon* 1 (Jan. 1878): 49. (Reprinted in *Songs of the Silent World*. Boston: Houghton Mifflin, 1891. 92–93.)

Pomeroy, Florence M. *Tristan and Iseult: An Epic Poem in Twelve Books*. London: The Bodley Head, 1958.

Porteous, Frances. "Knight of the Grail." In *Knight of the Grail*. Driffield, Yorkshire: The Guild Press, 1962. 7–8.

Reedman, Janet P. "Morgan's Lament." *The Round Table* 4.1&2 (1987): 54.

Reese, Lizette Woodworth. "Guinevere in Almesbury Convent." In *A Handful of Lavender*. 1892. Portland, Maine: Thomas B. Mosher, 1915. 8.

Roche, Judith. "Morganna La Fey: The Lessons." In *Ghosts*. Port Townsend, WA: Empty Bowl, 1984. 45.

Schwader, Ann K. "Merlin." *The Round Table* 4.1&2 (1987): 12.

Singer, Sarah. "Guinevere, the Nun." *The Round Table* 5 (1989): 53.

Skinner, Margo. "Quest Now." In *Grails: Quests, Visitations, and Other Occurrences*. Ed. Richard Gilliam, Martin H. Greenberg, and Edward E. Kramer.

Atlanta: Unnameable Press, 1992. 444–45.

Smith, Evelyn. *The Kitchen Knight*. In *Form Room Plays*. London: Dent, 1926.

Smith, Stevie. "The Blue from Heaven (A Legend of King Arthur of Britain)." In *Selected Poems*. Norfolk, CT: New Directions, 1964. 24–25.

———. "The Frozen Lake." In *Selected Poems*. Norfolk, CT: New Directions, 1964. 10–12.

Stephens, Genevieve. "The Dark Tower." In *A Round Table of Contemporary Arthurian Poetry*. Ed. Barbara Tepa Lupack and Alan Lupack. Rochester, NY: Round Table Publications, 1993. 5. (A Merlin and Vivien poem.)

Sweetman, Elinor. "Pastoral of Galahad." In *Pastorals and Other Poems*. London: Dent, 1899. 38–44.

———. "Pastoral of Lancelot." In *Pastorals and Other Poems*. London: Dent, 1899. 45–53.

Tatum, Edith. *The Awakening of Iseult*. Oglethorpe University, GA: Oglethorpe University Press, 1933. (Originally printed in *Neale's Monthly* 2 [Aug. 1913].)

Teasdale, Sara. "At Tintagil." In *Dark of the Moon*. New York: Macmillan, 1926. 20. (Reprinted in *The Collected Poems of Sara Teasdale*. New York: Macmillan, 1937. 165.)

———. "Galahad in the Castle of the Maidens." In *Helen of Troy and Other Poems*. New York: Macmillan, 1911. 85.

———. "Guenevere." In *Helen of Troy and Other Poems*. New York: Macmillan, 1911. 27–29

Tolmie, Sarah. "The Story of the Meeting of Cuculainn and Arthur." In *A Round Table of Contemporary Arthurian Poetry*. Ed. Barbara Tepa Lupack and Alan Lupack. Rochester, NY: Round Table Publications, 1993. 20–28.

Trask, Diana. *Under King Constantine*. 2d ed.; New York: Anson D. F. Randolph and Co., 1893. (Contains three long poems set in the time of King Constantine, immediately after Arthur's passing: "Sanpeur," "Kathanal," and "Christalan.")

Turnbull, E. Lucia and H. Dalwey. *Through the Gates of Remembrance*. London: Nelson, 1933.

Tynan, Katharine. "The Chapel of the Grail." In *Ballads and Lyrics*. London: Kegan, Paul, Trench, Trübner & Co., 1891. 139–42.

Vincent, Karen. "The Keeper." In *An Arthurian Miscellany*. Ed. Barbara Tepa Lupack and Alan Lupack. Rochester, NY: Round Table Publications, 1998. 13. (A poem about the Lady of the Lake.)

Webb, Holly. "Carmen Sine Nomine." In *An Arthurian Miscellany*. Ed. Barbara Tepa

Lupack and Alan Lupack. Rochester, NY: Round Table Publications, 1998. 14–16. (A poem about Pellinore and the Questing Beast.)

Weinberger, Mildred. *Elaine: A Poetic Drama. Poet-Lore* 34 (1923): 72–110.

Weston, Jessie. "Knights of King Arthur's Court." In *The Rose Tree of Hildesheim and Other Poems*. London: David Nutt, 1896. 47–58.

White, Gail. "The Testament of Guinevach." In *A Round Table of Contemporary Arthurian Poetry*. Ed. Barbara Tepa Lupack and Alan Lupack. Rochester, NY: Round Table Publications, 1993. 46–47.

Whitney, Helen Hay. "When Tristan Sailed." In *Gypsy Verses*. New York: Duffield, 1907. 25–26.

Widdemer, Margaret. "Merlin Is Wise." In *Ballads and Lyrics*. New York: Harcourt, Brace & Co., 1925. 104–05.

Williams, Antonia R. *Isolt: A New Telling*. London: Published by the author, 1900.

Wilson, Barbara Ker. *Legends of the Round Table*. Ill. Maria Calati. Feltham, Middlesex: Paul Hamlyn, 1966.

Wisniewski, Kay Newburger. "Percivale." In *A Round Table of Contemporary Arthurian Poetry*. Ed. Barbara Tepa Lupack and Alan Lupack. Rochester, NY: Round Table Publications, 1993. 12.

Yeo, Margaret. *The Everlasting Quest*. Decorated by Martin Travers. London: The Society of SS. Peter & Paul, 1915.

"The Ylle Cutt Mantell, a Romaunt of the Tyme of Gud Kynge Arthur." In *The Democratic Review*, New Series 14, No. 71 (May 1844): 465–76. (Published anonymously but said in the text to be by "a daughter of Eve.")

Yolen, Jane. "The Question of the Grail." In *Grails: Quests, Visitations, and Other Occurrences*. ROC, 1994. Ed. Richard Gilliam, Martin H. Greenberg, and Edward E. Kramer. Atlanta: Unnameable Press, 1992. 9. (Reprinted in *Grails: Quests of the Dawn*. Ed. Richard Gilliam, Martin H. Greenberg, and Edward E. Kramer. New York: ROC, 1994. 1.)

———. "The Question of the Sword." In *Excalibur*. Ed. Richard Gilliam, Martin H. Greenberg, and Edward E. Kramer. New York: Warner Books, 1995. 1–2.

Yolen, Jane, and Adam Stemple. "Amesbury Song." In *Camelot*. Ed. Jane Yolen. Ill. Winslow Pels. New York: Philomel Books, 1995. 176–78.

Young, Ella. "The San-Grail." In *The Rose of Heaven: Poems*. Dublin: Candle Press, 1920. 25–26.

———. "A Song That Trostan Made." In *The Weird of Fionavar*. Dublin: The Talbot Press, 1922. 13.

———. "Trostan Made This." In *The Weird of Fionavar*. Dublin: The Talbot Press, 1922. 14.